REVOLUTIONARY EMANCIPATION

Antislavery, Abolition, and the Atlantic World
R. J. M. Blackett and James Brewer Stewart, Series Editors

REVOLUTIONARY EMANCIPATION

SLAVERY AND ABOLITIONISM
IN THE
BRITISH WEST INDIES

CLAUDIUS K. FERGUS

Louisiana State University Press
Baton Rouge

Published by Louisiana State University Press
Copyright © 2013 by Louisiana State University Press
All rights reserved
Manufactured in the United States of America
First printing

DESIGNER: Michelle A. Neustrom
TYPEFACE: Ingeborg
PRINTER: McNaughton & Gunn, Inc.
BINDER: Dekker Bookbinding

LIBRARY OF CONGRESS CATALOGING-IN-PUBLICATION DATA

Fergus, Claudius K., 1950–
    Revolutionary emancipation : slavery and abolitionism in the British West
Indies / Claudius K. Fergus.
        p. cm.
    Includes bibliographical references and index.
    ISBN 978-0-8071-4988-1 (cloth : alk. paper) — ISBN 978-0-8071-4989-8 (pdf)
— ISBN 978-0-8071-4990-4 (epub) — ISBN 978-0-8071-4991-1 (mobi) 1. Slav-
ery—West Indies, British—History—19th century. 2. Slave trade—West Indies,
British—History—19th century. I. Title.
    HT1093.F47 2013
    306.3'6209729—dc23
                                                                2012027976

The paper in this book meets the guidelines for permanence
and durability of the Committee on Production Guidelines for Book
Longevity of the Council on Library Resources. ♾

This study is dedicated to my mother, Stella Bouville.

CONTENTS

PREFACE

The intellectual controversy over Britain's abolition of its transatlantic slave trade and colonial slavery is well known; a brief comment on some of the seminal contributors to the debate puts the current study into perspective. Given the modern Caribbean's proud tradition of radical intellectualism, it is hardly surprising that radical Pan-Africanism under the influence of international socialism of the 1930s accentuated attacks against the hegemony of an imperialist historiography that silenced diaspora Africans as agency in the history of the region and glorified Christian morality over economic imperatives in the regeneration of empire. The best-known Anglophone flag bearers of the emerging nationalist historiography, C. L. R. James and Eric Williams, collectively invalidated the "Quashie" portraiture of enslaved Africans and iconic humanitarian abolition. Although published in 1944, Williams's epochal *Capitalism and Slavery* was truly a product of the revolutionary 1930s. Notwithstanding earlier stirrings in other scholarly quarters, *Capitalism and Slavery* was embryonic to the dichotomy in the historiography of abolition. Williams transferred to the study of British abolitionism a Hegelian-Marxist dialect first applied to James's *Black Jacobins* (1938).[1] Since the earliest responses to *Capitalism and Slavery,* the controversy over the transformation of Britain's old regime of sugar, slavery, and slave trading has been polarized between the prerogatives of economic determinism and the impulse of moral imperium. Attempts to close the ideological gap have considerably enriched the study of Atlantic history, but so far, these pedagogies have defied reconcilement.

The formal marriage of moral imperium and abolitionism dates back to Thomas Clarkson's *History of the Rise, Progress and Accomplishment of the Ab-*

olition of the African Slave Trade by the British Parliament (1808), its timely publication an epitaph to the general Abolition Act and a glorification of the Abolition Society. Moral imperium defined the historiography of abolition-ism throughout the nineteenth century as a triumph of white, Anglo-Saxon Protestantism.[2] Several leading scholars, among the most noteworthy being Reginald Coupland and Frank Klingberg, rescripted the same pedagogy in the early twentieth century.[3] The Clarkson-Klingberg-Coupland combination continues to sway neo-imperialist scholars, among the most influential of whom have been Roger Anstey, David Brion Davis, and Seymour Drescher, a triad that consciously complement each other.

The modern historiography of subaltern agency in British emancipation is also rooted in *Capitalism and Slavery,* though unmistakably inspired by *The Black Jacobins.* Williams concurs with James on the dominant theme of resistance and the impact of its cataclysmic moments in Jamaica, Demerara, and Haiti on the consciousness of colonials and metropolitans alike. Follow-ing in James's footsteps, Williams strongly advocates a pivotal role to the en-slaved in their own emancipation. More particularly, he positions the Baptist War as the final nail in the coffin of British colonial slavery; his conclusion, "Emancipation from above, or emancipation from below. But EMANCIPATION," has imprinted the historiography of subaltern antislavery. Yet, he concludes, "the Negroes had been stimulated to freedom by the development of the very wealth which their labor had created."[4] Thus, Williams's logic remains quint-essentially economic determinism.

The current study is conceived wholly within the subaltern but differs centrally from James's and Williams's perspectives. It interprets the struggle for freedom as a reaction to enslavement, regardless of the economic fortunes of the colonies. In this regard the biographies of emancipated Africans and other African-descended contemporaries provide invaluable lessons and are liberally cited in this study. The work also incorporates an African-centered worldview into the narrative of resistance, enriching the literature on the Af-rican experience during the slavery era. Among more recent scholars the work of Richard Hart deserves special mention. From his own admission he began to articulate the main theme of his major work, *Slaves Who Abolished Slavery,* since about 1940 and thus stands shoulder to shoulder with James and Wil-liams in advancing a new subaltern historiography of abolitionism. Operat-ing within the environment of the "new nationalist upsurge" of the 1930s, all three scholars were "unashamedly political" while adding substance to a new "scientific history" of colonial slavery and the Atlantic world.[5] One of the latest, noteworthy contributors to this genre is Gelien Matthews.[6]

The current monograph grew out of my doctoral work at the University of the West Indies, which argued that Britain's abolition of its Atlantic slave trade and African emancipation were key strategies in the reconstruction of its West Indian colonies in the aftermath of Jamaica's Tacky's War of 1760, the first major slave insurrection in the Americas.[7] The theme of revolutionary emancipationism, which appeared as an ill-defined tributary in my earlier work (for want of sustainable evidence), has become the primary stream in the present study. The interpretation of emancipationist insurgency as revolutionary is supported by established scholars. Hegel postulated, "The moment of revolution comes when the slave recognizes that his or her *primary identity* lies with the other slaves and as a result withdraws both labour and recognition."[8] More specifically, Williams asserts, "The moment he [the African captive] was placed on the small tubs which made the Middle Passage, that moment he became a revolutionary, actual and potential."[9]

The study is partly located within the economics of abolition and emancipation, though radically shifting the focus from arresting economic decline of the colonies to arresting their insecurity sustained by revolutionary emancipationism. The rejection of revolutionary emancipationism as the primary agency in the abolition of the slave trade enjoys a curious consensus among historians, regardless of ideological persuasion. Several cases underscore this verdict. Anstey contends that the threat to security from continuing to import captives from Africa and the imperative of cheaper labor, which made Creoles more cost-effective than native Africans, "were less than compelling" factors in abolition and definitely not "provable."[10] More recently Davis has argued, "It would be difficult to show that fear of another Haitian Revolution motivated Parliament's crucial votes in 1806 abolishing the slave trade to rival foreign markets, which prepared the way in 1807 for abolishing the British slave trade altogether."[11] Drescher, a co-contributor to the same volume, was more resolute in rejecting the impact of colonial insecurity on the outcome of the abolition debate. Accordingly, he asserts, "The motion for abolition was grounded on an explicitly non-insurrectionary premise about the prior behaviour of British slaves."[12] With equal fortitude, in one of his latest published contributions on the subject, Drescher judicially rejects João Pedro Marques's claim that the Haitian Revolution "had a positive impact in the acceleration of the abolition of the slave trade" as "an overstatement."[13] He then presents his case for liberating the "fear factor" from every aspect of abolitionism. Despite his clever portrayal of Haitian revolutionaries as "Black Jacobins," James posits that British parliamentarians discussed colonial security merely "to keep the people quiet"; Williams echoes a similar refrain in *Capitalism and Slavery*. Although slightly shifting position in a later work, *From Columbus to Castro: The History of the Caribbean, 1492–1969,* Williams remains ambivalent on the significance of internal security to the outcome of abolition.[14]

Against this accumulated rejection of the primacy of security, and thus the pivotal role of revolutionary emancipation in British abolitionism, the current study demonstrates that the plantocracy's psychopathic fear of Africans and the dread of revolutionary emancipation by British abolitionists were fundamental to the selection of reform strategies by colonials and metropolitan abolitionists alike. Among these strategies the uppermost priority was the search for security through abolition of the slave trade and the complete creolization of labor. The added-on imperative to make plantation labor efficient informed common concerns by both metropolitans and colonials over the elimination of some of the most dehumanizing and cruel practices of plantation slavery, especially against women.

The study explores the impact of revolutionary emancipationism from Tacky's War through the Haitian Revolution to Jamaica's "Baptist War" (1831). It proposes that Tacky's War was the pivotal moment in the launch of abolitionism. It also posits that the Haitian Revolution was the pivotal moment for abolition of Britain's transatlantic trade in enslaved Africans. Finally, it concurs with historians of the subaltern that the Baptist War was the pivotal moment for African emancipation in the British colonies but provides hitherto unexamined evidence. The study links the Haitian Revolution to the simultaneous emancipationist revolts in the Lesser Antilles as part of a single phenomenon. The following hypotheses are intertwined with this outlook: that legislation to abolish the slave trade (1805 to 1807) was a tactical response to the crisis of colonial security; that the first phase of imperial intervention in the reconstruction or remodeling of the colonial system was informed by government's acknowledgment of this crisis; and that the enslaved class exploited this intervention, ultimately destroying the confidence of political authorities to provide adequate security, thus culminating in statutory emancipation.

In treating the problem of amelioration and abolitionism, the study incorporates the perspective of imperial trusteeship but in a radically different way from George Mellor and the imperialist school. Simply stated, trusteeship was the phase of parliamentary intervention in amelioration. The perspective of trusteeship provides a historical platform on which to assemble key stakeholders that directly and indirectly impacted the remodeling of the colonial system. These agencies included enslaved and enslavers, missionary societies, other metropolitan activists, and the imperial government. The problem of slavery reform in the wider British West Indies is accentuated in a case study of the island of Trinidad, especially after its conquest in 1797. The selection of Trinidad was made with three basic considerations in mind. First, the direct rule of the Crown established it as the first colony in which imperial intervention could be harnessed without the political obstructionism endemic in the Legislative Colonies; second, Trinidad shared all the socioindustrial characteristics of the old colonies, thus justifying the same attention to the reform of its slavery system; and third, the colony was an ideal political laboratory for assessing the ideology and program of imperial trusteeship.

For this study I consulted a number of libraries and archives, including the Trinidad and Tobago National Archives; the Main Library at the St. Augustine Campus of the University of the West Indies (UWI); the National Archives of St. Vincent and the Grenadines; the Public Records Office; the British Library; Colindale Newspaper Library; the School of Oriental and African Studies; Rhodes House Library; Bodleian Library; and Lambeth Palace in the United Kingdom; in France I conducted research at the Centre des Archives d'Outre-Mer, now the Archives Nationales d'Outre-Mer, Aix-en-Provence.

I owe special gratitude to several people: Selwyn H. H. Carrington, who motivated me to undertake this study and chaperoned me through London on my first visit; Bridget Brereton, for her moral support and encouragement; the late Fitzroy André Baptiste, my thesis supervisor and mentor, who largely influenced the strong African diasporic cultural content in the work; librarians at the UWI, especially the late Gloria Baptiste, Kim Gransaul, Kathleen Helenese-Paul, and Glenroy Taitt; John Campbell and Elma Joyeau-Campbell (no relation), for their invaluable technical support in typing the early draft of the manuscript; K. O. Laurence, for facilitating research funding when most needed; Jerome Handler, for kindly providing me with copies of the Barbados Assembly's 1816 "Bussa" inquiry and newspaper clippings on the epic debate between him and Hilary McD. Beckles; the reviewers for Louisiana State University Press, for enlightened criticism and suggestions that contributed significantly to an improved final product; and my mother, Stella Bouville, who provided general support and encouragement and to whom I dedicate this work. For whatever deficiencies that might still remain, I take full responsibility.

REVOLUTIONARY EMANCIPATION

1

EXPLICATING THE "GRAND EVILS"
OF COLONIALISM

The Supreme Evil

W hen the French National Assembly legislated the general abolition of slavery in 1794, the slave trade was also abolished ipso
facto. On the contrary, British abolitionists doggedly justified
distinguishing slavery from the slave trade on the teleological
premise that no other evil "was comparable to that of the African Slave Trade."[1] Contemporary voices explicitly acknowledged two evils
of the colonial system: the barbarism of African enslavement and the horrors
of the Atlantic slave trade. Most were predisposed to consider them "distinct
from each other" or else perfunctorily dismissed them as necessary evils.[2]
Unquestionably, the evidence adduced at the parliamentary inquiries into the
slave trade between 1788 and 1791 was more than adequate to condemn the
commoditization and enslavement of Africans as crimes against humanity,
even by the standards of the day.

Although some philanthropically minded, colonial-based Quakers had
begun to rail against both evils since the seventeenth century,[3] the politi-
cization of abolition had more to do with the slave trade as a feeder for an
even greater evil than slavery itself, often captioned as "internal commotion,"
"internal violence," or "internal insurrection" and appropriately embodied
in the term *revolutionary emancipationism*. Abolitionist luminary Henry
Brougham implicitly included revolutionary emancipation as the greatest of
the "grand evils" confronting colonial security.[4] Indeed, ranked by vested interest, slavery was the least problematic of the grand evils, insurrection the
greatest. Contemporary logic on the cause of this threat informed the priori-
tizing of ending the trade over emancipation. Paradoxically, to revolution-

ary emancipators the military option was the most viable physic to the evil of slavery.

A standard question posed to witnesses at the parliamentary inquiry was whether an African was less "susceptible of the sentiment of liberty as a free peasant in England." It is to England's credit that a minority of white contemporaries had sufficient confidence in their conviction of the natural rights of humanity to condemn the racism implicit in such an assumption. One senior naval officer contended that there was "no comparison between a set of free men in a land of liberty and protection, and a set of people who were treated in many respects like cattle."[5] Even fewer whites, however, dared to admit that rebellions were not motivated by African savagery but rather by desperation to recover or secure their liberty. One exception was Barbados-born Reverend Robert Nicholls, who informed the parliamentary committee of 1790–91 that freedom was the motive behind the "two great rebellions mentioned by Long," referring to Tacky's War in 1760 and its Hanover sequel six years later.[6] Refusing to be railroaded, he affirmed, "I consider liberty as the first comfort in life, as well as an inalienable right. I consider the want of it as lessening the comforts of life."[7] Africans were not invited to testify before the committee, although the abolitionist Sons of Africa successfully tabled at least one memorandum.[8]

The Sons of Africa was a seminal abolition society in England, founded in 1786, one year before the better-known Society for Effecting the Gradual Abolition of the Slave Trade. Among the well-known names of the Sons of Africa were Olaudah Equiano and Ottobah Cugoano.[9] Many Africans, including Equiano and Cugoano, penned (or dictated) poignant declarations of their rights to liberty, happiness, and justice in autobiographies that to a large degree are also biographies of slavery, the slave trade, and emancipation. Trained in the art of combat before his capture, Equiano explained why the conditions of West Indian slavery thrust the enslaved into a perpetual struggle for freedom: "When you make men slaves you deprive them of half their virtue, you set them in your own conduct an example of fraud, rapine, and cruelty, and compel them to live with you in a state of war."[10] Much more explicitly than any other metropolitan-based abolitionists, Cugoano justified revolutionary violence as a tool of emancipation and even anticipated the Haitian Revolution.[11] Decades later Mary Prince added her voice to the still relevant question. Toward the end of her graphic narrative about her multiple experiences of enslavement, she contended that Africans' right to freedom and happiness could be no less than that of English subjects. Accordingly, she asked rhetorically, "How can slaves be happy when they have the halter round their neck and the whip upon their back?"[12]

Not surprisingly, one of the enduring clichés of the slavery era was the notion that Africans were natural enemies of the plantocracy and, by extension, the colonial system: from quintessential religious foe to quintessential political and military foe. The doctrine of slaves as natural enemies dates back to the classical period in Western thought.[13] The sentiment was inherited by colonizers of the New World. From the earliest phase of the Sugar Revolution colonists manifested a psychopathological unease about the Africans they enslaved. Richard Ligon and John Oldmixton have given us some of the earliest dimensions of this self-inflicted paranoia. When Ligon visited Barbados in the late 1640s, whites were already outnumbered by Africans two to one. He saw this as an ominous development because Africans were "accounted a bloody people where they think they have power or advantages; and the more bloody, by how much they are more fearful than others."[14] Planters' phobia intensified as the ratio of whites to blacks diminished. By the early 1700s the plantation revolution, fueled by sugar and African enslavement, had spread from Barbados to several other colonies, including those of other European nations. Against this background John Oldmixton considered "revolutionary blacks" as the "common enemies" of all Christian nations.[15] The natural enemy cliché reappeared in late-eighteenth-century debates on the right to liberty; ironically, it also resonated among those who proudly distinguished themselves as "Friends of the Negro."[16]

Afrophobia was bolstered by pseudoscientific racism, to which Edward Long was a major contributor. Long was one of Jamaica's wealthiest planters, a legislator, and a man of letters, thus one of the colony's ablest spokesmen. In quoting Montesquieu, he iterated, "Such people as these are the natural enemies of the society; and their number must be dangerous."[17] James Ramsay was influenced by Long on many issues relating to slavery. A resident Kittitian cleric and surgeon for nineteen years, Ramsay had held substantial property in Africans. His description of Africans as enemies echoed Long as well as his personal experience: "Masters and slaves are in every respect opposite terms; the persons to whom they are applied are natural enemies to each other."[18] Brougham, one of Britain's leading abolitionists, never visited the West Indies, but up to the very end of slavery lived in mortal dread of African insurrection. With impetuosity and imperious pride, he penned the most poignant images of racial antagonism: "The negroes . . . are the enemies most to be dreaded in America by all Europeans, they are the natural enemies of white men, who are distinguished by indelible marks in body, *and by marks almost indelible in mind*."[19] The backdrop was Napoleon's invasion to reinstate slavery in Haiti with England's secret backing of the enterprise made public.

Enslaved Africans also considered European enslavers their mutual enemy but restricted the indictment to enemies of liberty and humanity. This distinction was succinctly expressed by Toussaint L'Ouverture and is important to an understanding of the boundaries of retribution that African insurgents and other emancipated people imposed on themselves;[20] it also explains the peaceful response to Emancipation Day in the British Caribbean, which baffled contemporary Europeans and many modern scholars. In the true "spirit of *ubuntu*," a southern African concept affirming the interconnectedness of all human beings, African antislavery struggles were not intended to destroy the enslavers but, rather, to win respect for the enslaved people's own humanity and create secure spaces of freedom for themselves. *Ubuntu* has recently become a subject of African ethics and moral philosophy, but it is deeply rooted in the worldview of traditional African communalism. Before its recent appearance as a major topic in the academy, *ubuntu* was "illustrated in songs and stories . . . traditional customs and instructions, and in the whole ethos or lifestyle."[21] The spirit of *ubuntu* is central to "the healing of breaches, the redressing of imbalances, the restoration of broken relationships"; it is "the very essence of being human."[22]

African antislavery was the antithesis of the nightmare of enslavement: from capture in Africa, in the holding bays on the coasts, aboard slavers of the Middle Passage, and in the Caribbean beginning with the very first cohort of forced migrants. It took various forms of "resistance," the most feared being shipboard mutinies and colonial insurrections or revolts. Slave ships were the first theaters of emancipationist uprisings beyond the "doors of no return."[23] The very first revolt on Caribbean soil may have occurred as early as 1502 in Cuba but certainly by 1522 in Hispaniola and 1527 in Puerto Rico; in Barbados planters preempted a plot to set fire to destroy the factories of a sugar plantation as early as the 1640s, the foundation phase of the Sugar Revolution.[24] From that time colonial regimes maintained a favorable balance of power by constantly mustering troops and conducting regular armed exercises in the presence of the enslaved to warn them of the ruthless consequences of insurgency.[25] Antiguan planters also experienced a significant uprising relatively early in their transition to a sugar economy.[26] By the 1710s the English colonies had experienced at least seven insurgencies and six aborted ones.[27] During Jamaica's transition from invasion in 1655 to formal cession by Spain in 1670, the island experienced its first "serious revolt" on an English plantation.[28] Up until emancipation it remained the colony most tormented by revolutionary upheavals. The eighty-year Anglo-Maroon wars in Jamaica (1660–1739) fueled a culture of insurrectionist emancipationism. Jamaican planters came to view the Maroons as "a plague on the body politic," while the response of whites in general was one "bordering on paranoia." [29] White Jamaicans avoided perpetual war against the Maroons by timely resort to the Cudjoe-Trelawney treaties.[30] Maroon oral tradition commemorates the event as a decisive victory.[31] Freedmen and Maroons everywhere remained protagonists of revolutionary emancipationism because many of their wives, children, and other close relations remained in slavery. They also clearly understood that they could never be truly free so long as slavery persisted.

The Cudjoe-Trelawney emancipation treaties did not guarantee security. Twenty years later an enslaved Akan speaker named Tacky led a major insurgency against the plantocracy. Long was an eyewitness; his analysis of events and recommendations for preempting a recurrence made an indelible impact on advocates of colonial reform. His *History of Jamaica* inscribed the name Tacky as the pivotal subaltern agent in colonial reform. Tacky's War sharpened awareness that enslaved labor was an economic gamble. Post-Tacky Jamaica was rife with revolutionary turmoil as well as new ideas for reconstructing the colonial paradigm. Long found a receptive audience for his notion that the chief actors of seditions and mutinies were "imported Africans," and he swayed reform-friendly contemporaries with his advocacy of creolization as the best counterpoise to insurrections. His ideas were mistakenly fashioned on the myth that the African-born were less predictable and potentially more rebellious than Creoles.[32] These ideas were not completely new. The perception that the principal protagonists of revolutionary emancipationism were unassimilated Africans had delayed Spain's first issue of the *Asiento* by almost two decades. Long is important to the history of colonial reformism because of his intellectual leadership in establishing creolization as the pragmatic rationale for abolishing the English slave trade. The positive balance from measuring the economic benefits of creolization against economic distress from emancipation wars fertilized the embryo of abolitionism and, in many respects, spurred the genesis of reform of the colonial system.

The Atlantic Traffic in African Captives

British participation in transatlantic trafficking in enslaved Africans began surreptitiously almost a century before the launch of its sugar revolution. By the end of the eighteenth century the British were by far the single largest carrier of African captives in an enterprise best described as big business.[33] Altogether British ships delivered some three million Africans to their own colonies as well as those of their imperial rivals. Captains of slavers included men of high status in English society. Many investors and participants in the trade held high office; some were humanitarians engaged in a variety of charities.[34] The parliamentary inquiry into the slave trade produced stunning revelations; among the most disturbing was the dependence of the trade on systematic plunder, kidnapping, and murder of captured Africans as well as endemic fraud.

The trafficking of African captives by Atlantic merchants was not always a Middle Passage affair. What became the transatlantic slave trade was a later expression of a slowly evolving commercial and colonizing enterprise within the eastern Atlantic, the embryo of an Atlantic world order in which slave trading became one of the defining features. Every facet of this evil—from the first Portuguese raiders to corrupted African politico-judicial authorities who supported the trade—was driven by the imperatives of mercantile capitalism.[35] Early papal intervention liberated the conscience of Christian traders from guilt or doubts about the morality of their undertaking. This is clearly demonstrated in the naming of slave ships after the most esteemed icons in Christianity, such as the *Jesus of Lubeck* and the *Ave Maria*. Ships were also commonly named after political defenders of the faith, including kings and princes such as the *Elizabeth* and the *Henrietta Marie;* yet others were embossed with titles more appropriate to their capitalist enterprise, such as the *Fortune*.[36] In general the nation that contracted the *Asiento* dominated the trade; this enviable status belonged to the British from 1713. By 1788 some two thirds of all Africans imported into "foreign" colonies were acquired from British merchants,[37] a factor that has impacted the historiography of abolition in a significant way.

Interestingly, Eric Williams treated rather perfunctorily the question of mortality in the slave trade, preferring instead to underscore its profitability; even in acknowledging that a captive in the hole of a slave ship "had less room than a man in a coffin," he insisted that abolitionists exaggerated the evils of the slave trade to score political points.[38] Nonetheless, the tales of survivors, participants, and observers reveal a sort of netherworld of unmitigated terrors troubling to the imagination. Captives were rounded up and driven as cattle, in some instances, over eight hundred miles to the coast, death lurking at every turn. Many who reached the coast but were rejected by buyers were murdered in factories and barracoons rather than be set free.[39] Female captives were routinely raped, others murdered in the dark holding bays in the many European castles and forts that dotted Africa's Atlantic coastline.[40] In the cargo hold of slaving ships, poor ventilation and tight packing deprived captives of adequate oxygen; the heat was so intense that dehydration occurred within a very short time. Captain John Ashley Hall recounted that after spending only a few minutes in the hold, his shirt was "so wet with perspiration, that I could have wrung it as if it had been steeped in water."[41] Equiano recounted the captive's personal experience: "The stench of the hold . . . was so intolerably loathsome, that it was dangerous to remain there for any time . . . The closeness of the place, and the heat of the climate, added to the number in the ship, which was so crowded that each had scarcely room to turn himself, almost suffocated us. This produced copious perspirations, so that the air soon became unfit for respiration, from a variety of loathsome smells, and brought on a sickness among the slaves, of which many died . . . The shrieks of the women, and the groans of the dying, rendered the whole a scene of horror almost inconceivable."[42] A carpenter employed in the Royal Navy confirmed that the hold was indeed like a graveyard yielding up its dead: "I have known them to go down well, and in the morning brought up dead, from the suffocated state they were in below."[43]

Thomas Clarkson was the first academic to quantify mortality in the English slave trade. His research revealed losses of between 8 and 33 percent, with an overall average of 21 percent.[44] This was phenomenally higher than any other branch of maritime migration, so much so that "more persons would be found dead in three slave-vessels from Bristol, in a given time, than in all other vessels put together, numerous as they were, belonging to this same port."[45] The Select Committee of Parliament inquiring into the slave trade documented even more disturbing losses, ranging from 25 to 50 percent per vessel.[46] Curtin, Miller, Lovejoy, and other modern statisticians have calculated middling losses of between 9 and 17 percent per ship for the whole British period.[47] Yet even the most conservative estimate is a sad tale of an immensely morbid traffic.[48]

Methods to deal with conditions aboard slavers did not mitigate their misery or save lives. Women were subjected to rape not only to satisfy the wanton lust of sailors but also as a ritual for "breaking them in."[49] Rapes were also common on slavers in the entrepôt traffic from Caribbean ports to final destinations.[50] For exercise captives were brought on deck, where the captain ordered them to dance and sing to the beat of the drum. These were not moments of merriment, however; songs invariably expressed the captives' fear of being beaten and starved as well as of the death they saw as only imminent.[51]

The vibrancy of the slave trade was intimately connected to the terror regime of plantation slavery, especially the sugar industry. Jamaica was by far the largest importer of captives: up to abolition of the trade over 1.2 million Africans were landed there, with slightly over 200,000 re-exported. Despite the self-perpetuating nature of slavery (children legally inheriting their mothers' status), by 1807 the population was less than 350,000. A similar picture emerged in England's second largest colony: between 1640 and 1807 Barbados imported over 600,000 African captives; by the later year, however, the enslaved population stood between 69,000 and 75,000.[52]

Decline from profit-driven, genocidal management was exacerbated by strategies to contain violent resistance. The arriving Africans most feared by West Indian proprietors were the "Coromantee," a generic term for captives from the Gold Coast. The Coromantee actually constituted a multiplicity of separate ethnic elements, including Ashanti, Fante, and Ga.[53] Akan was the lingua franca across a wide swath of this region. Coromantee leadership was evident in all the major revolts and documented plots from Jamaica to Suriname. Although Barbadian law prohibited their entry, they still constituted the largest subgroup in that colony.[54] By the close of the eighteenth century a wide cross-section of colonial and metropolitan interests had accepted Long's prognosis that future peace depended on curbing the revolutionary spirit of the Coromantee by creolizing the labor force.

The Challenge of Morality in Slave Society

Early colonizers to the West Indies were primarily about economic exploitation, not the transfer of civilization. Recruiters routinely targeted the societal "scum of scums" from the metropolis, garnished with a sprinkling of men of "high character."[55] In this diasporic milieu church and family lost their traditional functions as "the moral cement of society."[56] The Sugar Revolution ensured no regeneration. Overindulgence was the order of the day, whether rum drinking, gambling, feasting, debauchery, or the myriad vices frowned upon by seventeenth-century moralists.[57] It was not that West Indian colonists preferred to live outside the authority of the church; the colonial church never claimed such authority. Early colonists, including the clergy, largely disdained the moral-ethical restraints commonly associated with religion in the mother country.

Ironically, but with true imperial arrogance, ameliorators were generally more appalled by the morality of enslaved Africans than that of enslavers. They presumed that a revolution in morality of the enslaved was the key to the amelioration of slavery and the success of creolization. Because Christianity emphasizes control of sexual behavior as paramount in moral education, the dominant explanation for the moral standards of the enslaved was their promiscuous lifestyle. Promiscuity was linked to low reproduction; thus, advocates of Christianized morality and creolization naturally put the spotlight on the family. It goes without saying that the only family that reformers validated was the Anglo-Saxon, Christian model.

Historians have wrongly postulated an African origin for the family patterns and values that emerged among the enslaved class. Frank Pitman's description is typical: "Marriage among the Negroes commonly perpetuated the characteristics of the institution as it existed in Africa and, in the long period before Christian missions, little or no attempt was made to inculcate Anglo-Saxon conceptions of marriage."[58] Contrary to such presumptions, Africans' persistence with marriage, in whatever form, qualifies as the most profound act of nonviolent resistance against enslavement. Enslavers systematically attacked the marriage institution by the arbitrary sale of family members, the emasculation of husbands compelled to witness the flogging and other degrading punishments of their wives and mothers, and the similar stripping of womanhood by compelling wives and mothers to witness the flogging of their husbands and sons. Such violations were tantamount to a denial of humanity, their termination the cause célèbre of resistance.[59]

Christianity universally associates promiscuity with polygamy. The comparison of polygamy and monogamy was essentially a weighing of African against Anglo-Saxon marriage and the extended family structure against the nuclear. Monogamous marriage was never a reliable monitor of family values; thus, the elevation of one cultural option above another is sociologically untenable. The assumption of the African family as a poor agency for sexual mores prevailed, despite contemporary knowledge that the social degradation of the enslaved was a product of social control strategies of planters. Planters' systematic reduction of the usefulness of enslaved Africans to labor functions would have rendered impracticable a transfer of the requisites for autochthonous African family structures and values—ties that bound lineage groups together rather than individuals. Thus, the African family and kinship relations were not re-created on slave plantations; rather, they were destroyed.

European belief in African promiscuity was legendary. It persisted among colonials because it complemented the stereotypical African savage, incapable of civilized emotions and sensibilities. The promiscuity patent remained African despite evidence to the contrary from colonial men of letters and reports from European adventurers to Africa.[60] In the earliest published account of the social life of enslaved Africans in a British plantation colony, the reference to husband-and-wife relations among the enslaved suggests compulsive monogamy.[61] Indeed, the lower ratio of enslaved women to men in all early colonies elevated wives to a prized possession and made monogamy the pragmatic option, except for a privileged few. Commenting on the conjugal relations of the enslaved in early-eighteenth-century Jamaica, Hans Sloane affirmed, "They have every one his wife, and are much concerned if they prove adulterous."[62] Interestingly, the planters themselves engaged in monogamy-polygamy manipulation of African unions as a tool of social control. As Richard Ligon observed, they might allow "a brave fellow, and one that has extraordinary qualities, two or three wives"; women, however, were "allowed" only one husband.[63]

"Marriage" was a conspicuous symbol of belonging and a precondition for raising children among African arrivants. Grenadian planter Gordon Turnbull affirmed that immediately after "seasoning," many newly arrived Africans "are married (*in their own way*) and have houses, gardens, hogs, and poultry of their own."[64] In giving similar testimony, Edward Long included the proviso, "pro tempore," reflecting his experience as a leading lawmaker as well as the harsh reality of the vulnerability of enslaved marriages to enslavers' predation and insensitivity in the selling of close-knit family members.[65] The best account of an enslaved marriage ceremony comes from the biography of Ashton Warner of St. Vincent. Warner was manumitted by his aunt while still "an infant at the breast" but was falsely re-enslaved at ten years of age. Warner related that as a young man of twenty-one, having asked Sally, a "field slave," to be his wife, "we stood up in her father's house, before her mother and her uncle, and her sisters, and holding each other by the hand, pledged our troth as husband and wife, and promised before God to be good and kind to each other, and to love and help each other, as long as we lived."[66] Warner recounted the brutal punishments meted out to his wife, even when pregnant, which might have made the most determined person reluctant to take a wife.[67] Mary Prince similarly described the sadomasochistic floggings she received in the presence of her husband, a freeman.[68]

Long's assessment of African promiscuity is instructive. He observed, "They are all married in their own way to a husband or wife," yet, he added, they "have other family connections, in every parish throughout the island; so that one of them, perhaps, has six or more husbands, or wives, in several different places . . . [but] only one is the object of particular steady attachment."[69] Accordingly, it was "by this means they find support when their own lands fail them, and houses of call and refreshment, whenever they are upon their travels."[70] This nexus of relations points to an economic and strategic response to plantation slavery; economic survival was enhanced and the prejudices and suspicions of lodging beyond the confines of the plantation mitigated. These connections might also have been networks of polyandry and manifestations of gender equality—a clear indication that it was slavery that reshaped the parameters of sexual and familial relations of Africans. It is obvious also that these networks of communication might easily serve as cells of organized resistance, including insurgency.

A different pattern of family values emerged among the slavocracy, wherein marriage was an aristocratic indulgence, and "by universal consent concubinage . . . stands established as a virtue."[71] Polygamy was also a virtue, mainly because of the preference for bachelor-planters and attorneys, some of whom left their wives and children in England.[72] As with all slave systems, the enslaved were vulnerable to enslavers' sexual predation. The rare presence of the enslaver's wife and children was no deterrence. The account of Thomas Thistlewood, overseer and proprietor of Egypt Plantation in mid-eighteenth-century Jamaica, remains one of the best personal confessions of moral depravity and sexual abuse.[73] Other plantation officers also commanded similar services from enslaved females. Biographies of formerly enslaved persons confirm the degradation and shame from the victims' perspectives.[74] To a large extent, because of sexual abuse, women constantly attacked drivers and overseers, verbally and physically, a struggle well documented in the period of imperial amelioration, from 1823 to 1834.

Enslaved women were producers of wealth in addition to being sex slaves. Internal slave trading was in part a sex trade. Enslavers sometimes sold enslaved women they had impregnated because the prospect of naturally increasing the stock of labor might enhance their value; they sold some of the prettiest females on the open sex market; enslavers also habitually compelled them to prostitute themselves for lusting visitors.[75] Enslaved girls were forced into sexual activity with multiple partners from as early as nine years of age, in consequence of which white males perpetuated a vicious cycle of incest. As one report stated, "Mulatto girls, during the flower of their age, are universally sacrificed to the lust of white men; in some instances to that of their own fathers."[76] In this milieu of immorality the virtue of kinship was repudiated by male colonists, who treated their progenies of miscegenation as aliens. Commenting on these offspring of iniquity, John Luffman noted, "As soon as born, they are despised, not only by the very authors, under God, of their being, but by every white, destitute of humane and liberal principles."[77]

The Anglican clergy also contributed to the malaise of colonial society. In the first instance the clergy was hopelessly underrepresented in the sugar colonies. The classic example was Barbados, the birthplace of the Sugar Revolution and the most densely populated colony. Although the island had the highest number of priests per capita by the end of the seventeenth century, the ratio was only one quarter of what obtained in England.[78] In the second instance the dereliction of duty and repudiation of ecclesiastical ethics substantially reduced the potential implied in this statistic because "many priests of the Church of England proved incompetent or worldly or immoral."[79] One priest who had laid claim to two livings without having taken holy orders "had been tolerated for twenty-four years" by successive governors.[80] The situation was no better elsewhere. In 1671 Governor Sir Charles Wheler of the Leeward Islands informed the king that of the four priests stationed there, three were unworthy of their station: among them, he reported, was "one drunken orthodox priest, one drunken sectary priest, and one drunken person that had no orders."[81] By 1800 nothing significant had changed.[82]

"A Concentration of Misery"

Contrary to the prevarications of abolitionists, slavery was no less evil than the slave trade. The end of the Middle Passage was the beginning of a new chapter of alienation, degradation, and death to the survivors of the crossing.

On the auction blocks the new arrivals were sold as cattle; this degradation was followed by branding them with the names of proprietors' estates and imposing new personal names that also applied to plantation cattle or social rejects.[83] Sale by "scramble" in the West Indies was responsible for the division of relatives and "countrymen."[84] Some would never see each other again. These emotionally charged moments traumatized even African bystanders not on the auction block, as Equiano recounted: "At or after a sale it was not uncommon to see negroes taken from their wives, wives taken from their husbands, and children from their parents, and sent off to other islands, and wherever else their merciless lords chose; and probably never more during life to see each other! Oftentimes my heart has bled at these partings; when the friends of the departed have been at the water side, and, with sighs and tears, have kept their eyes fixed on the vessel till it went out of sight."[85] Even before recovering from the shock of survival, many were destined for immediate labor on the plantations; true seasoning was a luxury that the demands of the sugar industry could seldom afford, while the most effective language of communication was the whip.[86]

At the commencement of African enslavement in the Caribbean it was clearly understood that subservience might be maintained only by brute force.[87] For this reason non-Christian Africans were not welcomed in the Spanish colonies before 1518. The early decimation of native populations made it expedient to import labor directly from Africa, producing the first recorded large-scale insurrection in 1522; ironically, some of the insurgents might have been Christians.[88] The *Siete Partidas,* which governed slavery in Spain, had to be gradually supplanted by colonial laws sanctioning even more inhumane practices for instilling fear in enslaved Africans.

To abolitionists the work routine and living conditions of the enslaved were inconsistent with the minimum expectations of humanity and thus denounced as evil. Indeed, the term *punishment* was simply a euphemism for physical and psychological degradation, diabolical torture, and sadism. The "concentration of misery" was supported by laws giving whites almost absolute power of life and death over the enslaved and Afro-Caribbean peoples in general.[89] Until well into the eighteenth century British proprietors certainly relied on terror alone for security rather than trust the disarming potential of Christianity, the latter a popular myth in French and Spanish colonies. Enslavers' afrophobia was crucial in defining this preference. Bryan Edwards admitted that the slavocracy achieved the "routinization of terrifying spectacles," which was heightened by mutilation of the bodies of dead Africans to impress on bystanders "not only with their power over life, but with their influence in the afterlife."[90]

Few historians engage the lurid details of European savagism against enslaved Africans. Yet this engagement is essential to the dialectic of managing and resisting slavery. It is also important to students of Caribbean history who continue to mythicize postslavery indenture of new immigrants as "another kind of slavery." Spanish and Portuguese colonizers were the first masters of terror against enslaved Africans. The special police laws that superseded the *Siete Partidas* had the full support of philosophers and theologians.[91] French and English colonists adopted Iberian strategies; with the backing of their own intellectuals, terror was easily accepted as "a necessary inducement to labour in tropical colonies."[92] Among British abolitionists who understood the psychology of terror, the most explicit description comes from James Stephen, who had firsthand experience of the West Indies: "A strange but fortunate prejudice, the creature of early terror, fostered by ignorance and habit, secured in great measure the tranquillity of these colonies before their revolutions; and forms the great security of all the Islands wherein slavery still prevails. I mean that *nameless and undefined idea of terror, connected in the mind of the negro slave, with the notion of resistance to a white man and a master.*"[93] To Stephen it was not the pain of punishment that kept the enslaved class in submission but, rather, "the strong and indefinite terror" to which they had been constantly exposed from infancy or since their arrival from Africa.[94] Not all ameliorators balked at the savagery meted out to Africans. Based on personal experience, Ramsay acknowledged that the interests of enslaved and enslavers are so diametrically opposite that "it is impossible to infuse any other principle than fear into the mind of a slave."[95] Brougham assured policy makers that "a perpetual terror of the lash is the only preventive of indolence."[96]

In actuality terror was a tool of reverse psychology to disguise the fear enslavers had for the enslaved. For the latter the injection of fear began literally in the womb, as pregnant women were often stripped naked and savagely brutalized. Tiny tots were not spared; Mary Prince witnessed the daily terrorizing of "two little slave boys in the house," whether they behaved "well or ill." She lamented, "I have seen their flesh ragged and raw with licks.—Lick—lick they were never secure one moment from a blow, and their lives were passed in continual fear."[97] Yet the concurrence of men like Brougham (with no direct experience of colonial slavery) on the arbitrary use of terror is testimony to a shared understanding of the primacy of the colonial economy to Britain as a world power; furthermore, the three referenced, imperialist spokesmen were all leading abolitionists and ameliorators. Although the following details particularize the plantation, it should be noted that dehumanization had no occupational barrier. Mary Prince recounted that her consignment to the salt pans of Bermuda was the cruelest of all her work experiences as an enslaved woman.[98] Animal husbandry and urban occupations were certainly not as hazardous to life as sugar production, but no enslaved person was safe from manic tyrants.

Colonials well understood that a successful insurgency represented the gravest threat to life, property, and power relations of a colony. The significance of insurrection is reflected in the degree of savage retaliations of the plantocracy and state against rebels and conspirators. Two suspects in an emancipationist conspiracy in seventeenth-century Barbados were strung up in chains for four days until they "confessed" to a planned large-scale rebellion; the leaders were "promptly executed."[99] Having suppressed a revolt in the 1680s, the Antiguan authorities ordered one ringleader to be "burned to ashes"; another participant owned by the governor "had his tongue cut out and a leg chopped off 'as a living Example to the rest.'"[100] These "punishments" were repeated on a grander scale in the aftermath of the alleged plot to rebel in 1736.[101] Following the Barbados uprising in 1692, forty-two alleged participants were judicially castrated.[102] Harsh treatment was guaranteed to emancipationist leaders, but the passion for absolute power sometimes resulted in plantation authorities inflicting retribution on every participant in an insurgency or suspected plot. Such was the case in Jamaica in 1685–86 when "every Negro caught during this rebellion was killed—burned alive, torn by dogs, or drawn and quartered."[103] White Jamaicans resorted to similar savagery in the aftermath of Tacky's War "to make a few terrible examples of some of the most guilty."[104] Indeed, slavery completely degraded enslaved and enslavers. One witness to the 1790 parliamentary inquiry into the slave trade described a scene that particularly disturbed him: a proprietor who instructed a surgeon to cut off the leg of a perfectly healthy enslaved man. The doctor refused; thereupon "the planter took up an iron bar, with which he broke the leg in pieces, and then he desired the surgeon to cut it off, which he did."[105] Female enslavers were no less sadistic. The wife of a clergyman at Port Royal was described as a "remarkably cruel woman" who would drop scalding hot wax on enslaved persons after a whipping.[106] Mary Prince experienced such a mistress, who would strip her naked and hang her up by her wrists before cutting her flesh open with the cart whip; this was "ordinary punishment for even a slight offence."[107]

Enslaved Africans bore these cruelties with superhuman valor, which over time white colonials and metropolitans misconstrued as the inability to feel pain. The most dramatic demonstrations of stoicism corresponded with the most terrifying, post-revolt retributions. Clarkson concluded that the callous punishments so commonly executed for even the most trivial offenses robbed whites of human sensitivity to Africans' pain and suffering: "The very slitting of ears has been considered an operation so perfectly devoid of pain as to have been performed for no other reason than that for which a brand is set upon a [sic] cattle, as *a mark of property.*"[108] A section leader in Tacky's War, sentenced to death by fire, "was made to sit on the ground, and his body being chained to an iron stake, the fire was applied to his feet. He uttered not a groan, and saw his legs reduced to ashes with utmost firmness and composure."[109] It is now known that such stoicism was intrinsic to the curriculum of institutions commonly called "secret societies," which proliferated in sub-Saharan Africa. Equiano's biography validates anthropological findings that even young boys taken captive in Africa might already have been schooled in the art of transcending physical pain.[110] Africans enslaved in the West Indies and elsewhere deployed this stoicism as a political weapon in their determination not to give their enslavers the pleasure of submission to their will. Accordingly, stoicism exacerbated the punishment syndrome on plantations.

Metropolitans and colonials shared the belief that "only subjection to the power of masters armed with absolute authority" could prevent African ascendancy over Europeans.[111] Above all else, the whip symbolized power. As Patterson recognized: "Whipping was not only a method of punishment. It was a conscious device to impress upon the slaves that they were slaves; it was a crucial form of slave control."[112] Theoretically, whipping was grounded in Judeo-Christian Scripture. Moses, the revered Jewish lawmaker, first prescribed the thirty-nine lashes, which became the standard for colonial legislatures and which planters generally claimed as the maximum inflicted.[113] Yet the means, if not the severity, of flogging challenged Scripture. Ramsay surmised that Moses might have imposed greater restraint had he known the cart whip, which was designed to torture rather than punish.[114] The whip was made of "cow's hide, about half an inch in breadth with large knots upon it in several places." [115] Whips could also be made of ebony, with natural protrusions to ensure maximum injuries. [116] These special designs made floggings of enslaved persons crueler than those inflicted on soldiers and sailors in the Royal Navy. Military officers testified that the whippings of enslaved people were "more severe, although they did not receive so many lashes; yet the punishment was more cruel on account of the size of the whip with which the punishment was inflicted." [117] Lieutenant John Simpson, who often witnessed regimental punishments, concurred: "The punishments of the soldiers were generally mild, compared with the whippings of the slaves in gaol or round the town." [118] To this explanation William Dickson added a touch of sadistic empiricism: that the customary thirty-nine lashes meted out to the enslaved were "more severe, perhaps, though less tedious than two hundred from the cat-o-nine-tails used in the army." [119]

Whipping of Africans began with their capture and trek to the barracoons and factories of Africa's slaving coasts; it greeted them on their arrival in the West Indies, forcefully separating family members who had survived the Middle Passage. According to John Wesley, "Here you may see mothers hanging over their daughters, bedewing their naked breasts with tears, and daughters clinging to their parents, till the whipping soon obliges them to part." [120] Whippings continued unabated during and after seasoning.

Whipping was the specialist occupation of a "jumper," who called at the homes of enslavers for whipping jobs, which he apparently enjoyed. To make a punishment more severe, after cutting the enslaved on one side of the back, the jumper changed direction "in order to cross and chequer it": "When this operation is over, the slave is again flogged, but in another way. This is done with a switch of ebony, the pickles of which open any bruises that may have been made on the back, and let out the congealed blood." [121] Enslaved people were often "hospitalized" after a whipping and carried lifetime scars, a measured objective of jumpers and enslavers. [122] According to one witness, victims were "sometimes swung off the ground up to a crane erected for that purpose, with great weights to their feet to stretch them out to make the wounds larger with the whip. Men and women were both served in the same manner." [123] Children might be spared the cart whip but not the cruelty of sadistic whippings and other forms of plantation terror. An eyewitness testified: "I have seen four or five negro boys and girls tied up by their hands to the ram-horns of a crane, and by means of the machine lifted from the ground. Their whole weight was suspended by their wrists. In this situation they were flogged with a bush of black ebony, which has ten times more prickles upon it than the green thorn of this country. The blood issued at every stroke, and to increase the pain, the bush was previously dipped into salt water." [124] Courts-martial authorized the most severe whippings. After the Demerara uprising in 1823, a court-martial ordered that several rebels be given between two hundred and a thousand lashes with the cart whip. A doctor was on hand to revive them from the many spells of unconsciousness; ten of the most brutalized spent up to three and a half months in the Colonial Hospital recuperating from their wounds. Those receiving the maximum number of lashes were also condemned to work in chains for the rest of their lives. [125]

Despite its importance as punishment, the whip was more crucial in the field, where it gained its reputation as the "badge of slavery." As an instrument of torture, the whip competed with other forms and instruments of brutality; in the fields, however, the whip ruled supreme. It was the only incentive to work or, indeed, the most effective disincentive for faulting the rhythm of the gang. A driver would continually flick his whip over their backs as if practicing for the next blow, promoting a constant fear of the lash as workers toiled. Driving the gang was a high-status job for an enslaved person. The driver was carefully chosen for his great physical strength. He had the full authority to flog whenever he perceived the slightest variation from the established rhythm; it did not matter whether the relaxation was from skulking or incapacity. There was no regard for age, sex, pregnancy, or postnatal complications. [126] Occasionally, the white overseer would do his own whipping. One eyewitness testified, "I observed the Negroes at work in the field with one or two White Men looking after them, and a Black Man or two, called a driver, keeping the whip constantly cracking over their heads while at work, and sometimes lashing them with it; which I thought a very oppressive situation; sometimes a White Man whipping them." [127] This scene was common to all colonies in the late eighteenth century. Plantation work was double punishment for many enslaved people, especially for those found guilty of marronage, revolt, and violence against whites. An overseer's desire for rhythmic gang work did not rule out enslaved laborers bearing a log of wood or heavy iron ball as much as fifty pounds in weight, attached to an ankle by an iron chain. [128] Field laborers also wore heavy iron collars around their necks, which carried "large triangles riveted on the outside of them, spreading about two feet." [129] These iron contraptions weighed as much as twelve pounds. Children were not spared these disabling punishments, which seemed to have increased in severity after the Haitian Revolution. In the early nineteenth century twelve-year-old girls were forced to wear padlocked neck chains weighing as much as eighteen pounds.[130]

The sugar works complemented field work in imposing superhuman demands on the enslaved, some of whom were made to work all night in the boiling house. This routine took a heavy toll and affected the quality of the sugar. Ramsay was an eyewitness to this wanton waste of human and material resources: "They sleep over their work; the sugar is ill-tempered, burnt in the boiler, and improperly struck; while the mill every now and then grinds off an hand, or an arm of those drowsy worn down creatures that feed on it."[131] He was appalled by the planters' insistence in working against their own economic interest.

The prime usefulness of the enslaved population was their labor; little else mattered to proprietors. From the age of two children were sent to collect grass, an activity that produced cuts and bruises, some of which developed into permanent sores.[132] Children from six to twelve years of age were organized into gangs, as much "to keep them out of mischief, as to ensure them gradually to the work of the sugar estate."[133] Not surprisingly, old, economically useless enslaved people were discarded without means of subsistence, in spite of laws to prevent this practice. One Jamaican planter developed a launching pad over a precipice to jettison those who were old and infirmed "into eternity."[134] Sometimes the elderly were set loose to roam the streets and live as vagrants and beggars; those retained on the estates were given less severe workloads, but the failure to complete them could nevertheless invite severe whippings.[135]

On the surface grass collecting and tending to provision grounds appeared to be light tasks, but the work was no less injurious than "cane-holing," traditionally considered the most backbreaking task for field workers.[136] Grass collecting was light enough to be done by children, but the real nature of the task left field workers with little time for sleep. Grass was collected mainly out of crop, when the work of the field gangs was more drudgery than burdensome. The emphasis on grass collecting at such times made the "slack season" no less inhumane than crop time, when field hands sometimes worked around the clock. A workday started as early as four o'clock in the morning and ended as late as midnight. The actual workday in the field usually ended at sunset, after which the same field gangs were sent to collect grass. Often grass was found at great distances from the fields, especially in times of drought. Each person had to bring a fixed quota or face punishment, a task that robbed exhausted field hands of much deserved rest. To Ramsay grass collecting was so "oppressive" that it was "the most frequent cause of running away,"[137] an option with its own severe consequences.

Sick laborers were worked to death and in some instances callously murdered.[138] Plantation officials often refused to believe complaints of ill health by enslaved persons. Yet illnesses were common in light of poor housing conditions and little time for proper personal hygiene. Doctors were of little use; often their visits were not to administer medical treatment to ailing patients but, rather, "to pronounce them past recovery."[139] Even if an enslaved person were hospitalized, the chance of survival was not enhanced because hospitals were often "filthy in the extreme" and "destitute of almost every convenience."[140] These evils were compounded by poor diet, which differed slightly in different colonies but was commonly poor and monotonous: "breakfast, dinner and supper being similar to each other, and, for the most part the same throughout the year."[141] Underfeeding was premeditated to break the will of Africans to resist and to accelerate the passage of the superannuated, so that they might not become an economic burden.[142] Food was a major import but generally not intended for enslaved laborers.[143] By the late eighteenth century, however, underfeeding was also a consequence of reduced profitability of the sugar industry.[144] Malnutrition and overcrowding made enslaved people highly susceptible to a variety of illnesses, such as dysentery, rickets, scurvy, yaws, and insect-borne diseases, most of which became fatal under conditions of overwork and poor health care.[145] The short time spent at "home" provided little rest and no comforts to the enslaved class. For some home was comparable to an open cow's shed, fully exposed to the damp; for the more fortunate it might be a little hut with clayed walls and a roof covered with cane trash, sometimes with plantain leaves. No bedding was provided; they usually slept on a hard plank, without even a change of their working garments.[146]

Plantation work routine and living conditions might have reduced fecundity among the enslaved, yet pregnancies were common. Pregnant women received no sympathy from enslavers, however, who compelled them to do the very "painful work" of weeding.[147] During Ramsay's sojourn in St. Kitts "nothing raised a manager's resentment sooner than to be informed that a Negress was with child."[148] Women were kept working in the fields up to the last month of pregnancy, resulting in many miscarriages.[149] Plantation owners and managers saw only the short-term, economic gain in aborted pregnancies because these women would waste no time in tending to their children. Even when women survived these horrors and successfully delivered their babies, the joy of motherhood was short-lived. A delivery often occurred "in a dark, damp, smoky hut, perhaps without a rag in which to wrap the child."[150] Only two weeks after giving birth, they had to resume their customary tasks, including the burden of weeding, with no one to care for their infants.[151] At best infants were carried on their mothers' backs in classic African tradition, but they were likely to be roasted by the sun and starved, lest the mothers invite savage cracks of the driver's whip for daring to interrupt the rhythm of the gang.[152]

Not surprisingly, infant mortality was phenomenally high for the first month of life. During the eighteenth century over 80 percent of the infants of enslaved mothers died within the first nine days of life.[153] From the 1760s conditions for postnatal care began to receive the attention of the few proprietary ameliorators, but there was no compulsion to secure better ones; by the 1780s conditions were still grim and primitive. A "lying-in woman" was allowed only three to four weeks for recovery. After this period of recuperation, she was sent to the field with child in one hand and hoe in the other, enjoying no respite from the cart whip. Estate management made no provision for childcare; the mother was obliged to place her naked infant in a furrow near her, without protection from the tropical elements. Only a few planters provided nurses, but picking grass was the only work from which they were exempt.[154] Amazingly, even to the end of slavery, pregnant women were not spared the cart whip and other sadistic punishments. Ashton Warner of St. Vincent recounted how the estate manager twice ordered flogging and confinement in stocks for his wife "when far advanced in pregnancy," while he stood a helpless witness; the floggings continued soon after childbirth.[155]

While rebellions and other acts of destructive resistance were obvious investor concerns, high mortality also represented a capital loss that was virtually impossible to quantify. Newly arrived captives seldom lived beyond nine years, while their landed cost rose steadily from about fourteen pounds in 1663 to as much as fifty pounds during the 1760s.[156] After the War of American Independence the price of prime captives escalated to sixty pounds.[157] By that time abolitionists were associating high mortality among enslaved adults with dependency on the Atlantic slave trade. To a large extent Long's *History of Jamaica* underscored this hypothesis. The period of seasoning accounted for the vast majority of deaths. Long condemned the situation as highly uneconomic and proposed more prudent management toward greater economy:

"To augment our negroes therefore by procreation, we must endeavour to remedy those evils which impede or frustrate its natural effect. And to conclude, if the waste of these men should become less, the price of them would fall; and the same demand would be kept up, by extending our plantation, which is now produced by mortality of these people; estates would be gradually well stocked, and rendered more flourishing; and the circumstances of the planter changed for the better."[158] In pleading the case for Jamaican plantership against charges of ill treatment, Long argued that planter terror was a necessary evil consistent with the dangers from large native African populations.[159] Thus, with respect to security and productivity, two critical facets of the colonial economy, the slave trade and slavery, stood condemned. On this legacy metropolitan-based abolitionists mounted their attack against the slave trade in order to achieve viability and security from amelioration.

2

HUMANITY ENCHAINED

Propertied Humanity

The Navigation Acts ended the short era of proprietary government but not the rule of the plantocracy.[1] One of the Crown's major concessions was nonintervention in domestic slavery. The planter-dominated assemblies aggressively defended this compromise as a right of charter beyond the reach of Crown and Parliament. No party seriously considered the humanity of the enslaved until the onset of proprietary amelioration in the 1760s. For the next four decades embryonic amelioration experiments progressed slowly and unsystematically. Notwithstanding, they ignited an early spark that attracted the attention of metropolitan abolitionists. Convinced by the feasibility of statutory amelioration, the Crown finally gave its stamp of approval toward the close of the century—its first political intervention on the side of the enslaved.

The framing of imperial intervention "as a trust" merged with the construction of moral imperium.[2] The process was seeded by a fortuitous convergence of Protestant humanism, political expediency, and economic necessity. Britain's emergence as one of Europe's great powers provided the initial stimulus, Protestant philanthropists articulated its political potential, and pseudoscientific racism defined its boundaries. Several leading clerics interpreted the dawn of this new cultural imperialism as an opportune moment for Protestant missionism. John Wesley, the father of Methodism, succinctly proclaimed, "I look upon the world as my parish."[3] William Carey, founder of the Baptist Missionary Society, concurred.[4] Adding a touch of jingoism, Reverend F. Randolph, chaplain to the royal family, boasted to Prime Minister Pitt that England's rise to high civilization was a work of genius of her own nationals in the fields of politics and the civil arts. Randolph preached the doctrine of manifest destiny, asserting that the military and commercial achievements of Englishmen bound them "to act as the Tutors and Guardians of mankind; and if we betray or abuse the Trust reposed in us, we prove ourselves unworthy of the Freedom we possess; and unfit the whole Employ of it; for which Providence may probably have designed us."[5] For the West Indies the bootstrap of this mission was amelioration. Architects of imperial trust idealized amelioration as the conscience of a reformed colonialism; there was, however, no intent to radicalize the social structure, even with the cooperation of colonial legislators.

The orientation of imperial policy toward trust first emerged during the trial of India's governor-general Warren Hastings and the related inquiry into the affairs of the East India Company.[6] Nevertheless, the first experiment was conducted in the West Indies as a counterpoise to the widespread emancipation wars in the eastern Caribbean and the emergence of Haiti as a Caribbean power and beacon of revolutionary emancipation.[7] The defining feature of the Caribbean model of trust was amelioration. Its primary challenge to moderate the arbitrary power of plantership was based on the popular but false belief that ameliorating slavery would preempt or defuse the impulse for revolutionary emancipationism and make the enslaved "more useful to themselves, their masters, and the state."[8] The futility in reining in proprietary absolutism provided the pragmatic rationale for pure Crown colony government in Trinidad and St. Lucia, modified Crown colony in Demerara, and Crown-directed amelioration from 1823 in all three colonies. Initial intervention began with demands to all assemblies to enact reformed amelioration slave laws with standard provisos for protecting enslaved persons, particularly women, against animalistic labor routines and planters' manic impulse for violence. The imperial push for statutory amelioration was supported by abolitionists and slave trade advocates alike. The common logic was economic necessity: to raise the competitiveness of colonial economies against French competition, achieve internal security, and manage labor in the event that the slave trade was abolished.[9]

Abolitionists conflated the economics of slavery with an imperative to humanize the enslaved. Deconstructing this humanity is critical to understanding the limits of metropolitan intervention on behalf of enslaved Africans, including the avoidance of emancipation in slave trade abolition and antislavery discourse. It is evident from the biographies of freedmen and freedwomen in the age of amelioration that their sense of humanity differed significantly from that of white ameliorators. Although Olaudah Equiano's *Interesting Narrative* was obviously tempered to placate his conservative patrons, and even though he also advocated amelioration as a halfway house, he was convinced that European humanity would be vindicated only "when the sable people shall gratefully commemorate the auspicious era of extensive freedom."[10] Equiano's subaltern humanity equates with the Xhosa-Zulu concept of "ubuntu," a conscience call of "humanity to humanity."[11] White ameliorators spoke a different language, translating aristocratic Aristotelian humanism into a virtue of British imperialism. Typical of the old school, Adam Smith had contended: "The amiable virtue of humanity, requires, surely, a sensibility much beyond what is possessed by the rude vulgar of mankind . . . As in the common degree of the intellectual qualities, there is no ability; so in the common degree of the moral, there is no virtue."[12] Such sentiments resonated widely in mid-eighteenth-century England. Any prospect for imperializing humanity was nevertheless circumscribed by the pathological fear that defined European-African relations in the colonies. White ameliorators had to reconcile the received notion of Africans as "natural enemies" with their new "Friends of the Negro" ascription. This apparent dichotomy was consistent with mainstream Methodism. In *The Character of a Methodist,* John Wesley referenced the Sermon on the Mount as he appealed to Methodists to repay hatred with neighborly love: "*For he loves his Enemies, yea and the enemies of* GOD; *the Evil and the Unthankful.*"[13] Protestants inherited the label "Enemies of Christ," imposed on Africans by the papacy in sanctioning the launch of the Atlantic slave trade.[14] The belief that Africans were political and cosmological enemies afforded evangelical abolitionists the highest redemptive possibilities. Thus, their desire to befriend enslaved Africans did not preclude supporting tyranny to secure European life and property. It is this conflation of principles that informed Peter Fryer's conceptualization of imperial trusteeship as the "cosmetic version" of pseudoscientific racism;[15] Alice Conklin's "constructive exploitation" offers an even more succinct description.[16]

Purveyors of trusteeship assumed intellectual and cultural superiority over subjugated peoples. This assumption was crucial in idealizing "trust" as the highest virtue of imperialism and the noblest objective of humanity; it stemmed from the notion that humanity was a virtue of "civilized" nations, to which Europeans claimed elite membership. Other peoples ranged from savage to primitive: collectively, they were the "inferior" or "colored" races of the earth. Trust was the gift of civilized nations to inferior races; its application was conditioned by their innate brutishness. This imperial arrogance was validated by the general acceptance of the findings of pseudoscientific racism. Ultimately, the objective of metropolitan intervention was not true justice or equity because, as Burke succinctly stated, "inferior races were doomed to live upon trust."[17] Their treatment at the hands of Europeans was conditioned by the very character traits contrived by colonials for their exploitation: shift-lessness, cunning, shamelessness, brutishness, untrustworthiness, and licentiousness, among other derogatory traits. Thus, medical doctor James Maycock could boast that the punishments of enslaved laborers of Barbados were "regulated more by principles of humanity than formerly"; likewise, a Jamaican planter considered his infliction of nine lashes with the cart whip "gentle admonition."[18.] This situation was no paradox. The simple fact is that so long as colonial powers and their slaveholding elites claimed intellectual property rights over definitions of humanity, happiness, and justice, amelioration could only at best be regulated tyranny.[19] Even the most radical phase of statutory amelioration faced no significant opposition to brutal and humiliating punishments consistent with the advance of "humanity and justice," the signature abolitionist mantra.

The irony in combining conventional violence with humanity and justice was best captioned in the enigmatic query "Am I Not a Man and a Brother?" inscribed on the Josiah Wedgewood medallion (the signature emblem of the antislavery movement). If anything, the words were a classic Freudian admission of imperial attitudes to enslavement of Africans. Subjected to critical appraisal, the emblem fell short of a realistic depiction of West Indian slavery: chains were a common symbol of imprisonment, even enslavement in general; but for West Indian slavery in particular, it was the cart whip. The medallion was sanitized of the scarification from cart whipping and other marks of torture that identified the body of an enslaved African; such realism might disturb polite society, the medallion's principal market. The medallion's logotype might better illustrate Rousseau's dictum "Man is born free but is everywhere in chains." Wedgewood was a subscriber to Equiano's first edition of *Interesting Narrative;*[20] although the medallion was already in circulation, it was never significantly modified. A more appropriate contemporary representation of the inhumanity of African enslavement was William Blake's 1796 illustration "A Negro Hung Alive by the Ribs to a Gallows," but this image was too shocking for conservative philanthropists. Wedgewood's medallion was a unique emblematizing of imperial arrogance and stereotypical condescension toward Africans. A case in point is John Steadman's assertion that Africans were known to carry their gratitude "to such a length, that they will even die for those who have shewn them any particular favour."[21] Thus, the medallion was more certainly a product of scientific racism than enlightened Christianity.

Montesquieu had declaimed, "If Negroes were allowed to be men, a doubt would arise whether their masters were Christians."[22] Notably, the European leadership in the abolitionist movement staked a claim not only to Christianity but also to sainthood. Nonetheless, the real challenge in recognizing African humanity was strictly a problem of economics, not religiosity. Had philanthropists recognized Africans as true men and brothers, their professed pursuit of justice must have entailed building a case for unconditional emancipation, not just amelioration. This distinction is what separated the abolitionism of Olaudah Equiano, Ottabah Cugoano, and fellow activists in the Sons of Africa from that of the most radical white antislavery advocates of the late eighteenth century. Cugoano was the most strident in demanding unconditional, immediate emancipation. In the very year of the launch of the London Anti-Slave Trade Society, Cugoano had called not only for immediate and total abolition of the trade but also for a proclamation of "universal emancipation of slaves" on the same day.[23] Six years later he openly expressed his disappointment in William Wilberforce for not resetting his objectives beyond abolishing the slave trade, even after the damning evidence of the slave trade inquiry by Parliament.[24] James Ramsay's insensitivity to African humanity was typical of British ameliorators, although he was more brutally frank than most: "I will not say to vindicate for them the common rights of humanity, but to secure to them the full exertion of their animal powers."[25] Even so, the enslaved might only qualify for this modicum of rights by accepting Christianity. This disguised preference for enslavement over liberty was typical of abolitionists' conceptualization of humanity. Ultimately, their appeal for humanity toward Africans was a gratification of their own sense of superiority.

The Dialectic of Private Property and Individual Freedom

The contention that all men have natural desires to be free and to own property was signature to the universalizing of aristocratic privileges into inalienable human rights. Notwithstanding the Enlightenment's explicit exclusion of

Africans from the new social contract, its declaration quickly filtered into the realm of English common law, which opened up an independent debate on the status of Africans within the empire. Western jurisprudence, philosophy, and religion had placed such a high value on private property that the very preservation of the social order depended on the preservation of property relations, including the institution of slavery.[26] In the West Indies enslaved humans were not only a form of private property but a labor force vital to the creation and maintenance of other forms of property. These interrelations of property created irreconcilable issues between colonists and metropolitans over the scope of amelioration against a common dread of emancipation.

The primacy of private property and white supremacism underscores an overarching problem in the study of Atlantic history.[27] This problem was central to the dichotomy between the rhetoric of immediatism and the devotion to gradualism on the question of abolition.[28] The problem, however, is seldom combined as a single feature of historical discourse. The primacy of private property in Western civilization presented an epistemic challenge to the antislavery movement and the imperial government, influencing their responses to prohibition of the slave trade and abolition of slavery. The following discourse attempts to put into historical perspective the problem of reconciling the natural right to liberty with the inviolable right to private property. It also elaborates the framework for understanding the nature of imperial trusteeship as applied to West Indian plantation colonies.

The application of common law to natural rights during the eighteenth and nineteenth centuries raised new problems of dominion, freedom, due process, justice, and equity. Consequently, the struggle for the restoration of liberty to enslaved Africans was undermined by the preeminence of human property in the colonial milieu and by those with a vested interest in plantation slavery. By and large the legal opinions of jurists in English courts of common pleas determined the limits of imperial justice. Because questions of law and justice were likely to be prejudiced by property considerations, property relations more often than not determined judgments of common law. From time to time throughout the eighteenth and early nineteenth centuries, judges were confronted with the burning issue of the legal status of Africans in England and the colonies. Although the pendulum of justice swung many times toward a clear and unequivocal declaration of African liberty, it never failed to return to its opposite pole in an equally clear and unequivocal defense of the right to private property in enslaved Africans. Even Britain's

Emancipation Act skillfully prioritized the protection of property over the liberty of contrived apprentices.

Contrary to the legal fallacy "that England was too pure an air for slaves to breathe in," enslavement of Africans was evident in England, at least since 1555, but disguised in common law under rights of property.[29] This was the case until Chief Justice Holt defended the natural right to liberty of resident Africans. The conclusion is drawn from his landmark judgment in 1706 in the case of *Smith vs. Brown and Cooper:* "Men may be the owners, and therefore cannot be the subject of property."[30] The ruling equalized the legal status of Africans in England with native Europeans, "for the common law takes no notice of Negroes being different from other men . . . there is no such thing as a slave by the law of England."[31] Legal judgments are not always unequivocal; the Holt ruling included sufficient ambiguities and exceptions pertaining to the right of property in humans to eliminate any serious threat to the slave trade or to slavery in the colonies.

Two decades later, in another landmark judgment, chief justice Sir Philip Yorke and solicitor general Lord Talbot swept away those ambiguities in favor of colonial slavery and the trafficking in enslaved Africans while preserving the legal myth of England's free airspace: "We are of opinion, that a slave, by coming from the West Indies, either with or without his master, to great Britain or Ireland, doth not become free . . . We are also of the opinion that the master may legally compel him to return to the plantations."[32] This judgment was significant for colonial slavery, coming at the apogee of the First Empire. The ruling was reinforced by the decisive intervention of Parliament three years later, with the first English statute to recognize enslaved Africans as private property. According to the act, "the houses, lands, negroes, and other heriditaments and real estates, situate or being within any of the said plantations belonging to any person indebted, shall be liable to and chargeable with just debts, duties and demands of what nature or kind soever, owing by any such person to his Majesty, or any of his subjects, and shall and may be assets for the satisfaction thereof."[33] This act underpinned the ruling of chief justice Lord Hardwicke (formerly Sir Philip Yorke): "I have no doubt but trover will lie for a Negro slave; it is as much property as any other thing."[34] Implicit in this judgment was the problem of the transmarine jurisdiction of metropolitan law. Hardwicke affirmed, "All our colonies are subject to the laws of England, although as to some purposes they have laws of their own."[35] The limited application of metropolitan law was a tacit surrender to the rights of colonial charter. The interpretation was crucial for allaying fears of vested interests in overseas colonies. Hardwicke reasoned that if "the moment a slave set foot in England he becomes free . . . why they should not be equally so when they set foot in Jamaica or any other plantation."[36] He also made a capital statement on the legality of slavery in England: "There were formerly villains [sic] or slaves in England . . . and although tenures were taken away, there are no laws that have destroyed servitude absolutely. Trover might be brought for a villain."[37] Thus, the struggle for African liberty was also, fundamentally, a struggle for the unconditional right to liberty of the English. Indeed, this was the principle on which England's first celebrated philanthropist, Granville Sharp, based his legal arguments in the famous James Somerset case.

The Somerset case is the most frequently cited as the point of departure toward an English moral imperium. Charles Stewart of Virginia, the legal owner of Somerset, took him to England on one of his visits. Somerset absconded but was later captured and handed over to the captain of a vessel bound for Jamaica. Before the vessel lifted anchor, however, Sharp intervened on behalf of the victim. In court Sharp invoked the maxim "Whatever was at Common Law, and is not taken away by statute, remaineth still."[38]

Chief justice Lord Mansfield's judgment on the Somerset case was one of the great landmarks in English jurisprudence during the eighteenth century, not only because of the subject it addressed but more so because by judicial law "an end was put to slavery in England."[39] Although generations of abolitionists, jurists, and historians have misinterpreted the import of the judgment, Mansfield had no doubt about its limited application: a case of habeas corpus. In delivering his judgment, he iterated that "the only question before us is, whether the cause on the return is sufficient?"[40] But ironically, the words that stirred the hearts of abolitionists were those that actually preserved colonial slavery, once the accepted limitation of England's transmarine jurisdiction is considered: "So high an act of dominion cannot be recognised by the law of the country where it is used. The power of a master over his slave has been extremely different, in different countries. The state of slavery is of such a nature, that it is incapable of being introduced on any reasons, moral or political; but only [by] positive law . . . It is so odious, that nothing can be suffered to support it but positive law. Whatever inconveniences, therefore, may follow from a decision, I cannot say this case is allowed or approved by the law of England."[41] In retrospect the judgment was an opiate to abolitionists rather than a catalyst in furthering the cause of unconditional freedom for enslaved Africans in the colonies. Their reaction is of signal importance to the history of colonial slavery. The only "inconveniences" that followed involved colonists classifying enslaved persons as "servants" or "apprentices" when visiting England.[42] In spite of this situation, abolitionists preferred to perpetuate the myth that the outcome of the case was definitive on the question of English liberty.

Judicial law on the legal status of Africans in England in the first half of the eighteenth century was made against the background of the rapid expansion of the English traffic in enslaved Africans, the pervasiveness of African enslavement in European colonies, and the growth of popular literature negating the humanity and culture of Africans—all of which contributed to the image of Africans as natural slaves. As Thomas Buxton succinctly stated, "The black factor made the man a slave."[43] Such stereotyping also challenged the interpretation of natural law and restricted Mansfield's ruling to England by conferring only "limited liberation" to African residents.

Edward Long's comments on the Somerset case ideally reflected the colonial nexus between the black factor and enslavement. In discerning the restricted application of the judgment, Long argued that if the laws of England had prohibited slavery, colonial planters would have been expressly prohibited from bringing enslaved persons to England.[44] Yet he remained guarded because of the somewhat ambiguously framed opinion of William Blackstone, one of England's most highly respected jurists: "That the law of *England* will protect the Negro in the enjoyment of his person, his liberty, and his property; yet, with regard to any rights which the master may have acquired to his perpetual services it will remain unaltered."[45] Long was perplexed; he queried the legal proposition that enslavers might "exercise a right of perpetual service, without restraining the Negro in his liberty, his power of locomotion, or of removing his person wherever his inclination may direct."[46]

It was obviously impossible to reconcile rights of humanity for Africans with the plantocracy's dependence on chattel slavery. Long preferred the authority of Chief Justice Powell, who had ruled that "the *Laws of England* take no notice of a Negroe."[47] Long, however, was confused by the legal distinction between *Negroe* and *slave*. Parliament had made enslaved "Negroes" legal property subject to seizure for debt, but the problem remained whether *Negroe* and *slave* were synonymous in English jurisprudence, given that the common law clearly recognized that Africans were not natural slaves. Indeed, Mansfield's carefully worded judgment was also an unqualified rejection of race in English judicature.[48]

As a colonial, Long's concern about the status of Africans under the common law was legitimate. Abolitionists were not troubled by the inherent dilemma, however, until some fifty years after Somerset. The new test case involved Grace Jones, who had resided in England between 1822 and 1823. She returned voluntarily with her mistress to Antigua, where she was seized by customs and "forfeited to the King, on the suggestion of having been illegally imported."[49] The Vice-Admiralty Court of Antigua ordered that Jones be returned to her mistress.[50] In 1827 Lord Justice Stowell heard the Crown's appeal against the judgment of the colonial court. Stowell ruled that Jones "was not a free person" once she had departed from England.[51] In his opinion Mansfield's judgment had only granted temporary freedom to a specific person entering the metropolis; it did not confer general manumission but was simply a law protecting enslaved persons from being taken out of the country by force.[52] In the Jones case the plaintiff had returned to Antigua on her own volition. Therefore, Stowell turned to Hardwicke (1749) and, by so doing, brought into question the progress of human rights for African peoples over the half-century since Somerset, but especially in the second decade of the abolition of Britain's Atlantic slave trade. Stowell justified his retreat to Hardwicke on the silence of abolitionists concerning the actual benefits of the Somerset case as well as on the unchanged situation since then. As Stowell explained: "The personal traffic in slaves resident in England had been as public and as authorised in London as in any other West India islands. They were sold on the Exchange and other public places of resort by parties themselves resident in London and with as little reserves as they would have been in any of our West India possessions."[53] Stowell actually blamed Mansfield for the predicament of English law on the right to liberty. He charged that Mansfield "long survived the change of law he had made, and yet never interposed in the slightest manner to correct the total misapprehension, if it is so to be considered, of the law which he himself had introduced."[54]

Stowell's indictment was unsubstantial. In 1785 Mansfield had ruled in another case of removal, that of Charlotte Howe, an enslaved African woman of long residence in England. He determined that her case needed special authority of positive law because "the case of Somerset, the negro slave, goes no further than to determine that the master of such a servant shall not have it in his power to take him out of the kingdom against his will."[55] This judgment came on the eve of the establishment of the Abolition Society, which nonetheless, preferred glorifying Sharp's pyrrhic victory. Clarkson praised Sharp, his personal friend, for "the great and glorious" judgment that, "having been determined after so deliberate an investigation of the law, can never be reversed while the British Constitution remains."[56] To Clarkson the crux of Mansfield's judgment was the elevation into law of the old adage "that as soon as ever any slave set his foot upon English territory, he became free."[57] The constitution remained intact, but the "glorious" judgment was a myth.

Stowell, who described himself as a "stern Abolitionist,"[58] confirmed that the maxim "Once free for an hour, free for ever! has never been once applied, since the case of Sommerset, to overrule the authority of transmarine law."[59] Like Mansfield, he was certainly conscious that his ruling was making law that could decide the fate of colonial slavery. Thus, his judgment was decidedly more favorable to colonial property than to African humanity. In a letter to Judge Story of Scotland he explained: "I am a friend to abolition generally, but I wish it to be effected with justice to individuals. Our Parliaments have long recognised it and could not have only invited, but actually compelled our colonies to adopt it, and how, under such circumstances, it is to be broken up at the sole expense of the colonist, I cannot see consistent with either common reason or common justice; it must be done at the common expense of both countries; and upon that part of the case very great difficulties exist. Our zealots are for leaping over them all, but in that disposition I cannot hold this to be within the wise or just part of the nation."[60]

In light of the fierce struggle for compensation by vested interests in the West Indies, Stowell's judgment was not surprising or unexpected. It was a fair reflection of the position of government and Parliament on amelioration. As he piloted the government's Amelioration Resolutions just three years prior to the Grace Jones ruling, secretary of state for foreign affairs George Canning hedged on the issue of monetary compensation to enslavers but unequivocally recognized the right to private property, including property in humans, as sacrosanct. William Huskisson, the then undersecretary of state for the colonies, was only slightly less equivocal, as "it appeared to him that the ownership in slaves was similar to other rights established by law."[61] He deprecated the violation of this right without adequate compensation to the owner. Correspondingly, Thomas Buxton, parliamentary successor to Wilberforce, did not expect the planters to assume the burden of reparations for enslavement. He was willing to allow proprietors time to complete what they had commenced until "every slave now living shall have found repose in the grave."[62] During the abolition debate William Baring succinctly stated the case for the West India Interest: "If that property was said to be stamped with the character of immorality and injustice, he should be glad to know what improved morality and justice there was in the privation of property, the acquisition of which the laws had allowed."[63]

The Grace Jones case was not the only one of its kind in which Stowell had presided, nor was Stowell the only judge involved in such cases in the last decade of slavery. Also in 1827, Stowell had to rule in another case involving a child who was born in England of an African woman but enslaved when she accompanied her mother to the West Indies. A second case was that of John Greaves, who ran away from enslavement in 1810 to safety in England. Although he served for ten years in the Royal Navy and had an English wife and two English-born children, he was arrested and charged as a runaway when he returned to Grenada twenty-two years later to visit his parents. A third case involved two children of a "gentleman of property" and an enslaved mother. The children were sent to England, where they received an "excellent education" but were enslaved as field laborers when they returned to the West Indies because their father's estate had changed hands. Jones and other similar cases that emerged during the amelioration prompted Dr. Stephen Lushington to call for the specific inclusion of such individuals in the Emancipation Act.[64]

Thus, while Stowell judiciously avoided deepening the rift between Britain and its colonies, he was also acting in conformity with the highest ideals of British jurisprudence. The case was of no less importance to colonial slavery than that of Somerset, though it has attracted little attention in the historiography of slavery. The Jones case put the lie to the Abolition Society's euphoria over the Mansfield judgment as a great victory for African liberty. English law had set such high value on private property that its protection took precedence over the welfare of the community. This assertion is borne out in contemporary thought. Adam Smith considered secular justice the highest virtue, yet in applying it to the social situation, he contended that "the most sacred laws of justice . . . those whose violation seems to call loudest for vengeance and punishment are laws which guard his property and possessions; and last of all come those which guard what are called his personal rights."[65] Blackstone had emphasized with even greater authority that "so great is the regard of our law for *private property,* that it will not authorise the least violation of it; no, not even for the *general good of the whole community.*"[66] Thus, while English law was clearly favorable to African freedom in England, jurists were not prepared to interfere with the sacred rights of private property in enslaved Africans, unless by an act of Parliament, while Parliament dared not decree emancipation unless first guaranteeing compensation and political security.

3

PRAGMATIZING AMELIORATION AND ABOLITION

Embryos of Change—The Colonial Impulse

Slavery reform and antislavery were contradictions inherent within slavery itself. Not surprisingly, both statutory amelioration and proselytizing, the two major facets of British slavery–era trusteeship, had their origins in the West Indies. Amelioration was the cornerstone of trusteeship, proselytizing its corollary. This perspective implicitly acknowledges a subaltern agency while transferring the accreditation for the genesis of British trusteeship from Edmund Burke to Edward Long.[1] Long was a pioneer-advocate for statutory amelioration as a means to a greater end: the total creolization of plantation labor. This was his major social response to the half-decade of sustained insurgency unleashed by Tacky's War of emancipation. This subaltern change dynamic is a radical reinterpretation of human agency in amelioration and slave trade abolition. At least since Du Bois's *Suppression of the Atlantic Slave Trade* the subaltern theme has pivoted on the Haitian Revolution.[2] In the current work the revolution was the rupture, but the pivotal event that informed the pragmatic rationale for abolition was Tacky's War. Long's prescription to preempt similar turmoil in the colonies was the first blueprint for politicizing the essentials of what might best be described as the embryo of imperial trusteeship.

England had dominated the sugar trade for the first hundred years of the Sugar Revolution. By the mid-eighteenth century the British dramatically lost their competitive advantage to the French, but more particularly to the booming economy of St. Dominique. Recovery became more difficult after the 1775 Prohibitory Act reclassified Britain's rebellious North American colonies as a foreign nation under the Navigation Laws. Ragatz, Williams, Carrington, and others have argued that these challenges were among the main triggers in the economic decline of the British colonies.[3] It is even more important, however, to recognize this period as one of socioeconomic adjustment and transition to a new colonial model hitched to amelioration and the natural increase of labor.

Dependent on slave labor, the sugar plantation was the most vicious capitalist system ever devised. Planters purchased new Africans to work them to death.[4] In the hundred years since the Navigation Acts, the average price of male laborers had risen 300 percent.[5] With the rapid expansion of French plantations, the prognosis was higher prices. During the 1660s a few visionary planters in Barbados and Jamaica, the two leading sugar colonies, sought to offset the cost of production by mitigating some of the most degrading and oppressive conditions of young women in order to promote fecundity and reduce infant mortality.[6] Ironically, Thomas Thistlewood, overseer of Egypt Plantation in Westmoreland, Jamaica, provides an early example of this development. Less ironically, the moderation of his tyranny was probably influenced by Phibbah, his most favored and astute concubine;[7] Phibbah's influence underscores the critical interventions of enslaved and emancipated persons in amelioration and abolition. In the first years following Thistlewood's arrival in 1750, he had treated his pregnant slaves in the same brutal, inhumane manner practiced by the slavocracy since the launch of the Sugar Revolution.[8] During the following decade, without diminishing his sexual assaults, Thistlewood slightly tempered his ill treatment of women by allowing a three-month maternity exemption from physical labor evenly divided before and after delivery.[9] With minor modifications this arrangement remained standard for ameliorators well into the nineteenth century.

The Society for the Propagation of the Gospel (SPG) also validated amelioration as the way forward in plantation management. In 1710 Christopher Codrington bequeathed two plantations to the SPG as models of a Christianized slave polity. Over the next half-century the Codrington project acquired some 450 Africans, but in time it surrendered to the same lure of profit making as the secular planter class. Even with added births, by 1760 overwork and extreme brutality reduced the population to about 250.[10] From the 1760s the managers of Codrington plantation adopted a new approach, however, diverting some of their funds toward improving the living conditions of their existing labor force, thus underscoring the delineation of that decade as a major landmark in amelioration.[11] The Barbados planters might have done more for creolization by giving early support to independent economic activities of the enslaved as existed in Jamaica and elsewhere.[12] Notwithstanding these shortcomings, by the launch of the abolition movement Barbados already had a Creole population of close to 90 percent; at the same time 65 percent of the enslaved Kittitian population was also Creole. By the turn of the nineteenth century Dominica and the Bahamas had successfully stabilized their enslaved labor force; the Windwards and Jamaica lagged behind proportionately but not in absolute numbers.[13] It would seem that the key policy for achieving more positive demographic trends was improving lying-in conditions. When combined with genuine midday rest, other leisure time, and adequate, locally raised provisions, sugar was less fatal.[14]

Although amelioration was certainly a response to the rising cost of new labor from Africa, concern over economy of scale curiously converged with the fear and alarm generated by Tacky's War. Revolts and plots were endemic to African enslavement, but Tacky's War and the Berbice uprising three years later were the first to stun the slavocracy with significant casualties, population displacement, and massive destruction of property.[15] Within three decades amelioration became the most favored formula for anti-insurgency, while Creole labor was poised to become the standard for assessing the viability of abolition. Although irrational when viewed retrospectively, belief in creolization was the genesis of change in the ancien régime of colonialism. The attraction of this nexus was precisely why amelioration became the flagship of abolitionists' lobbies and why Long's *History of Jamaica* was seminal in pragmatizing trusteeship.

Long first attracted public attention in Britain through a series of pamphlets in the wake of the 1772 Mansfield judgment. His *History* was a rich mix of xenophobic diatribe, rare anthropological insights, and seminal proposals for colonial reform. Its publication catapulted him to the position of pioneer spokesman on the mix of statutory amelioration and creolization. Tacky's War, with its trickle-down insurgencies over six successive years, was the point of departure. The balance sheet for this war included sixty white fatalities, some six hundred thousand pounds in damage to property, and the untallied cost of new defenses against future uprisings. Despite severe retributions by the slavocracy, plots continued intermittently, climaxing in 1766 in an uprising in which nineteen whites lost their lives.[16] Long argued that the mainspring of insurgency since the 1739 Maroon treaties had consistently been those Africans newly arrived in the colony, "especially as no small number of them had been warriors in Afric [*sic*] or criminals."[17] Jamaican absentee Bryan Edwards, with ties to one of the plantations overrun by Tacky's forces, later confirmed Long's prognosis.[18] In authenticating the warrior claim, Equiano recalled that Igbo men and women were equally involved in the armed defense of their communities, that the entire community was constituted as a kind of militia, and that even young boys were trained in the arts of war.[19] Through astute marketing Equiano's biography instantly became one of the most popular antislavery works. He himself had ensured that it reached the hands of leading metropolitan abolitionists by personal mail.

Long did not explicitly call for abolition but surmised that creolization was the only antidote to insurrection. By the time *History of Jamaica* was published, Creoles were already a major component of Jamaica's plantation labor. While Long's advocacy of creolization may have been economically sound, it was nevertheless politically flawed. As a student of pseudoscientific racism, Long instinctively disdained authentic scientific methodology, and as a consequence, the plank of his reformism rested on the misconception that native Africans "are chiefly awed into subjection, by the superior multitude of Creole Blacks, with whom they dare not confederate, nor solicit their concurrence in any plan of opposition to the white inhabitants."[20] An analysis of the anatomy of Caribbean revolts would show that this proposition was fatally flawed. As early as the 1680s, a Barbadian governor had feared "that the 'Creolian generation' of young slaves . . . would soon strike against their masters."[21] Most of the leaders in the 1736 Antigua conspiracy were "privileged Creoles" exempt from field labor.[22] In 1776 a predominantly Creole cohort planned a new uprising in Hanover, western Jamaica; this was a major upset to the theory of Creole subservience, just two years after the publication of Long's *History*.[23] The myth of the subservient Creole also survived the emancipation wars of the 1790s, which contained myriad examples of Creole-African collaboration, including the principal theater, St. Domingue, but such details were largely hidden from the metropolitan public.[24] Thus, it was Long's assessment of Tacky's War that influenced political opinion and which was accepted as the authentic anatomy of insurgency, until the shocks of the three large-scale Creole-led emancipation uprisings in Barbados, Demerara, and Jamaica, all within two decades.

The mortality of African-born was alarming: roughly 50 percent of the 42,000 Africans who landed between 1761 and 1768 had died. Calculating each immigrant at £35, this wastage of life represented a capital loss of £735,000, not including the opportunity cost from future production and reproduction; Creoles, however, had achieved sustainability in the same period.[25] Notwithstanding his extreme racism, Long's support for amelioration marked the transition to politicizing the socioeconomics of African enslavement as a rationale for a new colonial architecture. For four decades his analysis reverberated in anti–slave trade pamphlets and parliamentary debates. Clearly limited to political and economic objectives, Long argued that only amelioration could increase the pool of Creole labor, which would eventually rescue planters from the worst habits of Africans. Although he expressed abhorrence for the abuse of absolute power, he justified enslavers' inhumanity as quid pro quo for the rage of the enslaved; amelioration would moderate both behaviors.[26]

The Long amelioration model incorporated religion as a force for social control. As a student of French colonial slavery, Long adopted as his model the 1685 *Code Noir,* which he reproduced fully in the appendix to his *History.* Accordingly, he ranked Roman Catholics as the most effective proselytizers because their rites catered to the African love of ceremonies and because Africans found compatible iconography in Catholicism; he noted that some French churches in the Caribbean even had black saints.[27] Even more significant to him, as a lawmaker, he easily saw through the ineffectiveness of the *Code Noir* in preventing cruelty. Thus, he resolved, "it is not enough to make laws; it is also necessary to provide for their execution."[28] Long was a genuine advocate of reform of colonial legislation and a limited application of the rule of law in amelioration. Although he explicitly rejected ill treatment as a cause of rebellions, he implicitly acknowledged it in his appeal for legislative action: "It would be an act of humanity, reflecting the highest honour on the legislature of Jamaica, if the gentlemen who compose it should, in imitation of the French, promulgate a code of laws and ordinances respecting the Negroes, more particularly in the treatment of them upon the plantations."[29] Long proposed that a reformed Jamaican slave law should curb planters' tyranny by regulating the punishment of enslaved persons. He hoped that planters' "dread of legal pains and penalties" would facilitate compliance. His most potent reform dynamic, however, was the corps of white servants on each plantation who might be enticed into becoming informers with the right inducements. Overall the proposed structure was remarkably similar to the 1789 Spanish *Code Noir,* which strongly influenced Britain's imperial model of amelioration. Long soberly acknowledged that the reform of slavery required more than legal reform; it also required the reform of colonial governance. Thus, he advised "that they may effect these, and many other beneficial consequences, is my sincere wish; and that they may be applied here successfully, not only to the correction of errors in our political, but in our domestic government likewise, should be the endeavour of every honest and intelligent planter of Jamaica."[30]

Beginning with James Ramsay, abolitionists consistently made Long their principal authority for creolization as the antidote for internal security, often quoting extensively from his *History of Jamaica* or simply extracting from it data that had become axiomatic by the 1790s. Ramsay's advocacy began the transformation of amelioration from private projects to imperial policy. He epitomized the immense difficulties that advocates of state regulation of slavery were destined to face from the intransigence of the colonial slavocracy. In spite of his prominent status in the Church of England, Ramsay was no darling of the planter class. His efforts to proselytize his own enslaved laborers in St. Kitts had made him "a rebel convict against the interest and majesty of plantership."[31] Following his return to England in 1783, Ramsay was instrumental in opening the gateway of political influence and patronage to Clarkson. Clarkson, in turn, added a new twist by engineering the framework to institutionalize abolitionism as a permanent fixture on the agenda of Parliament.[32] Other powerful antislavery advocates with ties to leading political figures included Equiano, Ottobah Cugoano, and their associates in the seminal antislavery society Sons of Africa. Although Equiano and Cugoano were propaganda fodder for white abolitionists, as Africans espousing emancipation and justifying insurgency as a natural response to enslavement, their activism had become too revolutionary for political guidance following the outbreak the Haitian Revolution. Thus, it was Ramsay who emerged as the first major spokesman for a comprehensive reform of colonial slavery. He was well qualified to lead this intellectual assault. Although he accepted plantation laborers as stock, he imperiously submitted that they could become responsible Christians, for which he worked out a novel scheme.[33]

His plan envisaged cautious indoctrination in selective Christian principles. Yet his personal experiment was a dismal failure, being limited to calling his labor force together on evenings to repeat "the Creed, the Lord's Prayer, and a few other prayers that were reckoned best adapted to them." These prayers were the fundamentals of Christianity in the Church of England as well as Roman Catholicism.[34] Ramsay admitted, however, that his enslaved laborers showed no enthusiasm for establishment religion. Indeed, one remarked that "he did not love such things, and that he, a Negroe, had nothing to do with the prayers of white people."[35] Yet Ramsay remained convinced that Christianization was the best option for social change and political stability. Thus, he contended: "Man, in order to become a good member of society, must be inspired with religious principles. That he may not counteract the common views, out of secret fraud, malice or selfishness, but to be carried on to every generous exertion by which the public happiness can be effected. Religion, then, must enter into every plan that has the general good or profit in view."[36] Ramsay did not completely rule out the state as an agent in the advancement of amelioration, but such intervention was reserved for compulsory religious instruction and government support of missionaries. Although he could easily refer to his own experience, his case for state intervention put the spotlight on one Robertson, whose failure to Christianize his enslaved laborers demonstrated "that nothing considerable can be done in it unless government interposed in earnest to carry it on." Ramsay was mindful that political intervention could dangerously undermine enslavers' authority and warned, "Before government can meddle with slaves, it must take them first within the bosom of society, advance their condition, protect them in their claims of human nature and make them objects of police."[37] Ramsay's dilemma was endemic to the abolitionist movement. It represented the impossibility of striking a compromise between extending limited rights to enslaved laborers and maintaining the colonial status quo. It was especially important not to antagonize the planter class, without whose cooperation any plan of amelioration was bound to fail.

Ramsay introduced into the debate on colonial slavery the first well-argued case for multifaceted economic returns from amelioration. He demonstrated that the planters' management and treatment of enslaved laborers were the most significant factors in the high cost of production and low returns on capital investment.[38] Laborers who worked all night in the boiling house produced low-grade sugar and suffered serious injuries. He argued further that the cost of cruelty, neglect, and overwork must be reckoned in terms of lost labor through illness, incapacity to perform labor, or inefficiency. Evaluating the limited examples of management reform, he concluded that "those masters are best served who feed and clothe their slaves well."[39] Ramsay provided empirical evidence that humane treatment neutralized factors that militated against natural increase. Over a period of eighteen years his labor force had expanded one hundred–fold from births alone.[40] However isolated, the common factor in all cases was the change in treatment and living conditions.

Ramsay did not confine his attention to the domestic economy and security but extended the benefits of amelioration to the metropolis. Progressive planters could bring new prosperity to the empire: "Instead of confining their demands, as at present, to a few coarse woollens and Osnaburgs, to a little grain, they would open up a new traffic in every branch of commerce, they would add to the strength and security of the colonies."[41] Equiano later made a similar case for abolition but extended the new market prospects to Africa: "As the inhuman traffic of slavery is to be taken into the consideration of the British legislature, I doubt not, if a system of commerce was established in Africa, the demand for manufactures would most rapidly augment, as the native inhabitants will insensibly adopt the British fashions, manners, customs, &c. In proportion to the civilization, so will be the consumption of British manufactures."[42] Equiano's appeal was an endorsement to recently launched projects of the Anti–Slave Trade Society in Sierra Leone. The orientation to commodity trade with Africa deepened as the Industrial Revolution made more demands for lubricants, which Africa was well poised to supply but which threatened to reduce an even greater proportion of the population to economic slavery.[43]

Ramsay was convinced that amelioration was a sound investment; conversely, the Atlantic slave trade had become an obstacle to colonial prosperity. He rejected the feasibility of regulating the slave trade; only its abolition made economic sense. Thus, he argued, "the abolition of the slave trade, far from giving the planter a claim to compensation, will really save him. Government will prevent him from continuing to involve himself unnecessarily in bankruptcy and ruin. The only means by which he can improve his condition is, as Long advises, to use prudent regulations in the right husbanding of his stock, and promoting its increase by natural means."[44] Ramsay was consistent in his appeal for more economic pragmatism. He pontificated, "Though slaves be now raised to a price that few old settled plantations can afford to give, yet this is all the care taken in most of them to raise a young generation; while Creoles or native West Indian negroes are universally acknowledged to be more hardy, diligent, and trusty than Africans."[45]

The stimulus for proselytizing as the primary catalyst of colonial reform also came from the West Indies via former enslaved visionaries and preachers. Oliver Furley contends that the first Moravian mission to the West Indies was undertaken in response to formerly enslaved Anthony Ulrich's appeal to the Moravian Church authority in Germany.[46] Furthermore, George Liele and

Moses Baker from Georgia in the United States, among other black preachers, were the pioneers of Baptist missions in Jamaica. By 1791 Liele and Baker controlled two chapels and congregations of hundreds, mostly free blacks, enslaved persons, and a few poor whites in Kingston and the outlying plantations.[47] It was Liele and Baker who persuaded the first white Baptist missionaries to evangelize Jamaica.[48] Other African American preachers pioneered evangelism in several other colonies.[49] Planters accommodated proselytizing largely because of a growing belief that Christianity might be an effective counter-subversive force. James Grainger, an absentee planter, reflected on this early development: "How shocking to philanthropy is it to think they are human beings, who are made to act from motives of fear only! Surely were Negroes instructed in the practical principles of Christianity, they would be rendered much better servants."[50] Christianity thus became a new facet of British plantation management. It also sowed the seeds of black liberation theology that defined the emancipation wars of the nineteenth century.

The narrow economic interest of West Indian plantership must be seen in the wider context of a new awareness by British metropolitan ideologues of the significance of missionism in imperial expansion and consolidation. Missionism was the foundation of the new morality of colonial exploitation in the second half of the eighteenth century. Britain's West Indian colonies became an experimental field for this cultural imperialism. West Indian planters, however, were determined to preserve their status quo and the right to deploy conventional deterrence against insurgencies, thus limiting the nature and pace of proselytizing.

The colonies also set the precedent for ameliorative slave laws. William Wilberforce had contended that even if Edmund Burke's draft Slave Code had been completed in 1780, as its author claimed, it had not become public knowledge before 1792.[51] Thus, it was the Jamaica Assembly's consolidated slave law and Grenada's Guardian Act that ushered in the new era of legislative reforms.[52] The Jamaica code was the offspring of Long's activism, but it was the Guardian Act that became the model for imperial reference as abolitionism picked up momentum. The Guardian Act revealed that colonial legislators clearly understood that absolute power was self-defeating. The legislation, passed in 1784, incorporated measures for the welfare of old and infirm laborers, "weekly Allowances of Provisions completely adequate to their maintenance" and an annual distribution of "decent & sufficient Cloathing."[53] The act forbade planters from subjecting enslaved laborers "to Night or Extra Labour, except in the Act of Manufactoring [*sic*] such Species of produce as necessarily requires the same"; in addition to fines for mutilating enslaved persons, the act deprived planters of their services. It exempted females with six or more children from servile labor and formulated a scale of tax rebates for planters who achieved varying levels of natural increase of enslaved laborers. It introduced the office of Guardian of Slaves, with every parish having three such officers responsible for enforcing its provisions.[54] The Guardian Act was reenacted in 1788 as "an Act for the Better Protection and Promoting the Increase and Population of Slaves."[55] Notwithstanding Jamaica's earlier flirtation with legislative amelioration, the imperial government considered the New Grenada Slave Act the most advanced reform legislation and recommended its protector of slaves to all colonial assemblies.[56]

The 1784 Grenada Code was a legacy of French rule and modeled on the *Code Noir;* it was also consistent with Long's amelioration model.[57] One of the new provisions was proprietary proselytizing. The ninth clause required proprietors to "instruct their Slaves in the Principles of the Christian Religion, & to do their utmost to fit them for Baptism, Which Ceremony the Clergymen are to perform gratis, & also to attend them in Sickness."[58] This provision was not radical because the majority of the enslaved class was already baptized, making them nominally Roman Catholic.[59] By 1789 most of the "old colonies" had drafted reformed slave codes modeled after the New Guardian Act. Colonial assemblies eagerly passed the new laws to preempt parliamentary intervention.[60] Notwithstanding the element of coercion, the new codes established the principles and possibilities that informed abolitionism down to emancipation.

Missionism as Social Control

From the inception of amelioration its leading spokesmen had advocated that the mitigation of slavery divorced from a resocialization in quietistic Christianity would fail to deliver the requisites for political security. The duty to implant a new Christian morality fell to Nonconformist or sectarian missionaries. Although the Church of England had launched the very first proselytizing project under the aegis of the SPG, by and large, missionaries of the late eighteenth and early nineteenth centuries were Nonconformist. Members of the British plantocracy were not as easily persuaded as their French and Spanish counterparts that Christianity could have a quieting effect on the enslaved.

Their belated confidence was tagged to the success of Moravian missionaries who had set up their first stations in the Danish colonies as early as 1732.[61] The Moravians were slaveholders and identified completely with the proprietary class. A couple of decades later two influential absentee Jamaican planters invited the Moravians to establish missions on their plantations.[62] By 1756 the Moravians had also established stations in Antigua, which soon became the most successful field of sectarianism, winning over two thousand converts in the first twenty years.[63] Not to be outdone, Methodists also staked an early claim in the new missionary frontier. In 1760 the speaker of the Antigua Assembly, Francis Gilbert, and his helper, Nathaniel, began enforcing Methodist rules on their immediate social circle, including enslaved converts.[64]

The first official political endorsement for proselytizing came in 1788, a happy coincidence for abolitionists who had recently launched the Abolition Society. The Methodist society boasted that it had brought about such dramatic reformation of Christianized laborers in Antigua that the traditional precaution of declaring martial law at Christmas had lost its significance and remained a "mere matter of form."[65] Planters' confidence was also boosted by magistrates' endorsement that "baptized Negroes" in the Danish colonies were "a greater security to them [the planters] than their forts."[66] By the turn of the century a "Christian revolution" was well under way, with a proliferation of missionary societies pursuing cultural imperialist agendas; many targeted the West Indies as their major field of operation.

Although they originated from varied ethnic backgrounds, many Africans known to have contributed in large numbers to the labor pool of West Indian colonies had a shared cosmology of human origin, persona, death, health and sickness as spiritual conditions, ancestral worship, magic, spirit possession, and songs and dances as worship, among other conventions.[67] These lines of cosmological continuities were a key component in the success of multiethnic alliances and effective leadership in insurgencies. To control the African mind it was necessary to suppress and manipulate key elements of their cosmology. Accordingly, the Moravians proscribed dancing for its over-sensuousness and presumed vulgarity as well as its potential as a medium for insurgency; converts caught in the act were condemned as "backsliders" and liable to expulsion from the church.[68] Missionaries tactfully incorporated singing as formal worship, however, a proselytizing method copied by other sectarians. Metropolitans instructed Caribbean-bound missionaries to exploit Africans' impulse for music by introducing Christian dogmas through the psalms.[69]

In the Old World early Christianity took root among oppressed classes partly because it guaranteed salvation in an afterlife and partly because of its potential as an ideology of resistance and revolution against political oppression. These were similar enticements to many enslaved Africans, for whom the only guarantee of freedom or salvation was transmigration. Unable to practice their native religions openly, many took to Christianity as a medium for paying discreet homage to their ancestral deities. African cosmology harmonized the spiritual with the physical; accordingly, nothing was done outside the context of religion.[70] This epistemology facilitated the incorporation of sectarianism as a tool of resistance to enslavement, a phenomenon manifested in the largest revolts in the nineteenth century. Among the strongest incentives for conversion were greater sanctioned mobility and opportunities for socialization beyond the immediate reach of the whip. These privileges played a key role in insurgency in the nineteenth century.

One thing the plantocracy feared more than proselytizing and liberation theology was obeah. Colonists applied the generic expression "obeah men" or "obeah women" to traditional African priests and priestesses such as the *akomfo* of the Ashanti and *hungan/manbo* of the Ewe, to other African mediums of the spirit world, and to practitioners of African science and esotericism, especially those trained in herbal secrets. While the plantocracy generally condemned them as "poisoners," the enslaved accepted them as natural leaders.[71] Those suspected of practicing obeah suffered torture and execution reserved for leaders of rebellions. One of the earliest documented cases links back to Tacky's War, one of whose principals was executed for his role in administering "the Fetish or solemn oath to the conspirators" and furnishing them with "a magical preparation which was to render them invulnerable."[72] To meet the threat that the "professors of obeah" posed to life and property, laws existed everywhere against drumming, secret meetings, and esotericism.

Christian baptism was a spiritual weapon against obeah. This political theology was shared by some enslaved persons and exploited by missionaries to win converts. Interestingly, the ideology transcended colonial slavery, as evidenced in early Christian missions in the Kingdom of Kongo, where the local elites regarded Roman Catholic missionaries as foreign *nganga* (native priests) who used *nkisi* (charms or fetishes) to influence events in the natural world.[73] Subordinate classes understood that "the most important function of the Christian priest was to protect the faithful against witchcraft."[74] As a result of the perceived magical properties of salt used in Catholic baptismal rites, there was a "keen demand" for that sacrament.[75] Ramsay testified that a similar attitude had emerged in St. Kitts, a Protestant colony: "Baptism is supposed to free a slave from the power of the negroe conjurer, and it being permitted, is considered in the master, as conferring of a favour, that is complete, when the rite is performed."[76] Despite the growing endorsements of quietist Christianity, the slow pace of proselytizing well into the nineteenth century ensured the viability of obeah as a powerful tool of resistance against enslavement.

Four decades after Ramsay, Wilberforce made a sterling appeal for the incorporation of Christianity as the mainspring of official amelioration. Wilberforce was confident that proselytizing was the only effective weapon in rooting out African religious practices. He declared: "Christianity never failed to chase away these vain terrors of darkness and paganism. No sooner did a Negro become a Christian, than the Obeah-man despaired of bringing him into subjection."[77] The imperial government bought into this confidence and embraced proselytizing as a key strategy of the imperial phase of amelioration from 1823, opting for sectarianism, however, against protestations of the established church.[78]

Contrary to the perception by Anglicans and Catholics that instructing the enslaved in Scripture would pose a threat to social order, sectarians chose scriptural instruction as the pathway to conversion. Sectarian missionaries treated backsliders as heretics to be "deprived of the means of Grace," or, simply put, excluded from the Eucharist; they might even be excommunicated.[79] The Methodist Society instructed missionaries to enforce expulsion where "conversion is not becometh the Gospel of CHRIST."[80] They were to ensure "that any member of Society who may relapse into his former habits, and become a polygamist, an adulterer, or an unclean person; who shall be idle and disorderly; disobedient to his owner (if a slave); who shall steal, or be in any other way immoral or irreligious; shall be put away, after due admonition, and proper attempts to reclaim him from the 'error of his way.'"[81] Thus, sectarian congregations remained small as much by their own commitment to scriptural codes as by the general hostility of planters to proselytizing. The ensuing church organization nurtured close-knit subcultures of enslaved laborers in relatively strong alliances with ministers of religion.

Sectarian missionaries were specially selected to deal with the problem of African enslavement and Christianization; those destined for the West Indies received similar instructions and were cautioned to treat the colonies as "stations of considerable delicacy." A Methodist instructional manual warned that a missionary's only business was "to promote the moral and religious improvement of the slaves to whom you may have access, without in the least degree, in public or private, interfering with their civil condition."[82] As a precaution, special lessons, catechisms, and sermons were prepared by the London society. In essence colonial quietism sought to provide divine authority for planter paternalism. A typical text based on Paul's Epistle to the Ephesians reads: "Servants, obey in all things your master according to the flesh: not with eye-service, as men pleasers, but in singleness of heart, fearing God: and whatsoever ye do, do it heartily as to the Lord, and not unto men: knowing of the Lord, ye shall receive the reward of the inheritance; for ye serve the LORD CHRIST. But he that doeth wrong shall receive for the wrong which he had done: and there is no respect of others."[83] Women, children, and "the less instructed of adult slaves" were the principal targets of missionary endeavor.[84] Independent of the missionaries, enslaved Christian women were believed to continue the indoctrination of their children by the "constant use of prayer" and keeping them "out of all wickedness."[85] Clearly, divine retribution was not bound by class distinctions. Consequently, even the most quietistic Scriptures provided fodder for revolutionary ideology. Enslaved Christian preachers in the early nineteenth century would appeal to the Bible in legitimating their protests against servitude.

Although missionaries directed Pauline reproofs at both masters and servants, they refrained from rebuking the plantocracy for inhumanity toward the enslaved. Instead, they expected the enslaved to reform their enslavers by supplication and condescension. Missionaries exhorted enslaved hearers and converts not to retaliate; they must endeavor to soften their enslaver's heart and to make him love them by doing all they could for him.[86] Thus, the price of amelioration was complete subservience. In reality colonial missionism was confirming and validating the slavocracy's claim that enslaved people did not seek revenge for brutish treatment because of their innate animality.

In the Caribbean missionaries' interpretation of sin and evil conformed to the slavocratic worldview: a "good master" was one who exercised his paternalistic duties by providing the barest necessities for his enslaved laborers; a "bad master" neglected these duties. Missionaries accepted whipping as appropriate punishment for the "badness" of enslaved persons.[87] Their sermons warned that resistance to enslavement was unworthy in God's sight and admonished the enslaved to bear with patience the excesses and oppression of their enslavers: "You ought not to disobey his orders, to steal from him, to tell lies, to run away from him, or do any other bad things towards him."[88] To offend against a good enslaver was "doubly bad." They warned their enslaved congregations: "When you do any badness, and your master punishes you, it is soon over; and many of you are apt to forget it in a few days afterwards. But god punishes bad people, one way or another, as long as they live; and if they do not leave off their badness and come good, will punish them worse than they can think of after they die."[89] Sectarianism ideally complemented proprietary paternalism, reinforcing stereotypes of plantation relations.

Enslaved people had mastered the drama of "fatalistic stupidity" in their repertoire of survival strategies. Within their own leisured spaces, especially when they gathered for storytelling around their fires at nights, these very individuals dramatically demonstrated "precision of ideas and accuracy of judgement," behavior usefully defined as "Anansism."[90] Anansi was the Spider God of the Akan-speaking peoples of the Gold Coast hinterland. He was the supreme African trickster-hero who survived the Middle Passage to become the most popular folklore hero of the enslaved Diaspora throughout the Caribbean and beyond. Other African trickster-heroes assimilated to Anansi. The enslaved applied Anansi psychology against their enslavers in order to preserve energy, reduce workload, avoid punishment, and earn private time and space. Edward Long observed this survival feature in Jamaica: when confronted by a "very intelligent, wary and active" overseer, the enslaved would leave no expedient untried, thwarting his plans, misunderstanding his orders, and reiterating complaints against him. If those tactics did not succeed, "they perplex him and worry him, especially if he is of an impatient, fretful turn, till he grows heartily sick of his charge, and voluntarily resigns it."[91] Against the systematic dehumanization of plantation enslavement, Anansi and similar African folklore preserved Africa's moral-ethical values and provided a philosophy of survival and resistance. In the popular imagination of Jamaican Maroons and their descendants, Anansi was their inspiration for military intelligence and martial science, including camouflage and ambush. According to a descendant of Jamaica's Windward Maroons, "Anansi started to talk his story . . . through we Maroons."[92] Missionaries understood that one of the primary challenges they faced was "to replace Anansi, the supreme ginal, with Christian the Pilgrim, who fought his way through life."[93]

Europeans well understood the politics of spiritual conquest. John Shebbeare, a contemporary of John Wesley, had pontificated, "He who rules the soul rules everything."[94] Missionaries admonished the enslaved to submit to the authority of their enslavers, even when it contradicted divine authority. They deprived converts of Holy Communion for committing adultery but required them to defer to their enslavers' lust. Plantation economy and security also took precedence over the divine injunction on Sabbath keeping. Here, again, the model was the Danish mission, where missionaries compelled enslaved converts to give complete "submission to their masters, and full obedience to their commands, even to working on the plantations, when so ordered, on Sundays."[95] To finally qualify for baptism enslaved converts vowed not to seek freedom by marronage.[96] For repudiating resistance to enslavement, they were appointed to positions of responsibility within plantation enterprises and sectarian church organizations. In a word missionary theology was completely functional to plantation slavery. Sectarians actively propagated the idiom of natural slavery in an age when such a concept was no longer intellectually tenable in Europe.

In the face of these difficulties, wives of missionaries and newly enslaved converts emerged as the real moral force in many mission stations. In these early missions enslaved Christians were "raised to the dignity of elders or helpers to superintend each the behaviour of the other sex, and to forward the work of instruction."[97] The most loyal and trusted converts were appointed to important pastoral offices; women were equal beneficiaries. The empowerment of female converts was facilitated by leadership roles played by women during the foundation phase of West Indian mission stations. This accommodation was especially important, as some males proved incapable of resisting the vices of tropical plantations and thus were unable to maintain high moral standards for converts to emulate.[98] The appointment of converts to positions of authority served the missions well, especially before the 1790s, when missionaries were few and generally not organized into societies. Indeed, it was often these converts, acting on their own initiatives, who kept the missions going whenever the sudden death or departure of a missionary created a vacuum in leadership. It was not unusual for a woman to fill the void.[99]

4

ABOLITIONISM AND EMPIRE

Metropolitan Counterpoint

To situate Edmund Burke's role in British imperial trusteeship, it is necessary to consider the significance of India in the emerging moral imperium. India features prominently in major studies on Britain's adoption of trust, yet there is a tendency among scholars to misconstrue Burke's significance to, as well as his motive for, trusteeship in India. A royal charter granted the East India Company full proprietary control over British India, including the executive, the military, and the judiciary.[1] Excessive power was a formula for excessive abuses. The first serious attempt to restrain the directors of the company was the Regulating Act of 1773, which established a Supreme Council and a Supreme Court at Bengal.[2] This and subsequent judicial reforms failed to check the company's absolutism in any significant way, yet Burke refused to support regulative legislation until the report of a Select Committee of Parliament in 1781 provided the fodder for his "one-man crusade for justice" for Indians.[3] Burke was largely responsible for two regulative bills; thereafter, he stoutly defended the right of Indians to self-rule.[4]

Burke could not contemplate a similar defense of African institutions or values when pleading the case for trusteeship in the West Indies. It is important to understand this distinction in order to afford Burke his true place in the evolution of imperial trusteeship. In spite of Burke's claim that British rule in India should be that of a trust, intervention before 1783 had little or nothing to do with philanthropy. This assertion is equally applicable after 1783, when he became the chief mouthpiece of the pressure group demanding control of the directors of the company. Peter Marshall argues that Burke's principal source of information on India was Philip Francis, whose interest

52

in imperial intervention was driven by "ambition and the desire for revenge" against the company.[5] Marshall explains that Francis did not have "the welfare of Indians as an end in itself, but he believed that Bengal was in a state of rapid decline and that the property of its inhabitants must be restored if it was to be of any practical value to Britain."[6] Clearly, the imperative of intervention was informed by the relationship between colonizers and subjects. Burke had a high regard for Indian civilization, especially its systems of government and jurisprudence. To him India was different from but not inferior to Europe. On the contrary, his attitude toward Africans was informed by propaganda of Africa's lack of government, law, and religion; consequently, Africans' place in the scheme of civilization was under European tutelage.[7] It is this distinction that made his Slave Code so radically different from his designs for India.

Questions over Indian sovereignty and the legitimacy and character of British dominion were similar to those addressed by moral philosophers of sixteenth-century Spain, yet there were some important distinctions. Spanish philanthropy centered on the Amerindian masses because of their importance as laborers and clients of missionaries. Spaniards also generally placed Amerindian cultures lower in the scale of civilization than their own; at best, Amerindians were "noble savages."[8] On the contrary, Burke's and, by extension, Britain's concern centered on the Indian ruling classes, which attracted attention largely because their members controlled the distribution of taxes and trade goods to the East India Company.[9] The Indian masses were never a factor in Burke's appeal for the preservation of Indian institutions from British imperialism. Notwithstanding these distinctions, one ought not to dismiss Burke's West Indian project.

Burke's plan was the most constructive prior to the imperial amelioration project launched in 1823. It was also consistent with amelioration priorities launched in the 1760s but with greater social content. Central to his "civilizing" scheme was the Christianization of the African family. The plan was based on the maxim that "the Government of a family is a principal means of forming men to fitness for freedom, & to become good citizens."[10] Consequently, he advocated the appointment of an "Inspector of Negroes" who must ensure that all healthy men between the ages of twenty-one and fifty years were provided with "a woman, not having children living, & not exceeding the age of the Man."[11] The plan promoted monogamous marriage by compelling all enslaved male laborers above the age of twenty-five years to "be married publicly in the face of the Church."[12] If necessary, the minister or inspector of Negroes must be authorized to order flogging for "all acts of adultery, unlawful concubinage, & fornication."[13] The plan included compulsory education for enslaved boys under the patronage and management of the Church of England. Under this scheme scholarships would be awarded to the most gifted to pursue further education in England under the direction of the bishop of London.[14]

Burke's cultural imperialism plan did not recognize wrongs against Africans committed by Europeans. He did not consider that slavery had destroyed the moral systems and institutions of Africans because he assumed that these frameworks never existed. Furthermore, he failed to address the hypocrisy of spreading Christianity to the enslaved class while remaining tolerant and supportive of a counterculture among the free population. That was a social flaw in the plan: a new moral order among the enslaved was unattainable outside of a new moral framework for enslavers. Thus, although constructive in what it proposed, the plan was fundamentally flawed and cosmetic because it failed to address the main problem of the African family. In this regard Burke might have learned from Bryan Edwards, Jamaican absentee landowner and member of Parliament. Edwards admitted that ameliorative regulations would avail the enslaved little or nothing unless proprietors' right to separate and alienate family members was deemed illegal.[15]

Burke's trusteeship for India was elitist. There was no guarantee of British juridical culture filtering down to the Indian masses. In the West Indies the planter class was the sociopolitical equivalent of Indian princes. When seen in this light, the distinction between Burke's concern for Indian natives and his concern for enslaved Africans narrows to the point of insignificance: both were elitist, and both placed full confidence in the existing power structure. Notwithstanding Burke's political status, Ramsay, Clarkson, and Equiano had a greater impact on the politics of amelioration in the later eighteenth century. Ramsay was schooled in the management of colonial slavery, Clarkson in the academy, and Equiano in the subaltern experience of enslavement; together they combined empiricism with diligent scholarship.

Clarkson's original interest in colonial slavery and slave trading arose out of a purely academic exercise. In the early 1780s Dr. Peckard of Cambridge University sponsored a prize for a Latin essay on slavery, a popular topic in philosophical and legal circles at the time. Clarkson wrote the winning essay, "Is it Right to Make Slaves of Others against Their Will?"[16] Its impact alienated members of his former social circle, with whom he had previously shared a casual acceptance of the trade as just another branch of imperial commerce. The essay immediately shuttled together disparate strands of contemporary abolitionists, beginning with a close group of philanthropists who originally came together to discuss the prize essay in the Senate House at the university. The network included Edmund Burke, William Dillwyn, Samuel Johnson (Dr. Johnson), James Ramsay, Granville Sharp, and other prominent moral philosophers and advocates of imperial trusteeship and their extended acquaintances.[17]

These ameliorators were not only interested in ideas but more so in being the architects of change. They underscored their commitment by their founding membership in the Society for the Gradual Abolition of the Slave Trade. The Abolition Society, launched in 1787, was the second association to create a major stir in political and commercial circles in England and the colonies within less than two years; the first, seldom recognized by historians, was the Sons of Africa, under the leadership of Equiano. Unlike the Sons of Africa, the Abolition Society included ultraconservative, successful men of business, politics, law, and the church; it was also favored with strong, intimate links to influential absentee planters and equally highly respected and influential Tories and Whigs in both houses of Parliament. These relationships made the society a major political movement for the reform of colonial slavery in England.[18] From 1727 to 1783 Quakers had moved futile resolutions and organized at least one petition against the slave trade. Whereas in 1727 the Quakers objected to slave trading because it was "not a commendable nor allowed practice,"[19] in 1783, when the first petition for abolishing the trade was presented to Parliament, the official objection merely reflected the influence of Enlightenment philosophy: that the trade was contrary "to the principles of humanity and justice."[20] With the establishment of the Abolition Society the new emphasis was economic and political, though still glossed with humanity and justice.

The year 1787 was fortuitous for the politics of slave trade abolitionism. The Abolition Society found a formidable ally in the manufacturing town of Manchester, the heart of the booming industrial north. There was also the early indication of an awakening of interest in abolition in Birmingham, another leading industrial town.[21] Seymour Drescher has argued that the conversion of the Abolition Society into the "first social reform movement" was the work of the Manchester Faustian manufacturers, who "launched the abolition campaign in 1787 independently of the London leadership."[22] He argues that without Manchester's political campaign, appeals to humanity and justice could expect to make no serious headway against vested interests. The ascribed seminal influence of the industrial towns fails to acknowledge Clarkson's, Equiano's, and Ramsay's prior injection of materialist motives for abolishing the slave trade.[23]

Not surprisingly, vested interests moved quickly to burst the abolitionist bubble by astutely co-opting allies from the Abolition Society. William Dolben, a member of the society and representative for Liverpool (the principal slave traders of the kingdom), piloted the Regulating Bill in Parliament. Its passage was a milestone in the history of abolitionism and a mark of the influence of the Sons of Africa, who had prompted Dolben to bring the bill.[24] Although Dolben constantly consulted Equiano,[25] he had not intended any serious change in attitude to slave trading. After a party of Liverpool merchants "had entertained him most lavishly with Turtle and Port," he praised them for being "liberal minded men."[26] Accordingly, he approached the question of the slave trade with greater sobriety and moderation, punctuated by apologies to slaving merchants and West Indian planters. He wished that members of Parliament would "understand that his bill did not at all interfere with the general question on this subject but had merely in view some temporary regulations for the safety of the lives of those poor people in the passage from the coast of Africa."[27]

Although Dolben expressed anguish over the method of tight packing aboard slavers, he and others basked in the hollow victory of the passage of the Regulating Act, which merely provided for an increase in the amount of space allowed for each person when packed in the hold of a slaver, which remained a vessel of trauma, diseases, and degradation. Clarkson's campaign against the bill reinforced Ramsay's arguments: if the slave trade was then a questionable contributor to the plantation system, its regulation would remove all doubts.[28] Clarkson had painstakingly produced empirical evidence to support Long's earlier claim that the slave trade was unprofitable.[29] Furthermore, if all the proposed measures of the bill were executed to the letter, there could be no hope of profit.[30] At that juncture it was evident that the campaign against the slave trade was more an attack against the rising cost of slaves than against the inhumanity of the trade. Even among the most ardent reformers, the perception of African barbarism shaped their definition of humanity. Such men persisted in the belief that Africans benefited from enslavement under European masters. This attitude was responsible for many leading philanthropists reserving judgment on the impolicy of the trade. As Burke explained, "The cause of humanity would be far more benefited by the continuance of the trade and servitude, regulated and reformed, than by the total destruction of both."[31]

For most British politicians and activist-ameliorators the slave trade was an issue distinct from slavery. It is therefore interesting to consider attitudes toward slavery and emancipation prior to 1830, especially in relation to colonial security. The slave trade lobby consistently accused abolitionists of politicizing the trade as a stratagem to secure general emancipation. Historians' acceptance of an emancipation agenda during the abolition debate in Parliament between 1805 and 1807 is an oversimplification of the problem. Most abolitionists were ultraconservative and reactionary on the question of slavery because of concerns for the safety of the colonies and the problem of compensation for the deprivation of human property.

Emancipation was integral to the economic recovery of the colonies and could not be avoided indefinitely. While abolitionists generally accepted the principle of Africans' natural right to freedom, they were steadfast ameliorators, not emancipators. For one thing the question of compensation was too complex to manage to the satisfaction of those with a vested interest in slavery. Moreover, any plan for general emancipation entailed the uncertainty of white rule in the region. Yet it would be unhistorical to deny that some abolitionists had a genuine, if somewhat hazy, vision of African emancipation. This apparent contradiction was evident in public declarations of Clarkson, Ramsay, and Sharp, among other abolitionists. John Majoribanks, a minor but radical abolitionist garrisoned in Jamaica from 1784 to 1787, epitomizes the dilemma of security and liberty that abolitionists faced in general. Although adamantly opposed to slavery, he remained committed to military protection of the system. In a very long poem, "Slavery: An Essay in Verse," he uniquely captured the terrors of slavery and made a strong appeal for amelioration. The poem also made a rare call by a Briton for unconditional abolition of both the slave trade and slavery prior to 1807. Yet in his final footnote Majoribanks penitently recanted, relegating emancipation to a "romantic, and as yet impractical, scheme."[32] Quoting from pamphlets written by Sharp and Elizabeth Heyrick, David Brion Davis tells us that both had issued calls for immediate emancipation in 1806 and 1824, respectively. Davis, however, does not discuss the political context of these demands; rather, for both activists emancipation was a prophylactic against divine retribution, a recurring theme in British and American antislavery thought.[33] No reference was made to Africans' right to freedom.

Most leading abolitions consistently conjured spurious defenses against harboring an emancipation agenda. In 1788, against the backdrop of his growing personal popularity as an abolitionist and the first wave of reaction against the launch of the Anti–Slave Trade Society, Ramsay raised the white flag of neutrality on the slavery question: "I shall first observe, that where this author treats of a general emancipation of slaves, he combats only a shadow; because the present plan aims only at the abolition of the African slave trade. It meddles not with the slaves already in the colonies; if it did, that sympathy, which first incited me to plead their claim to better treatment, would force me to range myself on the author's side, and protest against the indiscrete measure."[34] Yet even as he argued against a hidden agenda, he had accepted that in principle "the slave has a natural right to freedom."[35] Nevertheless, he rejected the feasibility of immediate emancipation on the classic justification that the enslaved African did not possess the capacity for liberty: "But it would be insidious not to declare, that humanity looks forward to full emancipation, whenever they shall be found capable of making a proper use of it. But, this may be left to the master's discretion, and the effect of future arrangements, which even the planter acknowledges to be necessary."[36] Clarkson was no less ambiguous. At the dawn of his abolitionist career he had categorically rejected the right of property in man and even provided funding to the French abolitionist society L'Amis des Noirs.[37] In answer to the 1790 parliamentary inquiry, however, he declared unequivocally, "I never was so absurd as to think of the emancipation of the Negroes at all; the sole object of my journey to Liverpool was, to collect facts for the abolition of the Slave Trade; this distinction between abolition and emancipation I set out with as a first principle, and have preserved to this day."[38] Clarkson was less equivocal toward emancipation in Africa. In planning the purchase of an island to expand the incipient Sierra Leone establishment, he instructed his brother to include all enslaved inhabitants in the transaction, with the express purpose of emancipating them "immediately" and "unconditionally" and employing them as wage laborers in various skilled capacities, including ship's pilots and carpenters.[39]

William Wilberforce continually vindicated himself from "the charge of wishing to make the Slaves free."[40] Although the ultimate objective of imperial amelioration was the transformation of the enslaved into a "free and happy peasantry," his condemnation of slavery as a "violation of the natural rights of human beings" was more rhetorical than prescriptive.[41] Instead of supporting immediate emancipation, he appealed for Christianization as a precondition for liberty and a vehicle for the restoration of natural rights,[42] a prescription for the indefinite continuation of slavery.

The same equivocation on African liberty resonated in the debate on the 1807 Abolition Bill. In moving the first reading, Lord Grenville passionately condemned the slave trade as "injustice" to Africans in Africa but advocated with equal vigor the continuation of slavery as "justice" to those in the West Indies: "But in giving liberty to the slaves on the islands, we should do the gravest injustice to them in giving them that which they would not know how to use, and which would be productive to them of injury. That liberty, the blessings of which we were enabled properly to estimate and appreciate, would be to them, in their state of ignorance and barbarism, a poison of the most baleful nature."[43] This was typical abolitionist hypocrisy. Barbarism was the consequence of planters' savagism, not a state of the Africans' development; likewise, colonials maintained the enslaved in ignorance as a tool of subservience and security.[44] Logically, Grenville's prognosis meant permanent enslavement for Africans. This was the principal flaw in the logic of gradualism advocated by abolitionists. The absurdity of Grenville's statement diminishes if it is understood that the primary objective of abolition was security for colonials. The right to private property was of much greater antiquity and more deeply rooted in European epistemology than the right to individual freedom. Emancipation could erode a substantial quantum of private property in the colonies. Clearly, abolitionists were caught in the same philosophical web of contradictions as Montesquieu and other moral philosophers of the Enlightenment, who dared not reconcile the rights of Africans within the universality of humankind.[45]

The blueprint of abolitionists' prescription of freedom, latent in Ramsayean gradualism, was finally unfolded at the launch of imperial-driven amelioration in 1823. The core concept in this blueprint was the transformation of slavery into a free peasantry, though still repudiating statutory emancipation. Clarkson defended his conversion to emancipationism, arguing, it "ought never to be forgot, that emancipation was included in the original idea of the abolition of the Slave Trade."[46] Yet this idea had gone no further than Ramsay's original proposition that the process of transformation must be through natural increase of the enslaved population. It is not unreasonable to conclude that abolitionists wished for a reformation of colonialism from slavery to free labor, yet they had no intention of preempting its evolution via statute. Their precedent was Europe's transition from slavery to free peasantries. As expressed by Wilmot Horton, "Slavery will merge into a sort of caste,"[47] the equivalent of *villeins en gros* and *villeins regardants*. Thus, a primary objective of imperial-driven amelioration was facilitating the process of transformation without any specific time frame.

Laissez-faire, the New Faith

Montesquieu was one of the earliest Enlightenment thinkers to empiricize the superiority of free labor;[48] Adam Smith's *Wealth of Nations,* however, was the first treatise on the subject. Smith condemned slavery as the dearest form of labor and commercial monopoly as a sacrifice of the general good in order to promote the interest of a minority.[49] Monopoly was also an obstacle to the efficiency of metropolitan and colonial economies alike. The unequivocal answer to monopoly was free trade; although he argued the case for free labor with equal vigor, he hesitated to recommend its extension to the West Indies because it would radically undermine property in enslaved Africans.

Ramsay was among the first abolitionists to assimilate laissez-faire doctrine to abolitionism and amelioration. In *Objections to the Abolition of the Slave Trade* he reiterated the Smithian creed of the superiority of free labor.[50] Speaking more directly from his own colonial experience, he added the corollary that the demise of a free man would add no cost to production because free men reproduced the next generation of laborers, whereas slaves were "regenerated" only by new purchases. Ramsay also rejected the claim that sugar could not be procured from foreign colonies. Of signal importance to his message was a vision of Britain at the dawn of a new imperial age in which the East, especially India, would play a key role. He argued that Britain had for long been importing foreign sugar at one third the cost of the British West Indian product and that cheap sources of free labor sugar were available from Batavia, Cochin China, and elsewhere in the East.[51] These were ill omens for West Indian colonists, but in the late eighteenth century the threat of competition was not serious enough to link amelioration to survival in a world of free trade. Yet it was this very nexus that gave the antislavery movement a new fillip after 1823.

James Stephen and Henry Brougham, two frontline abolitionists at the turn of the century, also made *The Wealth of Nations* their canon for a new imperial model, flirting with the free trade–cum–free labor doctrine to inject into it economic pragmatism for abolition of the slave trade. Both also endorsed Ramsay's application of Smith's theory of the superiority of free labor to the greater capacity of the colonies to consume British manufactures.[52] In the new age of industrialization and the expansion of India's sugar industry, the quest for free trade created a crisis in metropolitan-colonial relations. In the unfolding drama the West Indian monopoly naturally became the focus of debate. In the process pro-slavery advocates were compelled to defend a case that was not entirely new to British slavery. The conviction of free trade ideologues transformed abolitionists into natural allies of industrialists and antimonopolists in general. This development was both pragmatic and paradoxical, saving the abolitionist movement from becoming irrelevant and moribund.

Slave trade abolition failed to achieve the much-vaunted change projected by ameliorators. Ironically, one of the impediments to amelioration was abolitionists' faith in the colonial slavocracy to regulate itself. Not surprisingly, there was a general waning of abolitionists' fervor following the passage of the general Abolition Act. One abolitionist who stayed the path was James Stephen; as attorney general, he persuaded new parliamentarian Henry Brougham to move a motion to plug one of the major loopholes in the Abolition Act by making slave trading an offense punishable by death; he also pushed through the Registration Order-in-Council and Registration Acts as a halfway house toward amelioration. On the other hand, Wilberforce confessed that he had "postponed efforts to help the slaves."[53] Unequal to the task of confronting the West India Interest on the question of slavery, he sought to hand over the mantle of parliamentary leader to Buxton, who "had not yet decided to assume such responsibility."[54] It was against this background of inertia that James Cropper emerged as the new messiah of metropolitan antislavery. Through Cropper's initiatives, supported by a few leading abolitionists, a new society was launched to conduct a campaign against the contumacious West Indian oligarchs. The shape of this campaign was largely worked out by Cropper, with Clarkson an able lieutenant and emissary.

David Brion Davis unequivocally establishes Cropper as a pacesetter of the new abolitionism, frequently dragging the sluggish band of "humanitarians" behind him. In 1822 Cropper established his own Liverpool Anti-Slavery Society for the Amelioration and Gradual Abolition of Slavery and constantly appealed to Clarkson and Macaulay to organize a similar society in London. Cropper initiated moves to bring the economic aspects of amelioration to the platform of public debate. To him the only hope of winning public support for antislavery was by openly attacking the systems of slavery and monopoly, especially if accompanied by a vast propaganda campaign. He revived the lobbying of Parliament by mobilizing his Quaker "friends" to organize petitions on the slavery question, while he personally led a deputation of Liverpool merchants to present the case for East India sugar duties before a parliamentary committee.[55] Thus, 1822 was 1788 rewritten.

In January 1823 the London-based Society for the Mitigation and Gradual Abolition of Slavery (the Anti-Slavery Society) held its first meeting. Less than four months later, Buxton unveiled the group's amelioration program in Parliament, an unequivocal proclamation of abolitionists' preference for slavery over immediate emancipation. His primary objective was the mitigation of abuse of power by the slavocracy. While proposing free birth, Buxton studiously disclaimed any prospect of statutory emancipation for the existing generation. The most salutary recommendations were the enforcement of marriage, the removal of restraints from manumission, the receiving of judicial testimony *quantum valeat,* the abolition of the cart whip, and the rejection of compensation.[56] The government, in collusion with the West India Interest, responded with counter-resolutions for greater security of the colonies while respecting the right to compensation.[57] The unanimous passage of the government's resolutions underscored the irrelevance of the Anti-Slavery Society's appeals to humanity and Christianity. The London society had rebuffed Cropper's advice to combine the commercial question with the humanitarian. Buxton's failure to command the authorship of official amelioration meant that the leadership of slavery reform had shifted to the West India Interest—a case of 1797 revisited.

The Anti-Slavery Society eventually regained some ground after embracing Cropper's advice—and his personal interests—but lost momentum within a very short time because of compromised altruism. Except for their concern with recent revolts in the colonies, meetings of the London committee reflected the effervescence of bourgeois leisure. Writing confidentially to fellow abolitionist Joseph Gurney, Buxton confessed that antislavery affairs frequently became muddled in flights of fancy of inebriated members: "You were present at the debate at my house & saw how ardent we were for a fierce and valiant attack on Slavery itself—I have been served in the same way four or five times. In council & after a few glasses of Champagne we are the havest of the haves—& scorn all cautions, councils, but our courage evaporates as fast as the liquour—& in point of fact we do nothing."[58] He further confided, "The wavering temerity with which we execute, is really one of the greatest difficulties we have to encounter—& I have learnt that we must be slow & very prudent in our determinations, & then resolute in carrying them into effect—but this history is only for your private ear—pray therefore keep it for yourself."[59] In retrospect this malaise contradicts the dread with which vested interest in plantation slavery presumably held the antislavery lobby. In spite of, and more likely because of, this malaise and the urgency unleashed by the 1823 Demerara uprising, the seed of radicalism was sown outside of the new society in the writing of Quaker activist Elizabeth Heyrick and the Methodist Society.[60] The few old guards within the progressive wing included Stephen and Clarkson. By 1830 a new generation of radicals formed their own wing, the Agency Committee. The first foray into radicalism was marked by support of imperial intervention to enforce the parliamentary resolutions for amelioration in all colonies. On the more fundamental question of the future of the West Indian colonies, the radicals argued for free trade in East India sugar within a new globalization of British commerce.

The Anti-Slavery Society's open defense of free trade and cheap sugar, whatever its origins, was as much a triumph for ameliorators of the late eighteenth century as it was for Adam Smith. The paradigm shift was critical to the future of antislavery politics in England. In order to promote East Indian sugar, there was widespread condemnation of the West Indian product as "blood sugar," reinforced by the charge that the British consumer was forced to support a contumacious plantocracy under the existing system of preferential sugar duties. By 1826 the new strategy made colonial slavery an issue in national elections for the first time.

Only a few "Friends of the Negro" had maintained any real interest in the sugar question after the Abolition Act.[61] Early in 1824 the Anti-Slavery Society adopted a free trade resolution because it was "deeply convinced of the moral guilt as well as the political inexpediency of Colonial Slavery."[62] In attempting to moralize politico-economic expediency, the society argued, "The continuance of these commercial regulations, which by imposing such higher duty on sugar the produce of free labour than on sugar grown by slaves, force the latter into consumption in this country, almost to the exclusion of the former."[63] There was truth in this claim but not the whole truth. The overriding concern was cheap sugar, not the way it was produced. As Eric Williams has argued, the same repugnance was not shown for imported sugar from Brazil, Cuba, India, Martinique, and Mauritius and cotton from the United States.[64]

The creation of constituencies of support against West Indian monopoly demanded scheming and nationwide propaganda. Few of the old guard of abolitionists could have rallied to the call as completely and competently as Stephen and Clarkson. Their main strategy was the tagging of antislavery to votes in national elections in order to galvanize political support in the new Parliament. New committees of the Anti-Slavery Society were set up on Clarkson's initiatives while on a grand tour of the country. Magistrates, clergymen of the Church of England and Ireland, and Tories as well as friends of government were planted in each committee for publicity and to guarantee conservatism.[65] In simple terms all the new committees had thrown their weight behind Cropper and advanced the struggle for free trade from advocacy to activism. As Clarkson explained, "It was agreed by all these . . . that they would be ready to come forward with Petitions to Parliament, to take off the Bounties and Drawbacks on West India Sugars, and to equalize the Duties on sugar from the East &c—and then, if Parliament should not comply with their Petitions, to do their best to promote abstinence from West India Sugar."[66] This was a veiled declaration of war and a determination to sacrifice the West Indian colonies if necessary to the new god of free trade. Whether pursued as an end in itself or a means to an end, equalization had assumed an urgency that was destined to create an irreconcilable chasm between abolitionists and West Indian plantership. In a letter to Buxton, Clarkson explained the new tactic as a line drawn in the sand: "If you were to equalize the Duties and take off the drawbacks (these being great supports of West India Slavery) the planters *must come into* our measures or be gradually ruined."[67] Those measures were expected to secure genuine amelioration for the enslaved class, the commonly desired but elusive prerequisite for improved productivity. For the new free trade evangelists amelioration would be the means by which planters might enjoy lower costs of producing sugar and enhance their competitiveness while eliminating the principal justifications for preferential treatment in a new and changing world of free trade.

Contrary to the antimonopolist lobby, West Indian planters clamored for a reduction in sugar duties to offset the cost of amelioration.[68] For the Anti-Slavery Society equalization would remain an imperative whatever the options they adopted to advance the cause of slavery reform. As far as Clarkson was concerned, the bright new jewel of India would more than compensate for the despoliation of the West Indies.[69] The new antislavery platform was strengthened by the publication of James Stephen's *England Enslaved by Her*

Own Colonies. The work was written against the background of an imperial policy-making environment favorable to free trade. Advocacy for laissez-faire had yielded early results in the free labor experiments in Trinidad in the first decade of the nineteenth century and in the India Act of 1813 ending the trade monopoly of the East India Company.[70] The British West Indian sugar monopoly was also undermined unobtrusively from 1813, when the French West Indian islands were allowed equal access to the British market.[71] Stephen was perplexed; he complained that French sugar was "now privileged like that of our West Indian Colonies; though for what reason it is thus preferred to the produce of Bengal, except that it is raised by the forced labor of Slaves, it is hard to imagine."[72] Thus, by 1823 free trade and free labor had already entered the arena of imperial policy. Economic liberalism was strengthened by the extension of the West Indian sugar preference to Mauritius in 1825 and the ending of commercial restrictions of the West Indian–American trade.[73] Although mercantilism still had more powerful defenders than detractors, free trade had become so irresistible that abolitionists could openly defend such a policy as justice, while they condemned monopoly and slavery as injustice.

Stephen publicly confessed that hitherto he had been a "feeble advocate" for mercantilism but that he need no longer be ashamed to recant, "for it would be a crowd of splendid converts who have now renounced the same erroneous faith."[74] He condemned as unfair to British consumers the recent relaxation of restrictions on the West Indies while maintaining them on the British merchant class. He argued: "The general principle is the favourite maxim of political economists that trade should be perfectly free. The colonial monopoly, therefore, ought clearly to have been abolished on both sides . . . As to protective duties, they should no longer have a place in our Custom-house vocabularies; the very name is heretical to the new faith; for commerce can be protected only 'by itself.'"[75] This was a clear rejection of the old ethos of imperial commerce and an orientation toward the ethos of free trade, the progress of which he described as "a great commercial and maritime revolution."[76]

Concomitant with the benefits of free trade were the benefits of free labor. In the West Indies the prospect for free labor was obfuscated by the ubiquitous stereotype of the lazy African. By the 1820s, however, reports of the success of the Haitian peasant economy began to challenge this stereotype.[77] Haiti was the product of revolutionary emancipation, but imperial reformers remained committed to gradualism in transforming their own enslaved laborers into free peasants. Disguising their own personal fears of emancipation, abolitionists aggressively argued that the progress of free labor was negated by planters' contumacy toward amelioration. They argued that this resistance was sustained only because of the support of protective duties.

To Wilmot Horton the combination of monopoly and slavery in a single matrix was confusing and economically illogical. In a pamphlet dedicated to exposing the inconsistencies of the new saints of free trade, Horton argued: "If there were not a single slave in the West Indies, the West Indians might protest *ex parte,* against any relaxation of duty, whether with respect to East Indians or to foreign sugar, on the grounds that sugar cultivation in the West Indian Islands had been fostered by British Acts, upon the principle of monopoly."[78] Even in conceding that there was a valid case for reducing the duties on East Indian and foreign sugars, Horton maintained that there was no sustainable nexus between "the question of slavery in the West Indies, and the question of the Commercial Monopoly given to the West Indian Colonies."[79] Horton was convinced that the gospel of free trade propagated by the Anti-Slavery Society was flawed in some of its fundamentals. Certainly, if as Cropper claimed, free trade and free labor were manifestations of "the great hand of God in the flow of goods toward their natural markets,"[80] then the case for emancipation in the West Indies was seriously compromised. On the one hand, Indian sugar was produced by unfree, if not chattel, labor, in spite of the society's claims to the contrary. As Horton was well aware, India's sugar works existed under definite "circumstances of unequivocal coercion, and absence of anything like the idea which is conveyed by the term *'freedom'* to the mind of an Englishman."[81] On the other hand, the cheap foreign sugar advocated by Stephen was, invariably, the produce of enslaved Africans. The only logic in this plan was the poorly disguised primacy of self-interest.

To Horton the dilemma created by the Anti-Slavery Society would preserve the slave labor system indefinitely: "It would not be inconsistent to assert that the West Indian Colonies ought not to have a monopoly, and at the same time to contend that the planter ought not to be deprived of the Services of his Slave without compensation."[82] Ultimately, government's position was that the planters should seek compensation in amelioration.[83] The West Indians countered that official amelioration increased the cost of producing sugar and threatened the survival of plantation economies. The ensuing stalemate ensured that gradualism remained the official policy for the reformation of the colonial system.

5

THE HAITIAN REVOLUTION AND OTHER EMANCIPATION WARS

The Haitian Revolution climaxed almost three hundred years of sustained revolutionary emancipationism. It was the pivotal moment in the contest between the right of Africans to liberty and the right of Europeans to property in them. It also provides the key to the ebb and flow of abolitionism between 1791 and 1807. The Haitian Revolution went beyond its French counterpart to break the chains of private property that bound Europeans to prevarication on the universal right to unconditional liberty. No contemporary European understood the psychology of the moment better than James Stephen. He called upon his countrymen to pray for Toussaint's safety—after his kidnapping and transportation to France in chains—"for this great & good man, this pious champion of the noblest of human causes & if they think with me they will go further—they will not pray for Toussaint only but that it will please the Almighty, to bring to nought the counsels of those who would perfidiously & bloodily restore the yoke that has been broken from the shoulders of our oppressed brethren in the West Indies, that he would graciously take their cause into his most holy protection & signalize his own wisdom, power and goodness by making it finally to triumph." He lamented the great emancipator's sacrifice of his children, "rather than betray the glorious cause."[1] Yet paradoxically, Stephen also dreaded the progress of revolutionary emancipation.

Consequent upon its extensive inquiry into the slave trade and slavery, Parliament passed a series of resolutions in 1792 committing itself to abolition of the trade. After much wrangling and anxiety to press ahead, the House of Commons resolved to advance the previously agreed date for final abolition from the first of January 1800 to the first of January 1796.[2] Within months of the resolutions, the West Indies was caught up in the throes of French revolutionary wars, further complicated the following year when France declared war on Britain, Holland, and Spain but more so when Britain launched its invasion of St. Domingue and other French colonies. The British enterprise in Haiti and its extended wars in defense of slavery demanded a revision of the 1792 resolutions. Ironically, it was Haitian independence that paved the way for restoring the status of the resolutions, thus precipitating the abolition of the slave trade.

The Haitian Revolution in Abolition Historiography

Against the backdrop of scientific racism and continuing dependence on slave-based economies, imperialists were determined to record the Haitian Revolution as a historical aberration.[3] Karl Marx was perhaps the first notable European scholar since James Stephen to deem the Haitian Revolution the most significant victory toward the advancement of universal freedom.[4] W. E. B. Du Bois must have arrived at the same conclusion, stating unequivocally that the success of the revolution "rendered more certain the final prohibition of the slave-trade by the United States in 1807."[5] Dessalines's utter destruction of Napoleon's *grande armée* was as profound as Toussaint's victory over Britain. The defeat of the *grande armée* permanently erased the institution of slavery from Haiti and set the stage for the transformation of the whole of Hispaniola—the first colony to experience European slavery—into the first province of universal freedom in the Americas. The defeat of Napoleon also secured the future westward expansion of the United States.[6] Notwithstanding its dramatic impacts, this cataclysmic war of emancipation remained the best-kept secret among white scholars during the nineteenth century. John William Fortescue was the first to break through the white veil of silence.[7] Even so, the Haitian Revolution remained significant mainly to African American historians. The U.S. occupation of Haiti in 1915 was soon followed by the launch of the *Journal of Negro History,* which provided an outlet for reassessing Haiti's anti-imperialist role in the hemisphere. Typical of this reaction was George W. Brown's essay "The Origins of Abolition in Santo Domingo."[8] Between the two world wars Pan-African scholars warmly embraced socialism as an ideology of anticolonialism and upheld the Russian Revolution as their compass to progress. Against this backdrop C. L. R. James produced his masterly study *The Black Jacobins,* deploying Marxist historicism to develop a new understanding of the African experience in European colonies; more particularly, he reinterpreted the Haitian Revolution as a Caribbean counterpart to the French and Russian revolutions.

Although James only briefly addressed the impact of the revolution on British abolitionism, the work raised two key questions in the historiography of the movement, namely the origins of the Anglo-Haitian war and the extent to which revolutionary emancipation determined the status of the 1792 resolutions. In addressing the first question, James argues that from the outbreak of Boukman's revolt in 1791, Pitt had intended to seize St. Domingue and transform the Caribbean Sea into a British lake.[9] James further argues that it was not until some eighteen months after the invasion that war minister Henry Dundas (the future Viscount Melville) had proclaimed that the expedition was "'not a war for riches or local aggrandizement but a war for security,'" though he "knew that not a single member of Parliament would believe him."[10] With respect to the second question, James dismisses the fear of Jacobinism in England as significant to the suspension of the 1792 resolutions; instead, he advanced the seminal idea of economic advantage vis-à-vis the sugar trade. Accordingly, once Britain gained control of St. Domingue, "instead of being abolitionists they would be the most powerful practitioners and advocates of the slave trade, on a scale exceeding anything they had done before."[11]

A second seminal application of historical materialism to changing North Atlantic–Caribbean historiography in the interwar years was Eric Williams's dissertation, "The Economic Factor in the Abolition of the British Atlantic Slave Trade," revised and published in 1944 as *Capitalism and Slavery.* Williams's primary focus was British abolition. Like James, he argues that prior to the outbreak of revolutionary war in Europe, Pitt's original interest in abolition was merely strategic: to curtail French sugar output, reduce the cost of sugar production, and secure the market for British producers. In echoing James's view on St. Domingue, Williams affirmed, "The very acceptance of the island meant logically the end of Pitt's interest in abolition."[12] Williams further contends that the real reason for Pitt's backpedaling was not the fear of Jacobinism as advanced by "Liberal historians" but the "simple" fact that "no man occupying so important a position as Prime Minister of England would have taken so important a step as abolishing the slave trade purely for humanitarian reasons."[13]

Roger Anstey presented one of the earliest cogent arguments that the abolition agenda of 1792 was altered because of emancipation wars in the West

Indies, the fear of Jacobinism in England, and revolutionary war in Europe. Making a clean break from James and Williams, Anstey argues that the major influence on Pitt's and Dundas's anti-abolition ethic was a combination of military and political expediency. He further posits that in 1794 the war minister voted against abolition because he anticipated resistance from the colonial assemblies, which could seriously compromise England's wartime revenues.[14] Two years later, when Dundas again sought to justify his hostility to abolition, the war minister simply offered a new corollary to colonial contumacy: "Prohibition of the trade from Africa . . . if passed into law in the present distracted state of the colonies, would throw them entirely into the power of the enemy."[15] In presenting this case, Anstey was closer to the truth than James and Williams. Yet while the plantocracy would certainly have resisted abolition, colonial assemblies would not have voted for alliance with France if only because of its emancipation decree of 1794; for the same reason British colonists would have done everything in their power not to allow their plantations to fall into enemy hands. Indeed, capitulation to demands for enlistment of enslaved laborers speaks to the extent of the plantocracy's accommodation of distasteful imperial impositions. Among other factors advanced by Anstey for the strong anti-abolition showing in the House of Lords was the "recoil from Jacobinism," which opened the door for the West Indians to reset the formula for abolition and effectively torpedo Abolition Day 1796. Accordingly, because conservatism "demanded opposition to change in the established imperial system, the evident connection between Jacobinism and abolition . . . must demand resistance to abolition."[16] Anstey expected these views to be accepted as historical maxims given that he did not attempt to establish a direct connection between abolition and the fear of Jacobinism. His representation of the aristocracy as "defenders of a traditional imperial interest" merely begs the question;[17] furthermore, it was against the backdrop of an even more expansionist France that the House of Lords passed the general Abolition Act of 1807, before the Commons had even begun its debate.

Prior to Anstey, Dale Porter had demonstrated that the connection between Jacobinism and abolition was not so evident. Instead, Porter asserts that anti-Jacobinism in England "cannot be accepted as a valid interpretation" of the negative voting in the House of Lords in the early 1790s.[18] He explains that in 1795 Pitt had come around to a pro-abolition position, only to be confronted by Dundas's argument "that more time was needed by planters, who under wartime conditions were unable to build up a stock of slaves sufficient to cushion the shock of abolition."[19] While there is some truth to Dundas's account of planters' needs, available evidence shows that his explanation was an ingenious cover for withholding sensitive information on recruitment of enslaved Africans as the Trojan Horse of the imperial army. The radical but tightly guarded policy of conscripting enslaved laborers was bound to compromise the official commitment to abolition. Indeed, by 1795 Dundas had already given the green light to military commanders to levy upon planters their prime labor force and, if necessary, to engage in "picking the Cargo" of arriving slave ships for additional recruits.[20] Such was the exigency imposed by France's tactical emancipation. Thus, the anticipated stock of enslaved labor to which Porter alluded could not be achieved, but just as well, Britain could not have maintained its colonies without abandoning abolition. Michael Craton correctly grasped this fact in his seminal *Testing the Chains*.[21]

Notwithstanding Porter's refutation and Craton's insightful deduction, by the mid-1980s Anstey's views on the subject had become the traditional ones, though continuously refined. One spinoff has been the tendency to explain the emancipation wars in the Lesser Antilles as the work of French agents provocateurs. This perspective is quite noticeable in David Geggus, *Slavery, War, and Revolution: The British Occupation of Saint Domingue, 1793–1798*. Arguably, Geggus is the leading English-language historian on revolutionary St. Domingue; his immense output has considerably enriched the historiography of the revolutionary decade. Although recognizing the decisive role of black militarism in the Lesser Antilles, Geggus, like many other historians, prioritizes French captains.[22] As such, he downplays the impact of black soldiers and insurgents on Europe's military failures in the Caribbean during the 1790s while making heavy weather of the French Republic in Britain's forced evacuation from Guadeloupe and St. Lucia. He also tempers the gallantry of African militarism in Haiti by emphasizing malaria and alcohol as factors in Britain's defeat and the decimation of Napoleon's crack forces in 1803.[23] In a recent essay on the subject, Geggus reiterates that scholars have overrated Haiti's value to abolition. He posits that contemporaries seemed unconvinced "by the argument that abolition was needed to defuse the threat of rebellion."[24] Interestingly, his only evidence presented for this far-reaching conclusion is Drescher's brief rebuttal in the bicentennial collection of essays that Geggus himself edited. In his contribution to the same volume Robin Blackburn firmly rejects Drescher's opinion but with such politeness its significance might well be overlooked.

Roger Buckley's *Slaves in Red Coats* is one of the best accounts linking black militarism to abolitionism in the period under study. He is one of the few historians to include a central role for African soldiery in a history of the British army in the revolutionary 1790s.[25] His earlier work on the formative years of the West India Regiment is essentially a history of soldiery by enslaved Africans. Buckley cogently argues that British military power in the Caribbean rested on the black regiments and corps but also recognizes that Britain's greatest opposition came from self-emancipated fighters. Furthermore, he is unique among the 1970s generation of scholars in recognizing the abolition paradox in the militarization of plantation labor. Buckley courageously recognizes revolutionary emancipation as the underpinning of official abolition policy. He astutely asserts, "The policy of purchasing slaves as soldiers influenced in no small way the efforts to end the slave trade."[26] Michael Duffy ranks with Buckley in centering black militarism in the Caribbean balance of power during the 1790s. More boldly than anyone before, though still garnished with temperance, he affirms, "At the most, the war may have provided the clinching arguments which finally undermined the antiabolitionist defense."[27] Notwithstanding these indicators, Anglophone scholars have generally negated the impact of revolutionary emancipationism on the Abolition Acts of 1806 and 1807. Many other excellent works on black militarism generally do not establish links to the problem of abolition of the slave trade.

Taking the "traditional view," Howard Temperley claims that the combination of French revolutionary and African emancipationist wars "strengthened the forces of conservatism and thereby weakened the appeal of measures based explicitly on notions of justice, humanity and religion."[28] Reinforcing Temperley, Peter Marshall argues that public opinion in Britain accepted that "both slavery and the slave trade were evil" and demanded their reformation or abolition, but "other things being equal," political and economic expediencies demanded otherwise.[29] He further asserts that such a course of action "was dangerous and impractical in the circumstances of the 1790s. The economic situation, the military campaigns in the West Indies, the dangerous examples of the Haiti revolts, all made changes inexpedient for the moment."[30] This prognosis is historical surrealism. Prior to the outbreak of the Haitian Revolution, the abolitionist leadership unequivocally disavowed support for black liberation. One of the few points of convergence from James to Marshall was the rejection of colonial security as a factor in the abolition of the slave trade. Yet the developments cited by Temperley and Marshall position the politics of abolitionism squarely within the economics of security. As argued earlier, humanitarianism was not the primary issue in abolition; without compelling materialist motives, it would have been impossible to swing public opinion in support of radical change. Indeed, none of the frontline spokesmen for amelioration or abolition appealed primarily to conscience, religion, justice, humanity, or even natural law. Abolitionists well understood that "men were always ready to obey their sympathies when it cost them nothing."[31]

Seymour Drescher's best-known work, *Econocide,* considers the broader picture of emancipation wars in the Caribbean but maintains that they had no significant impact on the resolutions of 1792. Instead, he contends that "although the revolting threat to the British colonies reached its height in 1795–1796, the Commons failed to sustain even its original resolution to abolish the trade by January 1, 1796."[32] Drescher, however, is best measured against the views of Williams.

Williams's central explanation for Britain's attitude toward abolishing the slave trade is the performance of sugar. Therefore, in shifting the main dynamic to colonial security in the current study, it is of capital importance to establish whether or not the government would have retained St. Domingue as a prize of war. The St. Domingue royalists had sought British protection only "until the general peace"; although the original proposal did not oblige Britain to restore the colony to France, some six months later such an agreement was reached.[33] Indeed, the available data are weighed against retention. Retrospectively, it is unthinkable that France would have ceded such a valuable colony to Britain on a return to peace. If anything, the Treaty of Amiens was a test case. Although Britain negotiated against a backdrop of military successes, it gave up all its conquests except Trinidad and Ceylon (Sri Lanka), neither of which was a French possession.[34] In debating British withdrawal from St. Domingue, James Fox had sharply criticized the government for squandering the nation's resources "to preserve a colony we were certain would be given up, and which at present was of no use whatever."[35] William Wilberforce supported this view.[36] Furthermore, in the aborted negotiations for peace in 1796, English plenipotentiaries had offered to evacuate St. Domingue and return France's other conquered colonies.[37] Thus, while Williams's assertions about Britain's imperial design on St. Domingue are hardly contestable, the prospect of permanence is missing; it begs the historian to look further for a more satisfactory explanation of the ups and downs of abolitionism to 1797.

Some quarter-century after the publication of *Capitalism and Slavery,* Williams revisited the Haitian Revolution only to flirt with revolutionary emancipationism rather than reconcile the phenomenon with the imperatives of sugar. In his last major work, *From Columbus to Castro,* he argues that the real explanation for the failure of abolitionism from 1787 to 1807 was St. Domingue.[38] Notwithstanding the emphasis on failure, he implicitly recognizes that the revolution was also decisive in changing the fortunes of abolitionists: "The extent to which Saint-Domingue changed the abolition picture in Britain is best brought out by the attempt of the abolitionists, in pursuit of what was the most generally acceptable aspect of the early abolition movement, to prevent the exportation of slaves to the conquered colonies of Trinidad and British Guiana."[39] This statement, however, only supports his earlier contention of the economic advantages of possessing the French colony; by addressing the first Abolition Act of 1806 forty pages after his reference to the 1805 abolition order-in-council that the act replicated, Williams successfully divorced those seminal legislative measures from the critical issue of revolutionary emancipationism.

Williams is typical of many historians who are either ambivalent or noncommittal on the impact of revolutionary emancipation on abolition legislation; on this issue he shares mutual ground with his most strident critics. In *Econocide* Drescher emphatically denies the impact of Haiti on the Abolition Acts of 1806 and 1807. Even though he acknowledges the success of black insurgency in overturning the enslaver-enslaved relations, he concludes, citing Lord Howick as his sole evidence, "The very idea of internal revolution in the British West Indies was treated as 'ridiculous.'"[40] Interestingly, Drescher and other recent critics of revolutionary emancipationism have failed to incorporate Michael Craton's assertion that Howick had firmly believed in a direct link between newly imported Africans and insurrection in the Caribbean.[41] The parliamentary records are replete with similar acknowledgments.

Unlike Williams's partial turnaround, Drescher has resolutely advocated his original views on the revolution. Published on the eve of the bicentenary of Haiti's independence, Geggus's collection of essays, *The Impact of the Haitian Revolution in the Atlantic World,* anticipated the renewed clash of ideologies as the bicentennial commemoration of Britain's and the United States's abolition acts approached. In his brief contribution to the volume, Drescher reiterated views expressed in *Econocide,* emphasizing the Haitian Revolution as a setback to the abolition process.[42] He defended his position on the subject just as doggedly in *Who Abolished Slavery?,* a recent collection of essays he coedited with Pieter Emmer.[43] Another major contributor to Geggus's bicentennial collection, David Brion Davis, one of the most influential scholars on Atlantic slavery in the latter twentieth century, conceives the impact of Haiti on abolitionism as "ambiguous" and argues, "It would be difficult to show that fear of another Haitian Revolution motivated Parliament's crucial votes in 1806 abolishing the slave trade to rival foreign markets, which prepared the way in 1807 for abolishing the British slave trade altogether."[44] The act of 1806 added nothing new, however, to the abolition order-in-council of the previous year, which abolished the Atlantic slave trade to "conquered colonies." The royal edict was the direct outcome of the debate on George Canning's motion of May 1802, in which the specter of another Haitian Revolution was most evident.

Revolutionary Emancipationism and the Suspension of the 1792 Resolutions

The Boukman uprising that ignited the Haitian Revolution was not the opening salvo of the emancipation wars of the 1790s. Warning tremors had occurred in Guadeloupe and Martinique a few months prior to the main event in St. Domingue.[45] What was certainly unprecedented was the scope of the revolution, its shatter zone ultimately extending throughout the Lesser Antilles, thus becoming the most intensely contested military struggle for freedom within any slave system in history. By 1795 the combined emancipationist forces had become the worst nightmare of Caribbean plantation colonies, climaxing in the decisive defeat of the British Empire at the hands of Toussaint L'Ouverture and France's grand army at the hands of Jean-Jacques Dessalines. Correspondingly, the revolution overturned the traditional balance of power in the Caribbean and the status of Africans from the "sinews of empire" to its military backbone, with a corresponding shift in the somatic image of its leadership from "imitators" of Europeanism to distinguished captains of conventional warfare. These psychological shockwaves demanded a revision of the resolutions of 1792.

The simultaneous revolts across the Caribbean were not isolated events but fronts of a common war against slavery—an expanded Haitian Revolution. Contrary to the views of some leading historians, the Haitian Revolution, with its satellite revolts in the eastern Caribbean, was pivotal to the passage of abolition legislation from 1805 to 1807; it was also the key factor in the adoption of amelioration by the British government. Whereas Abolition Day 1796 was suspended because of revolutionary emancipationism and the exigencies of military conscription, abolition was embraced between 1805 and 1807 as the principal weapon against the contagion of emancipation. This dialectic is the key to understanding the politics of abolition following the 1792 resolutions.

At the outbreak of the Anglo-French war Dundas calculated that the possession of St. Domingue would be economically advantageous to Britain and might well be the trump card to lessen the maritime power of France.[46] In the initial stages of invasion Britain had offered protection to royalist planters against Jacobins and independent African warlords.[47] The first object of defense, however, was the protection of Jamaica, Britain's premier colony; possession of St. Domingue would provide an anti-emancipationist buffer to the neighboring island.[48] Speaking retrospectively in 1797, after the worst phase of the emancipation wars in the Lesser Antilles, Dundas questioned rhetorically: "Was there any man who would agree, that if the Negroes, being in that state [of insurrection], had been permitted to proceed, and gaining strength had extirpated the planters, Jamaica would be worth one year's purchase; or that the lives and properties of the planters of Jamaica would be safe? What saved Jamaica from the same sort of invasion as Grenada? St. Domingo was in our possession."[49] Thus, whether for economic gain or defense, St. Domingue demanded occupation. In light of the contribution of the sugar colonies to the revenues of both powers, this was no surprise. The thesis of economic advantage expounded by James and Williams cannot adequately account for Pitt's apparent ambivalence toward abolition. Although the logic of imperialism supports James's and Williams's explanation of the invasion, by 1794 that logic had changed: the revolution of the enslaved had redefined the struggle as a war for security. Indeed, if imperial policy shifted from pro-abolition to pro-trade, both positions were consistent with the imperatives of security. The more immediate cause of Pitt's new anti-abolition stance, however, was Dundas's commitment to building standing armies of enslaved Africans as the main line of defense against revolutionary emancipationism and French republicanism. Interestingly, both James and Williams accuse Dundas of insincerity in asserting that security was the main objective of the

West Indian war.[50] Yet the war minister's explanation not only made sense; it was the only thread that held together all other issues. It also added an element of consistency to Pitt's politics, especially his attitude to abolitionism.

The pendulum of abolitionism in the 1790s pivoted around the large-scale conscription of enslaved soldiers to neutralize French emancipation. Ongoing conscription seriously compromised the slave system. The success of revolutionary emancipationism in St. Domingue heightened paranoia over the fate of plantation colonies elsewhere. While the center of revolutionary emancipationism was Haiti, the Lesser Antilles was truly the revolution's eastern front. With the outbreak of revolutionary war in Europe further complicating the situation, neither France nor England had the capability to engage in an effective ground war in the Caribbean.[51] Where the French fell short on conventional resources, however, they capitalized on plans and activities of the enslaved populations to break free from the shackles of slavery.[52] The result was the rapid deployment of black regiments and informal alliances with black warlords.

Emancipation had become an aspect of the power play between Royalists and Jacobins before the British occupation of St. Domingue. In June 1793, having allied with Maroons to defeat Royalist governor General César Galbaud, Jacobin commissioner Léger Félicité Sonthonax won over the majority of the governor's black conscripts by promising to confirm the freedom Galbaud had offered them. One month before the British invasion, Sonthonax unilaterally proclaimed general emancipation (with conditionality) to the North Province in order to preempt Spanish offers of freedom to the two principal black warlords, Georges Biassou and Toussaint L'Ouverture, and to mobilize all available manpower for the impending invasion.[53] The expulsion of Galbaud marked the end of white supremacy in St. Domingue.[54] Against this setting British invasion was a blueprint for disaster. Emancipation was differently deployed in Martinique and with different consequences. Although the newly emancipated were critical in repulsing the first British attack, only the "most courageous" were constituted into two permanent battalions of "corps de chasseurs."[55] The island capitulated when the British renewed their assault in February 1794.[56]

The British invasion of St. Domingue began in September 1793. Although white Royalist collaborators had promised easy victory, the small expeditionary force of some 560 soldiers, including a "corps of black slaves" drawn from Jamaica, belied the significance of the enterprise.[57] French collaborator

Vernault de Charmilly secured the main ports of Jeremie and Mole St. Nicolas for the invaders.[58] The only significant achievements of British arms were "some military posts"; by 1794 the advance had ended, and the campaign deteriorated into an exasperating war of attrition against Maroon warlords and *nouveaux libres* Africans, many in French and Spanish uniforms, until the humiliating evacuation in 1798.[59]

The French convention formally ratified Sonthonax's emancipation decree by legislation dated 4 February 1794; in just over two months the executive council mandated all administrative units and tribunals to implement the law with immediate effect. The motion for emancipation was moved by self-manumitted Jean-Baptiste Bellay, the chief spokesman of a delegation of the "new Deputies of St. Domingo," who boasted that six hundred thousand recently freed "men of colour . . . have sworn to live free, to support the Republic, one and indivisible, and to crush the English and the Spaniards if they shall dare to appear."[60] Having listened to Bellay, Deputy Lavasseur remarked untruthfully, "When drawing up the constitution of the French people we paid no attention to the unhappy Negroes."[61] Attention was certainly paid but freedom denied. Robespierre, among others, had argued for the retention of slavery in 1791 because of the importance of St. Domingue and other sugar colonies to the economy of metropolitan France.[62]

In reciprocating Bellay's military overture, Deputy La Croix moved that the convention "decree that all the Men of colour are French Citizens, and that they shall enjoy the blessings of the Constitution we have decreed."[63] Behind the show of revolutionary idealism was the recognition that emancipation was the best weapon to destabilize the British and the best option for the leading slave-trading ports of France to recoup huge property investments, especially in St. Domingue.[64] Accordingly, another deputy inserted the military overlay, demanding "that whenever our Armies should set foot on the Colonies of foreign Powers, they should publish this Decree."[65] On that note Deputy Danton was more specific: though he lauded the convention for having done "justice to Humanity," he moved a resolution to ensure that the strategic value of the decree was fully embraced by sending it to the Committee of Public Safety. Thus, 4 February 1794 was more than Emancipation Day; as Danton perceived it: *"This day is Death to the English People."*[66]

The French emancipation decree coincided with a new motion for abolition presented by Wilberforce. The effect of the news threw the British political directorate into immediate panic. Pitt linked the decree and the turmoil in the islands as "the strongest reason in support of the Bill," which got the approval of the Commons with a significant majority.[67] In attempting to demonstrate the hopelessness of the military equation in Haiti, Member of Parliament St. John claimed that during the early months of invasion anti-British forces consisted of white troops divided into 6,000 elite National Guards from Paris and 9,000 auxiliaries customarily garrisoned in the colony; the white troops were supplemented by 10,000 "discipline blacks," or regular conscripts; added to these conventional forces were the "professed enemies" of slavery, consisting of "a number of revolted Negroes, amounting to 40,000, who would fall upon either party, if they could do it with hopes of success."[68] Although the British forces were continually supplemented by reinforcements under elite officers, at no time were they a serious match for the enemy they faced, either in terms of numbers or field tactics. Military dispatches show in no uncertain terms that Britain's ability to conduct war in St. Domingue was circumscribed by black insurgency elsewhere in the Caribbean, the main hotbeds being Dominica, Grenada, Guadeloupe, Jamaica, St. Lucia, and St. Vincent. Of critical importance to the success of emancipationist strategies was effective leadership in almost every insurgent colony.

Undoubtedly, the most famous of all insurgent warlords was Toussaint L'Ouverture, a general in the French army but commander-in-chief of semi-independent African and "mulatto" warlords, many of whom had captained their own guerrilla bands before Toussaint had officially joined the revolution. Other outstanding insurrectionist leaders of the period included Magloire Pélage of Guadeloupe, Louis Delgrès (affectionately called the "Toussaint L'Ouverture of Guadeloupe"), Julien Fédon of Grenada, Maroon chief Farcelle of Dominica, Garifuna chief Chatoyer, and his brother, Chief Duvalle, of St. Vincent. When Napoleon sent his grand army to reimpose slavery in the Caribbean in 1802, Delgrès was the principal leader of the resistance in Guadeloupe, fighting to the last man. Many insurgent leaders in the Lesser Antilles remain nameless, although the records of their exploits are indisputable. These "brigands," as the black liberation fighters were obstinately described by their French and English enemies, were the masters of guerrilla warfare, acknowledged by European generals as uniquely African.[69] Guerrilla leaders astutely incorporated African military science to reinforce their positions as divinely inspired leaders. Many cultist leaders doubled as warlords, dispensing metaphysical protection against enemy weapons, including bullets. By this psychology they inspired extraordinary acts of heroism. Martial spiritualism was deeply rooted in continental African military science, which allowed a significant role for female spiritualists.[70]

Opinions on the strategic importance of any colony differed between French and British military intelligence and among modern historians. To British military commanders Martinique was the "Island of the first Importance" and the first colony during the revolutionary war in which black soldiers outnumbered regular English troops.[71] To hold Martinique indefinitely, however, it was necessary to control St. Lucia.[72] To the French St. Lucia was the island of "first importance in the Windward Islands."[73] Obviously, the English were also well aware of the strategic importance of St. Lucia, for immediately after taking Martinique, a force of some six thousand under the command of the duke of Kent (father of Queen Victoria), occupied the island but surrendered it soon after, mainly because of the counteroffensives of black fighters led by Pélage.[74] For its loyalty to republicanism St. Lucia earned the sobriquet "Saint-Lucie la fidèle" and was officially recognized as the "bridgehead of patriotic propaganda" in the region.[75] French and British dispatches concur that St. Lucia was the command center of the brigands.

As early as 1790, Guadeloupe had taken the lead as the prime hotbed of revolt and revolutionary emancipationism.[76] By the end of 1794, in spite of draining every garrison to supply the island, the British were ousted a mere two months after their first invasion, leaving the colony as the "new power in Caribbean politics."[77] It soon became obvious to the British high command that neither their prestigious sea power nor a significant enlargement of ground troops would be appropriate for the preservation of sovereignty against the alliance of African insurgents and French republicans. In the wake of the evacuation of Guadeloupe, General John Vaughan, commander of British forces in the West Indies, warned his line minister, "A force under 6000 men is unequal to the protection of all the colonies in these Seas; whether to defend the old ones against foreign attack; or to secure the property and persons of the many conquered ones against internal Commotions."[78]

By 1795 French master strategist Victor Hugues was trying desperately to convince the revolutionary emancipators to unite under the French banner. The carrot dangled before the brigands was the national convention's emancipation decree. In his contribution to the debate on the withdrawal of British troops from Haiti, Wilberforce attested to this new development: "Victor Hugues with 1,100 men had, by landing in Guadeloupe and joining the Negroes, been able to expel the British troops, and to organise and direct the whole black force of the Leeward Islands."[79] Indeed, the easy movement of insurgents among the islands transformed the several revolts into a common war against slavery. Mobility was facilitated by monetary offers. In a proclamation addressed to the "Citizens of Martinique and other Antillean Colonies," Hugues promised, "All black citizens serving in the British army . . . who would return to the army of the Republic with arms and equipment will be readmitted according to his rank, if desired, and he will be given a grant of thirty livres."[80] Consistent with armed revolts was the widespread burning of plantations and real estate. Fire empowered the least physically endowed and allowed them a unique opportunity for active combat, including women. In April 1795 General Vaughan reported that almost every plantation on the windward side of St. Vincent had been destroyed by fire, which facilitated the Black Caribs' retention of full possession of that part of the island, while self-liberated Africans held most of the rest of the colony.[81] That year insurgent fires also ravaged Grenada and St. Lucia, among other colonies, blazing a fiery path to sovereignty, however tentative.[82] By the start of 1796 "Grenada was a black republic under arms."[83]

To preempt the complete destruction of colonial property, martial law was declared everywhere, hilltop forts were reinforced, and nightly patrols instituted along coastlines. In spite of those measures, Vaughan likened the situation in the Leewards to a tinderbox.[84] Trinidad was not spared the revolutionary ferment sweeping the region; as early as 1790, French patriots had begun to identify with the tricolor flag.[85] In 1795 a planned insurrection was aborted by the arrival of five Spanish warships.[86]

Williams had argued, "When Saint Domingue was lost to France, the slave trade became merely a humanitarian question."[87] A more appropriate assessment of the 1790s is that with French deployment of emancipation as a tool of imperial strategy, abolitionism became more absolutely a military question.[88] The dispatches between military commanders in colonial hotspots and the home government demonstrate clearly that military strategy in the Caribbean was shaping political decisions in England. One such issue was precisely the massive deployment of enslaved soldiers.

The British response to French emancipation as a tool of war quickly overtook the economic enticement of St. Domingue as the dominant factor in suspending the abolition agenda of 1792. Britain was forced to copy the French strategy of arming the black population, enslaved and free. Like the French, English generals on the ground had taken the initiative, against objections of the war minister. The first field of experiment was Martinique. With only four to five hundred white soldiers at his disposal, General Vaughan conscripted as many as five thousand Africans, "all armed with muskets and bayonets."[89] The elite Black Carolina Corps, a legacy of the War of American Independence, was placed under Lieutenant Colonel Soter; recruits included free and enslaved blacks, who became the backbone of defense of the island.[90]

The generals had a hard time convincing the home government or even the colonial legislatures that it was a good strategy; both authorities considered the experiment too dangerous.[91] Clearly, the expulsion from Guadeloupe was decisive, for immediately following it Vaughan appealed to Dundas for a rapid deployment of black soldiers, even if it meant commissioning ships to go to Africa to recruit them.[92] In several official dispatches military officers in various colonies reported the resistance of colonial governments to compel planters to enlist their workers even for their own defense.[93] Notwithstanding these early setbacks, Vaughan asserted his prerogative as field marshal and issued appeals to colonial legislatures to sacrifice part of their labor force rather than lose all to the enemy.[94] Antiguan planters had boasted of creating a model of subservience by Christianization; the capitulation of its assembly within one week of receiving Vaughan's memorandum symbolizes the desperation of the plantocracy everywhere. The assembly issued an order for the immediate requisitioning of at least seven hundred enslaved persons for fatigue duty and combat.[95] In the meantime Vaughan was sending home glowing reports of the success of the Black Carolina Corps and its role in maintaining British occupation of two key French colonies. In one report he acclaimed, "It is to the Black Corps under Lieut. Colonel Soter that we owe the possession of Martinico at this Moment."[96] It was also due to the lately raised Corps of Blacks under Captain Malcolm that they retained their footing in St. Lucia.[97] Undoubtedly, such reports helped to win Dundas over to a policy of total war by arming the enslaved population. Official resistance was finally broken during April 1795. The British high command instructed Vaughan to form a "Negro Cavalry" to function as a military police force, levy regular troops from among the enslaved plantation laborers, and purchase other enslaved persons to make up any shortfalls.[98] Imperial endorsement did not automatically end colonial contumacy, which only broke when the crisis of security hit each legislature. Facing invasion from colored insurgents from Guadeloupe and other external threats, the Council of War of the Leeward Islands directed the mobilization of three corps, each comprising four hundred enslaved men, armed proportionately with muskets, cutlasses, and pikes and outfitted in military uniforms. The council embarked on full-scale mobilization, mandating every estate to furnish various quantities of war materials, including mules, horses, and cattle.[99] Under heavy pressure from the Black Caribs, the legislature of St. Vincent consented to levy 4 percent of each plantation gang to serve in the Black Corps for the duration of the war.[100] Although reluctant to cooperate, every colony eventually capitulated and made its contribution to the expansion of the black military. Indeed, the plan could not have been implemented without the cooperation of the legislatures and plantocracy. Once off the ground, the scale of conscription proved fatal to the progress of the 1792 resolutions.

The rapid buildup of the West India Regiments, Black Corps, and fatigue auxiliaries put a severe strain on the most productive plantation sector. Fatigue duty was urgently required for the construction of fortifications.[101] Conscription of this kind could be substantial, consisting of as many as three thousand Africans at one time;[102] other levies were for active combat. Army commanders issued orders to levy only "prime new slaves" between the ages of sixteen and twenty-two years.[103] Altogether, some ninety thousand Africans were conscripted for military service; of this allotment some seventy-seven thousand, more than half of whom probably served as noncombatants, came from the plantations.[104]

Recruitment also strained the imperial coffers. Purchase prices for plantation-based conscripts varied from a low of £56 sterling to a high of £70, depending mainly on age and fitness to bear arms.[105] In addition, recruits had to be outfitted and paid, fighting men receiving equal pay to white regulars. In many instances hiring was the means of conscripting enslaved persons. One Black Corps stationed in Martinique cost over £2,000 local currency per month paid to the legal owners, in addition to a stipend of 4 pennies sterling per day per soldier.[106] By 1797 the military was "picking" as much as one third of a slaver's cargo, for which purchase prices ranged from £60 to £70 sterling.[107] At that time the annual estimated cost of maintaining a colonial regiment was a whopping £400,000-plus sterling.[108] The buildup continued even as Britain negotiated for peace with France in 1801, when government agreed to purchase plantation-based Africans to complete the Eleventh West India Regiment, at a cost of some £40,000 sterling.[109] Generals also continued the policy of purchasing directly from slave ships; by 1808 over thirteen thousand combatants had been so acquired since the recruitment had begun.[110]

To many politicians the war budget and war fatalities were inseparable because for them the real cost of war was balanced against the glory of victory. It is uncertain whether East Indian magnate Jenkinson (later Lord Hawkesbury) was deceived by Dundas or was party to the conspiracy to cover up the dismal performance of the British military in the Caribbean. In his contribution to the state of the nation debate in 1796, Jenkinson defended the government's extraordinary war expenditures; he boasted that with the strategic conquests since 1793, including St. Domingue and Martinique, there had never been "a more glorious and successful war."[111] Yet nothing had changed since Fox had observed, "There is little hope of our being in possession of any part of St. Domingo; and we are far from being without well-grounded apprehensions for the safety of Martinico and the other conquered islands."[112]

Parliamentary critics emphasized the fatalities and high cost of war without any significant gains to show. This picture was obviously a major consideration in the motion by St. John for full withdrawal from St. Domingue. The mover revealed, "In 1794 the bills were £296,000; in 1795, £772,000; in 1796, £2,211,000; and in January 1797, alone £700,000." Bills drawn for the St. Domingue campaign were £4 million compared to "the large army on the continent."[113] St. John lamented that after four years of war the British army "only possessed three places, which we had gained within the first ten days after landing"; this alone "was a strong argument in favour of withdrawing our troops from that island."[114] He then waded into the fundamental issue: "Though we possessed the best harbour [Mole St. Nicolas] in the place, yet we by no means secured our trade."[115] Although those figures were significant, the overall picture was much worse because the real cost of war must include the wars of emancipation across the Caribbean; advanced pay for foreign mercenaries; discharged mulattoes and free blacks; substantial bribes to ensure the safe evacuation of troops from St. Domingue; and financing the continuing claims by French planters, which were approved by various English generals during the occupation.[116] If Dundas had had his way, he would never have accounted for much of this money; as troops prepared for evacuation, he instructed Major General John Knox that he should offer unquantifiable bribes to war chiefs of Haiti to negotiate commercial advantages for Britain; these monies "could not appear in the public accounts of the Commissary General."[117] Such claims added considerably to the cost of the West Indian war. Indeed, Stephen estimated that the full cost of defending the colonies was roughly £150 million, including millions to colonies to repair war damages.[118]

In calling for the withdrawal of troops from St. Domingue, St John argued that the demand for increased sums for the Haitian mission must be reconciled with "the sad catalogue of the deaths of our unfortunate countrymen."[119] Returns tabled in Parliament accounted for 7,500 deaths to 30 September 1796.[120] Geggus estimates that by the evacuation in 1798 losses amounted to at least 12,500, from a total deployment of just over 20,000 troops.[121] These are conservative estimates. For the same period Blackburn's tally is 20,000.[122] Fatalities were even heavier in the Windward Islands, where Lieutenant General Ralph Abercromby's campaign alone cost the lives of some 14,000 troops, with an additional 7,000 incapacitated.[123] Total English fatalities throughout the Caribbean ranged between 50,000 and 70,000, inclusive of other white troops serving in the British army; to this must be added some 30,000 casualties in the Royal Navy.[124] In addition, the number of French casualties in St. Domingue would not have been lost on the minds of Britain's political class; of the 60,000 troops sent to the colony, "most never returned."[125] Modern historians who devalue the impact of revolutionary emancipation on statutory abolition also tend to inflate accidental poisoning and yellow fever over combat as the primary causes of fatalities among European troops.[126]

Military setbacks and war casualties were hidden from the British public in the conservative media. In evaluating the casualty report in the *London Gazette,* James Fox lamented, "I have compared it with other accounts on which I admit I have not the highest reliance, those detailed in the *London Gazette;* and I find a considerable difference between the loss of men as stated in the *Gazette* and that of the paper which now lies on our table"; he noted, "We must not only look to the army in Flanders, but we must look to our army wherever it is stationed, whether in the East or West Indies, or on the continent."[127] Leading abolitionist James Stephen was also skeptical of the official reporting of the war in the Lesser Antilles, having heard from "very good authority" that ministers chose not to publish a third aborted attempt on Morne Fortune in St. Lucia and also having received Abercromby's misgivings that a siege on the fortress would surely ruin the army.[128] Although Dundas grudgingly admitted that the massive deployment of black regiments was critical to the preservation of British sovereignty in the region, he persisted with his politics of deception. As British forces prepared to evacuate St. Domingue, he advised General Cuyler under "secret" cover to exercise caution in ongoing recruitment, lest the public become aware of the real "circumstances of the purchases made on the part of the government."[129]

The conspiracy of silence maintained by the respectable media and government over details of the war in the West Indies was broken by the *Morning Post,* a maverick newspaper, according to the standards of contemporary journalism. Sources of information reaching the *Morning Post* included private letters from colonists and copies of correspondence from military officers. Obviously proud of its image, the *Morning Post* frequently referred to itself as the "Paper of the People." Its editors were conscious of their role in disseminating information too sensitive for the official and conservative media. A crosscheck of the *Morning Post*'s coverage of the Anglo-Haitian war with official records supports its claim to authenticity. In the initial months of the war editorials tended to be supplementary to the official *Gazette,* as seen in its covering note to a series of letters from the West Indies: "It is with concern we inform the Public, that in addition to the letters in the Gazette, fresh accounts of a still more gloomy nature, from the West Indies, were brought yesterday by Colonel Francis Dundas, Sir Charles Grey, and Sir John Jervis."[130] With growing criticism against it from officialdom, however, the *Morning Post* waded into its detractors, as in an editorial from early January 1795: "Even public report does not answer the desperate situation of our *late conquests* in the Western world. The hirelings of the Ministry do not cease to launch out into daily invective against the PAPER OF THE PEOPLE, which has repeatedly warned the Community at large against the bold speculation adopted and entered into by a few hardy adventurers on the Exchange. Behold at length an awful lesson to the credulous of this country. St. Domingo is already, we hear, from respectable authority in possession of its former masters."[131] It is true that in early 1795 the alliance between Toussaint and the French was still holding, but the *Morning Post* did not yet consider the independent insurgency of the formerly enslaved warlords who were prepared to set their own conditions for emancipation rather than accept it as a boon of the French government.

Throughout 1795 and 1796 reports from several points across the Caribbean painted the same dismal picture of the British army as military underdogs to black and colored insurgents in alliance with French regulars and mercenaries. One writer from Antigua complained, "Our situation in the West Indies is truly alarming"; the writer projected that the deplorable situation in Guadeloupe was likely to worsen because with the military training from "a Representative of the National Convention," the island would have an effective army of twenty to thirty thousand men, "all Blacks." He concluded, "I wish my family were away from this, either in England or America."[152] This and similar letters belie Drescher's assertion that "British planters on the spot did not clamor to be saved from African 'seeds of destruction.'"[153] Paradoxically, by 1796 the British war effort in St. Domingue was heavily reliant on black fighters, while white troops were mostly confined to garrison duties or relegated to what General Maitland called "nominal British Soldiers," working on those estates whose owners had hired out their enslaved laborers for war duties.[154]

The rapid buildup of black regiments paved the way for the entry of Lieutenant General Abercromby in command of the largest English army ever deployed in the Caribbean and the largest force ever to be deployed from English shores.[135] The ground forces numbered over sixteen thousand white regulars, to be augmented with more than three thousand "Blacks" from Barbados (the first port of call), expressly for fatigue duty.[136] At the time of embarkation in February 1796 the colonies were facing their worst political crisis since their founding years in the seventeenth century. The future of Britain's West Indian empire rested on the outcome of Abercromby's expedition. The general was also fully aware of the burden of his mission.[137] Major General Dundas expressed this critical moment in their history thus: "It is my conviction unalterably fixed that either with a view to Peace or War, and whatever may be the success of his Majesty's Arms in other Quarters or in other directions a compleat [sic] success in the West Indies is essential to the Interests if I will add to the *contentment* of this country—no success in other Quarters will palliate a neglect there—failures in their Quarters may be palliated if to a certain degree remedied by success of consequent security in our distant possessions."[138] Abercromby was caught between the priorities of the king, his war minister, and the military's high command.[139] The king, a staunch defender of the slave trade, was well informed on the significance of St. Domingue to British interests in the West Indies. Concerning the primary objective of Abercromby's expedition, he stated, "I really expect it may secure the Possession of St. Domingo, without which Acquisition I cannot think our Possessions in the Islands secure, and that Peace can be best of short duration."[140] Dundas shared the king's concern over the spread of revolutionary emancipation but placed Guadeloupe and St. Lucia on equal footing with St. Domingue in the strategy of containment.[141] Thus, Dundas instructed the general: "The first great service expected from you, according to the plan of Campaign formed prior to your departure, was the reduction of Guadeloupe & St Lucia."[142] Dundas knew the importance of St. Domingue to Jamaica but also understood that the eastern Caribbean was the gateway to the Caribbean. Precisely for this reason, he enticed Abercromby to dedicate all his forces to preserving British power in the Lesser Antilles, "instead of proceeding after making a certain progress to Saint Domingo."[143] Ultimately, Dundas reconciled the king's wishes with his own priorities and persuaded Abercromby to act according to his assessment of the situation on the ground: "If in your judgement, these attacks [on St. Domingue] can be attempted with a reasonable prospect of their not interfering to prevent the execution of my Secret and separate Instructions, you will be at liberty to regulate your proceedings accordingly."[144]

Abercromby's campaign accorded with Dundas's priority in saving the Lesser Antilles. St. Lucia capitulated to a force of twelve thousand,[145] a statistic that spoke to the importance of the island to black militarism in the region. Correspondingly, the great loss of troops suffered by Abercromby spoke to the toughness of the resistance encountered; the cost in British lives was truly "alarming."[146] By 1797 the nuclei of revolutionary emancipation in colonies formerly under the British flag were either defeated or scattered and on the retreat, away from the main centers of habitation. Nonetheless, the colonies did not return to the political status ante 1793; many black fighters from St. Lucia evacuated the island to assist their comrades in St. Vincent and Grenada.[147] Thus, the evacuation from St. Domingue was effected against the backdrop of continuing insurgency and guerrilla activities in the Lesser Antilles.[148] The critical situation is perhaps best borne out in a peace treaty between the Dominica government and Maroon warlord Chief Farcelle and in the imperial government's offer of special conditions for the surrender of Maroon chiefs of Guadeloupe and St. Lucia.[149] Moreover, revolutionary emancipationism in the Lesser Antilles had saved the revolution in St. Domingue.[150] Contrary to Eric Williams, the decision to withdraw from St. Domingue was indeed the turning point for the transatlantic slave trade. The defeat of Britain laid the foundation for the entry of a new generation of abolitionists best able to articulate the new reality in the Caribbean. Even Wilberforce bought into the new dispensation, although he continued to hold brief for humanitarianism. Yet it is important to note that even Wilberforce recognized that revolutionary emancipation was providing a new synergy in abolition politics. During the debate on St. John's motion for withdrawal from St. Domingue, he contributed, perhaps unwittingly, to the awe of black militarism and the dread of revolutionary emancipationism, by noting en passant: "They [the enslaved in the French Antilles] were no longer like the inhabitants of India, too low for the storm that was passing over them: they stood erect, and influenced its directions."[151] Although the motion was defeated, the issue did not die; from that time no debate on amelioration or abolition ever failed to feature extensive discussion on St. Domingue and Haiti. Significantly, debate on the withdrawal of troops exposed for the first time the dire straits of the British military, its staggering casualty rate and high recurrent cost. These issues constituted the essence of debates on the abolition of the slave trade after 1796 and the British enterprise in Trinidad.

Abolitionism and the New Balance of Power

The debate on the slave trade was intimately connected to the conduct of revolutionary war and revolutionary emancipationism. The emancipation wars in several Caribbean colonies revalidated Edward Long's hypothesis that the holding of large populations of native Africans in slavery was a potential time bomb and recipe for economic ruin. More dramatically, the new reality was that enslaved Africans acting as a collective, regardless of birth, were prepared and able to seize the moment to effect their own emancipation.

It is therefore necessary to reposition the genesis of the politics of abolitionism within the context of Tacky's War.[152] During the abolition debate in April 1791, Pitt expounded the problem of insecurity created by imported labor from Africa. That debate took place prior to the outbreak of insurgency in St. Domingue but after a major revolt in Guadeloupe.[153] Following Ramsay and Long, Pitt argued that if the enslaved population were allowed to increase naturally, it could provide the answer to endemic insecurity. He used his skills in "political arithmetic" to inject the necessary empiricism into the debate.[154] Pitt bought into Long's assessment that Creole labor was already self-sustaining in all colonies since midcentury and cited an example of actual increase in births over deaths in Dominica. He estimated that the deaths of newly imported Africans accounted for almost all the "extraordinary deaths which would cease as soon as the importations ceased."[155]

In February 1792 an advocate of colonial reform commented prophetically, "The St Domingo business, tho' it certainly ought not, has & will affect the Sentiments of many in the house, as it has already done of many out of it."[156] St. Domingue was too important a market to British slave merchants not to become a hot topic of conversation among all vested interests. Indeed, in his contribution to the abolition motion two months later, Pitt examined the implications of the slave trade for colonial security: "It is no small satisfaction to me . . . that among the many arguments for prohibiting the slave trade which crowd upon my mind, the internal security of our West India possessions against internal commotions, as well as foreign enemies, is amongst the most prominent."[157] At that time the French were yet to launch their revolutionary wars or to contemplate emancipation. Pitt berated the West Indians for anticipating the extension of the St. Domingue rebellion to British colonies because of his government's support for amelioration rather than their own labor policy and treatment of their enslaved laborers. Unlike Long, he explicitly condemned ill treatment as a major cause of mortality. Indeed, after the heartrending revelations of the parliamentary Select Committee on the Slave Trade, only the most obstinate apologists could have drawn any other conclusion. Pitt also questioned the political sanity of his West Indian detractors in the House of Commons: "Why should you persist in introducing those latent principles of conflagration, which, if they should but once burst forth, may annihilate in a single day the industry of a hundred years? Why would you subject yourselves, with open eyes, to the imminent risk of a calamity, which may throw you back a whole century in your profits, in your cultivation, in your progress to the emancipation of your slaves?"[158] Pitt adopted the view current among abolitionists that the need for brute force in the management of enslaved laborers militated against experiments in amelioration: "If any argument can in the slightest degree justify the severity that is now so generally practised in the treatment of the slaves, it must be the introduction of these Africans. It is the introduction of these Africans that renders all idea of emancipation for the present so chimerical; and the very notion of it so dreadful. It is the introduction of these Africans that keeps down the condition of all plantation slaves. Whatever system of treatment is deemed necessary by the planters to be adopted towards these new Africans extends itself to the other slaves also."[159] Drescher acknowledges with judicial circumspection that the success of black fighters in the Anglo-Haitian war "destroyed forever the myth of impregnability" of the West Indian planter class.[160] From 1797 abolition of the transatlantic slave trade and amelioration of slavery became inextricably linked to the defeat of Britain in Haiti. Haiti's emergence as the new independent power in the Caribbean and the prospects of recreating a new Haiti elsewhere made all colonies with large tracts of arable Crown lands a prime subject of colonial policy.

Abercromby had targeted Trinidad and Puerto Rico to compensate for the St. Domingue fiasco.[161] Trinidad was taken in February 1797 without a fight, but the Puerto Rico campaign ended in another humiliating defeat for Britain, the plan of invasion based on wrong intelligence.[162] In the months immediately following the capture of Trinidad, George Rose informed General Cornelius Cuyler, commander in charge of land forces in the Leeward and Windward Islands: "Mr. Pitt has an *insuperable Objection* to any Grants or Sales of Lands in the West India Islands, which can by possibility lead to a cultivation of them, as that could not happen without occasioning an importation of Negroes for the purpose."[163] The following year Pitt warned the Commons that the continued importation of new Africans would endanger the "internal tranquility" of the colonies and that it was incumbent on the government to "press the necessity of our immediate and total abolition for the salvation of these very islands."[164] This warning against alienation of Crown lands extended to newly conquered St. Lucia as well as the former "Black Carib" possessions in Dominica and St. Vincent. To the British these Black Caribs were indeed "Negroes," thus another constituency of the black enemy in the Caribbean.[165] Although the Crown lands issue applied equally to Trinidad, at the time of George Canning's motion in 1802, the island was the only "ceded colony" in British hands.[166]

The year 1797 was also propitious for defenders of the slave trade. Two months after the capture of Trinidad, the West Indians, led by absentee Jamaican planter Charles Ellis, scored a major parliamentary victory over the abolitionist party.[167] The motion overturned the abolition-amelioration equation: whereas abolitionists pursued abolition as a precursor to amelioration, the West Indians made amelioration the keynote formula for effecting the gradual abolition of the slave trade. Within months the government was instructing colonial governors to draft reformed slave codes in accordance with the spirit of the motion. Paradoxically, Ellis bought wholesale into the economics of security inherent in amelioration and creolization as advanced by Long, Ramsay, Equiano, Clarkson, Pitt, and other reform-conscious ideologues. He warned:

> In addition to this immediate and self-evident interest, a new and collateral motive, but not a less powerful one, has arisen from the events which have lately taken place in that part of the world. St. Domingo is nearly become a negro colony, and the revolution lately operated in that island has made

her a most dangerous neighbour . . . In such circumstances, and with such interests, is it in nature that the African trade should be considered by us in any other light than that of a necessary evil? Can stronger motives be required, than are in our case combined, to insure an honest zeal in the execution of a plan, for the purpose of obviating the necessity of that trade?[168]

The motion was passed by an overwhelming majority.[169] The enthusiasm for the plan had grave consequences for the abolition movement. In responding to the motion, Wilberforce confessed, "As the plea for justice and humanity had been so often urged upon this subject, and urged in vain, he was afraid it was hopeless."[170] British hardships in St. Domingue did not only impact the West Indians but also took a toll on Wilberforce. The veteran campaigner unequivocally articulated the language of revolutionary emancipation, but by so doing, he was inadvertently positioning himself to be checkmated by the West Indians: "By persisting in the system of importation, the period might soon arrive when rivers of blood would flow. He would therefore say to those who only looked to their property in the West Indies. Abolish the importation of slaves at this moment, as the first step towards the salvation of those islands. Natural causes would produce natural effects; and there was no reason for this or any other country hoping that Providence would protect it from the consequences of injustice."[171] In order to dislodge the West Indians, a new crop of orators was needed to raise the specter of Haiti from Ellis's "collateral motive" to center stage of imperial interest.

The heroism of black combatants in the Caribbean had become legend by 1802; the high point was reached with Toussaint's invasion of Spanish Santo Domingo and the abolition of slavery there.[172] The imperial potential of a united Hispaniola was a frightening prospect. The performance of black soldiers, whether deployed to overthrow the slave system or preserve it as soldiers of colonial powers, helped to swing the debate on the slave trade in favor of abolitionists. The pivotal moment was the commencement of debate on the future settlement of Trinidad.

James Stephen and Henry Brougham were convinced that the numerical superiority of black fighters in St. Domingue was the key to their success against the forces of slavery, but they ascribed an even greater importance to the proliferation of native Africans, the consequence of the rapid development of the colony during the late eighteenth century. Although Stephen had the courage to recognize Haitian emancipation as a triumph for humanity, nonetheless he apprehended revolutionary Haiti as "the *new enemy* to be encountered" in imperial rivalry in the Caribbean, but particularly as agent for the "dreaded progress of emancipation."[173] In a well-timed polemic titled *Crisis of the Sugar Colonies* Stephen presented the British prime minister a portrait of an enslaved people whose soldiering was superior to that of the Europeans. To him the rhetoric of humanitarianism had sentimental value, but only pragmatism could resolve the crisis of security. Thus, he earnestly reminded Prime Minister Addington, "My arguments have been addressed, not to the *conscience* of a British Statesman, but to his *prudence* alone; and, but that it would argue great moral insensibility in the writer, as well as do violence to right feelings, it would perhaps be wise to rest my case here; without attempting to strengthen it by what with some minds is a most dangerous support, an appeal to higher principles, than those of political expediency."[174]

The military prowess of enslaved Africans was part of the cultural baggage brought from Africa, where many boys, adult males, and females had significant military experience before capture and sale into slavery. Knowingly or not, during the 1780s captains of slavers had shipped to St. Domingue tens of thousands of Africans who had fought in ongoing wars in Dahomey, the Kongo, and other coastal and hinterland states.[175] Judging from the bustling trade in guns since the sixteenth century, many would already have been familiar with the use of guns and gunpowder before their capture. For the second half of the eighteenth century England alone exported between 333,000 and 444,000 guns annually to Africa.[176] Africans' familiarity with gun technology was an important factor in the success of insurgent forces since Tacky's War; it might also help to explain the easy adjustment and battlefield successes of conscripted Africans in European infantries. Furthermore, the choice of dying on the battlefield or dying on the plantation was no choice at all—thus their proverbial courage, which Stephen ranked as second to the natural advantages of climate and knowledge of the local terrain.[177] The results of these distinctions are reflected in the first three years of war in St. Domingue, the British rate of attrition through diseases being just over 40 percent while that of their black troops was only 3 percent.[178] The Africans' military strategies were no less decisive, however, particularly the resort to guerrilla warfare long associated with Caribbean Maroons, which certainly exacerbated the effects of diseases on European troops.[179]

Brougham was more brutally frank in his assessment of the new balance of power in the West Indies as he expounded the threat from black militarism.

In agreeing with Stephen, Brougham asserted, "With such a power as the new black republic no European colony can form a league against any other European colony, or any negro state."[180] He argued, "The peculiar circumstances of the West Indian islands, and the internal policy of modern Europe, would render independence of any one of *those* colonies peculiarly dangerous to the rest, and would render the colonial regimen a greater source of weakness to them than to any other establishments of the same kind."[181] He further contended that "the interests of all the whites in the West Indies are one and the same."[182] For this reason he gave his wholehearted support to the French campaign to restore slavery in Haiti while calling on the British government to ally with France in order to defeat the "natural enemy."[183] To him French hegemony in the Caribbean was less to be feared than black emancipation and independence. He concluded, "The greatest of dangers to the West Indian community lies in the success of the negroes, and that the reestablishment of the old system in the French islands can alone insure the permanent superiority of the Europeans, either there or in other colonies."[184] The government did not need prompting. Lord Grenville's speech to the House of Lords on the Definition Treaty of Peace (Treaty of Amiens) combined ambivalence with doublespeak on the question of covertly facilitating or conspiring with Napoleon to depose Toussaint and reimpose slavery in Haiti. In one breath Grenville feigned neutrality: "In direct opposition to our entreaties and threats, France had sent an armament to the West Indies."[185] Yet with a twist of disingenuousness, he was reluctant to "discuss the question whether it would or would not be better for this country if St. Domingo was under the dominion of France."[186] He insisted that the only reason his government had deployed a sizable fleet was simply to "watch" the French ships but confessed, "In the West Indies we had restored to France Martinique and Tobago, and had facilitated the means of recovering St. Domingo."[187] With the failure of the French campaign in Haiti, history threatened to repeat itself in the colony of Trinidad under the sway of British capitalism. This specter reset the course of abolition toward its final resolution in 1807.

6

FROM REVOLUTION TO ABOLITION

The Trinidad Question

Britain's capture of Trinidad in 1797, its defeat in St. Domingue, and the success of West Indian gradualism were pivotal events in the countdown to abolition. Metropolitan civil society involvement was unquestionably intrinsic to the politics of abolitionism, but the larger undercurrent of change in parliamentary abolitionism flowed from events and developments in the colonies. Implementation of the final phase of the 1792 resolutions earmarked for 1796 was overtaken by the exigency of black military conscription. One year after the proposed Abolition Day, Parliament's endorsement of amelioration struck a crippling blow to the abolitionist party, effectively shifting the captaincy of colonial reconstruction to the West India Interest.[1] Led by Charles Ellis, the West Indians sold amelioration to Parliament as the panacea for arresting demographic attrition of the enslaved; thus, they proposed an unmapped gradualism as the best formula for abolition. William Wilberforce was well aware that Parliament's support of the motion "would do away its own solemn pledge" of 1792.[2] Equally important, the success of Ellis's motion ensured that the original deadline for total abolition in 1800 as well as Denmark's promise to abolish the trade in 1803 would not provide new political fuel for immediate abolition.[3]

The loss of support for immediatism was underscored by the contentious Trinidad Question. Imperial strategy demanded capture of the island long recognized as a serious threat to Britain's southern colonies.[4] In the early 1790s the island was linked to the presence of immigrants (white and free colored republicans and enslaved people) from St. Domingue; the "dangerous principles of equality" they imported warranted the destruction of the island if it could not be conquered.[5] Notwithstanding these allegations, Abercromby's pretext for attacking Trinidad was that it had dispatched reinforcements to assist the Fédon insurrectionists in Grenada.[6]

Capitalists welcomed the capture of Trinidad as adequate compensation for the loss of St. Domingue. Yet within a few years the former Spanish possession would become a new nightmare for abolitionists. The island's economic potential pivoted the colony to center stage on two of the most pressing questions of the day: the abolition of the transatlantic slave trade and the future of colonialism. The debate on the island's future spawned new life within the abolition movement; abolitionists skillfully refashioned a common war trophy into the principal nursery for experiments in a new colonial paradigm central to which was abolition of the slave trade.[7]

Conquest was followed immediately by intense propaganda to sell the island to British investors as the new jewel in the English Crown. In one of his early reports governor Lieutenant Colonel Thomas Picton commented, "The Island itself after Cuba and Hispaniola is incontestably the finest in all the West Indies whether the general fertility of the soil or the extent of cultivable lands be considered."[8] Trinidad was a late starter in plantation economy, having its first sugar mill only in 1787. Ten years later a plantation revolution was in full swing, with 159 sugar estates in addition to 130 estates under coffee, 60 under cocoa, and 103 under cotton.[9] By 1802 the number of sugar estates had increased to almost 200, of which Picton himself owned several.[10]

The island's exaggerated economic prospects alarmed abolitionists. A contemporary labor estimate of at least one million deepened the specter of another St. Domingue in the making.[11] As early as 1800, three fourths of Britain's slave trade was already going to the newly conquered colonies of Demerara, Suriname, and Trinidad.[12] Trinidad's share amounted to 5,861 imported between 1798 and 1801; of this number 4,409 came directly from Africa.[13] The formal cession of the island triggered a sharp rise in labor imports into the colony, motivated by Addington's support of land grants to new colonists. In the two-year period from 5 January 1802 to 5 January 1804, the island received 10,270 African captives.[14] Against this backdrop the alarm raised by abolitionists prioritized the Trinidad Question as a crisis of first importance to the future of the British West Indies.

The cession of Trinidad was the clarion call for the dramatic entry of Henry Brougham, George Canning, and James Stephen to the center stage of abolitionism. For several months Canning overshadowed Wilberforce as chief parliamentary spokesman on abolition; outside Parliament the new principals of abolition were Stephen and Brougham. In the aftermath of Britain's defeat in Haiti, the appeal to security and anti-emancipationism was definitely more pragmatic than to humanity and justice.

Canning skillfully swung the debate from the "main question" of general abolition to the "subordinate question" of restriction of the slave trade while changing the focus from humanity and justice to security and anti-emancipationism.[15] In response to Canning's first parliamentary resolution in March 1802, the government promised to provide specific information on Trinidad, including a record of all land deals since the conquest.[16] The following month Canning introduced a new motion on the settlement of the island, arguably the most significant speech in the history of the abolition movement.

As undersecretary of state for foreign affairs, Canning functioned at the command center of the Anglo-French war.[17] This scenario places a major part of the predicament of Britain's failed military campaign, and failed colony in Haiti, almost equally on the shoulders of Canning and Dundas. More than most abolitionists and policy makers, Canning had firsthand knowledge of the effectiveness of African guerrilla warfare. On the eve of his historic second motion to the House of Commons, he wrote to William Windham:

There remains only to speak of Trinidad. My Motion comes on next Thursday.—I do not ask you to attend (even supposing your uncomfortable feelings & embarrassments to have subsided a little) because I would much rather you should be absent than oppose me . . . The ground, which I chiefly rest upon is not the abolitionist, anti-negro baiting, ground, of which I know you are afraid:—but simply this.—That in the present state of the Colonies we ought to look for *strength,* rather than for rapid augmentation of wealth—that we have our choice whether to make Trinidad a new sugar-growing, negro-driving Colony, productive indeed, but weak, & exposed, & inviting attack in preparation—or to create there a place of military strength, a fortress for the defence of our other Colonies; & to lay the foundation of a new system of colonization for future military purposes[;] I think I can prove this. I may be mistaken: but if I go *near* to prove it, you will not be against our making the trial, however, that I state for your information only. Do not betray me to the Enemy. I had rather they should come prepared only to hunt Negroes.—In addition to this, I think I can show a necessary waste of human (i.e. Negro) life in the sudden sugar-settlement of Trinidad, at which the most cold blooded panygerist [*sic*] of Exports Imports ought to hesitate. But this is merely *subsidiary.* The argument upon which I should rely *with you,* is the other. And whether I convince you or not, I can assure you, & do most solemnly, that I am in my conscience convince [*sic*] myself of the truth of which I contend for. This sometimes is the best chance of convincing others.[18]

As secretary at war for the period 1794 to 1801, Windham was a close associate of Dundas and Canning. Upon appointment to office, Windham abandoned support for abolition, having been assigned the major responsibility for recruiting enslaved soldiers.[19] Canning's letter was obviously intended to neutralize one of his main opponents but one who clearly understood the military options in the Caribbean.

Canning's motion was premised on "the great importance of preventing the dangers and mischiefs which must arise from the excessive increase of the importation of negroes from Africa . . . without restriction into the island of Trinidad."[20] To achieve this goal, the Crown must not authorize grants or sales of new lands; future grants must exclude employment of native Africans, until Parliament regulate the importation of labor from Africa into the island.[21] The motion concluded on a note reflecting the new security focus of abolitionists: that the plan adopted for the development of Trinidad must be "the least likely to interfere with the wish expressed by this House for the gradual diminution, and ultimate termination, of the African slave trade, and the most conducive to the stability and security of the interests of the colonies, and of the West Indian commerce of this kingdom."[22] Canning harbored no pretensions to humanitarianism, though he was truly "a rising . . . star in the abolition firmament."[23] Nevertheless, he was keenly aware of the lure of political philanthropy and especially the desire for an abolition policy for Trinidad to preempt the unimaginable suffering of new Africans, about a million of whom might be required to bring the island to optimum cultivation of export staples.[24] Yet he downplayed the humanitarian principle, emphasizing that his motion was less concerned with the horrors of slavery than "by every consideration of the security of the colonies, and of the true policy of this country, under the present circumstances of the world."[25] Canning's focus on Trinidad and limited abolition was a new departure from the "general principle."[26] This compromise clearly stemmed from Canning's acute awareness that the slave trade was still a viable source of recruitment for the

West India Regiments; therefore, it made sense to opt for regulation rather than total prohibition.

Canning was acutely aware that the early domino effect of the Haitian Revolution could happen again. In countering the viability of Haiti as a regional force for emancipation, some scholars reference the diplomacy of Britain and the United States in securing Haiti's neutrality and collaboration in preempting French invasion of Jamaica. A similar logic could be applied to the disavowal of violence and pledge of loyalty by enslaved converts to missionary Christianity, yet all the principals in the revolts in Barbados in 1816, Demerara in 1823, and Jamaica in 1831 were Christians. Moreover, Haiti had provided seminal assistance to Creole nationalists to overthrow Spanish rule in Venezuela and later occupied the whole of Spanish Santo Domingo.[27] Indeed, there was even greater concern over the security of Jamaica than there had been in the early 1790s. Thus, the duke of Portland wrote to Governor Nugent that any black state in the Caribbean would be more dangerous to Jamaica than the restoration of French power.[28] Portland had become home secretary in time to deal with the escalation of emancipation wars in the eastern Caribbean and the balancing of security issues at home with those of the colonies. This fear was articulated even more stridently and publicly by Canning, Stephen, and Brougham. Thus, the relevance of Haiti to abolitionism was not its diplomatic neutrality but, rather, the probability of subversion either by direct expansionism or simply by being a model and inspiration to all enslaved peoples in the hemisphere.

The vulnerability of all colonies placed an obligation on Britain's imperial directorate to design a new colonial architecture. Although claiming disingenuously that the danger of revolutionary emancipation was "too delicate to be agitated," Canning's cleverly crafted rhetorical questions presented a daunting specter of Haiti as a military power, which he combined with the prospects of Trinidad as a new Haiti, if the new colony were allowed to develop into a full-fledged sugar colony. "Was it possible to look at the present state of the colonial world without feeling considerable awe and apprehension?" he asked.

> The struggle now subsisting in St. Domingo, whichever way it might terminate, could not be but productive of great evil and danger to our colonies; in the one event a great moral danger, if the negroes should not be thor-

oughly subdued; in the other case, of complete success to the French arms, a great military danger. In either of these events, what was the use to which it would be most desirable to have turned our new acquisition? Would the moral danger be best guarded against by having established a new negro colony, by importation from Africa? Would the military safety of Trinidad be best ascertained by a population from which, in the time of attack, you would have as much dread as from the enemy; a population which, while you defended it with one hand, you must keep down with the other?[29]

Central to Canning's argument was his conviction that the future of Britain in the West Indies would depend on internal security, not sugar.[30] By his masterful oration Canning united the "subordinate question" of restriction to the "main question" of general abolition. He argued that the 1792 resolution for gradual abolition was still the official position of Parliament and ought to be the principle guiding policy on the settlement of new colonies.[31] As such, unregulated distribution of lands in Trinidad would be nothing less than a repudiation of 1792.

Since Ramsay's earliest advocacy, abolitionists' vision of a new colonial system had centered on the character of the laboring population and a reform of colonial governance. Accordingly, Canning argued that the key to transforming internal weakness to internal strength was by propagating a "natural population" in place of an "artificial one"; to name this process he coined the term *creole colonization*.[32] In the case of Trinidad the natural population might be veterans discharged from the West India Regiment as well as the metropolitan army and free Creoles from the old colonies. He recommended that land grants be made to them all in order to induce permanent residence. The new settlers must aim for self-reliance by raising cattle, vegetables, and nontraditional staples.[33] He also considered "peons" from Venezuela good candidates for a hardy militia.[34] Another source was Trinidad's "native Indians"; Canning was sanguine about their potential for demographic increase, particularly because of a favorable balance of sexes.

Although Prime Minister Addington pledged his support for the motion, he was not particularly convinced by Canning's claim that the slave trade to the older British colonies would diminish by regulating the Trinidad slave market alone. But he thought it "a wise policy to increase, as much as possible, the White and Creole population."[35] He also informed the Commons that his government had already initiated measures to control the grants or sales of Crown lands; a commission had also been appointed to carry out a survey of the island.[36] Nonetheless, the success of Canning's motion recaptured the ground that abolitionists had lost in 1797. Within months the general principles of the motion were adopted as official policy, thus bringing the question of general abolition once again into focus.

Stephen's published analysis of Haiti and his assessment of Trinidad as ideal for a new experiment in colonization perfectly complemented Canning's parliamentary motion. Interestingly, both spokesmen had addressed the British public within weeks of each other. Curiously mirroring Canning, Stephen weighed the prospects of Trinidad under conventional colonization against a new colonial paradigm. In the first instance the development of a new plantation colony in the "neighborhood" of St. Domingue was a time bomb, "less irrational, than it would be to build a town near the crater of Vesuvius."[37] On the other hand, he interpreted the cession of the island as an "inestimable treasury" that transcended its considerable commercial and strategic importance to Britain; its annexation was fated to lay the foundation for a new system of colonialism: "You have in this great acquisition, the means of most favourably trying an experiment of unspeakable importance to mankind; an experiment never tried before; and of which the success might in future produce such extensive good, as to indemnify humanity for all the evils of the late dreadful war: Africa might here after be delivered by it from the devastation of the Slave Trade; and a new system founded in the West Indies, gradually, but surely corrective, of all of the evils of the old."[38] Unlike Canning, Stephen insisted that it was the duty of Parliament to abolish the slave trade "totally and immediately."[39] Like Canning, he expressed his commitment to a free labor preference in opening up Trinidad. Yet Stephen's experimental model was substantially different, based exclusively on "Free Negroes," initially sourced from the existing slave trade.[40] Stephen's formula endorsed the moratorium on alienating Trinidad's Crown lands while prohibiting the importation of chattel labor.[41] Stephen defined the status of Africans in the proposed system as "the known relation of indented servant . . . whose labour would be remunerated by wages fixed by law" and whose overall situation "must be clearly and anxiously fixed by positive law and guarded by the most vigorous sanctions."[42] The most critical reform must be the absolute prohibition of the whip, denounced as "utterly inconsistent with the happy formation of a new system."[43] Charged with the responsibility of overseeing this amelioration model would be a special magistracy composed of men "of great respectability, independent of the community in which they live, and prohibited from holding landed property in the Island."[44] They must be invested with extraordinary judicial powers and "should be obliged to record the evidence on which they proceed, in order to secure and facilitate the due investigation of their judgements, upon appeals to a higher tribunal in this country."[45]

Brougham's *Colonial Policy* offered a third major analysis of the Haitian Question and imperatives for colonial reform. The work was written with the hindsight of Canning's and Stephen's proposals; not surprisingly, both plans fell under Brougham's critical lenses. Brougham shared the view that the ultimate interest in colonies was "the increase of wealth, and the security both of the colonial government and the power of the mother country from all the efforts of external and internal violence."[46] It would seem that Brougham also borrowed extensively from Wilberforce, particularly ideas concerning colonial slavery and the unmitigated racist stereotype of lazy, savage Africans.[47] Accordingly, Brougham unequivocally rejected both Canning's and Stephen's abolition models as unfeasible. In the first instance Brougham was suspicious of a settlement plan based on the importation of enslaved laborers from the old colonies; such a plan, by emptying those colonies of seasoned and Creole laborers, would ultimately increase the dangers they might face from new imports from Africa brought over to fill the void.[48] In the second instance the importation of free Africans was an even worse proposition; only two sources could be practically considered. The first was the West Indian colonies, which he ruled out because "the free negroes in the West Indies are, with very few exceptions . . . equally averse to all sorts of labour which do not contribute to the supply of their immediate and most urgent wants."[49] The second option was Africa, but Brougham argued that native Africans as free laborers must be fraught with immense capital risks to investors and injustice to such Africans; there was also a higher risk of emancipation wars. He satirized, "I must be allowed to suspect, that, in order to people Trinidad and the other unsettled colonies with negroes who will work for hire, they must discover a new race of Africans industrious in their country, or invent some method of operating instantaneously upon the tribes already known."[50]

Brougham argued that because a wage economy was alien to West Africa, only compulsion could produce the desired result. This imperative would necessarily mean equipping new proprietors with "the power of inflicting moderate chastisement," an authority that would inevitably perpetuate an unjust system accentuated by racial prejudice. For the proposed "free negro system" to be free of conventional prejudices, it would necessitate the creation of a new generation of white proprietors, but moderation of abuses would be impossible to effect because of the compulsion for cultural and racial bias. Brougham conceded that the tyranny of the ruling class was inimical to the prosperity of the colonies; he acknowledged, however, that "the most fatal of all the consequences . . . are those that immediately affect the[ir] security."[51] He also condemned Stephen's analogy with white colonial indentureship as flawed because bonded whites "were always men accustomed at home to labour for hire; driven from their country by want of employment, or the prospects of greater wealth, and eager to find work in the new world. They were, therefore, exactly in the situation from which the greatest exertions of industry might be expected, whether for profit or for hire."[52] Significantly, Brougham saw nothing wrong with the colonial structure; indeed, as he saw it, "the slave system has now become so radically incorporated with the colonial system, as to form an essential part of it."[53] Accordingly, he rejected the return to a policy of tropical colonization based predominantly on white settlers, insisting, "As long as the colonies are cultivated, the population must consist of a mixed and variegated tribe."[54] For him the challenge facing imperial legislators was the improvement of social relations between enslavers and enslaved. Like Canning, Brougham coined a new expression, "new-modeling," to define his colonial construct. He strongly advised, "The only plan which can be admitted into our thoughts must proceed upon the principle of new-modeling the present structure of society."[55] Accordingly, he suggested that task work was the best plan to conduce to the efficient use of enslaved labor and should be compulsory; to him tasking was the panacea to the evils of the plantation system. Indeed, alleviating the drudgery of enslaved laborers' daily routine might certainly satisfy abolitionists' conscience. Tasking already had a history in some colonies and was definitely more productive than the gang model. Although most planters still frowned upon tasking because of the free time it afforded enslaved persons, support for the approach came from leading West Indians, including Charles Ellis, who anticipated that tasking would lead very rapidly to hired labor.[56]

Brougham was satisfied with slavery as a labor system but viewed the slave trade as anathema to the future of colonialism. Like Canning and Stephen, he believed that the focus on producing wealth made economic sense only if the political climate was stable and secure. He argued, "The security system is of so much more consequence to both the mother country and the body of the colonies, in comparison with the increase of wealth (however disproportionate those considerations may be in the estimation of individuals), that the commercial benefits arising from the rapid importation of new slaves, can in no sense of the word compensate for the grand evils which flow directly from the same source. And we may confidently state this as one of the chief defects in the structure of West Indian society."[57] Thus, because of Brougham's apprehension of revolutionary emancipation, he stood firmly for immediate abolition of the slave trade. Notwithstanding fundamental differences, many aspects of the three architectural models for a new colonialism were incorporated into government's plans for cushioning abolition, in policing abolition legislation, and in framing the project in imperial amelioration from 1823.

Experimenting with Abolition

It is more than coincidence that abolition of the British branch of the slave trade was successfully legislated in the wake of Haiti's second defeat of France. The British government had given logistic and diplomatic support to Napoleon for his invasion of Haiti.[58] The Haitian victory and declaration of independence in 1804 were quickly followed by Britain's abolition order-in-council in August 1805 and the dispatching of a top-secret mission to China to recruit new settlers. The preamble to both the abolition decree and the principal memorandum for Chinese immigration spoke unambiguously to the issues of colonial security.[59] The Chinese plan was first proposed in 1802 by a senior military officer in response to the cession of the island. The rebellions in St. Domingue and the eastern Caribbean did not lessen faith in the politics of natural increase and creolization; if anything, these objectives became more urgent. Furthermore, abolition and amelioration became more critical to the safety of the colonies. On this score the rapid multiplication of missionary societies in the 1790s and their focus on the West Indies were pragmatic as well as symbolic.[60]

Haiti's decisive defeat of France and the sequel in political independence underscored the warnings of Canning, Stephen, Brougham, and other leading abolitionists that immediate measures be adopted to preempt the advance of revolutionary emancipation. In that regard the government took the path of least resistance by resorting to the legislative prerogative of the Crown. The 1805 order-in-council immediately restricted the importation of new captives from Africa to Trinidad and the five "conquered colonies" (Berbice, Demerara, St. Lucia, Suriname, and Tobago) up to the end of 1806, after which that branch of the transatlantic trade was earmarked for total abolition.[61] The conquered colonies were post-Amiens reconquests. The official motive for prohibition was the preemption of capital investments in colonies that were more than likely to be surrendered to imperial rivals on a return to peace. The accompanying circular dispatch began and ended with an appeal to the respective governors to be mindful of the general objective of the decree: preempting the French and Dutch the benefit of large-scale British capital until territorial claims were permanently settled.[62] There was, first, an absolute prohibition on the importation of Africans "for the purpose of cultivating Lands not hitherto in Cultivation" and, second, a prescription for harsh penalties for willful contravention of provisions of the order.[63]

The official pretext for the order-in-council was not necessarily its primary purpose. Many historians uncritically repeat the official view. Yet British capital followed speculative markets regardless of sovereignty.[64] A major reason advanced for the invasion of French colonies in 1793–94 was that military occupation was the only way to recover the huge debts they owed British merchants.[65] Despite Lord Hawkesbury's warnings in 1806, successive British governments continued to allow their manufacturers, merchants, brokers, and other capitalists "to furnish the very pabulum of the slave trade," mainly to Brazil, one of Britain's principal rivals in the international sugar market.[66] Another view not explored by historians is the real possibility that capital investments could also have been lost to "people of color." "Mulatto" general Magloire Pélage warned about such a possibility in Martinique.[67] The fear of color may also be deduced from the plan of Chinese immigration to Trinidad. Further, various sources indicate that, contrary to official pledges, Crown lands were being distributed to foreign planters and military officers before and after the cession of Trinidad. Similarly, as Drescher argues, "In 1797, at the very moment the British government held up land sales in Trinidad, slaving capital was allowed to flow in the millions of pounds to Demerara."[68] Winston McGowan reiterates the same point.[69] On the eve of Wilberforce's abolition motion in 1799—and in the wake of the military withdrawal from St. Domingue—Pitt sought Liverpool's support for restriction of the slave trade by including the potential loss of new capital to conquered colonies, but more significantly, he confessed, "What I wish to propose rests almost wholly on Political Grounds, and has in view the future security of our West

India Possessions."[70] Thus, historians need to question whether the greater apprehension was the loss of capital to rival colonial powers or the loss of capital to black emancipators. In 1806 a parliamentary act upheld 1 January 1807 as Abolition Day for Trinidad and the conquered colonies. If the debate on that bill did not fully explore the issue of colonial security, it was largely because the act was merely intended "to give effect to the Order in Council."

Because prohibition of the slave trade struck at the base of the colonial economy, the first abolition legislation included concessions to avoid financial and economic ruin without fundamentally compromising the legislative objectives. The principal concession was a licensing system allowing proprietors or managers of existing plantations to import new captives equal to the number of productive laborers lost through attrition over a given period. In order to guard against corruption, total imports were fixed at a "liberal maximum" of 3 percent of the slave population, a figure ultimately derived from the political arithmetic of creolization from Edward Long to William Pitt. By 1807 the acknowledged demographics ranged from 3.5 percent excess of deaths over births at the peak of development of the plantation regime in Jamaica to a negligible 1/24 percent by 1800.[71] The decree placed a total ban on imports from Africa from 1 January 1807; planters could import from the old colonies but only to maintain existing numbers.[72] In order to guard against transfers from existing estates to new cultivation within a conquered colony, penalties included the rescinding of import licenses.[73] For local policing the law provided for the creation of an office of Registry of Slaves to be managed by a specially appointed officer. The new system required that enslaved persons be classed according to sex, maturity (child or adult), and origin (African or Creole);[74] it also obliged planters to submit a list of births and deaths as well as sales and purchases to the Registrar of Slaves every six months. To guard against any demand for new laborers occasioned by ill treatment or overwork, a "petition" for purchase had to be accompanied by certification from a plantation doctor.[75] Ships illegally importing Africans risked forfeiture of the healthiest and strongest male captives, equal to the excess of the licensed number for any particular ship, while captains of unlicensed ships risked forfeiture of all captives on board.[76] Upon request commanders in the Royal Navy were bound to assist governors in apprehending ships suspected of breaching the law.[77] Africans forfeited under this order were not set free but became the property of the Crown, thus creating a new class of enslaved persons called "Colony Negroes" to be employed in public works or the domestic service of the governor of a colony covered by the abolition edict; alternatively, they could be dispatched to any of the old colonies, to be employed according to the discretion of the incumbent governor. The West India Regiments also benefited from conscription of the fittest males.[78]

Secretary for war and the colonies Lord Castlereagh foresaw difficulty in achieving complete success of the abolition decree. Loopholes were evident in the numerous concessions favoring circumvention rather than compliance, especially in wartime. The colonial situation was no better. In Trinidad a breakdown in administration weakened the potential for properly policing the measures. Lieutenant Colonel Briarly of the Vice-Admiralty Court was an opponent of General Hislop, a governor with populist inclinations. The clash of personalities compromised enforcement of the commercial restrictions: efforts by one official to be impartial were sometimes countered with mischievous abuse of power by the other.[79]

Neither the abolition decree of 1805 nor its parliamentary replica, the Abolition Act of 1806, explicitly threatened the slave trade to the old colonies, but the signs were ominous. Once the trade was legally prohibited in its most lucrative markets, the extension to a general abolition in already creolized colonies became more possible than probable. Indeed, the limited prohibition act of 1806 was quickly followed by an "Act for the General Abolition of the Slave Trade." It is noteworthy that the bill was first passed in the House of Lords, which had previously frustrated all attempts at general prohibition.

Drescher and other advocates of moral abolitionism stand firm on the view that "the motion for abolition was grounded on an explicitly non-insurrectionary premise about the prior behaviour of British slaves."[80] This statement does not reflect a careful reading of the dread of insurrection in abolitionist discourse. In his contribution to the 1805 motion that the House of Commons consider a new abolition bill, foreign secretary James Fox asked rhetorically, "Was it a theory that the West India islands were in a very alarming state?"[81] Fox further premised his general abolition resolution in June 1806 with the assurance that a successful outcome would place the colonies "in a state of safety beyond anything that could be effected by fleets or armies."[82] Lord Grenville, the secretary at war and a foreign secretary for most of the 1790s, was no less assured of the efficacy of abolition on colonial security as he piloted the 1807 general abolition bill in the House of Lords. In moving the second reading, Grenville warned, "So far from the abolition of the slave trade having a tendency to produce those horrors in our islands, I contend that it is the only measure that can prevent them . . . the abolition of the trade is the only way of avoiding, in your own islands, the horrors which have afflicted St. Domingo."[83] On the third reading of the bill the earl of Buckinghamshire gave his support to the measure "because the abolition was the only means of preventing those evils which must otherwise necessarily result from the multiplication of slaves in the West Indies."[84] Similar sentiments dominated pro-abolition contributors to the bill in the House of Commons. In leading the debate on the second reading, Lord Howick declared, "Were I called to state my belief of what would be the measure of the greatest security and advantage to the West India Islands, I would state this very measure."[85]

While Wilberforce persisted in cloaking imperialism with a conscience, he was well aware of the greater imperative of colonial security. Being a close friend and ally of Pitt and Fox, Wilberforce must have been privy to the military calamities in the Caribbean. His response to Ellis's 1797 amelioration motion was infused with images of an impending racial war if the slave trade continued unabated. In Wilberforce's first motion for abolition in Pitt's second ministry (1804), he contextualized the wanton loss of British troops in putting down insurgencies as well as defending the colonies against foreign attacks: "How long the country would be able to bear these successive drains of men; how long our population could answer these repeated demands, he could not take on himself to anticipate; but surely the system which rendered them necessary could not be easily defended. The present situation of St. Domingo, it was impossible for him to pass over without some notice. Was it wise, he would ask to increase the number of new negroes in our West India islands, under the present circumstances of the colonies?"[86] Drawing heavily upon Long's analysis of insurgent-prone imported Africans and the implications of the strategic locations of independent Haiti and revolutionary Guadeloupe, Wilberforce echoed the solemn warning of his abolitionist allies: "Was it forgotten that St. Domingo was almost in sight of Jamaica, and that Guadeloupe was in the centre of the Leeward islands? The abolition of the slave trade appeared to be called for by every consideration of justice, of policy, and of humanity."[87] Interestingly, Wilberforce's contemporaries were fully aware that the abolitionists' mantra, humanity and justice, had more currency as international diplomacy than in domestic politics. The relevance of the expression in the bill was hotly debated in committee. In his contribution the earl of Westmoreland revealed that members of Parliament had agreed finally to include the phrase *justice and humanity* purely for its diplomatic impact, believing "that by retaining these words, foreign powers might be humbugged into a concurrence in the abolition."[88] Britain could not seriously expect its imperial rivals to follow it into abolition because of philanthropy or religious sentiment; besides, their political cultures would not have facilitated it. Yet few contemporaries were prepared to admit to hypocrisy, as Westmoreland clearly conceded: "Upon what principle of logic it was to be proved that if the slave trade was contrary to justice and humanity, it was not also contrary to justice and humanity to keep the negroes who had been procured by means of the trade, in a state of perpetual slavery."[89] If few spokesmen alluded directly to emancipationist wars, it is largely because of the success of the government in covering up the facts of the revolutionary 1790s.

7

IMPERATIVES OF CREOLE COLONIZATION

The Politics of Free Labor

Within four months of Canning's Creole colonization blueprint, the British government was moving full speed to implement some of its key proposals. Secretary of state for the colonies Lord Hobart explained to Governor Picton, "The peculiar situation of the West Indian Colonies at the present period, and the opinions which have been expressed in this Country against permitting the importation of Slaves from Africa to Trinidad, may make it necessary to have recourse to other than the common modes for the Settlement and improvement of that valuable acquisition."[1] Hobart required Picton to assess the prospects for "a Colony of White Inhabitants of the labouring class" in order to bring areas of the country with the best drainage and moderate rainfall into early cultivation.[2] The inducements extended to a wide spectrum of white immigrants, including demobilized soldiers and Dissenters from Ireland and Scotland.[3] Under the proposed settlement scheme each corporal would receive ten acres and each lieutenant seventy-five acres.[4] Dissenters would be contracted under five-year indentures with wages fixed by law; at the end of their contracts a token acreage would be granted as inducement for permanent residence: heads of such families would be given five acres; to every other free person, three acres; and for every child, two acres.[5]

The demographics of Creole colonization intertwined with internal security in a matrix of checks and balances. The principal role of containing politically ambitious Dissenters was assigned to war veterans located on higher ground and organized into a voluntary corps.[6] The colonization scheme included emancipated Africans with military experience, a master strategy to convert legendary enemies into allies of white rule. The preferred Africans were the most trustworthy soldiers of the West India Regiments, who were expected to become small farmers after demobilization.[7] Britain's prior experience in cooperative defense with emancipated Africans inspired confidence in the proposed security arrangement; the first experiments were the Maroon treaties in Jamaica; the latest occurred during the 1790s, when the Dominica government negotiated a similar alliance with Maroon chief Farcelle.[8] In Trinidad these allies were liable to military conscription should the need arise but under the command of white officers.[9]

Hobart's plan included a drive for self-sufficiency in food production. Diversifying and strengthening the island's domestic economy received strong support from prominent colonists. John Sanderson, lawyer and political activist, publicly rejected the extension of the plantation system and expansion of sugar cultivation, preferring small estates or farms on which a wide range of crops could be grown, including rice, maize, breadfruit, and pigeon peas, and in the savannah lands pasture and cattle rearing. He envisaged that the farmers owning ten to twenty acres could achieve not only self-sufficiency but also surpluses for export.[10]

The resort to white yeomanry was a colonial anachronism and made sense only as a deficiency expedient. The unfitness of whites for tropical labor had become proverbial. The overturning of this fallacy came too late to be considered a viable solution to the colonial labor problem. Slavery had become so pervasive that no European would willingly work side by side with an African. More fundamentally, manual labor was akin to slavery and racial degradation. To subject whites to agricultural labor in a plantation colony would dangerously subvert the mores that made enslaved Africans and blacks in general outcasts in colonial society.

The most grandiose Creole colonization project was the Chinese immigration scheme. The initial plan of July 1802 was proposed by Captain William Layman of the Royal Navy in response to Hobart's public invitation to contribute to the new-modeling of colonialism. The plan was modified and expanded several times over a period of four years. Layman's selection of Trinidad as the preferred nursery to propagate a Chinese diaspora as a buffer for black militarism makes him a coauthor of the new colonialism. The ideological framework of the plan was rather similar to the outlines articulated by Canning and Stephen. Layman argued that Chinese immigration might be the best "substitute for the Slave Trade"; it might also promote the interest of the East India Company as a counterpoise to the growing influence of the

United States with China and India. The scheme, expanded throughout the West Indies, might prevent dependence on the United States for supplies and make Trinidad an entrepôt for imports from China and India destined for South America.[11] Within months the British government set up a secret committee to manage the scheme and dispatched a copy of the plan to the Trinidad government. The project committee conceived an initial phase of some three thousand Chinese settlers.[12] The willingness of the imperial government and private investors to engage in such a costly enterprise underscored the imperative of security against black nationalism and potential expansionism. In 1803 the imperial government elevated the project into the flagship plan for ending the slave trade and securing the colonies against a possible recurrence of what had happened in Haiti. The memorandum promised the best security against the "Negro Government" in Haiti:

> The Events which have recently happened at St. Domingo necessarily awaken all those apprehensions which the Establishment of a Negro Government in that Island gave rise to some years ago and render it indispensable that every practicable measure of precaution should be adopted to guard against the British Possessions in the West Indies as well as against any future indisposition of a power so constituted, as against the danger of a spirit of Insurrection being excited amongst the Negroes in Our Colonies. It is conceived that no Measure would so effectually tend to provide a Security against this danger as that of introducing a free race of cultivators into Our Colonies who from habits and feelings would be kept distinct from the Negroes and who from Interest would be inseparably attached to the European Proprietors.[13]

Several memoranda and instructions to East India Company officials were penned within the first six months of the committee's existence. Among them was a "Secret Memorandum" from one Mr. J. Sullivan to the chairman of the East India Company, which took a direct interest in the scheme.[14] The Far Eastern governors' response to the threat of black militarism in the West Indies is worth noting. Robert Townshend Farquhar, lieutenant governor of Prince of Wales Island (now Penang), declared, "It must be obvious to those who contemplate the convulsions that have lately taken place in the West Indies, together with their probable consequences, that the project of substituting Chinese Labourers in lieu of African Slaves, if it can be carried effectively into execution, embraces objects, both in a Political and Commercial point of view of the utmost importance to the British nation."[15] The governor's observation is a candid snapshot of imperial logic in justifying abolition of the slave trade; moreover, his observation demonstrates a remarkable unity of imperial mind-set in matters relating to colonial security.

Had the "Mahratta War" of 1804 not compromised the India stage in the plan, the Chinese might have arrived before the landmark abolition order-in-council; instead, they disembarked in Port of Spain to a warm welcome by the authorities a little more than one year later.[16] Consistent with the new policy of Creole colonization, Hobart had instructed the Trinidad government to set aside tracts of land and facilitate the Chinese as independent cultivators of rice and even sugarcane.[17] By the time of their arrival, however, conditions had changed, and planters were obviously determined to reduce them to wage laborers. Instead of receiving land grants, they were divided into groups of two and three and contracted out to planters.[18] According to Sanderson, planters insisted on dividing the Chinese so that the plan would fail and they could fall back on the recruitment of Africans.[19] Except for "headmen," the stipulated wages were comparable with post-emancipation Barbadian plantation laborers, among the worst in the Caribbean.[20] Not surprisingly, within a year thirty to forty Chinese opted to take advantage of the return passage;[21] by 1814 there were only thirty left, and by 1824 the number was further reduced to twelve.[22]

The failure of Chinese immigration was guaranteed even with the best cooperation of planters. The personal risks taken by the recruiting agent had been so tremendous that the imperial government had given him a special dispensation to violate the Navigation Laws by importing into Trinidad Oriental goods, from which he would earn a personal commission of 5 percent.[23] Unfortunately for McQueen, the Trinidadian authorities ordered the forfeiture of his cargo.[24] With this act the material incentives for the high risks and inconveniences were removed. The credibility of the imperial government for any future operations was also seriously undermined. With the failure of Chinese immigration went the last hope, before emancipation, of the expansion of the plantation economy by organized immigration. From the metropolitan perspective the colony's destiny seemed to be inextricably linked to the least desirable type of laborer, the African, enslaved or free.

Although the Chinese scheme fell through after the initial voyage, the idea of Asian immigration as a substitute for enslaved Africans survived. Trinidadian governor Ralph Woodford (1813–28) avidly supported a small farms policy. In 1814 he submitted a proposal to the imperial government to entice artisans, peasants, and entire families from India to immigrate with their own headmen and religious leaders; they would be free to select their own residential sites, aiming at self-sufficiency in food; they would not be obligated to work on sugar plantations, but they should have an "inclination" to do so.[25] Had such expectation borne fruit, Trinidadian sugar planters would have availed themselves of cheap Indian labor and possibly satisfied the original speculations of the early postconquest years by becoming Britain's premier sugar colony.

William Burnley, one of the biggest sugar planters in Trinidad and self-appointed spokesman for British colonists, also supported Indian immigration but with some modifications to the governor's plan. Burnley envisaged that Indian immigration had the potential to bring about "the early extinction of that baneful system of slavery which is the [most] radical evil of all we are called upon to remedy."[26] He could see no viable future in the plan to settle the island with "a few disbanded soldiers from Europe, or a few indented negroes from Africa."[27] India as a new, major source of cheap labor obviously resonated in other parts of the empire; Mauritius received its first Indian immigrants only three years after Woodford's proposal, launching an era of labor recruitment from that country for the next hundred years.

The best result for Creole colonization prototypes was the settlement of discharged black soldiers who had served in the West Indies and North America. If not for the fear of black militarism, the colony might have benefited from deployments of the ten thousand troops of the West India Regiment emancipated by an act of Parliament in 1807.[28] Military emancipation was a major capitulation for Parliament, coming after several years of determination to renege on all promises of land and freedom to African soldiers conscripted since 1794. After the peace treaties ending the Napoleonic Wars, many of the regiments were disbanded, but upon discharge, over twelve hundred soldiers were immediately redeployed into garrison-pioneer companies.[29] This was a shameful act of betrayal because pioneers were deemed unsuitable for combat, and black soldiers had always considered pioneer duties a form of military punishment worse than flogging. Some discharged soldiers were shipped to a remote Honduras territory, but many thousand more were transported to Sierra Leone, where they could not impact the slavery question.[30] The few veterans finally settled in Trinidad with their families were a token gesture to the emancipation promises of the 1790s and the actual military emancipation law of 1807. The self-styled "Merikins" had fought in the Anglo-American War of 1812–14; beginning in 1815, they arrived at irregular intervals under the protection of the governor.[31] A few discharged soldiers of the West India Regiment began to augment this class of free settlers from 1816.[32]

The black veterans were well received by Woodford. Behind the apparent generosity of governmental obligation and protection, however, mistrust and prejudice determined the welfare and fate of the new settlers. The need to pre-empt cooperation or coalition between the two streams of war veterans guided their geographic distribution. Generally, the Merikins were located in Naparima, in the southwest of the island, the "West Indians" in Quarré and Manzanilla in the northeast. Even within each zone regimental villages were sited relatively far from each other; security was further enhanced by having two white officers stationed at each village.[33] This arrangement fulfilled Hobart's original idea of facilitating re-conscription should the need arise. Land grants to black war veterans were generous when compared with allocations to their white counterparts. In Naparima each Merikin received sixteen acres, the same as that allocated to free coloreds under the 1784 Cedula of Population. In Manzanilla and Quarré single men received eight acres each, while families received twice that amount.[34]

The proverbial deck was stacked against the progress of newly manumitted even more than against vintage freedmen. The discharged soldiers were no exception. Commandant Mitchell compelled the veterans in the southern Company Villages to work on his wife's estates as quid pro quo for "protection." Although they were considered free laborers, they were treated as slaves.[35] Mitchell also fraudulently appropriated two thirds of their wages toward a "hospital fund," from which they derived no benefits and which actually went into his personal account.[36] The economic potential of land ownership was reduced because they were settled "on wastelands of the Crown."[37] These disadvantages notwithstanding, the former soldiers zealously guarded their independence; they resisted indenture and became major suppliers of rice and plantains to locally based military units.[38] Some thirty to forty miles of forests and poorly maintained trails separated the northeastern settlements from the market in Port of Spain. Many carried their produce on their heads over this distance.[39] The planters envied their independence and apprehended their potential for destabilizing the enslaved population, but Woodford was not fazed by such fulminations and lauded the veterans' industry and high morals.[40] The shortage of women and the lack of medical facilities set back the social development of the settlements. Not surprisingly, some of the northeastern settlers migrated to Port of Spain.[41] Similar disabilities drove the southerners more and more into dependence on the plantation economy and society; many actually lived on the plantations. Indeed, a true sense of community was virtually impossible for new freedmen, who continued to be bound by kinship relations to enslaved persons; these restrictions robbed them of the full economic potential of kinship. To some extent the neglect of the black settlers by the colonial state was also an indictment against the imperial government and the Church of England.

It was evident that slavery limited the market for economic activities of manumitted persons, whether agriculturists, craftsmen, or traders. The hostility of white colonials compelled many of the self-manumitted to hire themselves out to enslavers.[42] Officialdom also frustrated the economic ambition of free blacks. Typical of such hostility was the treatment of a disbanded soldier brought before the chief of police, who also exercised magisterial functions. The former soldier was charged with plying for labor as a porter without a license and fined; unable to pay, he was incarcerated for two days.[43] Neither imperial nor colonial government paid any attention to these structural injustices. Instead, attitudes continued to be shaped by the stereotypical African, who preferred the comforts and security of enslavement to the challenges and hardships of economic independence.

Abolition in Action or Inaction?

Abolition lacked effective sanctions to deter illicit traders; government also lacked the political will to enforce the act. The general abolition act maintained toleration of the intercolonial slave trade established in the 1806 act it had superseded. This compromise facilitated clandestine human trafficking for an additional two decades, often with the complicity of colonial officials. The concession also facilitated the reduction of free persons to slavery under the pretext of improving their conditions in host colonies. Interestingly, the intercolonial compromise was not offensive to abolitionists. Indeed, it was consistent with the mind-set that linked the probability of insurrections and emancipation wars with an unbroken African spirit. Abolitionists believed that an intercolonial traffic would supply new colonies with tractable laborers. Such trafficking was expected to pose little or no threat to the stability and security of colonial life and property. Much more worrisome to abolitionists was the lack of measures to enforce abolition of the transatlantic traffic. The United States, acting independently, and many slave-trading nations yielding to Britain's diplomatic pressures, passed abolition acts but lacked the political will to stop the trade. British abolition could have met the same fate had Parliament not incrementally passed amending legislation to close the many loopholes in the original act. Long after it came into effect, British slavers continued to set out from their traditional ports in Liverpool and Bristol under the protection of foreign flags. The list of arrested ships before the Admiralty Court tells of a multinational conspiracy against abolition: the *Fortune* (formerly, the *William and Mary*), flying American colors; the *Diana*, flying Swedish colors; and the *Golupchick*, flying Russian colors; and many more.[44] To some extent moral suasion was also lacking; no law prohibited British merchants and manufacturers from supplying foreign slave ships with trade goods.

After years of inaction, abolitionists renewed their interest in amelioration while demanding zero tolerance for slave trading. To achieve this goal, they agitated for two pieces of enabling legislation, a Slave Registry Act and a Felony Act. In June 1810 the House of Commons adopted Brougham's motion calling upon Parliament to express strong indignation against the open violation of the Abolition Act and to take into consideration measures for the speedy and effective end to such practice.[45] The following year Brougham successfully introduced a bill elevating slave trading to a felony but failed to have it condemned as piracy.[46] "Felons" faced a maximum of three to five years' hard labor or transportation of not more than fourteen years; lesser offenses under the act were merely considered misdemeanors.[47] The Felony Act, like the General Abolition Act, suffered from ineffective policing and likewise failed to bring an end to illicit slave trading.

Following closely was the Registry Order-in-Council (later to become an act of Parliament), the brainchild of James Stephen. To Stephen a Registry of Slaves was a logical follow-up to the Abolition Act.[48] He lamented the delay in enacting police measures but blamed the rapid changes in the executive and the laxity of Spencer Perceval's administration, of which he himself was attorney general and thus equally culpable. With remarkable candor he admitted, "I cannot I fear defend my own public conduct in consistency with those principles which I am known to hold sacred."[49] Thus, he persuaded Wilberforce to bring in a Registry Bill to give effect to the prohibition of the transatlantic slave trade to Trinidad.[50] For some historians the Trinidad Registration Order-in-Council of 1812 represented the first stage in the evolution of metropolitan-engineered amelioration. Several factors favored Trinidad for the registration experiment. First, its location was ideal for smuggling; more significantly, the West India Interest owed too little of its wealth and power to Trinidad for registration to provoke the degree of recalcitrance common to older colonies.[51] Above all, Crown colony constitution ensured that planters' protests could not be easily upgraded to legislative obstruction. The registration decree required every resident in the island to make an original return of every enslaved individual.[52] To George Stephen it was the Registry Act that "gave the finishing stroke to the Slave Trade Abolition and Felony Acts."[53] This was an exaggeration. Every five years or so, up to 1829, acts were being passed to bring closure to the trade.[54] British mercantile support for the slave trade was even more resilient; up to the 1840s British cruisers avoided the all-out destruction of trading posts, some of which were stocked with British slave-trading goods.[55]

The British government made no attempt to extend registration to the legislative colonies until the postwar period. Stephen viewed deferral as a tactical move dictated by the uncertainty of adequate parliamentary support and the perception of a smaller scale of smuggling. He admitted, however, "The same law is there only less urgently necessary not less applicable and proper."[56] For him the trafficking in Africans from the old colonies to Trinidad amounted to a crisis demanding immediate redress. He argued, "The use of Trinidad is nevertheless so shocking in the way of humanity, so dangerous in its example and consequence to the Crown and security of abolition principles that it ought to be remedied if possible without further delay whatever else may be the indirect or collateral consequences."[57] It is difficult to reconcile Stephen's alarm with historical data. The enslaved population rose by 1,052 between 1802 and 1806, but in 1810 there was an actual decline over the previous two years.[58] The returns submitted to the Commissary of Population for the years 1809 to 1811 show that for the entire period 1802 to 1811, the average net annual increase was less than 160.[59] David Eltis also found that importation of new Africans into Trinidad after 1810 was negligible.[60] Other scholars have failed to establish an Africa link among clandestine imports after 1812, which could not have been on a grand scale.[61] The Registry Ordinance was a useful regulating law, but Hobart's relatively successful land policy of 1802 also significantly impacted slave imports.

The Registration Ordinance was a useful instrument by which to judge the economic feasibility of mitigating slavery. The warrant of office of the Registrar of Slaves gave him sole responsibility for registration and thus made him the principal officer of amelioration prior to 1824. On appointment the registrar was subject to a bond of two thousand pounds sterling and other sureties of one thousand pounds each; he could not be "the owner, part owner, or mortgagee, of any Slaves."[62] A further incentive to promote compliance was the substantial reward of three hundred pounds sterling to be shared equally between the governor and any informant giving indictable evidence of fraudulent returns.[63] To qualify for the post, Henry Murray transferred his holdings in human property to his wife.[64] Measured against the standards of the day, this maneuver was neither unethical nor illegal, since officeholders were all enslavers, including judges, the attorney general, Roman Catholic and Protestant clergy, and even the governor. Nonetheless, the practice was certainly a problem of trusteeship, as Stephen clearly recognized.

The Registry Ordinance was an enabling law, not a slave code. It empowered the registrar to enforce a purely economic measure: the elimination of human trafficking. In order to ensure maximum efficiency, all judicial institutions and personnel were classified as agencies to promote compliance.[65] The decree did not address the condition of the enslaved. Had it done so, it would have demonstrated a vital shift in the principle of intervention held by abolitionists. Planters feared such a situation because of its unsettling effects on the enslaved population. Instead, the ordinance made special provisions for protecting enslavers most vulnerable to exploitation, such as married women, lunatics, and the disabled.[66] Thus, instead of threatening disorder, there were clear indications of concern for the rights of property in enslaved persons.

Two principles in the Registry Ordinance were new to British colonial slavery and posed a potential threat to conventional enslaver-enslaved relations: compulsory manumission and the judicial evidence of enslaved persons in cases of fraudulent returns. These reforms, however, were more revealing of the powerlessness of the enslaved than a possible reformation of slavery. Under the ordinance every unregistered person enslaved within the colony was a potential beneficiary of judicial manumission. In actuality several conditions swung the advantage toward the claimant or enslaver. As a consequence, the law was a greater threat to freedom than to slavery. Under its provisos a free black or colored person could be enslaved until the next annual returns, which must then be used to ascertain the legal status of the unfortunate individual.[67] Similarly, the "right" to judicial testimony was facetious because the credibility of the enslaved could be easily negated upon objections by those with vested interest in the case.[68]

Stephen was incensed over the delay in the first registration exercise. Although he admitted that some of the causes "are in considerable degree reasonable and well founded," he remained highly suspicious that mischief and conspiracy to commit fraud were behind the second and third extensions of deadlines. To him such extensions were "much more than the clerical labour required" for compilation and verification, as Murray had suggested. Instead, Stephen was suspicious of "a strange and most unaccountable proportion in the number of personal slaves in Trinidad, by the ultimate returns."[69] The returns at 31 December 1813, verified by the registrar of slaves, showed 25,717 enslaved persons, 18 percent above the average for the years 1809 to 1811.[70]

The statistical disparity between the arrival of the Registration Order-in-Council and the completion of the first registration exercise fueled speculation of large-scale smuggling. To Stephen the high number of "personal slaves" in the late returns was sufficient evidence to indict the "mercantile importer."[71] Governor Woodford admitted that illegal imports continued unabated but insisted that their numbers "will not appear very surprising."[72] Indeed, the returns clearly indicated that the majority of late submissions came from urban enslavers having one to three personal slaves. The geographical isolation of many proprietors, the prevalence of illiteracy, and linguistic pluralism added a mix of indifference, inadvertence, and fraud.

Of fifty-three estates submitting late returns, thirty provided figures lower than those of 1811; six showed no change; there were no comparative data on four estates, which accounted for a total of only sixty-one enslaved persons.[73] Woodford argued that the major causes of delay were "the total Ignorance in which many of the free colored Owners lived" and the remoteness of the eastern districts from Port of Spain.[74] Because most of the late returns of so-called personal slaves originated with urban-dwelling free coloreds, the state would commit an injustice in "converting the penalties of Neglect and Disobedience into serious hardships."[75] Therefore, Woodford supported the opinion of the solicitor general and two other legal authorities that it would be an abuse of power to apply the penalties of the law in a high-handed manner against colonists, who were so inured to "the total Indifference of the orders of the Government that they are perfectly unaccustomed to obey any which does not happen to suit some object of personal convenience."[76] Such a course of action would surely "ruin the aged and ignorant owner of one or two domestic slaves."[77] Delays could also be attributed to improper communication because the proclamation was only in English, which was not the language of the majority. Furthermore, some politically distinguished enslavers challenged the constitutionality of the ordinance. Among them was James Audain, who held the prestigious position of Alcalde of the First Instance and owned sixteen personal slaves.[78] Even the government's "Colony Negroes" were registered late by the inspector of colony Negroes.[79] Thus, while there were obvious acts of deliberate resistance, more often than not, delays in registration were not politically motivated.

The resistance to registration in Trinidad was different from that encountered elsewhere. Berbice and Demerara resisted with the same fervor as the old colonies. In Trinidad more political energy was dissipated in resisting sectarianism than registration. Historians' emphasis on resistance generally failed to take into account the character of the enslaver classes in the colony, a factor no less important than the absence of an assembly. Compliance was politically expedient to different classes of enslavers for different reasons. In 1813 free coloreds legally owned 31.5 percent of enslaved persons and 37.7 percent of total estates.[80] This large share of the real "property" of the colony made the free colored response to registration politically important. Through compliance they demonstrated unswerving loyalty to the Crown. This response was a shield against the growing hostilities and prejudices toward them by white colonists and the state. Political disunity and mutual suspicion among the white colonists compounded the antagonism between them and the free coloreds. Like the free coloreds, the political interests of white French planters could be served best by compliance. So long as France was engaged in war with the rest of Europe, the French in Trinidad were destined to be regarded as enemies. Open resistance to registration could easily bring their loyalty to the British Crown into question. To the English compliance was politically advantageous in the continuing struggle for British laws. Thus, the social and economic power of the enslaver classes was not easily transformed into political unity necessary for sustained resistance. Consequently, the truer significance of registration in Trinidad was not the staged resistance—this was natural and expected by vested interest—but the futility of resistance. Proprietors recognized their weakness and attempted to make mileage by representing their compliance as the response of a law-abiding and responsible class; compliance underscored their desire "to avoid giving an example of disobedience and causing trouble."[81]

In spite of Woodford's misgivings, the end of the first registration exercise was quickly followed by the Trinidad government's determination to crackdown on defaulters. To this end the governor directed the attorney general to investigate all relevant cases. The investigation revealed ongoing attempts to smuggle enslaved persons into the colony. Those suspected of fraudulent imports were prosecuted, and forfeitures were made "apprentices" of the Crown.[82]

Diverse individuals sought licenses to import enslaved laborers into Trinidad, mainly from Barbados, Dominica, Grenada, and St. Vincent.[83] For large numbers the governor had to obtain permission from the Colonial Office.[84] Certainly, the much higher prices for enslaved persons in the newly ceded colonies of Demerara and Trinidad attracted profiteers. Whereas in Antigua and Barbados an enslaved adult was valued at thirty-five to forty pounds sterling, the seller received as much as eighty to ninety pounds in Demerara and Trinidad.[85] A hallmark of this traffic was the large number of visitors from the older colonies "attended" by several "domestic slaves" who became the property of new owners soon after landing and had their status downgraded to "field slaves."[86] The total number of licensed imports into Trinidad between 1813 and 1825 amounted to roughly sixty-three hundred.[87] This number was small in absolute terms but represented a significant proportion of the existing labor pool of the island. Without this traffic the economy would have been in crisis well before emancipation. The authorities were not unmindful of the abuse of the licensing system: importers of labor were compelled to pay hefty fees that went into the pockets of officials,[88] and suspected cases of fraudulent applications came under ongoing investigations.[89]

In 1824 the Consolidated Slave Act finally condemned the slave trade, including its intercolonial expression, as piracy punishable by death without benefit of clergy.[90] A loophole was nevertheless found in simply challenging the new law. Once an appeal was lodged, a case could drag on for years with no resolution. Williams is convinced that this act "did not nor was it meant to abolish this slave trade."[91] Indeed, even after further restrictions in 1828, "domestics" and "fisherman" continued to be imported under special license.[92]

8

❧

NEW-MODELING IN ACTION

Capitulation and Conflict

The adoption of Canning's vision for Trinidad as a new colonial paradigm linked the island's destiny to the future of colonial slavery. The contradictions inherent in the Trinidad model climaxed in Jamaica's Baptist War, compelling the abandonment of gradualism and the adoption of a new remedy in immediate emancipation. Post-abolition colonial policy was overshadowed by the Felony Act and the contentious registration order-in-council. Thus, the year 1813 saw the first transition to civilian governorship under Sir Ralph Woodford. His main mandate was to ensure the success of registration, manage the inflows of Africans into the colony, and facilitate royal absolutism under the new Crown-colony constitution. Although Woodford's substantive successors were military officers, their tenures witnessed even more assertive interventions of the Crown with respect to the treatment and status of enslaved Africans and free coloreds, the enforcement of abolition, and the climax of the experiment in "new-modeling" the colony gradually away from slave labor. Central to Trinidad's new-modeling was the legal-constitutional reengineering of different imperial traditions. The resulting conflicts and compromises imprinted the colonialism of the early nineteenth century. Berbice, Demerara, and St. Lucia underwent similar post-abolition grafting but with different degrees of imperial intervention.

Any reconcilement of abolitionists' and capitalists' expectations had to take account of the political and economic realities of Trinidad. The island was a frontier colony, a delicate war trophy that might yet be a pawn in the final settlement of the Napoleonic Wars; it was at the doorsteps of the volatile Spanish Main; and the majority of its population was influenced by revolution in France and the colonies. Even as stakeholders debated the constitution, the colonial regime became increasingly draconian toward nonwhites. It dispensed with the ameliorative pretensions of the 1789 *Cédula Real* (commonly called the Spanish *Code Noir*) in preference for the more draconian *Siete Partidas* and *Recopilación de Leyes de los Reynos de las Indias;* it also sought to trample upon the rights of free coloreds conferred by the 1783 Cedula of Population, the civil constitution of early modern Trinidad.

While supporting a liberal policy toward free people of African descent, the Cedula of Population preserved the fiat of West Indian caste. Racial prejudice was evident in the disproportionate distribution of land and, consequently, wealth and status. In the scramble to qualify for large land grants, fortune-hunting immigrants in Grenada rounded up impoverished freedmen, whose status was downgraded aboard ship.[1] Governor Chacon offered no protection to them.[2] Likewise, the allocation of land grants reinforced social stratification. The cedula specified that four and two-sevenths *fanegas* of land (about thirty-two acres) be given to each free white settler but only half that amount to each free nonwhite—an obvious surrender to the dictum of white superiority.[3]

Spanish liberalism toward free coloreds was critical to colonial security in an era of heightened imperial rivalry.[4] Commensurate with this agenda, the land grants to free coloreds was significant. Two *fanegas* (about sixteen acres) allowed the lowliest free colored with no capital resources (including no enslaved workers) to become a freeholder. Industrious immigrant freemen might easily insulate themselves from extreme want and destitution common to the majority of their class in other islands. In a real sense this settlement policy was a new experiment in race relations, the genesis of the vogue "colony of experiment," the well-known sobriquet of early British Trinidad. Chacon broke down other racial barriers that elsewhere set the free colored as a marginal entity among the free population. One consequence of this demographic experiment was the resetting of social distinctions of Trinidad's plantation society to two classes, freemen and slaves.

On appointing General Picton military governor, Abercromby confessed to leaving him in a militarily weak and politically fragile situation. To compensate, he assured Picton that he was responsible to no one, so long as his powers were used to retain the island for Britain.[5] In 1801 Picton was mandated to establish a council of advice comprising three to five proprietors to assist with its administration. In keeping with the traditions of military governance, however, he notified the council that his executive powers remained absolute.[6]

Not surprisingly, the treatment of enslaved persons worsened under Picton, who used martial law to subvert proprietors' authority. The governor was also president of the Cabildo, in whose jail enslaved prisoners, especially the chain gangs, were brutally punished.[7] The most common punishment for running away was cutting off the ears of the hapless Maroons, even against the wishes of enslavers, as in the case of Pierre Warner, whose enslaver testified that he "always found him to be a sober, honest and industrious slave."[8] A female runaway named Present was taken into the custody of the Cabildo at around 3:00 p.m. and hanged by sunrise the next day despite her enslaver's remonstration that she had no bad quality and was perfectly honest.[9]

With the cession of Trinidad, the imperial government needed to mitigate the fears of the abolition party as well as acquire accurate information on Trinidad. To satisfy both objectives, a three-man commission of government was set up in 1802, in which Picton was relegated to military affairs. William Fullarton, first commissioner and chairman, was responsible for civil affairs, while Commodore Samuel Hood was responsible for naval affairs.[10] Fullarton lost no time in demanding that the Cabildo adhere to due process under Spanish law. He assumed the position of supreme patriarch of the enslaved and insisted that no whipping be administered in the public jail without his authority.[11] Fullarton was a disciple of Edmund Burke and admired the statesman-philosopher's commitment to the epic trial of Governor-General Hastings for abuses committed against the people of India.[12] It is fair to assume that many of the political difficulties that Fullarton experienced in Trinidad sprang from his misinterpretation of Burkean trusteeship. Furthermore, Picton's continuing patronage of the proprietary class and Cabildo officers obviated any possibility of applying Burke's philosophy to Trinidad. By cultivating the loyalty of the elite for his own political agenda, Picton ensured that Fullartonian humanism did not take root in the colony. Furthermore, neither the imperial government nor the Abolition Society favored the kind of intervention articulated by Fullarton. Picton was a man of the times, Fullarton of the future. Seen in this light, the dissolution of the commission and Fullarton's recall were symbolic concessions to abolitionists and vested interest alike.

Following the abandonment of the commission experiment, Major General Thomas Hislop was appointed governor. From his first year in office he emphatically embraced the politics of white supremacy, stripping the free coloreds of most of the political and civil liberties granted by the Cedula of

Population and preserved under the Articles of Capitulation.[13] The increase in wealth and education of free coloreds since the Cedula fueled jealousy among the white population. Furthermore, free coloreds' role in the Haitian Revolution and Fédon's insurgency in Grenada left British colonists deeply suspicious of their loyalty. The continuing environment of war, revolution, and general insecurity made it easy for whites to justify their persecution of free coloreds and reduce the privileges of the enslaved. In 1804 the Board of Council promulgated the first police regulations against free coloreds.[14] Unlike the British, the French *Code Noir* had designated all freedmen citizens with full political and civil rights, yet everywhere free coloreds were treated as natural "enemies of whites" and too dangerous to be allowed any influence in colonial assemblies, including those proposed for the French colonies prior to the outbreak of the Haitian Revolution.[15] Not surprisingly, therefore, the curtailment of free colored liberty featured among recommendations to the imperial government for the internal security of the island. The council extended the definition of *enemy* to include local republicans but conveniently referred only to free coloreds. The most humiliating infringement was a night curfew usually applied only to the enslaved class. Enslaved persons found on the streets during curfew hours, beginning at nine o'clock, were liable to arrest; a fifteen-minute grace separated free coloreds from the same fate, unless they were in possession of a written permit from the governor and a lighted lantern or candle. To avoid arrest, enslaved persons must be similarly illuminated and in possession of a pass from their enslavers, who, ironically, might well be free coloreds.[16]

By 1810 Hislop had become irrelevant to the abolitionist party in Britain. The concerted effort to make Parliament aware that the general Abolition Act needed police measures for effective implementation ensured that Trinidad was brought once more to the center stage of imperial policy. James Stephen recognized the need for a new breed of governor, less intimate with the plantocracy than Hislop. In this new dispensation governors must not only be guided by "temporal" but also by "spiritual usefulness."[17] Thus, Stephen averred, "As our managers must be men who have learnt the business of planting and it will not be difficult to find such men uninfected with feelings of prejudices very opposite to our views, it is of importance to have other agents on the spot independent of them and in constant intercourse with the slaves."[18] This call was a tacit recognition of the impossibility of effecting fundamental social reform without isolating all with a vested interest in slavery from political office. Stephen condemned Hislop as a "rogue" who had violated the trust placed in him to uphold the "humane" laws of the colony.[19] He interpreted Hislop's persecution of free coloreds as retrograde, taking the colony back "to the usuall [*sic*] injustice & oppression which are so shamefully practiced against them in all parts of the West Indies."[20] He accused Hislop of bartering his obligation to protect the free coloreds for popularity among the whites. He also considered the situation so threatening to public order and the principles of justice as to warrant that "*Gen! Hislop should be recalled.*"[21] This was the end of an era. The new era was characterized by enlightened gubernatorial absolutism under a permanently instituted Crown-colony system of government.

Constitution, Law, and Power Relations

The British had conducted experiments in direct rule in Grenada and Canada following the Peace of Paris in 1763. After almost three decades of constitutional wrangling, the Crown finally conceded chartered status and internal self-government to the Grenadian colonists.[22] Following the occupation of St. Domingue and Martinique in the mid-1790s, the decision to maintain the laws of France set a new precedent for British conquests.[23] British rule in St. Domingue brought home to imperial decision makers and political analysts more than a new experience of constitution making. It also forcefully brought home a new experience of slavery in the West Indies: the gallantry of African soldiers, the tactical proficiency of their officers, and the ravages of a full-scale emancipation war. This experience served to reinforce the need for a new kind of colonial governance.

Picton was one of the earliest advocates of direct rule for Trinidad. Across the Atlantic, Stephen and Canning stridently supported the same policy. Stephen temporarily broke rank with the abolitionist party in 1802 because of his advocacy for Crown-colony rule. He argued that such governance was urgently necessary in order to reform the "bad interior system" of the legislative colonies, which so oppressed the enslaved that revolts similar to that of St. Domingue were more than likely to occur in their own colonies.[24] For Stephen the need to remedy the laws of slavery amounted to an "emergency" that demanded an act of Parliament.[25] As attorney general, Stephen was well placed to persuade the Perceval administration to link enforcement of the Abolition Act to the constitutional question in Trinidad. He confessed to Perceval: "I am not one of those who think the legitimate influence of the Crown too large. I hold the very opposite."[26] Stephen found a protégé in Chief Justice George Smith, who concurred that a colonial constitution ought to reflect the interests and obligations of government, which, in the case of Trinidad, was the protection of the enslaved population from the abuse of power of their enslavers.[27] Yet Smith's objective in protecting the enslaved was limited to the economics of natural increase. Thus, he concluded, "Policy not less than humanity calls aloud for such a system of government as may insure to this class of human creatures that protection which is essential to their increase, a practical, not a nominal protection."[28] He insisted, "This protection can only be afforded by an authority over which the master of the slaves has no control and to which he must submit."[29]

On the eve of the constitutional settlement in 1810, the free coloreds became fearful of a political conspiracy to marginalize them. Their latest petition to the governor demanded the restoration of their status quo ante the conquest.[30] The free coloreds included some of the wealthiest and best-educated colonials. Hislop was determined to humble them all. While assuring the petitioners that there was no reason for apprehension—because details of the new constitution were not yet in the public domain—he set up a Committee of the Board of Council to investigate the signatories.[31] He mandated the committee to ascertain those who were British-born, those who were subjects by adoption, and those who had no just claim to citizenship under any circumstances.[32] Hislop's tactic was brutally pragmatic, purposely intended to create dissension among their ranks. Free coloreds of post-Cedula migration accounted for about 60 percent of the free male population,[33] which might have made a significant difference in ethnic power relations under an elective assembly. It would be impolitic to enfranchise the preconquest free coloreds without extending the same right to all of this caste. Hislop's prime concern was the preservation of effective power as a patrimony of the whites, especially the British. Thus, he informed the petitioners that he lacked the authority to forward petitions from them to the imperial government; he was, however, willing to receive them in council.[34] This feigned forbearance made Hislop no better than Picton. For those not considered white, the rule of law began and ended in the colony, unless appeals for redress were successfully directed through unofficial and clandestine means to higher authorities in Britain.

Under the Crown colony constitution, the Council of Advice became a permanent institution of government.[35] The governor's power was subject to review only by the Crown. Where there was disagreement between governor and council, members might seek redress directly from the imperial government. The members of council, selected by the governor, must be among "the most respectable of the inhabitants of the Island,"[36] in effect, only white settlers. Legalized prejudice against the free coloreds effectively robbed them of the cloak of respectability; the social conventions of the colony would have ruled them out in any case. In Trinidad it was considered fashionable for white "gentlemen" to have colored women as housekeepers, a euphemism for concubines.[37] Although their planter-consorts allowed them the privileges of legal wives, they dared not marry them, dine with them, or even be seen in public with them.[38] This racial prejudice compounded the political problem of enfranchisement of the free coloreds. Sharing the same political chamber with colored men was as reprehensible to whites as sharing their table with colored women.

The Trinidad constitutional problem had implications for conquered colonies that were never under British rule prior to the French revolutionary wars. Two of them, Demerara and Trinidad, had the greatest potential for derailing abolition should the Crown surrender chartered rights to the plantocracy. Secretary of state for the colonies Lord Liverpool made the race problem his ace of cards for denying Trinidad an elective assembly on the basis of its unique demography, but even if it was no different from other colonies, "the determination of Government would probably be to negative such a Proposition."[39] Dominica was the only other colony with a free colored majority. It had an elected assembly but did not match the demographic complexity of Trinidad. The legal equality of all free inhabitants in Trinidad was established by the Cedula of Population and guaranteed by the Articles of Capitulation. The colony also had to contend with the cosmopolitanism of its white inhabitants, most of whom were considered aliens with no history of parliamentary government.[40] The Crown-colony decree was a formula to resolve those issues. The government justified its retention of absolute power over new colonies as essential to its obligation to abolition. The decree postulated that Crown-colony rule was the best means of avoiding subversion by vested interests in Parliament and subordinate colonial legislatures determined to preserve the oligarchic status quo.[41]

Based on the Law of Nations (international law) and principles of natural law, neither free coloreds nor French aliens could be justifiably excluded from the franchise, yet it was impolitic to include them because of race and nationality.[42] Liverpool recognized that if the empowerment of the free coloreds under the Cedula of Population and Articles of Capitulation were carried over to an elected assembly, the imperial government must preserve those rights. Such a path to enfranchisement might well have led to a premiering of the Morant Bay rebellion in Trinidad.

Notwithstanding the Liverpool Constitution, the political machinery for the experiment in new-modeling was still defective. The principles that continued to guide its operations were virtually untouched by the Crown-colony order-in-council. Although Stephen admitted its defect, his new-modeling had called for corrective surgery only to the legislature and governorship while leaving the gangrene in the rest of the body politic. It was not that he was unaware of the uselessness of cosmetic changes; he had cited the Emancipation Decree of the French National Convention, which had originated from a clear understanding that meaningful change must take into consideration not only reform of the "civil organization" of the central authority but also the reform of an "administration general and particular."[43] With respect to Trinidad's slave system, this administrative machinery was the protectorate of the commandants.

The retention of legislative power by the Crown was complemented by the expedient of maintaining white elitism. The governor's prerogative might have frustrated the politically ambitious, but it certainly did not reduce the proprietary class to having "no more political weight than the poorest labourer."[44] Crown-colony government did not equalize the political influence of all free males; neither did it essentially alter the relations of power as obtained in the legislative colonies. More effectively than restrictive franchises, Crown-colony government excluded the free coloreds and neutralized the French. It effectively stifled colonial politics but ultimately entrenched the planter class in power even more securely than the old representative system. Even when token concessions were made to free coloreds, the system did not distribute political influence below the wealthy and professional elites.

The Crown's reservation of power over legislation was no guarantee that lawmaking ceased to be a tool of sectional and vested interest. The fallacy of a new dispensation in colonial legislation was exposed by the elder Stephen in 1826: "Of all the errors in policy it is the most palpable, to commit the structure and management of difficult and delicate measures to those who avowedly dislike the principles on which they are founded; and who wish not for their success, but their failure: nor is there in this respect any difference between Slave-holders elected into a Colonial Assembly, and Slave-holders elected sitting in a Council, or Court of Policy, under the authority of the Crown."[45] By that time there was already enough evidence of racial and religious prejudice in Crown-colony legislation, particularly with respect to the persecution of free coloreds and Methodist missionaries. Crown-colony was a system of governing, not a principle of law or judicature. Once the legislative process is understood, the fallacy exposed by Stephen becomes even more sinister. Orders-in-council originated more often than not within the colony itself: Stephen's advice to Perceval to instruct Hislop to prepare the draft of a "plan of constitution and laws" for Trinidad was typical of the process of lawmaking under a Crown-colony system; a similar instruction to Woodford accounted for the amelioration order-in-council of 1824.[46] The principle that the official on the spot was better placed to advise was applied to the content and purpose of legislation. There was also the ignorance of Spanish law by ministers responsible for colonial affairs. Even the younger James Stephen, principal legal advisor to the government on colonial affairs, confessed ignorance.[47] The governor, in concert with his council, produced drafts of legislation and transmitted them to the Colonial Office, where they were reviewed and transformed into orders-in-council, to be proclaimed without amendments unless specially authorized by the Crown. Orders-in-council often required amending legislation, to which governors responded by issuing local proclamations with a shelf life of two years if not assented to by the Crown or repealed by a subsequent order-in-council.[48]

Legal theorists claim that interpretation is the essence of law and that the meaning of a law must be interpreted within the context of the social environment that gave rise to it.[49] This explanation supports the assertion that the spirit of the law is as important a guide to jurists as the letter. If this claim were applied to the Articles of Capitulation, articles 11 and 12 favored retention rather than a complete overthrow of Spanish laws. Article 12 was particularly sensitive to a change in legal systems. It stated in part: "The free coloured people who have been acknowledged as such by the laws of Spain shall be protected in their liberty, persons and property, like the other inhabitants, they taking the oath of allegiance and demeaning themselves as become good and peaceable subjects of His Britannic Majesty."[50] Although a major critic of the system, activist-lawyer John Sanderson conceded that there was virtue in preserving the "spirit of the Spanish law" as a guide to a remodeled colonial system.[51] The legal persecution of free coloreds by British officialdom had only violated the Cedula of Population. In other Spanish colonies free coloreds remained subject to a wide range of prejudicial legislation that supported sadistic punishments.[52] Article 45 of the Cedula of Population preserved this sordid aspect of Spanish colonialism. Legal discrimination after the conquest was merely a return to tradition.

The Articles of Capitulation did not address the treatment of enslaved persons. The free coloreds could appeal to article 12 as well as the spirit of the capitulation, but in the absence of any provision for the enslaved class, Picton's Slave Code of 1800 became the new *Code Noir* for Trinidad. When Chief Justice Smith declared, "The Spanish slave owner is obliged to maintain his manumitted slave in sickness, infirmity and old age," however, he was clearly referring to the *Cédula Real* or *Code Noir* of 1789. Immediately upon assuming office, Smith wrote to Stephen suggesting that five hundred copies be printed in French, Spanish, and English.[53] Smith would soon learn the harsh reality of proprietary absolutism: knowledge of the law was one thing, enforcement another. Interestingly, the weight of historical evidence indicates that the *Code Noir* was a dead letter in Trinidad well before the conquest. Sanderson had strongly contended that the legislation was never in force in the colony.[54] This was also the conclusion drawn by the Royal commissioners inquiring into all colonial justice systems following the launch of imperial amelioration. The commissioners compiled a comprehensive list of laws current in Trinidad; they did not include the *Cédula Real*.[55] Eminent historian Franklin Knight arrived at the same conclusion, affirming that the *Cedula* "was not even read in the colonies."[56] Based mainly on misinformation from Smith, Stephen "admitted that the Spanish laws though general and expressly retained have not been executed for the protection and benefit of slaves. Their neglect has been so intense and systematic that the Oidor thinks an instruction from His Majesty's Governance necessary to restore this efficacy."[57] The political will to do so produced Britain's first slave code, the amelioration order-in-council, in 1824.

Smith's zeal for the Spanish slave laws was founded upon contemporary propaganda and personal ambition. The enslaved class had never had the semblance of legal protection before the conquest. Furthermore, contrary to popular claims, the *Siete Partidas* was severe toward enslaved persons. For runaways punishment varied according to the extent of marronage: for four days' absence the penalty was fifty lashes; for just under four months, two hundred lashes; for more than six months, death by hanging.[58] For assaulting a white person, the punishment for the first offense was one hundred lashes and the nailing of the hands; for a second offense a hand was cut off.[59] For robbery, rape, or murder an enslaved person was liable to mutilation and a slow, painful death.[60] The code gave an enslaver absolute power over an enslaved person except the right to kill,[61] but even if an enslaver should murder an enslaved person, he or she was unlikely to face prosecution because the law stated that "a slave cannot accuse his master except in special cases."[62] Evidence in permissible cases was extracted by torturing the enslaved witness, who invariably corroborated the enslaver's claims.[63] The *Recopilación* was even more draconian.

The continuing imbroglio over the status and execution of the laws of the colony had much to do with the transition from Spanish to English rule. Spanish law ceased to be practicable on Chacon's capitulation, yet upon vesting Picton with the mantle of military governor, Abercromby instructed: "Execute Spanish law as well as you can."[64] By eliminating the *Audencia* of Caracas, the highest colonial court of appeal, "the judicial system of Trinidad became immediately defective, according to the Spanish law, in its most valuable jurisdiction."[65] Consequently, the entire superstructure of law and justice was vested in one man. Christoval de Robles, a top-ranking Spanish official, explained the awesome the powers devolved upon Picton: "The circumstances of the conquest have combined in you the whole power of government. You are supreme political, criminal, civil, and military judge. You unite in your person the separate powers of the Governor, Tribunals, and Royal Audencia of Caracas; Our laws enable you to judge summarily without recusation or appeal . . . If you do substantial justice, you are only answerable to God and your conscience."[66] Under any governor this power was a formula for legalized terror.

Because of the power of propaganda and general ignorance of the legal authority for enslaver-enslaved relations in Trinidad, the "spirit of Spanish law" was adopted by the British government as the philosophical blueprint of slavery reform throughout the British West Indies. As the model colony, Trinidad was given an administrative structure through which Spanish law (at least theoretically) could be manifested in a new social compact. In this experiment enslaved laborers would experience a level of legal protection unthinkable under Spanish governance or the oligarchies of Britain's old colonies and unmatched in other Crown colonies.

Imperatives of Religious Orthodoxy

Throughout the slavery period the Roman Catholic and Anglican churches remained uncompromising on intellectual and psychological disempowerment of enslaved Africans, especially with regard to deprivation of literacy and any possible opportunity for church leadership. This platform made them implacable enemies of all sectarians. Before the conquest the inhabitants of Trinidad were mainly Roman Catholics. The situation remained unchanged largely because the post-cession land and labor policy put the brake on Protestant immigration and also because of the Church of England's traditional opposition to proselytizing the enslaved class. By 1810 the island constituted a motley population: generally, the French and Spanish were Catholics, so, too, the Irish, Scots, and a significant proportion of the free coloreds. Free coloreds of British ancestry were the fastest-growing class of free people, rising from about 47 percent of the British population in 1802 to almost 63 percent by 1810;[67] most of them were Protestant. The majority of Protestants were adherents of the Church of England and Ireland, a few were Scottish Presbyterians and German Hanoverians, and a small number of free coloreds were Methodists. Amerindians were all Catholics, while most enslaved persons were nominally Catholic.[68]

Papal bulls had conferred on the Spanish monarch the titles of patron and secular head of the Catholic Church in Spanish America. This authority devolved upon Spanish colonial governors, who became the official vice patrons of the church.[69] Article 11 of the Articles of Capitulation guaranteed freedom of conscience to freedmen of Trinidad but was silent on the immediate authority over the church. On the other hand, article 11 of the Commission and Instructions, which established the quasi-Crown-colony constitution of 1801, was more explicit; it instructed Picton to maintain Roman Catholicism "according to its former legal Establishment."[70] This compromise implied that Catholicism was not merely the religion of the majority but the established religion of the colony. Yet, according to Vincent Leahy, "only by an Act of Parliament could the formal establishment of the Roman Catholic Church have been preserved in Trinidad. This measure was not taken."[71] Nonetheless, the Crown's acknowledgment of Picton as vice patron by the bishop of Angostura (in the Spanish Main) conferred legitimacy.[72]

A Protestant governor as vice patron of the Roman Catholic Church was one of the many aberrations of the conquest. Governor Woodford wore the title with dignity while remaining secular head of the Protestant Church of

England and Ireland. Local ordinances and official dispatches of the imperial government treated both churches as established. Nonetheless, the roots of hostility between English Protestants and Catholics were deeply buried in the past. The English Toleration Act of 1688 explicitly excluded papists or popish recusants from the benefits of religious toleration.[73] Under Woodford the political marriage of the Catholic and Protestant churches was a catalyst for building bridges between the two dominant religious traditions.

Before Woodford's tenure, the white British inhabitants were bent on establishing themselves as a superior class, which exacerbated the tensions between them and white French colonists. Woodford's religious policy emphasized cooperation between Protestants and Catholics. He led by example, often attending mass in the Catholic Church. He boasted with some justification that during his administration there was not "the slightest symptom of disagreement between Protestants and Catholics."[74] This image of harmony was important for him to win the support of the British government for his antisectarian policy, which was clearly opposed to the principle of rapprochement that the British government had adopted toward sectarianism in the old colonies and the Guianas.[75]

At the beginning of Woodford's tenure there were only two Roman Catholic chapels, both in need of rebuilding. In 1816 priority was given to the construction of the first Protestant church above all other public works.[76] Although the construction of the Catholic church was equally important to Woodford, the project was denied funding from the imperial government. Undaunted, the governor kept up an ongoing request for more Catholic priests as well as Protestant clergy and catechists, some of whom were to establish a Protestant bridgehead among the disbanded black soldiers of the northeast.[77]

In 1822 the imperial government promised to support Protestant orthodoxy.[78] Obviously delighted, Woodford wrote to the bishop of London: "It has long been wanted & the Missionaries that will be sent out under such control, being Clergymen of the Church, will be well received."[79] This excitement, however, did not necessarily mean that Woodford's relationship with Catholics was a marriage of convenience, which could be shaken by aggressive missionism by his own church. Indeed, he continued to seek funding from the imperial government to support his Catholic policy. Unfortunately, the Crown was not willing to commit public money to a religious experiment that could not be defended in Britain publicly. In dismay Woodford wrote to the bishop of London: "We are however without the Instruction proposed; & I do not know what to make of the treasury as to Churches, for instead of building them, they have refused a roof for one in this town, the walls of which have been raised by Subscription & a partial application of the Public Funds."[80] The strong action taken by the imperial treasury against Catholicism in Trinidad led the governor to believe that there was no intention "to follow up the views that are held out as intended towards the Slaves."[81] Indeed, the Crown was not even committed to advancing the cause of Protestant missionism; the pledge made in 1822 was never honored.[82] Moreover, the discredit of the Crown regarding Christianization of enslaved persons was matched by abolitionists' disinterest in their physical welfare.

Woodford's support for Catholic hegemony was pragmatic. He shared the attitude of Protestant High Church colonials of limiting enslaved persons' participation in Christianity to baptism and recitation of prayers.[83] In this regard he was quite happy with the well-established tradition of joint prayer sessions of proprietors and laborers on French and Spanish estates but lamented the absence of the practice on the estates of British proprietors. Because he would not defer to the sectarians, he actively encouraged Catholicization; for him this was a politically safer course to pursue. Although the imperial government was also aware of the deficiencies of the Protestant Church, however, it clearly articulated a preference for sectarians as agents of proselytization.

The formal sectarian penetration into the religious milieu of the colony began in 1809 with Methodist missionaries. Roman Catholics and "orthodox" Protestants greeted them with systematic resistance. For Trinidad the association of sectarianism with labor unrest was magnified by the outbreak of revolutionary war in Venezuela. Creole nationalists in Venezuela lured large numbers of Maroons across the Gulf of Paria with promises of emancipation, should they enlist with rebel patriots.[84] By 1815 there was at least one regiment of Maroon conscripts at Guiria, led by "mulatto" general José Rivero.[85] The problem of the Latin revolution was compounded by news of an emancipationist uprising in Barbados in 1816. Thus, the presence of a single missionary in Trinidad that year created a "source of uneasiness" for Woodford.[86] The government planned to meet the challenge of sectarianism by constructing "orthodox" Christian churches and chapels throughout the main centers of enslavement.[87] The commencement of Methodist proselytizing also coincided with the renewal of repressive legislation against the free coloreds. The new church had attracted a few "respectable" inhabitants, but it was essentially a "colored" church. As such, it was bound to become the target of political vendetta as well as doctrinal war.

The task of Thomas Talboys, the first Methodist missionary to Trinidad, was initially one of organizer rather than founder, for he had met a small congregation of 36 Methodists led by a colored woman.[88] Membership grew rapidly following Talboys's arrival. By the standards of the day congregations were relatively large, with 140 members by 1812.[89] Talboys built a chapel in Port of Spain and proclaimed enthusiastically that "several openings presented themselves in the country, on the Plantations."[90]

The Trinidad press sensitized the white population to the dangerous combination of sectarianism and colored Jacobinism. Although the *Trinidad Gazette* stopped short of condemning the Methodists, they were nevertheless portrayed as enemies of orthodoxy, "taring [*sic*] at the very vitals of the church."[91] In Jamaica the press had been particularly important in maintaining class and religious strife against the sectarians.[92] In both islands the press branded sectarian activities as bad for the peace and prosperity of the colonies and the morals of the enslaved.[93]

The hostility against Methodism also had an official flavor. Governor Hislop personally threatened to put an end to Talboys's "bad conduct" if he refused to stop preaching.[94] In addition, a petition signed by a "large proportion of respectable inhabitants" was laid by the governor before the council. In it Talboys was accused of "holding forth doctrines destructive of the good order & peaceable conduct of the free colored inhabitants and slaves of this Island and for profanely administering sacraments contrary to the rules of our established religions."[95] The petitioners accused Methodist preachers in Jamaica of propagating "dangerous principles of Equality," with "fatal consequences" to the citizenry.[96] They asked that Talboys be deported as his Jamaican colleagues had been.[97]

Ironically, Talboys escaped deportation on the basis of a sworn statement by Mr. Clapham, the curate of the Protestant Church, an "inhabitant of respectability," who gave a favorable testimonial. Although the council deferred to rights preserved by the "10th Article of His Majesty's Instructions," they invoked section 5 of the English Toleration Act, which they claimed had not repealed the Tests and Corporation Acts that debarred Dissenters from holding public office.[98] In 1811 Hislop issued a proclamation regulating the opening and closing hours of Talboys's chapel and obliging preachers to adhere strictly to the Bible.[99] The most vexatious and intolerable measures, however, were the prohibitions on administering the sacraments of baptism and the Eucharist and performing marriages and burials.[100]

Talboys was recalled by the district committee, but the mission survived.[101] His successor, George Poole, broke up the society into groups of twenty people, claiming that "by this means the Law protect us."[102] By 1817 a thriving Sunday school served over one hundred children.[103] More significantly, some of the most prominent English planters took the initial steps to open up the borders of the plantation polities. Patrons such as Charles Goin, Robert Neilson, and Commandant Townshend Pasea were indicative of the march of Methodism.[104] The plantation economy had also begun to benefit directly from Methodist indoctrination. Converts were put in positions of trust, such as boiler men, drivers, and watchmen.[105] Yet religious prejudice was often stronger than the lure of profits and the imperatives of efficient management. Methodist neophytes belonging to proprietors hostile to Methodism were relegated to the field gangs as punishment and a deterrent to other prospective converts.[106]

The all-out assault on Methodists earned Trinidad notoriety as the ultimate test of faith. Even Woolley, an indefatigable veteran of West Indian missionism, on learning of his appointment to Trinidad, asked woefully, "What evils befall me?"[107] He considered the Trinidad leg of his missionary career as a cross he would have to bear and feared the futility of his labor.[108] But as fate would have it, Woolley was the one to win the admiration and surrender of officialdom.

The status of Hislop's restrictions was eventually condemned by the law officers of the king's bench as unconstitutional. The legal experts confirmed that all Dissenters were protected by the Toleration Act 7 and 8 William 3, c. 35; in the case of baptism and burial they were protected by Act 25, George 3, c. 75; the right of administering the Lord's Supper was recognized by Act 13, George 3, c. 22.[109] The Trinidad council, however, preferred to disregard the highest legal authority of the empire and shelter behind Spanish law. Thus, Woolley was also summoned by the council to sign a bond immediately upon his arrival in the colony.[110] Interestingly, Woolley also appealed to Spanish law in rejecting the council's demands. He argued "that there was nothing in the Spanish code of which I was aware, to affect my case."[111] Furthermore, while the Articles of Capitulation did not address the religion of the conquerors, the "Instructions" to Picton in 1801 clearly provided for the protection of "Evangelicals."[112]

The stalemate between orthodoxy and dissent was resolved following Earl Bathurst's response to Woolley.[113] Although the council recognized the authority of Bathurst's letter, it made a last stand for orthodoxy. The council accepted Woolley as a person of respectability to whom every protection would be afforded. This recognition would be accorded, however, only if he were willing to give up the right to baptize, marry, and bury.[114] Woolley was confounded by this show of recalcitrance. He "was at a loss to conceive how they could associate the idea of liberty they had promised, with the bondage to which I was now called upon to submit."[115] His utter rejection of the proposal brought about the eventual capitulation of the council on the advice of the attorney general.

Woolley's victory was timely. The local society had suffered immensely from lack of leadership; many had abandoned Methodism. Woolley disbanded the survivors and launched a new beginning. By the end of 1821 prospects started to look brighter for the mission. The Trinidad society benefited from the illegal importation of "domestic slaves," many of whom were already converts to sectarianism.[116] This situation accounted partly for the relatively strong showing of the society in the face of official restrictions when compared with the demographically stronger Protestant colonies. With the reversal in the political situation came a widening of support of the plantocracy. Woolley's cross could now be borne with an air of exuberance. He boasted confidently, "The field opens up before me, and under the direct patronage of the Governor."[117] The society established a foothold as far as Sangre Grande, thirty miles east of Port of Spain, where the governor promised a free plot of land for a chapel.[118] A few "very respectable persons" attended the Port of Spain chapel.[119] Such was the promise wrought by the growing support of the colony's elites that the mission seemed destined to take on the character of a third establishment church.[120] Woolley rebuked the London committee for its failure to meet his repeated demand for more missionaries for rural Trinidad. He warned that "the Spanish Priests will soon invade those places, and then the day will be lost forever."[121]

Woodford developed great respect for Woolley, assuring him of his personal protection: "Mr. Woolley I shall not consent to your being removed from Trinidad, your friends may send who they like to assist you with your work . . . here, there has been so much uneasyness [sic], and I am now so fully satisfied, that I cannot allow you to be removed."[122] Woodford's unease was fueled by media reports on the parliamentary resolutions on amelioration; it became increasingly transparent that his humility and generosity were tactical and not a vindication of sectarianism. Woolley himself recognized that the governor's compliment was personal.[123] Woodford's reservation was underscored by his response to the Barbadian planters' burning of the Methodists' chapel on that island; although he condemned the attack, he thought that "it nevertheless shows what the feeling is towards the Sectarians."[124]

The promise of a major role for Methodism in imperial amelioration was undermined by the society's first public condemnation of slavery as sin in 1825.[125] Three Jamaica Methodist missionaries issued the joint statement without consulting the London committee, which suddenly found itself caught between its commitment to quietism and its commitment to missionism. The metropolitans were forced to make a public statement to appease the Jamaican plantocracy and save their missionaries from a political backlash. The committee declared that while the enslaved had a sacred Christian duty to submit to their enslavers and that while it would not compromise its instructions to instill obedience in the enslaved, it considered the system of slavery to be wholly inconsistent with Christianity; slavery was an evil to be terminated as soon as practicable by the wisdom and benevolence of a Christian government.[126] Yet there was no immediate change to a policy "favouring emancipation";[127] that change came after 1830, triggered by the rising tide of militancy by the enslaved. Nonetheless, once the London committee's declaration became public in Trinidad, proprietors generally refused Woolley's request to preach to their enslaved laborers. The following is a typical response: "Sir, have not your Committee told us that slavery is inconsistent with Christianity how then can we admit you to our slaves here."[128] Woolley acknowledged that the society's condemnation of slavery amounted to political suicide. He told his superiors in London: "Your Committee have ruined your Missions in the West Indies . . . I know not what to do . . . there is scarce an English Estate in the space of 30 miles over which I have travelled but I could have obtained permission to visit had it not been for the public arousal of the Com^{ee} Slavery is inconsistent with Christianity."[129] By the end of 1828 the few estates in the northwest still opened to Methodist preaching were finally closed. Direct contact with plantation laborers survived only in Arima and Carapichaima,[130] yet there was virtually no hope in effective indoctrination for want of a chapel.[131] This state of affairs continued down to emancipation. In 1833 one tenth of the enslaved population was considered Protestant;[132] of this class only forty-six were Methodists.[133]

As a religious movement in Trinidad, Methodism was a failure. Yet its struggle for religious equality remains one of the great contributions to imperial reform, especially in terms of the uniform application of British law and principles of jurisprudence. Free coloreds in the church joined the struggle for religious toleration to the struggle for colored emancipation. Although the Methodist plantation enterprise failed, the free coloreds were redeemed in 1829 by the second round of statutory emancipation.[134] This victory positioned the free coloreds as significant contributors to the paradigm of moral imperium, mainly with respect to the reassertion of the Crown's transmarine power in protecting the rights of every British subject and the unconditional right to one's freedom of conscience.

9

THE LAUNCH OF IMPERIAL AMELIORATION

The Balance of Amelioration to 1823

Postconquest economic policy in Trinidad frustrated the limited objectives of amelioration. The lure of Trinidad's virgin soils and high sugar prices presented major challenges to the imperial government's policy of curbing the plantation revolution. Despite the largely successful land policy, sugar estates increased from 192 to 221 between 1802 and 1813.[1] Although the average plantation labor force was greatly enlarged under English ownership, the phenomenal increase in sugar production from 1805 was disproportionate to the growth of the labor force. Sugar exports rose from 4.9 million pounds in 1799 to 15 million pounds within ten years; with only a slight increase in the official labor force, exports rose to 18.5 million pounds by 1813. At 1833 this figure had doubled to 37.7 million pounds, despite an officially declining labor force. Estate expansion also continued apace, with total acreage under cane doubling between 1808 and 1832.[2] Cocoa, the second biggest money earner, also rapidly expanded production until 1827, when prices declined dramatically and precipitated the abandonment of many estates.[3] The rapid expansion of the economy, the falling wartime prices for sugar, the maintenance of high wartime duties, and the large investments in steam technology all combined to sustain old attitudes of extracting the maximum labor in the shortest possible time.[4] The short-term profit outlook made estate management more oppressive as ownership changed hands from French and Spanish proprietors to English mortgage houses. Increasingly, it was not the planters who called the shots but the mortgagees, as in the old colonies.[5] As William Burnley lamented, the Trinidad planter was increasingly becoming only "the Tenant of an English mortgagee, and the foreman of his manufactory."[6] Abolitionists also recognized this development as a major problem for amelioration.[7]

Increased cultivation in Trinidad did not impact the average number of laborers per estate, thus denying the island the demographics of a true plantation colony. In Trinidad the small gang was common to all types of plantation staples. At the turn of the century Mayaro (on the southeast coast) was "virtually covered with sugar plantations," although the 120 settlers and 380 laborers there were more akin to peasant than plantation demography; Guayaguayare, in the distant southeastern corner of the colony, with 66 planters and 400 laborers, was equally removed from true plantation status.[8] By 1813 there were 205 estates in the colony with 1 to 5 laborers; 103 estates with 6 to 10 laborers; 234 estates with 11 to 50 laborers; 83 estates with 51 to 100 laborers; and a mere 26 estates with more than 100 laborers. Of the 109 estates with more than 50 laborers, 96 were pure sugarcane plantations, 3 grew cane and coffee, and 1 cane and cocoa. On the other hand, of the 542 estates with 1 to 50 laborers, 125, or 23 percent, were cane.[9] Many small farmers occupied lands granted after 1802 under a proviso to grow food crops rather than export staples. The phenomenon of estates with less than 10 laborers was compounded by the large size of "domestics," a subgroup of "personal slaves." Many were hired out and worked in plantation gangs. The number engaged in staple production was, therefore, much larger than supposed in the censuses.[10]

Small work gangs and Roman Catholic paternalism influenced enslaver-enslaved relations on estates under French and Spanish management. On these estates paternalism was reinforced by proprietors becoming godparents of enslaved infants and by compulsory evening prayers conducted by the proprietor or his wife. Proprietors usually stood the cost of baptisms, though the fee was often waived by priests. Enslavers also exchanged gifts with the enslaved at Christmastime.[11] This apparent intimacy was integral to the successful operation of privileges, which might include opportunities to visit friends and relatives on distant plantations, participate in Sunday markets, hold dances and wakes, access provision grounds, rear livestock, and "own" private property, including income from personal economic activities. Long-established privileges became conventions in plantation polities and could not be taken away or reduced without just cause; correspondingly, the enslaved claimed them as "rights" that planters would not willingly debate, even in the older colonies with a tradition of greater plantocratic contumacy toward the humanization of labor. Lacking judicial writ, rights defined by conventions remained conditional. Enslavers' power to withdraw or manipulate privilege lured them into a false sense of security. Evidence suggests that they were blind to the possibility that the enslaved might have considered the system of privilege as hard-won struggles against complete dehumanization. Some of the most trusted laborers were poisoners and masterminds of insurgency.[12] Therefore, notwithstanding the appearance of proprietary control over the nexus of plantations relations, the real substance or spirit of paternalism was the enslaved laborers' conditional repudiation of revolutionary violence to undermine or overthrow the slave system.

By 1823 some economically enlightened proprietors had already adopted new techniques of management and control that, in their minds, enhanced the welfare of their laborers. Perhaps the most salutary change was the adoption of task work, a subject of imperial interest since 1790. This genre of labor had begun to gain some popularity in Trinidad before the imperial government adopted it as a critical aspect of official amelioration. It was not an easy choice for planters to make, and most remained wedded to the old gang-and-driver system. Among the pioneers of this challenging experiment was Commandant Brunton, who confessed, "I have always been in the habit during crop season to task my mill, Boiling house, and Cutting Gangs, but I have found a difficulty in tasking the Weeding Gang."[13] Another tasking pioneer, Commandant Danglade, agreed that it was "highly advantageous in certain sorts of work."[14] Tasking created a nonmonetary incentive in free time earned by the enslaved after the completion of a set task. Whenever an enslaved person calculated a personal advantage from tasking, productivity definitely increased. Planters also resorted more to the use of a bell or conch shell, instead of the dreadful sound of the cart whip's lash, to awaken laborers to the toil of a new day.[15] Some planters had also begun to substitute confinement at night in lieu of flogging, while others found that work as a form of punishment seemed to have had a better effect than whipping.[16] Psychological punishment included denying molasses and water to a laborer while in the field or a portion of rum if wet while working.[17]

Colonial governors promoted their own patriarchy in dispatches to the Colonial Office while exaggerating and even fabricating the benefits of ameliorated labor under paternalistic proprietors and managers. They invariably interpreted reform policies as actual accomplishments. In Trinidad this propaganda began with Governor Picton, when he boasted unjustifiably, "During the Six years of my command at Trinidad more was done for the protection and comfort of this class [of enslaved] than in any other Settlement under his Majesty's Government."[18] Picton's sole claim as protector was his Slave Ordinance of 1800.

The historical literature is silent on the fact that Picton, like all governors of British colonies in the late eighteenth century, was instructed by the imperial government to draft a code of law for the urgent amelioration of slavery as warranted by Ellis's successful amelioration motion in 1797.[19] Although Picton had the Spanish *Code Noir* and meliorative laws of the old colonies as models, his ordinance failed to match their pragmatism and in many respects was much more draconian, especially toward women.[20] Not surprisingly, the ordinance did not receive royal assent and was allowed to lapse, despite occasional references to it by Picton's successors.[21] In order to fill the vacuum, the Spanish *Code Noir* was sanctioned but condemned to remain a dead letter, even under the immense judicial prerogatives commanded by its immediate trustee, Chief Judge Smith. Trinidad planters were more beholden to the commandants of quarters and the Cabildo than to royal officialdom. Under those conditions high mortality continued to defeat the main goal of abolition.

The failure of enslaved laborers to sustain or increase their numbers by natural means was not a problem of fertility, as Ramsay had discovered in St. Kitts. This situation was also evident in the returns of slaves for the period 1813 to 1822. Mortality statistics were those of a typical frontier colony. On average one of every three babies born to enslaved women was not expected to live to its tenth birthday; overall the life expectancy of a newborn was only seventeen years.[22] Survivability of infants was affected by the high cost of midwifery, which could be as much as thirty-six pounds in difficult cases. For natural deliveries the fee for enslaved persons was nine pounds.[23] Not surprisingly, enslaved women were generally abandoned to the most primitive and hazardous conditions for lying-in and postnatal care. The returns showed 4,825 births from 1813 to 1822; this number was offset, however, by the deaths of 5,661 children under ten years of age and an overall death toll of 7,631.[24] In considering Philip Curtin's assessment that the enslaved of the preconquest era had achieved self-sustainable growth,[25] it would be fair to conclude that the plantation regime had become more oppressive in the second decade after Amiens.

Not long after Woodford's arrival in the colony, he wrongly deduced that excessive consumption of alcohol was largely responsible for the high mortality. Several years later he came closer to the truth when he confessed that "the labor of the slaves has in general been increased for the purpose of enabling the planters to repair the losses sustained in their numbers and the depreciation of their produce."[26] For the enslaved this was a vicious cycle: they were being overworked in order to compensate for the decline of the labor force caused by misguided management practices and inhumane treatment. Nonetheless, Woodford maintained that even with increased hardships, slavery in Trinidad was unmatched by the ease with which laborers worked and passed their time of day. Often relying on reports of commandants of quarters, he mythicized an idyllic life on cocoa estates.[27] Obviously misled by the small gangs and the less rigid work routine on cocoa estates, Woodford's major concern was not the preservation of alleged comforts but the need to convince the Colonial Office to support his efforts to "sell" Trinidad to prospective investors, especially in cocoa.[28] With respect to sugar cultivation—which he was willing to admit posed a great hazard to the health and life of an enslaved laborer—nature itself came to the defense of the laborer's privileged lifestyle. Woodford proudly boasted, "In the new lands of Trinidad, it is sufficient to clear the surface and to lay the cane in the soil where it will for 18 or 20 years throw out fresh canes."[29]

Woodford's portraits of easygoing, contented enslaved laborers insulated planters' tyranny from external scrutiny. Yet by 1823 change was too slow and haphazard to inspire abolitionists with hope of natural increase. In spite of the general success of registration, the experiment had failed to improve the lot of the laborer. This situation was adequately summed up in Woodford's observation that "the comforts of the slaves depend upon themselves and their own industry, and their health upon their own imprudencies [sic], or the quality of the work they are required to perform."[30] In other colonies conditions had also worsened for enslaved persons, in spite of the passing of registration acts and ameliorative legislation. These failures provided the political ammunition for abolitionists to play a more dominant role in imperial policy for the next ten years.

The Enslaved and the Question of Judicial Protection

Although Edmund Burke strongly favored the rule of law to regulate slavery and improve the condition of enslaved laborers, he was cognizant of the oligarchic prejudices of colonial assemblies. His Reform Code was predicated on the universally sound principle that an accused cannot be a judge in his own case; therefore, the imperial government must play the role of trustee. Dispensing completely with plantation authorities, the code resolved that the attorney general "exercise the Trust & Employment of Protector of Negroes."[31] However sincere, guardianship could not guarantee protection; such security could only be realized by empowering the enslaved with the judicial oath. The unconditional right of enslaved persons to give evidence in court was irreconcilable with white supremacy. The token concession granted under the registration order-in-council did not threaten the authority structure of slavery. Yet the question of political authority was central to the progress of imperial trusteeship. Abolitionists generally agreed that the authority for directing amelioration should remain within the colony. Up to the 1820s the debate hinged on two options: the proprietor and the government. In the context of the times there was no qualitative difference; both authorities either marginalized or completely disdained the interests of the enslaved.

Prior to the 1780s all enactments regulating slavery were police laws. Even so, the rule of law played no role in enslaver-enslaved relations. As Ramsay explained: "Except in a very few points it is almost impossible for law to come between a master and his slave. A cruel or capricious man can tease and waste his slave in a thousand ways that law cannot check, nor authority reach."[32] He was particularly wary of imperial intervention. In this regard he urged the British legislature to "be cautious how it meddles with the state of slaves in the colonies, lest, while attempting to regulate their treatment, it confirms the bonds of slavery. If regulations be necessary, the island assemblies should enforce them."[33] Other abolitionists concurred. Wilberforce warned of the incompatibility of slavery and freedom, and the futility of uniting slavery and freedom under the law.[34] Instead, abolitionists supported the view that a new focus on breeding would necessitate better feeding and milder "discipline." Breeding would lead naturally to the expansion of benefits, to "*innumerable other particulars, which an act of Assembly could neither specify nor enforce.*"[35] Yet this situation was hardly better than the treatment of plantation cattle.

Wilberforce shared Ramsay's opinion that laws could not mitigate slavery, even if the slave trade were to be abolished. In one of his earliest motions on the slave trade Wilberforce warned his peers, "This plan of amending the situation of the slaves, and securing their good treatment by laws, was not inefficacious only, but unsafe."[36] He argued that enslaved persons ought not to be given the right of due process because "to give them the power of appealing to laws, would be to awaken in them a sense of dignity of their nature."[37] While the state might safely confer a modicum of rights to the enslaved, it was "dangerous" to impart to them a "sudden communication of the consciousness of civil rights."[38] The consistency and power of conviction in these statements demonstrate that the central problem for Wilberforce, Ramsay, and other leading advocates of amelioration was the danger of instituting the rule of law in the colonies. Their remonstrance contradicts the view that Wilberforce had opposed a West Indian–sponsored motion for extending "due protection under the law" to enslaved laborers "out of sheer distrust the West Indian Assemblies could really be prevailed upon to do anything effective."[39] On the contrary, it was the enslaved whom Wilberforce distrusted. He and like-minded abolitionists clearly recognized that it was the arbitrary use of force that kept enslaved laborers under subjection. Wilberforce's solution was classic waffling: "You must conduct them to the situation, having first prepared them for it, and not bring the situation to them. To be under the protection of the laws was, in fact, to be a free man; and to invite slavery and freedom in one condition, was a vain attempt; they were in fact incompatible, and could never coalesce."[40] Translated into reality, this duplicity left the full burden of amelioration squarely on the enslaved. Even considering the irreconcilability of slavery and freedom, the bigger issue was that white dominion and private property were at stake. For these reasons abolitionists and colonists were at one in acknowledging that the power of the enslaver over the enslaved must not be eroded. It was this reality that shaped the parliamentary "resolutions" of 1797 on the role of the Crown in amelioration. Then Parliament had gone beyond the leadership of the Abolition Society and placed the authority to ameliorate the slave system under colonial legislators,[41] yet Parliament wished to limit its role to facilitator. The problem was definitely not one of charter, for colonial legislators were simply not considered by the select committee on the slave trade as proper subjects of their deliberations.[42] Clearly, the major consideration was that imperial legislation might deprive colonists of the prerogative of terror. Abolitionists such as Henry Brougham willingly conceded this position and leaned toward planter absolutism. Writing at the turn of the century, he declared, "The modifications of slavery established by law in favour of the negroes would, without rendering their situation much more tolerable, give them far greater opportunity to disturb the peace of the colony."[43] The real reason for his objection to the rule of law, however, was the demographic superiority of a people destined to pursue perpetual opposition to the whites.[44]

The danger from granting enslaved persons legal rights was avoided by willingly surrendering to colonials all rights of legislation concerning slavery. This deference was not an expression of confidence in colonial legislators but an expedient for colonial security. Parliamentarians knew of the sham reforms of colonial legislation. They were aware that even when reformed slave codes addressed the abuse of planters' power, colonial legislators persistently refused to include the right of enslaved persons to give evidence against enslavers in a court of law.[45] A *Times* correspondent expounded the dilemma in commenting on the 1788 Jamaican slave code: "These regulations to people unacquainted with the West Indies appear much in favour of the negroes; but though the situation of the legislators may have been good, they will in general be of no effect, for it is well known that the negroes cannot give evidence against white people, which may be right in their present state of debasement, wherein they are not taught the restraint of Christian principle to oaths."[46] In general the rejection of judicial evidence of enslaved persons was based on the principle that "the negro slave is not impressed with the sacred obligation of an oath."[47] This position was partly informed by the stereotype of the enslaved as compulsive liars and partly by the claim that they were not practicing Christians. During the debate on imperial amelioration Dr. Stephen Lushington, son of an East India Company director and member of the Anti-Slavery Society, maintained that there was no expectation of truthful testimony "where there was no conscientious conviction of the sin and danger of perjury."[48] Wilmot Horton, undersecretary of state for the colonies, extolled the corollary that an enslaved person's certification of fitness to take an oath was indicative of his advancement in civilization.[49] Interestingly, the origin of this dogma had nothing to do with Christianity or Western civilization. According to Michael Grant, it was more likely a Christian adaptation of Roman jurisprudence, which sanctioned the torture of slaves to qualify them to give evidence in court because they were otherwise incapable of telling the truth.[50] English jurist David Walker concurred that the judicial oath was not peculiar to Christianity and even predated it; he also agreed that the practice always contained a spiritual dimension. The oath was "an assertion or promise made in the belief that supernatural retribution will fall on the taker if he violates what he swears to do."[51] Interestingly, Edward Long acknowledged that enslaved elders and religious leaders used grave dirt to invoke the powers of the spirit world in dispensing their own justice. He concluded, "The dirt is a material ingredient in their solemn oaths."[52] This practice was common to Caribbean slavery. The grave dirt guaranteed "damnation and confusion to them who will be false" to their oath.[53]

Clearly, concerns of jurisprudence were only a pretext for denying enslaved persons the right to give evidence against the slavocracy. Reformed slave codes took no notice of Christianized Africans as different in law from their "pagan" counterparts. Indeed, the problem transcended theology. The ethos of colonial slavocracies was grounded not in religion but in gentlemanly honor and ethnocentrism. Honor and racism continued to determine the slavocracy's resistance to extend the oath to the enslaved. An enslaved person's belief in God, Christian or otherwise, was not sufficient to breach the honor system of white colonials or to upset the principle of white supremacy. Furthermore, enslavers' immunity from prosecution for wrongs against enslaved persons had a long history in European slavery.[54] Investing enslaved persons with the right to give evidence was arming them with the protection of law. This principle was diametrically opposed to proprietary absolutism as a tool of security. As Horton explained, however captivating the principle of admitting testimony of enslaved persons *quantum valeat,* "he must be aware how difficult it would be to reduce it to practice in a society where slaves impact the general value to property."[55]

This swing in favor of slave evidence by abolitionists was evident first in Buxton's motion for amelioration in 1823. Three months after his failed amelioration motion, the Anti-Slavery Society recognized that without the right of enslaved persons to give evidence in court, "many other provisions in their favour must be greatly diminished."[56] Brougham also went to the polar opposite on the question of evidence. Whereas in 1803 he felt that evidence of enslaved persons was "utterly inadmissible,"[57] in the 1820s he became an assiduous campaigner for the right of enslaved persons to give evidence in court, arguing there was no reason to refuse to admit that those "whose evidence was required, should not be left in the same situation as a witness in this country, where the court was to judge of the admissibility of testimony. In our courts, a Pagan, Mohometan, or a person of no religion at all . . . was taken, he was examined. It was not requisite that the person should believe in revealed religion; but if he were found, on preliminary examination, to be a person who admitted the existence of a God, and a future state, his evidence was straight forward admitted."[58]

Up to emancipation, however, the few colonies that surrendered to pressure from the imperial government to allow judicial evidence from enslaved persons did so under new security of certification by a licensed clergyman, and thus the honor system of the plantocracy remained inviolate. Ironically, even as Jamaican planters persisted in denigrating the value of testimony of enslaved persons, insurgents in the 1831–32 "Baptist War" were sworn to secrecy on the Bible as well as the Ashanti *okomfo* oath.[59] Yet members of the plantocracy correctly recognized that their power and authority as enslavers could only be preserved if they enjoyed immunity from the testimony of the enslaved class. Indeed, in Trinidad it was the right to testify against their enslavers that the enslaved exploited to bring the slave system close to collapse.

The Amelioration Order-in-Council

Although the Crown had an indisputable right to impose amelioration on Trinidad, it did not do so arbitrarily. The amelioration resolutions moved by Buxton in May 1823 launched his career as parliamentary successor to Wilberforce. Interestingly, Buxton was even more wedded to gradualism than his predecessor. Although proposing the extinction of slavery throughout the empire, he equivocated: "not, however, the rapid termination of that state— not the sudden emancipation of the negro, but . . . first fitting and qualifying the slave for the enjoyment of freedom." He projected amelioration as the beginning of the final phase of slavery yet reassured the British people, "We are far from meaning to attempt to cut down slavery in the full maturity of its vigour."[60] Uppermost in his mind was the perception of rebellion that had accompanied every attempt at colonial reform since 1787.

The major amelioration resolutions moved by Buxton were that the testimony of slaves be received *quantum valeat;* that the *onus probandi* must be on the claimant contesting free status; that manumissions be free of restraints and must accord with Spanish law; that no colonial governor, judge, or attorney general be the owner of enslaved persons; that marriage of enslaved persons be sanctioned and enforced; that religious instruction be provided for them, with Sunday a day of rest and worship; that there be a mandatory lapse of twenty-four hours in cases of punishments ordered by enslavers; and that all children born "after a certain day" be freed.[61] The proposal for free birth from the onset of amelioration was consistent with abolitionists' apprehension of sudden emancipation; as projected, it would not be until "twenty or thirty years' time all the young, the vigorous, and those rising into life, will be free."[62] Yet it was obvious that this projected freedom, divorced from the freedom of mothers, was a recipe for unregulated but compulsory indentureship. On the whole Buxton's speech, richly injected with sarcasm, was a brutal display of callousness, which offered no hope of real freedom within the foreseeable future for the existing generation of enslaved:

> To a nation steeped in iniquity, can less be said than this: "We do not ask that you should suffer punishment; we do not ask that you should undergo deep humiliation, we do not ask that you shall make reparation to those you have wronged; we do not even say, cease to enjoy those acts of criminality which you have begun; but take the full benefit and fruition of past and present injustice; complete what you have commenced; screw from your slave all that his bones and his muscles will yield you: only stop there; and when every slave now living shall have found repose in the grave, then let it be said, that the country is satiated with slavery, and has done with it forever." This, after all, is the main point. It secures, a distant indeed, but a certain extinction of slavery.[63]

The metropolitan government stage-managed the ensuing debate to placate the West India Interest with counterproposals; although founded in large measure on Buxton's resolutions, the government's motion avoided the threat of imperial intervention, but just as significantly, it avoided a commitment to compensation.[64] The outcome of this compromise was the Trinidad Order-in-Council of 1824, Britain's first slave code.

A few weeks after the resolutions the imperial government took the first steps to prepare the enslaved for significant changes while making every effort to disguise the metropolitan origins of the reforms. The Colonial Office also saw the need to prepare proprietors for these changes by way of a ministerial dispatch, accompanied by a copy of Buxton's resolutions and Canning's speech of the same date.[65] The dispatch also outlined the imperial government's policy on compensation. The Crown demanded immediate implementation of two measures: the prohibition of the whip in the field and the prohibition on flogging females.[66] Other reforms awaited the order-in-council, Britain's *code noir*.

Woodford mandated commandants of quarters to provide copies of the proposals to every estate owner or manager. The governor warned that he would admit no discussion on the two mandates but solicited comments on other measures, including suggestions for the "most lenient substitute" for female punishment.[67] Woodford strongly advised proprietors to embrace the unqualified advantages to be gained from a "cheerful concurrence . . . whereby this concession to the female slaves, will appear as the spontaneous goodwill of the owner."[68] In follow-up correspondence to commandants he outlined specific details of the pending order-in-council, among which was the intention of the imperial government to promote proselytization and subsidize the recruitment of adequate "Clergymen under Episcopal Control."[69]

During the early 1820s the island was divided into thirty-two quarters, including Port of Spain. The authority for the city was the Cabildo, a local administrative body of elected officials.[70] In charge of other quarters were commandants, responsible only to the governor. Only the wealthiest planters were appointed to this office. Each commandant was responsible for policing within his quarter. As *alcaldes,* commandants were magistrates and justices of the peace who administered summary justice; as justices of the peace, they were ex officio assistant protectors of slaves.[71] In every quarter the homes of commandants served as seats of informal assemblies. Subgroups of leading planters submitted their own opinions on the proposals, and these were appended to the commandant's reply.[72] Planters were mindful of the possible injury to their authority by placing their enslaved laborers under the trust of the Crown. Despite council resolutions to prohibit the printing of the parliamentary reforms, they were still "clandestinely printed" in the *Port of Spain Gazette.*[73] With this purported betrayal, the potential advantage from disguising the real authority behind the sudden benevolence was lost.

Most reforms, including the most vexatious and problematic to enforce, found favor with the planter class, including the legal testimony of enslaved persons, marriage, and the promotion of religious instruction. Planters' well-politicized benevolence tempered their opposition to the parliamentary proposals. Because they claimed to punish only the most deserving cases, it was expedient that they agree to the proposal to delay punishment for twenty-four hours. Generally, planters were not averse to withdrawing the whip from the field; they simply left it close by, in the driver's house.[74] The whip would continue to be the principal incentive to labor because industrial resistance was classified as "domestic offences" and punishable by flogging. There was considerable resentment over the prohibition on flogging females; planters hoped at least for the right to use a switch applied over the shoulders.[75] Woodford's shrewdness in canvassing planters' opinion throughout the island was a landmark in public relations. Commandants and other leading planters could freely remonstrate against the indiscretion of imperial authorities and contribute toward consensus. In no small way this dialogue helped to diffuse a potentially explosive situation, given a form of government with no constitutional means of obstructing the legislative prerogatives of the Crown.

The board of council debated the imperial government's proposals and planters' responses. The "female question" and the government's silence on compensation were the major highlights. On the latter subject Burnley's stance was the most pertinent. He argued that because compensation was not alluded to, it was obviously not intended.[76] He roundly condemned some planters' eagerness to comply without the guarantee of compensation as the act of cowards "who permit their fears to overpower their judgements."[77] Although he recognized their powerlessness under the system of Crown-colony government, he was not prepared to give his unqualified support to the reforms.

The imperial government's order of "an absolute prohibition to inflict the punishment of flogging [females] under any circumstances" was a radical departure from the traditional mode of managing enslaved females.[78] Yet it was obvious from the responses of the plantocracy and the board of council that the female question transcended slavery and extended into the realm of gender relations. The prohibition brought chauvinism decidedly under political fire. The council's debate legitimized the views of proprietors. Colonel Aretas Young submitted that "all corporal punishments are bad"; however, he considered enslaved women to be "as bad and worse than men requiring more temper and address to manage."[79] Thus, he sought the continued use of the cat-o'-nine tails. With similar chauvinistic airs the chief judge expressed his abhorrence of the use of the cart whip as an incentive to labor but also hastened to recommend the cat-o'nine tails.[80] More than any other councillor, Burnley confessed an undisguised abhorrence for the prohibition on whipping females: "The idea appears to me to be so monstrous and extraordinary."[81] He invoked two historical assumptions to justify his abhorrence. First, "Stripes and slavery are terms to be found in juxtaposition in every language whatever existed . . . one cannot exist without the other." Second, as regards the "natural" status of women, he argued, "The history of all past and a view of all present societies will I think convince us that the fixed and natural state of women is subordinate to and dependent upon the men in civilized communities."[82] Thus, it appeared to him that the amelioration experiment was attempting "to arrest an immutable law of nature."[83]

Woodford's attitude to women was no less chauvinistic. In subscribing to the right of male domination, he intended to include in his draft ordinance the popular demand for retention of the right to flog women, albeit in a "less severe and indecent mode." This proposal was utterly rejected by the Colonial Office. Horton confided to Woodford that Earl Bathurst was not prepared to sanction any type of "corrective punishment" against enslaved females not already sanctioned by law.[84] He charged that Woodford's proposition that planters could legally carry a switch was a misinterpretation of his dispatches on the issue. Horton explained, "The distinction between a switch and a whip is infinitely too undefined" not to create an abuse if one were to be permitted and the other prohibited.[85] Thus, he instructed Woodford to ensure that his draft ordinance carry the precise will of the government into full and practical effect.[86] Bathurst was also incensed over the latitude for remonstrance that Woodford had allowed his council. Clearly, the colonial secretary was not satisfied with the council's claim that their acceptance of the imperial measures was based on the condition that no further demands for amelioration were required of them.[87] Bathurst deemed such a presumption to be "founded on a principle inadmissible in the utmost degree."[88]

Governor Woodford drafted the amelioration order-in-council after canvassing the opinions of his council in the hope of softening the inevitable rupture between enslavers and enslaved. Such protocol accorded with Crown-colony governance but was also prompted by the startling confession of James Stephen Jr.: "My knowledge of the law of Spain is slight and superficial."[89] The Colonial Office was set on framing amelioration on Spanish law, and Stephen was their legal advisor. Woodford's draft ordinance, like Buxton's resolutions, hinged on Christianization and progressive manumission; Woodford, however, was much more radical than Buxton on the latter point. The governor realized that the manumission of children only, as Buxton proposed, could produce no useful advantages for them unless mothers were first emancipated. Thus, he proposed that the emancipation process begin with the manumission of women.[90] But Woodford was not prepared to compromise planters' property rights in prospective manumittants and insisted that the imperial government provide adequate compensation for every case. In the spirit of compromise the imperial government substituted Woodford's proposal for that of self-manumission without an enslaver's consent while totally disregarding state compensation.[91]

If the ethics of amelioration was proselytization, the engine of reform was the protector and guardian of slaves. Before 1824 the office of *Síndico Procurador* (Syndic Procurador General), or Protector of Slaves, was entrusted to some of the largest proprietors, despite a decree prohibiting the office-holder from having any direct vested interest in slavery.[92] Henry Fuller, the last incumbent before amelioration, had enlarged his holdings to two sugar estates, a cocoa estate, and over two hundred enslaved laborers.[93] The new amelioration experiment made this contradiction untenable. Under slavery's ancien régime the term *guardian* or *protector of slaves* was an oxymoron. This exposé emerged in a joint statement of "concerned planters" professing that enslavers had hardly ever disputed the functions of the guardian, "whilst he was understood to administer justice with an even hand, and to perform the office of judge and arbiter between Master and Slave; for he was supposed essentially and fairly to execute the proper duty of a guardian when he directed the punishment of a slave for misconduct."[94] Burnley was adamant that the guardian of slaves should be the guardian of property. The old guardianship was justified on the classic interpretation that the interest of the enslaved was the extended interest of the enslaver. Free colored advocate Jean-Baptiste Philippe concurred with Burnley but branded both protector and governor the "friends of slavery, not the slaves." Philippe exposed the web of contradictions in a stinging indictment against the system: "The 'Protector of Slaves' may, by possibility, at the same moment, unite in his own person the opposite characters of criminal and judge."[95] He accused protectors of encouraging dissension between enslavers and enslaved to justify visiting the offending estates as arbiter. Each visit warranted payment of a string of fees that went to the protector of slaves. The amelioration order-in-council reversed this tradition. The guardian was now the protector of the enslaved and must "act in such a manner as may be most conducive to the benefit and advantage of any such slave."[96] His official role was that of advocate functioning through the courts "as the Protector only of the slave."[97]

In the new dispensation the protector of slaves must not be the owner or proprietor of any plantation or the manager, overseer, agent, or attorney of a plantation or estate with an interest in slavery, not even in his wife's name.[98] Any deviation from these conditions would be interpreted as de facto abdication of office, followed by forfeiture of salary. In order to offset the disadvantages of having to forgo a lucrative source of income as well as to promote the integrity of the office, the salary of protector of slaves was pegged at six thousand dollars per annum local currency, two thousand dollars higher than the defunct procurador syndic–cum–guardian of slaves.[99] The same restrictions did not apply to commandants of quarters, who were all ex officio assistant protectors of slaves, thus largely maintaining the status quo ante the new British *code noir*. Within the context of gradualism this deference to conservatism made sense. Yet, because enslaved laborers identified commandants as governors of plantation tyranny, this compromise contributed to sustained opposition: many enslaved persons protesting ill treatment simply ignored the local assistants and complained directly to the protector, Henry Gloster.

Woodford handpicked Gloster for the post of protector of slaves. Strongly in the appointee's favor was his competence in Spanish, French, and the patois (creolized French and English) of the majority of the enslaved. At the time of his appointment to office, he was the solicitor general and *Fiscal* to the Royal *Audencia*. His father, Archibald Gloster, had a long and distinguished service as attorney general and chief justice in several West Indian colonies.[100] Unlike other Crown-colony protectors, he earned the distinction of transforming the enslaved into a quasi-subject. Toward the end of slavery Gloster reviewed his tenure as an extremely difficult and sensitive one in which the rule of law was as important to him as the confidence of the laboring and proprietary classes. His philosophy was "to give satisfaction over whom he was placed, to conciliate the Planters by exercising with temperance and moderation the extreme powers entrusted to him; and finally so as to execute the provisions of the Law."[101] He was also mindful that Colonial Office officials had a keen eye for failure to observe due process.[102]

Under the amelioration order-in-council an enslaved person no longer needed the proprietor's written permission for marriage; he could apply directly to the protector or the commandant of the quarter in which his fiancée resided (cl. 22). The protector or assistant was bound to issue a marriage license. Except for the mechanism of manumission, however, no regulation facilitated common residence, a major deterrent to marriage. The order-in-council also protected the "property" of enslaved persons by establishing a savings bank under the direct control and inspection of the protector (cl. 26). The bank accepted all kinds of currency, of which there were many in circulation, at 5 percent interest. Branches were immediately set up in nine quarters, mainly to preempt unnecessary absenteeism by depositors. To protect against illegal acquisitions, enslaved depositors could freely remit into their accounts a maximum of twenty dollars in any given week. Even if enslavers might have "good and sufficient cause" to object, the protector could order the bank's manager to receive the disputed amount (cl. 25–27). In 1828 Woodford extended the bank to "all industrious classes" of the colony, thus making it the first truly public bank in the British Caribbean, the forerunner, if not the prototype, of the Colonial Bank established in 1837.[103]

The British government's flirtation with Spanish law was evident in many provisions of the order-in-council. Based on the premise that material goods traditionally owned (peculium) by the enslaved had always been "free from the control or influence of their masters," the imperial government converted a revocable privilege into a legal, highly contentious right "to acquire, hold, and enjoy property" (cl. 24). In dismissing objections raised in Parliament that the right of enslaved persons to private property was a contradiction in law, the government affirmed that every enslaved person was competent to purchase, own, and dispose of unlimited amounts of lands, cattle, and any other kind of property "and to bring, maintain, prosecute, and defend any suit or action in any court of justice, for or in respect of such property, as fully and amply to all intents and purposes, as if he or she were of free condition" (cl. 24). Ironically, while paying homage to enslaved Africans' right to private property, the amelioration code upheld the right to human property as no less sacrosanct.

Despite the unprecedented enfranchisement that the amelioration order-in-council conceded to the enslaved, the code was fundamentally a declaration of enlightened proprietary paternalism. One of its outstanding omissions was its failure to define the "duties" of the enslaved or "obligations" of enslavers, yet the official Plantation Record Book explicitly detailed a range of offenses intended to keep the enslaved in check, from going to work in proper time to tending to provision grounds and maintaining proper conduct at prayers. The list covered every attitude and behavior deemed inimical to colonial property and the sociopolitical order.[104] Thus, the record book actually underscored the slavocracy's customary trivialization of the social life of the enslaved. It also provided a window to the overwhelming rights retained by proprietors, including the right to inflict severe punishment. Furthermore, the cart whip was still legal. Proprietors could still legally imprison their enslaved laborers in private plantation jails or subject them to the discomforts and humiliation of confinement in stocks; they also retained the sadistic right to humiliate enslaved women in public, sometimes with their heads shaved clean.[105] Key officials in the Colonial Office endorsed the subjection of women to shame and disgrace. They wished to eliminate the "indecent exposure" associated with flogging women but not to curb their punishment or put them on equal footing with their white counterparts.[106] The amelioration law was thus a compromise between men of property and power in Trinidad and Britain; it represented a balance between the concerns of planters and council, on the one hand, and those of the West India Interest, Parliament, and Crown, on the other; it also attempted to standardize enslaver-enslaved relations while seeking to moderate planters' tyranny in line with the bourgeois conscience of Protestant abolitionists. The new law was fraught with potential for litigation. Further reconcilement was in the interest of both enslavers and enslaved.

In spite of the fulminations of Colonial Office officials, the Trinidad order-in-council contained glaring contradictions on the contentious female question. On the one hand, the original order provided that "it shall not be lawful to correct or punish by flogging, or whipping, any female slave" (cl. 13); on the other hand, the proprietors' right to flog enslaved women was preserved in the legal distinction between administering "stripes" and "flogging or whipping." Indeed, clause 14 clearly permitted the use of stripes to punish "any female slave, or any male slave," outside the purview of protectors; furthermore, a proprietor was not obliged to record three or less stripes. Proprietors were not satisfied that their power of "correction" over young females should be equally restricted. They alleged that the whip was essential to the "education" and training of young females. They demanded quixotically: "How is the education which young females have hitherto received, how is the attention to moral duties and the ordinary decencies of life now to be enforced?"[107] In criticizing the amelioration code, the Cabildo cited the legal contradiction in the right to flog free women of color while abolishing the flogging of enslaved women.[108] A faction of the council led by Burnley rejected the code because many measures could provoke unnecessary litigation if neglected or misinterpreted.[109] The protestors claimed that the lengthy delays in determining matters by the Lords of Appeal in England were detrimental to the propertied class. What they did not say was that the slow pace of justice was also the best shelter to preserve illegal property in humans. Nonetheless, the question of delays was justified; a single case could take several years before being reviewed by the Privy Council.[110]

The Colonial Office considered all objections, observations, and queries. The replies justified the large number of concerns. One of the most threatening measures of the original code was the provision for forfeiture of enslaved laborers ill treated by enslavers. The Colonial Office assured planters that forfeiture would apply only to the most serious cases, to be determined after due process in English court.[111] In any case no private individual could benefit from forfeiture because the plaintiffs would become wards of the Crown.[112] The Colonial Office emphasized that enslaved persons could not legally work for hire on their free days, even for their own benefit. But the basic fabric of plantation culture remained inviolate: "domestics" and others needed for security of the state or their plantations were no longer entitled to labor exemption, and a major concession was made for crop time when the prohibition on Sunday labor was put into temporary abeyance.[113] In addition, planter paternalism and male ego received a booster with the restoration of the right to flog girls up to ten years old.[114]

The Colonial Office incorporated the amendments in a revised amelioration order-in-council dated January 1825.[115] New grievances and uncertainties marred the arrival of the revised code. Policy makers in the Colonial Office were not prepared, however, to entertain indefinitely the delaying tactics of disgruntled colonists. In March 1825 Bathurst sent out the final amendments, together with an ultimatum to commandants that the measures must be rigidly enforced.[116] After failing to get the necessary amendments to restore their full social power and guarantee customary productivity, planters placed an even greater emphasis on compensation, which they linked more obstinately to compliance with the order. The reticence of the imperial government on compensation did not reflect the spirit of the 1823 resolutions, but silence testified to Canning's astuteness in setting the trauma of general emancipation as far back as possible.

10

CONSTITUTIONAL MILITANCY

Justice on Trial

I
n accordance with the amelioration ordinance, legal battles between enslavers and enslaved were fought at three levels. Minor domestic offenses were decided by the protector or his assistants.[1] Complaints of serious infringements of the law, including capital offenses, were adjudicated in the criminal courts.[2] An intermediate jurisdiction was created by the proclamation of 23 June 1824. This amendment was expressly designed to satisfy proprietors' demand that enslaved laborers receive greater punishment than what was authorized under proprietary authority.[3] The amending ordinance widened the magisterial net over amelioration. In Port of Spain this new authority was vested in the *alcaldes ordinarios,* the *alcaldes de barrio,* and the chief of police. No change was made to rural jurisdiction. The protector of slaves also retained jurisdiction over the whole island.

The new *code noir* inadvertently preserved Britain's reputation as the most brutal slave system. The *Cédula Real* of 1789 reduced to twenty-five the maximum strokes permissible under an enslaver's authority; Picton's ordinance reverted to the Mosaic prescription of thirty-nine strokes. Curiously, the model amelioration ordinance empowered proprietors to inflict a maximum of forty stripes on male laborers or confine them to the public stocks, in addition to subjecting them to the humiliation of wearing a "distinguishing dress or mark."[4] Female laborers were subject to imprisonment in the royal jail with or without hard labor in the treadmill for a maximum of one month. The principle of returning enslaved persons to resident plantations for punishment commensurate with the nature of the accusation was incorporated in this tier of jurisdiction to eliminate malicious persecution of proprietors by the newly enfranchised laboring class. The ordinance also gave enslaved persons the right of appeal against their enslavers, a feature of Spanish slave laws. Of particular interest was the obligation of judicial officers to hear complaints of enslaved laborers ex parte, without regard to extenuation.[5] This condition altered considerably a measure that otherwise might have greatly modified the potential of the enslaved class to radicalize the amelioration experiment.

Judgments were summary in the three tiers of arbitration. Appeals were only allowed against decisions of the criminal courts but subject to the colony's constitution. To offset delays consistent with appeals from these jurisdictions to the Crown, the Colonial Office reviewed all serious cases even when no appeals or complaints were lodged. This practice imposed on the protector of slaves and the local courts an obligation to be guided by basic principles of British jurisprudence. In addition, it made justice cheap and accessible to the most unprivileged persons and expedited or preempted appeals to the Privy Council.[6]

The amelioration ordinance only tacitly acknowledged the right of the enslaved to complain against their enslavers. Nothing in the legislation provided a mechanism for pursuing this right without obstruction. Instead, the benefits of amelioration depended on the Spanish principle of external intervention. The protector of slaves was obliged to investigate every complaint and to rule only after summoning all parties concerned as well as all necessary material witnesses. In cases of alleged misdemeanors by proprietors the protector was bound to refer them to a "judicial authority," meaning, the criminal courts. Misdemeanors were offenses such as punishing an enslaved person for a second time within twenty-four hours, carrying a whip in the field, and willfully making false entries in the plantation record book. Free persons guilty of misdemeanors under the amelioration ordinance were liable to a fine not less than fifty pounds sterling or more than five hundred pounds, but the records show that fines were almost always far less than the legal minimum.

Although members of the enslaved class were not officially educated about their rights under the amelioration, they were determined to put the system to the test. Many proprietors were no better informed. Thus, both enslaved and enslavers, locked in a battle of opposing interests, defined their responses according to their cultural values and traditions. The enslaved's apparent reverence for Buxton and King George as "massa" was symbolic and significant; the adoption of these imperial icons demonstrated that no gratitude or loyalty was owed to plantation enslavers for specific relaxations of the terrors of slavery. So long as their enslavers chose to defy Buxton or the king, the enslaved were determined to define their own responses. For the most part enslaved persons explicitly rejected the missionary prescription that they must patiently bear their oppression with subservience; instead, they transformed a merely regulative measure into a tool of social revolt. Their engagement with the colony's authority structure was a culture clash, with Eshu (Esu) and Anansi defining the ethics of justice and providing the energy of perseverance. Eshu is the Yoruba deity known as the "Guardian of the Crossroads" but also "a divine trickster, a disguise artist, a mischief-maker, a rebel, a challenger of orthodoxy, a shape-shifter, and an enforcer deity."[7] A well-known Ewe-Fon equivalent is Legba, or Elegba. Anansi, the Ashanti trickster-hero, embodied the essence of other African trickster-heroes. The accumulated forces of negation of plantation slavery compelled enslaved Africans to rely on those aspects of their ancestral cultures that accommodated the circumvention of morality and ethics, without fear of spiritual retribution. African moral philosophy of a middle ground offered a psychosomatic resolution to ethical exigencies. On a regular basis enslaved persons had their enslavers summoned before the protectorate or the criminal courts to justify "punitive" or "corrective" actions. Often matters were already settled privately between the two parties, yet enslaved persons might surprise plantation authorities by having them summoned before the protectors for the same grievance. On several occasions the enslaved would then reluctantly concede the defendants' explanation. This "persecution," as planters called it, lasted to the end of slavery.[8] In such instances victory was in turning upside down the traditional enslaver-enslaved relations of authority.

The limited authority of the protectorate exacerbated the tensions between enslavers and enslaved. In cases in which protectors ordered confinement in stocks, the punishment was carried out on the estates under supervision of plantation authorities. Thus, magisterial arbitration did not save an enslaved person from the wrath of vengeful proprietors. Yet enslaved persons defiantly rejected the authority of enslavers; they protested against excessive workloads, claimed customary privileges as legal rights and zealously guarded their right to their free time. Their perception of threats and attempts to deprive them of customary rights elicited responses of defiance aptly described as positive action but officially recorded as refusing to work, insubordination, disobedience, not coming to work in proper time, or absconding, among others; at any given moment these actions were easily extended into a work stoppage or strike.[9] In short the enslaved transformed amelioration into a contestation between privileges and rights as the ethos of power relations between the proprietary class and the laboring class. In this contest women were no less visible than men.

The record book identified no gender-specific offenses, although there was a gender propensity to certain acts of resistance. Theft and violence, with some kind of weapon, were generally committed by men, whereas assaulting drivers and overseers was mostly a female reaction. In this regard women were often reacting to sexual slavery or to particular acts of unfair treatment meted out to them by drivers and overseers for being spurned. Charges of absconding and running away were recorded mostly against males. For obvious reasons men could survive better the hazards of long-distance travel through untamed forests or vagrancy in Port of Spain. Urban employment also favored male runaways. Notwithstanding these disparities, running away also ranked high among acts of resistance committed by women. By comparison, in the half-year ending 24 September 1828, this was the second, most frequently committed offense by males; among females it ranked fourth. Women were equally committed to "riotous conduct," "disobedience," and "neglect of duty."[10]

Field labor made some women muscular and even physically stronger than men, which disconcerted many proprietors and drivers and earned those women the enviable title "domestic boxers."[11] Such women were often contemptuous of the orders of overseers and managers; they laughed at their commands and intimidated them by hinting at violent retaliation.[12] Women also delighted in taunting plantation authorities with cynical and insolent remarks or obscene gestures when punished or threatened with punishment.[13]

Women's defiance of plantation authority peaked between the passage of the Emancipation Act and the onset of the apprenticeship system. Confinement was no deterrent to hardened rebels. Often the resort to stocks provoked them into greater cynicism. Some women in the old colonies were obliged to curtsy and thank the jumper after a severe flogging.[14] During the amelioration they cynically expressed their "gratitude" in order to taunt their oppressors. With "a very low curtsey" and "the most ironical smile of insolence," some responded to being put in bed stocks with "Thank you massa, much obliged for let me sit down softly."[15] Some were offered reprieve from the stocks on the promise of good behavior. This approach worked in some cases, but for women such as Maria del Rosario good behavior might mean giving up their weekends of urban pleasures, which they were not prepared to forsake, even with the certainty of being made to wear the collar on their return.[16]

Two critical aspects of control in the juridical framework for ameliora-tion were the right to give evidence on oath and the lodging of complaints with various judicial authorities. Both were intended to operate against the enslaved. In the first instance, under the original amelioration code, only a member of the clergy could certify an enslaved person's competence to take the oath.[17] The dominance of the "established" churches was a distinct disad-vantage to qualification. In other Crown colonies the situation was no differ-ent. At the end of 1826 one clergyman of the London Missionary Society in Berbice submitted 113 names of enslaved persons fit to give evidence in court; the minister of the Church of England claimed that it was "not in his power to furnish any."[18] This circumstance was no different from the traditional safeguards enjoyed by enslavers and sanctioned by the registration law of 1812. In the second instance, in order to lodge a complaint with the various arbitration authorities, enslaved laborers depended on a pass issued by plan-tation authorities, against whom the complaints were being made.

In 1826 Woodford issued a proclamation partially removing the legal arti-fice against sworn testimony, thus transforming one of the slavocracy's most effective securities into the most legally threatening provision for ameliora-tion.[19] Under the new proclamation the credibility of enslaved persons' testi-mony was subject to the same test as that of free persons. Enslaved laborers were still prohibited, however, from giving evidence in any matter in which proprietors were directly involved, and in capital cases no enslaved person could give evidence against whites. In reality proprietors were not protected by such proscriptions. By 1826 it had already become acceptable for enslaved persons to give evidence under oath. It was the trial judge, not the clergyman, who decided the competence of enslaved persons to give such evidence.[20] The likelihood of punishment for false or unsubstantiated accusations did not deter the enslaved from bringing defamatory charges against enslavers. Although some enslaved persons were returned to their plantations to be punished for unproven accusations, Henry Gloster and some other protec-tors yielded to leniency.[21] In every quarter enslaved litigants often bypassed commandants they perceived as obstacles to justice, preferring direct cor-respondence with Gloster in Port of Spain.[22]

The protector of slaves took keen interest in all matters before him, be-yond the legal obligations of office. Although Gloster might have harbored genuine notions of equity, he really operated a unique blend of liberal pa-ternalism and colonial elitism. Whenever proprietors were found guilty of misdemeanors, they were likely to go away with a warning or a very light fine. Planter Wells, for example, was found guilty of inflicting severe blows on his female laborer and her infant child; he was fined six pounds. Mr. Charade was found guilty of illegally cart whipping and scourging a male laborer, for which he was fined ten pounds. On the other hand, the same tribunal sentenced five enslaved persons from one to seven years' hard labor for "absconding"; in addition, they were given 80 to 150 stripes each. Two other enslaved persons were sentenced to ten years' hard labor for attempting to poison their enslaver.[23] Even with witnesses, an enslaver's denial was enough for a dismissal. The case of Manuel Basso is typical. Basso complained to the protector that his enslaver, Henry Coryat, gave him 30 lashes immediately following the complainant's return from seeing assistant protector Commandant Le Chevalier de Verteuil. The commandant had given Basso a letter of reprieve for a minor offense. Three eyewitnesses testified for Basso, including the enslaved person who had administered the flogging. Coryat countered that only 12 lashes were administered after the stipulated twenty-four hours. He produced a copy of his record book and quarterly returns to support his claim. He also produced two white witnesses, who, according to sworn testimony by every enslaved witness, were never on the scene of the alleged offense. Gloster dismissed the case and wrote to the chevalier: "The declaration of Mr. Coryat coupled with the statements made upon oath by Mr. [Don José María] Camino and the free Spaniard Raymundo Carera satisfy me, that the slaves you examined are not worthy of belief."[24]

Gloster's loyalty to the cult of property was another factor influencing his magisterial judgments. One critical area in which the defense of the enslaved and the defense of property came into sharp conflict was marronage. A case in point is Carlyle Pompey, a runaway of more than three years. The lawyers provided for his defense refused to offer any witnesses, and the protector himself claimed that he could make no defense. No plea of mitigation was made. The court sentenced Pompey to one hundred stripes in the marketplace and twelve-pound leg irons for twelve years.[25] Yet even for runaways there was some measure of protection in due process. A case in point is Thomas Barrow, who was accused of escaping from the royal jail. The attorney general led the prosecution but requested a postponement of the trial because of the absence of his key witness, Patrick Denohoe, the overseer of the chain gang. To the attorney general's astonishment the judge ruled, "The trial must proceed; Patrick Denohoe is fined the sum of Five Pounds sterling."[26] Barrow was found "not guilty."

Not surprisingly, the reforms most vexatious to the plantocracy were those concerning the office of protector of slaves. The zeal with which Gloster performed his role was particularly disheartening to the proprietary class, whose members branded him a traitor. Burnley was particularly resentful of Gloster's manumission of Judy Dinzy, who had invoked the recently proclaimed Consolidated Slave Act to claim her freedom.[27] He accused Gloster of being too strict in his interpretation of his oath of office, contending that strict justice demanded that Gloster be "the Protector also, of Slave owners."[28] He was even more aggrieved after Gloster severely castigated him as assistant protector for sentencing Judy Brush to fifteen days confinement and labor in the treadmill for improper conduct and disrespect toward an estate manager. Brush appealed the sentence, and even though the court concurred with the guilty verdict, she won a judgment for appraisal and eventual manumission.[29]

Burnley justified his inveterate opposition to amelioration on moral-ethical grounds. He was aware that the policy of reform pursued by the Colonial Office was not uniform among all Crown colonies and that Trinidad planters were the only imperial guinea pigs. Benjamin D'Urban, governor of Demerara, had modified the royal proscription on flogging to allow for its implementation in less than twenty-four hours of an alleged offense; he modified a provision to allow the delegation of the protector's role of attorney to an enslaved person; he also disavowed manumission because "Dutch law gives no such right whatever to a slave."[30] In spite of these loopholes, Bathurst was reluctant to invoke the authority of the Crown. He confided in D'Urban: "I am disposed not only to waive the exercise of this right, but even to forebear pressing upon the Court of Policy a strict and rigorous adherence to all the Provisions of the Trinidad Order, provided that in spirit and in substance their measures and the Trinidad Order are the same."[31] Bathurst validated his expedient on grounds of security: reforms originating with the planters outweighed by far those from imperial authorities. Burnley knew of Bathurst's letter to D'Urban and became even more recalcitrant about manumission and other reforms, for which he believed the imperial government ought to grant monetary compensation.[32]

The management of amelioration in other Crown colonies was also less liberal than in Trinidad. In Demerara the protector, Colonel Young, complained that the enslaved indulged in litigation "as a cloak for idleness." He believed that their complaints against their enslavers were criminal acts. In St. Lucia the governor claimed that there was no need for a protector because the planters were more like parents than masters.[33] Complaints by the Trinidad Council and planters against the protector were indicative of the success that enslaved persons had made in influencing the work of that office; moreover, complaints were indicative of the enslaved's triumph over the regulative pass system. As in every plantation colony, an enslaved person was compelled by law to have a pass beyond a defined perimeter of his or her plantation base. Failing this, he or she might be treated as a runaway. The issuing of such passes, however, was the prerogative of plantation authorities and became one of the bulwarks of proprietary paternalism.[34] Had the enslaved deferred to the cult of paternalism, proprietors might have retained control of litigation. Complaints of plantation management such as "neglect of duty" and "absconding, running away" were manifestations of civil disobedience and the breakdown of the pass system. During the amelioration period enslaved persons absconded mainly as individuals, but circumstances sometimes compelled action in concert.[35]

The amelioration code did not explain how the protector must exercise his judicial role, except to ensure the correctness of returns and to be an advocate to the enslaved. His responsibilities tied him down to his office in Port of Spain. The early inclination of the enslaved to appeal directly to the protector ensured that his office remained a tribunal for complaints that should have remained within a quarter. Burnley further claimed that Woodford's circular to commandants dated 21 August 1824 seemed to have given the green light to enslaved persons to visit the protector without enslavers' consent.[36] Once complaints were lodged, summonses followed, and citations were left with the town agents for delivery, but often several days or even weeks might elapse before a proprietor would know of a complaint against him.[37] In the meantime the litigants took leave of all authority, "amusing themselves in Port of Spain under the shade of the Trees in the Court Yard."[38]

The constitutional revolt of the enslaved in Trinidad does not feature in the historiography of resistance. Accordingly, Trinidad has been wrongly assumed to be a place of relative calm during the nineteenth century as against the uprisings in Barbados, Demerara, and Jamaica. Eugene Genovese aptly conveys the received view thus: "British power in the Caribbean had become overwhelming by the time of annexation, and the prospects for peaceful emancipation were steadily brightening. The slaves bided their time."[39] The facts defy this assumption. A new breed of runaways was created, motivated by the desire for revenge by judicial means. Many refused to return to their plantation bases, choosing to live in town. In the context of the time this ac-

tion might be considered an abuse of freedom. Despite the governor's proclamation of August 1824, the Cabildo authorized judicial floggings of protected
persons up to a maximum of twelve stripes. Even free blacks and coloreds—
as well as poor whites—were liable to imprisonment and fines for roaming
the streets at night.[40] Although it was well known by the authorities that Port
of Spain abounded with Maroons, the "black factor" had lost its significance
as a badge of slavery in Trinidad. The board of council was forced to concede that invoking police measures might exacerbate the problem, because
"free persons might be taken up on suspicion of being runaway Slaves, from
their not being in possession of any Document to show that they were free."[41]
Thus, the growing number of the free black and colored population was also
contributing to a breakdown of the essential principles and safeguards of
plantation slavery.

Summation and Verdict

By 1830 there was a sharp decline in the recorded number as well as the severity of punishments on estates. Even the largest estates recorded negligible
punishments compared with the first years of the experiment. This remained
true for 1831, one of the most traumatic years for amelioration. The trend
is borne out in the protector of slaves' reports for 1831 and 1832. A drop
in punishments, however, was not necessarily indicative of a proportionate
reduction in acts of resistance by the enslaved. More likely, it was a reaction
to the refusal of the imperial government to compensate proprietors for loss
of labor during the trial and imprisonment of enslaved persons or for the
considerable time lost in answering complaints lodged by the enslaved. To
proprietors arbitration was uneconomic; they preferred to surrender to the
new liberties of the enslaved, some of which constituted traditionally serious
offenses. Even so, Gloster presumed that striking an enslaved person out of
passion occurred more frequently than reported. He also understood that the
enslaved was less likely to tolerate such molestation. Thus, he recommended
the drafting of a "systematic code of domestic punishments," which he intended to follow up with a few exemplary prosecutions in order to bring an
end to these indignities against the enslaved.[42] The final revised amelioration
code of 1831 eventually reflected Gloster's concerns.

In 1830 the new amelioration order united the offices of registrar of slaves
and protector of slaves under Gloster.[43] The new code prohibited the protec-

tor and his assistants from functioning as magistrates. Instead, they were to function only as advocates of the enslaved. One of the delicate but necessary compromises was maintaining the right of assistant protectors to hold property in enslaved persons. Because of the inordinate delays in implementation, the 1830 order was superseded by the Amelioration Order-in-Council of November 1831, embodying all the new measures of the aborted code. In addition, the latest code threatened to usurp significantly the private authority of the plantation regime. Under clause 11 of the 1831 code the protector had the right "to enter into and upon any estate, plantation, hut, house," or other private domain to communicate with a laborer.[44] By giving parity to the testimony of enslaved persons for all purposes as of free persons (cl. 87), the new code ended the age-old juridical immunity of enslavers and whites in general. Clause 8 decreed that the protector must terminate all benefits with slaveholding, which of necessity extended to his wife. Yet the imperial government persisted in treating "domestic slaves" differently; thus, it was still legal for the protector to hire enslaved persons as domestics where no free candidate was available.

Even if the revised amelioration order-in-council of 1831 might have triggered Jamaica's Baptist War, it is not true that metropolitan abolitionism was driving Caribbean insurgency; rather, Caribbean insurgency was changing the politics of metropolitan abolitionism. Nevertheless, the emphasis on the contumacy of the plantocracy is misplaced. Rather, credit should be given to the constitutional resistors of Trinidad in forcing the hand of the Colonial Office to institute the draconian reforms of the revised code, thus sending a clear message to the Jamaican emancipators that the system of slavery could collapse with a final push. The Trinidad Board of Council had repeatedly appealed for reform of the protector's office. Concessions made by the Crown, however, tended to increase the distance between the protector and the proprietary class.

The 1831 amelioration ordinance recognized the economic consequences of brutality against females. It prohibited the punishment of women for offenses to which they were particularly prone but which were peculiar to pregnant women. They were no longer to be punished for alleged or actual indolence, disobedience, neglect of work, lateness in work, abusive language, violent demeanor, bad work, neglect of stock, and feigning sickness.[45] The code made special provisions for women "known to be in a state of pregnancy" (cl. 92). They, together with children under the age of fourteen years and elderly persons over sixty years old, were exempt from all-night work (cl. 94). Furthermore, an enslaved laborer was no longer obliged to give more than nine hours of productive labor per day (cl. 90 and 91). Provisions for food, clothing, and household conditions were elaborately detailed; to prevent fraud and mischief, the law demanded that all provisions "shall be sound and fit for consumption and of good merchantable quality" (cl. 88); similar precautions were made where land was allotted for provision grounds. Missionism was elevated to a new level: under clauses 100 and 101 all enslaved persons ten years of age and older could exercise their right to attend any Christian church or chapel within six miles of their residence; they had six hours to do so, between the hours of 5:00 a.m. and 7:00 p.m. every Sunday, Good Friday, and Christmas Day.

If the operation of amelioration in Trinidad was a failure, as most historians claim, it could not be blamed on the contumacy of the plantocracy. To do so is to misconstrue the real objectives of amelioration: improved security, improved productivity, and natural increase of the laboring class. The improvement in the condition of the enslaved was a means to these ends. As such, the failure of amelioration resulted from the too rapid disintegration of the conventional relations of slavery, a development that was undesired and unanticipated by the architects of amelioration. Only in increased productivity was amelioration redeemed.

The application of the order-in-council to Trinidad was not an indictment against the planter class. The first amelioration code was known to its framers to be defective in several respects. The challenges of both enslaved and enslavers exposed many more defects. Even though enslavers in Trinidad had not actually welcomed amelioration, the records are replete with evidence that many of the leading planters cooperated in various aspects of the experiment. After initial misgivings, the spirit of cooperation was evident in the accommodation of Methodist missions. It was also evident in many judgments of commandants, the protector of slaves, and the criminal courts; these judgments were reviewed by Colonial Office officials, who were increasingly critical of the colonial regime. Perhaps one of the most outstanding public examples of moderation by officialdom was the judgment in the trial of enslaved laborers from Carenage for allegedly plotting a revolt. The governor took preemptive action by having the regular troops and militia in readiness. The judge presiding over the preliminary inquiry found, however, that there was no ground for prosecution: the defendants had only been discussing the rumor of a revolt in Grenada.[46] The conduct of the case was a far cry from similar trials under Picton and Hislop. Earlier in the century torture had been used to wring "confessions" from the enslaved, who suffered the harshest punishments under the *Recopilación*.[47] Trinidad plantation society had demonstrated a certain receptivity to ongoing reforms. Both enslavers and enslaved received the stamp of official confidence: secretary of state for the colonies Lord Goderich felt that Trinidad held out the best prospect for acquiescence in the law.[48] Similarly, Governor Grant boasted that of all the sugar islands "in none of them could the slaves be more easily managed and reconciled to their work than here."[49] This was all good propaganda. The official validation implies that considerable adjustments had been made by both classes, resulting in an uneasy and fragile reconciliation that changed the face of slavery without destroying it. Perhaps the most convincing evidence of accommodation was in increased productivity. Whereas in 1809 productivity in sugar was 1,963 pounds per capita, in 1829 it had risen to a peak of 3,657 pounds.[50]

Contrary to the assessment of Goderich and Grant, the compromises that had doubled the output of sugar and avoided insurgency obviously did not really succeed in getting enslaved persons to acquiesce in slavery. The arrival of the 1831 order-in-council dramatized this reality. The receipt of the new code was set against the backdrop of emancipation of the "Colony Negroes."[51] This development added a sense of legitimacy to the outbreak of strikes, work stoppages, and other open acts of defiance that followed the receipt of the new order. From Palmiste and Plein Palais estates in the south to Cascade in the north, the enslaved rejected the new code as a betrayal of their anticipated freedom. They organized several strikes and work stoppages over unjust allocation of tasks, unsuitable provision grounds, and unjust punishments, all defined by the enslaved. On Palmiste the enslaved protested that they had consented to removal from Tortola on a promise of freedom after seven years but were still enslaved though ten years had since passed. At Plein Palais the strikers threatened the commandant with violence when he attempted to arbitrate. Enslaved laborers on Concord estate refused to assist in putting out a fire that threatened to destroy the property of its "humane owner." This state of "considerable discontent and insubordination" remained for several months in many quarters.[52] The wider range of rights granted to the enslaved fueled a greater range of demands, creating a very complex and politically dangerous situation. In particular enslaved women relentlessly brought suit to protect themselves from whippings, other physical assaults, and deprivations of basic needs; some brought suit as advocates for pregnant and sick friends.[53] These developments marked the climax of amelioration. The decade of constitutional resistance by the enslaved awakened the planter class to its fragility. The enslaved succeeded in radically undermining the cult of paternalism. They advanced the cause of justice far greater than their reformist "friends" in the imperial metropolis had hoped because true justice was reclaiming their humanity. This was the real spirit of their constitutional revolt.

Against the background of widespread discontent among the enslaved, the newly instituted Trinidad Council of Government debated amendments to the 1831 amelioration order-in-council.[54] Before the end of 1832 the "representatives of tax payers" in the council won the right to amend the royal order. One of their most serious grievances was the reduction of the workday to nine hours. The secretary of state for the colonies was unwilling to upset or forsake the status quo. Consequently, he conceded an extension to a twelve-hour day for workers involved in factory production and a ten-hour day for field gangs. He rescinded the provision, however, that rest periods be part of the workday.[55] On the council's part it conceded in principle the need for radical advancement in the material conditions of the enslaved. It agreed to pay wages as stipulated in the original code and to compensate the manufacturing gang by adding three and a half pounds of salt fish to its weekly allowance and five pounds of the same to engineers and boilermen.[56] For an extra three hours of compulsory factory labor during crop time, it agreed to pay an extra allowance of three pounds of fish per week.[57]

The legal reduction in compulsory labor did not affect economic production. Enslaved and planters alike had learned to exploit the loopholes in the laws and the deficiencies in the administrative machine necessary for their enforcement. One manager of several estates confessed, years later, that the nine-hour day "was never attended to very strictly, and by giving the slaves a small compensation, the owners had so much influence that they readily got a great deal more than the Order in Council allowed to be exacted from them."[58] The "small compensation" averaged five pennies per day, for which enslaved persons worked the customary eighteen hours.[59] This was a criminal confession. Gloster had issued a comprehensive schedule of wages in October 1824. Among the different categories skilled slaves were to be paid six shillings currency per diem for extra labor and field laborers four shillings per diem.[60]

The really significant victory for the plantocracy was not the amendments to the order-in-council but the passage of a local ordinance before the proposed amendments to the order were brought to the Council of Government for debate.[61] The ordinance of 12 May 1832 redefined "offences" and their associated punishments and took immediate effect. It introduced three significant changes. The first was economic: clauses 11 and 12 altered the enslaved's unlimited right to property granted under the 1824 order-in-council and imposed penalties for possession of, and trafficking in, export staples or even in "foods wares or merchandizes."[62] The second was political: clauses 20 and 26 through 29 addressed the deep-seated concern about the security of planters' property against the deliberate action or inaction of enslaved persons.[63] The third was administrative: the court for misdemeanors was decentralized and widened to include the entire membership of the council, the *Regidores* of the Cabildo, the *Alcaldes Ordinarios,* the *Corregidores* of Missions, and the chief of police.[64] For the purposes of the ordinance these officers qualified as "magistrates" and were vested with the same power as the protector of slaves and assistant protectors for summoning witnesses under the 1831 order-in-council.[65] All were enslavers, including the chief justice; the provision therefore violated the founding principles of the imperial amelioration experiment.

The widening of arbitration in enslaver-enslaved conflicts was intended to redress the grievances of enslavers over the inconvenience and time wasting in responding to summonses to attend hearings in Port of Spain. No longer would enslaved persons be sent back to their enslavers for punishment in misdemeanor cases; only magistrates were now empowered to punish for this class of offenses, but by giving up this authority, proprietors lost nothing.[66] Instead, they were saved from the contempt and cynicism of the enslaved when under "correctional punishment." The amendment also significantly increased the severity of whippings and confinement that enslaved persons would ordinarily have received from their enslavers.[67] Notwithstanding these draconian measures, the ordinance failed to curb the restless yearning of enslaved persons to subvert the authority of the slavocracy; indeed, they were encouraged by the high rate of success against this traditional authority. Although the penalties imposed on enslavers were merely fines and warnings against recurrences,[68] successful suits gave enslaved persons a ray of hope that perhaps freedom might work to their advantage. In an immeasurable way Gloster had contributed to the political stability of the colony at a most difficult time of its history.

The ordinance of May 1832 is instructive. First, contrary to the vexatious outcry of some proprietors, the economy was not about to collapse from the want of law that preserved the proprietors' authority and sought to secure their property. Second, the ordinance acknowledged the outstanding achievement of the enslaved class in defeating the system of planter paternalism in just one decade. The traditional honor of gentleman-planters was no longer inviolate. It was also an admission that planters' deployment of terror had lost its relevance in the management of the economy. They now needed to legislate for recognition of their authority, their peace of mind subject to the whims of the enslaved. The demographic consequence of the fall of the paternalistic system was seen in the retreat of paternalist proprietors to the safer environs of Port of Spain or in emigration, leaving their estates in the hands of managers.[69] The ordinance was a Pyrrhic victory nine years too late to salvage the social framework of slavery, which had broken down irretrievably in its fundamentals. The political response of the enslaved to Emancipation Day was a demonstration of this reality. By 1832 Trinidad had already evolved into the pseudo-landlord-serf relations that defined the apprenticeship system in its mature stage in the legislative colonies. Indeed, the basic principles and features of apprenticeship were mere refinements and elaborations of the amelioration in Trinidad. Notwithstanding these advancements, it was also evident that only violence could accelerate general emancipation.

11

BREAKING THE CHAINS

The Failure of Gradualism

By the 1820s it was evident that colonial reformers had to contend with a rapidly industrializing metropolitan economy, central to which was the need to transform the volatile labor system for optimum productivity and security. There was yet no urgency to suggest, however, that radical change was on the horizon. Even the intervention of the metropolis in amelioration was experimental, focused largely on the Crown colonies, and still gradualist. The swing to radical change was driven by metropolitan desperation to preempt the ever-widening paths of destruction from major insurgencies launched by the enslaved in the post-slave trade abolition era. Colonial reformers and metropolitan abolitionists had consistently promoted creolization as a panacea to insurgency. If this theory were valid, the region would have seen a drastic reduction in the number and scale of emancipationist revolts in the nineteenth century. Furthermore, if the hypothesis of subservience through Christianization were applied to enslaved Creoles, the revolutionary potential of this class ought to have dissipated completely or been drastically reduced. Instead, enslaved Creoles, especially the Christians among them, became the mainspring of insurgency against the slave system.

The theory of security in separating newly landed Africans according to ethnicity and language was another dangerous deception.[1] Ironically, assimilating new arrivals with Creoles and already seasoned native Africans ensured rapid transmission of a plantation lingua franca evident in the English Caribbean since the 1680s.[2] Furthermore, one must question the ability of most colonial buyers to distinguish African languages that they could not speak and which they treated with contumely. The proven clandestine networking of the enslaved is another feature of plantation slavery that defeated divide-and-dominate strategies. Secret meetings, such as those documented by Edward Long, were motivated by a desire for community with others sharing a common native language and culture. The shift in strategy from the mid-eighteenth century to achieve greater security through controlled importation of new captives, and then by general abolition, had also failed.

From the birth of the Abolition Society right down to 1831, abolitionists, whatever their religious convictions, had subscribed to the principle of caution on the question of slavery. This principle defined Buxton's anomalous proposals for amelioration in 1823. Notwithstanding the Anti-Slavery Society's conservative approach to reform, the apparent turnabout to emancipationism was unsettling to many, including one-time ardent abolitionist George Canning, who was greatly perplexed over Buxton's combination of emancipation and abolition of the slave trade as if they had always been a single issue. Canning reminded MPs, "In all former discussions, in all former votes against the slave trade, it cannot be surely forgotten, that the ulterior purpose of emancipation was studiously disclaimed."[3] He explained that while he did not interpret political support of abolition of the slave trade as a trade-off for the indefinite continuation of slavery, he would readily concede that "slavery, not willingly, but necessarily, was allowed to continue."[4] This was top-down social engineering of slavery, not freedom; it provided continuing fodder for violent, popular resistance by the enslaved. The plan incited the worse revolts in the British colonies, advancing the emancipation timetable by several decades. The preemptive Emancipation Act is the salutary legacy.

Christianized Creole leadership was the new phenomenon in emancipationist uprisings in the nineteenth century. Insurgent captains invariably occupied the highest status among the enslaved class.[5] They successfully syncretized Christianity with traditional African cosmology, preaching the gospel of equality, temporal freedom, and earthly bliss, thus creating a revolutionary creed contrary to the quietism of plantation missionism. A case in point was a black preacher in Demerara who overturned the Hamitic Curse and placed it squarely on the white man: "The fust man, Adam, was a black man; and when him son *Sugar Cain,* kill him brother *Sable,* him be quite afraid to show him face, and turn white wid fear—and ever since dat all the Pickky ninies of *Sugar Cain* are de white man."[6] Although enslaved Catholics in Trinidad were not privileged with influential positions of deacons and catechists, they nevertheless used the religion to shape a secularized theology of liberation. One well-known chant had a revolutionary refrain parodying the Eucharistic sacrament: "The bread that we eat is the white man's flesh, *San Domingo!* The blood that we drink is the white man's blood, *San Domingo!*"[7] Blood is a universal symbol of ultimate sacrifice, and blood rituals on the eve of revolts were common; they sanctified the projects about to be undertaken and expiated from divine punishment those who might engage in brutal acts out of necessity. The view that nineteenth-century insurgencies were reactions to metropolitan antislavery and that the 1831–32 Jamaican revolt in particular was premised on a misinterpretation of the 1831 order-in-council as statutory emancipation is misleading.[8] A rereading of the evidence clearly suggests a messianic impulse making for a Black Baptist–cum–myal crusade for liberty. The Jamaican Assembly's report revealed that rebel William Buchanan had told overseer William Anand that the insurrection was "not the work of man alone"; rather, it was "the work of the Lord." The belief in divine guidance is also evident in several testimonies, such as that of rebel Thomas Gordon, who informed Reverend John M'Intyre that "the word of God said that freedom belonged to them" and that emancipation "was the work God gave them to do—they must be ready for it."[9]

The Barbados "Bussa Rebellion" underscored the crisis of reform in the plantation system. Franklyn, a Creole principal in the rebellion, was solemnly baptized in the Anglican Church, a rare occurrence in Barbados.[10] Furthermore, the colony had the largest percentage of enslaved Creoles in the British Caribbean, yet the rebellion rivaled the scale of Tacky's War. The Bussa Rebellion involved as many as twenty thousand enslaved persons from at least seventy-five different plantations and one hundred other holdings of various classifications and inflicted some £170,000 sterling worth of damage on the colony.[11] The insurgency was the first signpost of revolutionary consciousness reinforced by Africanized Christian liberation theology. The second signpost was the Demerara uprising in 1823, when some thirty thousand laborers from sixty plantations confronted their enslavers and the governor with mixed demands for freedom and wages.[12] To preempt a renewal of the war, eight companies of imperial troops arrived in 1824, garrisoned in strategically located barracks.[13] The Jamaica Baptist War of 1831–32 was the third signpost. The scale of this uprising was the most frightening, involving as many as sixty thousand enslaved laborers from over two hundred estates.[14] The war resulted in damage to property estimated at roughly over £1.5 million in the county of Cornwall alone, in addition to nearly £162,000 for its suppression, excluding unqualified sums paid to Maroons to hunt down insurgents who refused to surrender.[15]

The impatience of the enslaved class for statutory freedom was matched by the impatience of metropolitan "Ultra Emancipationists" for the equalization of East Indian sugar duties.[16] Missionary societies were also alarmed that their enslaved converts had been reshaping Christianity to suit their own political agenda. This unwelcome development, together with the growing hostility of the plantocracy toward sectarianism, drove a number of missionary stalwarts into open alliance with the immediatists within the Anti-Slavery Society.[17] No doubt, the missionary leadership had become aware that the best means of consolidating their foothold in the West Indies was through statutory emancipation; with such a feat they might win back enslaved converts who had already vested confidence in their own black pastors. Should the enslaved class emancipate itself, the cause of Protestant missionism in the West Indies might be jeopardized and, with it, social control of post-emancipation society.

By 1830 it had become manifest to those with their pulse on the colonies that political stability rested on the continued belief of the enslaved that "King George" would give them their freedom and that the imperial authorities would not allow the plantocracy to frustrate its operation. This attitude toward interventionist imperial legislation was evident since 1816.[18] Although by no means the cause, the condemnation of slavery by metropolitans and their declaration of universal liberty certainly legitimized the struggle for emancipation by the enslaved class. It was also becoming increasingly evident to abolitionists that piecemeal amelioration was a dangerous gamble. Methodists took the lead in change appeal. At their 1830 conference in Leeds they issued a definitive call for each candidate in the national elections "to unequivocally pledge himself to vote for the speedy & *total abolition* of *colonial slavery*."[19] This was civil society. Members of Parliament made no move toward emancipation until the first reports of the Baptist War.

Trumped by the Methodists, the Anti-Slavery Society galvanized into the primary political force in England, increasingly convinced of the determination of the enslaved class for self-liberation. The first reaction resulted in the formation of the Agency Committee, a pressure group within the Anti-Slavery Society. Among their major financiers were Cropper and Joseph Sturge, a Birmingham corn merchant. Impatient for results, the committee commissioned five agents to spread antislavery propaganda throughout Britain.[20] Yet the committee scored its earliest victory against the defenders of gradualism within the society itself. As a consequence, the society embraced the new radical position that the enslaved class was ready for emancipation, a view it began to sell to the nation in the spring of 1831. It now assured that "no risk to the safety of the white inhabitants could arise; on the contrary we verily believe, that the continuance of slavery rendered desolation and bloodshed much more probable; and that if the country does not repent of the sin of slavery and cast it from her, it may by the just retribution of Providence, terminate in a convulsion destructive alike of life and property."[21] This was not a new discovery but certainly a radical reworking of eschatological retribution. When the slave trade was believed to be the primary source of insurgency, the standard justification for excluding emancipation from abolition of the trade was the fear that sudden emancipation would unleash catastrophic violence. The ferocity of revolts in the post-abolition period compelled a belated acknowledgment that the real cause of insurgency was slavery itself. As Stephen Sr. succinctly stated, "It is in vain that experience has universally attested to the contrary, by showing that enfranchisement, when introduced by the arm of the law, has everywhere been safe, and disastrous only when obtained by insurgent violence."[22] Consequently, the society vigorously embraced its revised eschatology and made emancipation the primary electoral issue. Like medieval Christians, abolitionists saw the hand of God in an impending emancipationist war, with loss of life and property similar to the great reckoning in Haiti. Notwithstanding the new reality, the society was hardpressed to reach consensus on philanthropic sentiment alone, as is evident from entries in its diary of events. In December 1828 a branch of the Lady Anti-Slavery Society presented the parent society with a "Plan for Early Well Ordered Negro Emancipation"; it was rejected. In February 1829 the chairman of the finance committee proposed that the society introduce a resolution in Parliament declaring all enslaved children free from 1 January 1830. This idea was rejected as "inexpedient" until Brougham's proposed motion on slave evidence was ascertained. The following month the society tabled a letter from Cropper recommending "the total extinction of slavery . . . in the period of thirty years." In April 1830 another proposal was made for the society to bring a bill to Parliament declaring all enslaved children free from 1 January 1831 but merely as a strategy "to prevent the further extension of slavery" until the legislative colonies adopt the 1823 amelioration resolutions.[23]

The Jamaica Baptist War of 1831 underpinned the radical shift to intervention and emancipation by the Agency Committee. There was strong apprehension that the war was only the spark of a major conflagration that would soon engulf all of the colonies. Indeed, rebel Linton, under sentence of death, maintained loyalty to his military oath, thus protecting uncaught rebels. To the 1832 Jamaican Assembly inquiry he acclaimed, "There are many people concerned in this business, but I will not speak of the chief heads, excepting Gardiner and Sharpe," who were already in custody. Nevertheless, he warned ominously, if statutory freedom did not come, "in about three to four years the negroes will break out again."[24] This scenario had a peculiar continuity with the planned uprising in 1815: while on his way to the gallows, the principal rebel declared that enough of his Igbo countrymen remained at large to prosecute the war for emancipation.[25] Instinctively coming to terms with such resoluteness, the first report of the Anti-Slavery Society on the latest uprising showed the irrelevance of preemptive amelioration. Consequently, the society moved one of its most poignant resolutions: "We think that nothing ought to be proposed to Parliament by Mr. Buxton or any other friend of the slave not acting in the name and by the authority of His Majesty's Government, short of immediate and General abolition of slavery in all the British Colonies by direct Parliamentary enactment . . . The dangers of immediate emancipation are all imaginary . . . We do not believe that in the total rejection of the claims of justice and humanity there will be greater safety. But if there were, it is only in such measures as Government should support with all its power."[26] The expression of confidence in the safety of general emancipation was politically expedient, or at best an act of self-deception, as events leading up to the passage of the Emancipation Act revealed.

The Agency Committee brought a new businesslike approach to the Anti-Slavery Society. In July 1832 the subcommittee declared its independence from the London Society and assumed a new name, the Agency Anti-Slavery Committee.[27] By this time the parent body also eschewed gradualism, and thus amelioration, because the writing was on the wall for all to read and desperation the order of the day. The radicalization of the society alienated its parliamentary leader. Reports of events in Jamaica and the rest of the West Indies added fuel to the political agenda of the Agency Committee. It smelled the death of slavery and the birth of new opportunities for East India sugar and free trade. Decisively outfoxed, Buxton wrote to his son condemning the hijacking of the society by the disciples of laissez-faire: "I cannot but feel myself the representative of a Body who cannot speak for themselves and for whom I must act without other guide than my own conscience."[28]

The leadership of the abolitionist lobby had long convinced itself that a military option to quell regional revolts or prevent secession was too costly and inevitably futile, hence the resort to diplomacy. Central to this new strategy was the dangling of emancipation before the enslaved and compensation before the planters. The tone of the explanatory text was desperate yet sober: "Unless immediate measures are taken for the entire removal of this great national crime, *the committee are of the opinion* that the mutual hostility now existing between the slave and the slave holder will lead to such a termination of the system as will involve the oppressor & the oppressed in one common calamity."[29]

Buxton was at one with the new mood. In another letter to his son he predicted, "*One* power of emancipating in one way or another is fast drawing to a close. I mean that they [the enslaved] will take the work into their own hands."[30] This warning certainly recalled the Haitian cataclysm; thus, he publicly berated his fellow parliamentarians, "The people of England would not support this loss of resources to crush the inalienable rights of mankind."[31] Yet he did not throw caution to the wind. In opening the debate on amelioration, Buxton had reminded Parliament of Pitt's earlier warning "'that it was impossible to increase the happiness, or enlarge the freedom of the negro, without in equal degree, adding to the security of the colonies, and of their inhabitants.'"[32] Ten years on, with emancipation on his doorstep, he was equally apprehensive that sudden emancipation without special security measures was a recipe for disaster. Thus, he advanced a landmark remedy: "If the emancipation of the Slaves were in my power, I could not dare to accomplish it without previous Police Regulations."[33] Without such contingencies he would not pilot a bill for immediate emancipation; he was convinced that if discharged improperly, statutory emancipation could unleash as much bloodletting as an emancipation war itself.

Notwithstanding Buxton's avowal, on the eve of the parliamentary debate on emancipation, the society approved a resolution "that slaves of the British Colonies have an undoubted and indefeasible right to their freedom, without delay and without condition."[34] The resolution supported the granting of "fair measures of relief" to planters, as Parliament might deem appropriate.[35] Unconditional emancipation, however, had a very short reign. Claiming to act on the suggestion of a friend, Buxton proposed a personal amendment to the resolution to take to Parliament: "That it is the duty of this House to take measures for effecting the entire and immediate abolition of Slavery in the British Dominions, with the least delay which will admit of due deliberation in framing such laws as may be necessary for the maintenance of order amongst the liberated Negroes, and for the promoting of industry."[36] The amendment shows clearly that Buxton's emphasis was not freedom but control. Many historians have grossly downplayed the politico-economic realities of emancipation. Indicative of this thinking is William Green: "In the transition from slave labour to free, the anti-slavery movement gave priority to freedom, not to production."[37] Yet while order and industry were imperatives of progress for any society, Buxton's proposals for conditional emancipation were obviously dictated by unrests in the colonies, probable regional civil wars, and the irreconcilable distrust and fear of Africans.

The resolution exonerated enslavers, but the implications were ominous for the soon-to-be-emancipated. The enabling laws to govern postslavery society would be framed by the very plantocrats—even in the Crown colonies—who had previously been condemned as "irresponsible."[38] Nothing in the resolution hinted at reforming colonial constitutions to allow for some degree of equity for the enslaved. *Order* and *industry* were watchwords of a ruling class imposed on a laboring population. Buxton clearly determined that emancipation should be in the interest of empire.

At Last! Emancipation?

The Emancipation Act dispelled completely any lingering doubt there might be that the problem of security was the main concern of abolitionists and the imperial government. For those who understood freedom to mean the right to own property, especially land, to have control of one's time, and to pursue one's economic interest, including the right to be adequately remunerated for one's labor, the Emancipation Act was a masterpiece of deception. The act was little more than the imposition of a political settlement to ensure the peaceful and smooth transition from one form of control to another.[39]

The two principal measures of the act were the granting of twenty million pounds sterling as partial compensation to legal claimants to property in the enslaved and the imposition of a four- to six-year apprenticeship. William Green echoes the popular myth that "members of Parliament were shocked by their extravagance," to which he adds, "So was the Colonial Office."[40] These assertions are baseless; there was no generosity in compensation. Parliamentary amelioration in 1823 was premised on the guarantee of "the safety of the Colonies, and a due regard to the rights of those whose properties were implicated."[41] Successive secretaries of state for the colonies and their subordinates upheld this position. Furthermore, in light of the centrality of private property in British law and jurisprudence, a loan to proprietors and entrepreneurs dependent on slave labor could not be considered "fair and equitable compensation."[42] Indeed, compensation definitely included apprenticeship, calculated at roughly fifteen million pounds.[43] Both forms of compensation were crucial to the security of the colonies. The cooperation of the plantocracy could not be guaranteed without compensation and strict police measures; alternately, the enslaved would surely rebel against colonial resistance to statutory emancipation. In reality twenty million pounds was a sound investment: it was not the price of freedom; rather, it was the price of retaining sovereignty over the colonies and control over the colonial economy.

The allocation of metropolitan-based stipendiary magistrates was indicative of the imperial government's intention to supersede the authority of colonial judicatures. A maximum of one hundred magistrates was promised, to be paid an annual stipend of three hundred pounds sterling from the imperial treasury.[44] Establishing a body of magistrates with no prior connection to slavery was, however, a red herring. No provision was made for notaries to assist them, nor was there any commitment by the Crown that the judicial actions of these magistrates would be free of litigation.[45]

Of the six metropolitan-based magistrates originally assigned to Trinidad, only two arrived in time for Emancipation Day. Yet as in almost all other colonies, the Trinidad government had made contingency plans, creating a corps of salaried "special magistrates" in the Trinidad draft Apprenticeship Act.[46] One official at the Colonial Office warned that personal interest or bias must not enter the making of appointments.[47] This caution, however, had no meaning where men of respect and authority were invariably members of the proprietary class and thus owners of human property. Accordingly, the governor's selection of "specials" showed complete disdain for the advice of the Colonial Office.[48] The problem was compounded by the procrastination of the imperial government. With less than two weeks to go before Emancipation Day and the nonarrival of the Crown magistrates, the Trinidad council passed a unanimous motion calling for superintending special justices to be sent to newly established police settlements to take charge of preparations for emancipation.[49] Altogether the council made ninety-nine appointments.[50]

The reaction of the enslaved class to the 1831 order-in-council exposed the vulnerability of Trinidad planters. From that time the planters were acutely aware that their safety and future depended on their successful response to emancipation. In order to be armed legislatively, a delegation of the board of council had secured from governor George Hill the continuance of the ordinance of 12 May 1832. The group confessed its fear of the "great evils" that might result from changing the regulations for the government of the enslaved in such a short space of time.[51] The ordinance had been one of the most salutary compromises to the proprietary class since the launch of registration. Its extension into the apprenticeship, together with new police measures, was a preemptive strategy to neutralize militant protests against the limited rights of the apprenticeship.[52]

The establishment of effective police forces had been a precondition of Buxton's support for statutory emancipation. Yet the proprietary class did not need to be goaded by the Colonial Office to prepare its own security. In May 1834 the Trinidad government divided the island into nine police districts, or settlements, excluding Port of Spain, which was constituted a special district.[53] The police ordinance called for the establishment of a house of correction furnished with a treadmill as well as a penal gang within each police settlement.[54] The new special magistracy, created by the Emancipation Act, was closely linked to the police. Indeed, the administrative arrangement was also referred to as "judicial districts." The chief special magistrate was obligated to make routine visits to all police stations in order to inspect police books, houses of correction, and the penal gangs.[55] The new police legislation was "converting for the first time, civil matters into criminal offences"; it was also pressing against the free population with many harsh and severe enactments hitherto unknown to the island's judicature.[56]

Less than two months before Emancipation Day, the police stations had not yet materialized. Fearing that the short interval was the calm before the storm, the council urgently passed a resolution in June 1834 stating, "It is imperatively necessary that immediate measures should be adopted for providing a Police force in the several divisions and districts into which the Colony may be divided so that the same may be made effective and ready to enter on the discharge of their duties on or before the 1st of August next."[57] The new police force consisted of ninety privates and ten sergeants.[58] The loyalty of the disbanded West India Regiment, preserved by segregation, bribes of land grants, and special privileges, was once again the mainstay of internal security. Privates or constables were recruited from the villages of demobilized black soldiers and paid up to two shillings and two pennies, or fifty pennies, sterling per day.[59] The sergeants were "proper persons" from the higher classes and paid as much as four shillings and four pennies, or one hundred pennies, sterling per day.[60] All members were to be armed and "organized and in readiness to aid the magistrates in the execution of their duty."[61]

Governor Hill resorted to diplomacy to preempt militant protestations. He went personally to various estates in the southwestern coast to explain the Emancipation Act to the enslaved population as it might affect their situation after 1 August 1834. This area was the heart of the plantation economy; Hill's move was therefore strategic and tactical. Should he succeed in appeasing enslaved laborers there, it might be easier to save the colony from anticipated unrest and bloodshed. During Hill's visit he received clear signals of "extreme discontent," finding it impossible to make the enslaved accept that there was a difference between slavery and apprenticeship. Hill failed to convince them that "King George" would abolish slavery but compel them to labor under the same conditions for six more years.[62] They rejected the platitudes of the governor, whom they classed as an "old rogue" who had schemed up the apprenticeship idea with their thievish masters.[63] Considering the life expectancy of enslaved persons, thousands of them must have feared that they would not survive the apprenticeship to enjoy unconditional liberty. There is a strong likelihood that the twelve-year apprenticeship plan originally proposed by colonial secretary Edward Stanley was designed expressly to raise up a new generation of Creole laborers: those children under six years of age who were set free immediately, and the class of older children who were, more likely than not, born in the colonies.[64]

The alarm bell had been sounded and not without reason. The enslaved worked normally up to the last day of July. Throughout the night, however, thousands began converging on the capital like multiple tributaries into a single confluence.[65] From every quarter they came with one intention: to declare their freedom to the governor. The solemnity and trauma of this march can only be imagined. It was an emphatic statement-in-action to all ideologues, priests, philosophers, and charlatans who had conspired to promote the myth of the African preference for servility over liberty. The moment was a dramatic expression of Hegel's philosophy of revolutionary freedom: "The moment of revolution comes when the slave recognizes that his or her *primary identity* lies with the other slaves and as a result withdraws both labour and recognition."[66] The drama was underscored by the powerlessness of enslavers against this concert of people power.

The members of the enslaved class of Trinidad were no less law-abiding than their counterparts in other colonies.[67] On Emancipation Day, however, they suspended praises to God until their enslavers renounced all proprietary rights in them. They were adamant that they required no apprenticeship because they already knew their business perfectly. Similar arguments were heard all over the island.[68] These demands indicated that the revolt against apprenticeship was not equally against the state or plantation labor but, rather, against a regime triumphantly proclaiming freedom while requiring them to acquiesce to continuing enslavement. In the early postslavery period Anglophone freedmen crisscrossed the region seeking employment in the sugar industry.

The protestors interpreted the governor's declaration of apprenticeship as a plot to circumvent the will of the king, but to the very last they relied only on nonviolence to secure their hard-earned freedom. The entire episode was a classic demonstration of civil disobedience, a full century before Mahatma Gandhi's articulation of the ideology of protest, wrongly ascribed as a unique product of Hindu philosophy. Despite the deep feelings of betrayal, the resisters were unarmed. In reporting the event, the *Port of Spain Gazette* unconsciously paid glowing tribute to this African philosophy of nonviolence, deservedly a great political legacy: "Not one cutlass, or even beanstalk, was to be seen amongst them; not a single individual was intoxicated, nor was one single act of either personal violence or robbery heard of; they had been instructed and well trained in the most effectual mode of embarrassing a Government, especially one so weak and irresolute as the Government of this Colony has shown itself."[69] There had been numerous other displays of civil disobedience and strikes in many colonies since the beginning of the century. Although violence was never intended, such contempt by a laboring class is always interpreted as a declaration of war by the economic and political elites, and violence is never far away, often instigated by the elites themselves. This was the experience of Barbados in 1816, Demerara in 1823, and Jamaica in 1831.

By rejecting worship and religious platitude on 1 August 1834, the enslaved class of Trinidad was also rejecting the hypocrisy of the Anti-Slavery Society while exposing the treachery of its leadership. In 1823 the society had won the hearts of the enslaved with its unequivocal rejection of the use of slave labor to repay the debt that Britain owed to the planters: "It would be repugnant to every idea of equity, if we were to discharge any debt we may owe to the Colonists, not from our own resources, but with the toil and sweat of our African brethren."[70] Yet in 1833 Buxton supported the apprenticeship, through which proprietors exacted a legal minimum of forty and a half hours per week of "toil and sweat" from their enslaved brethren. His compliance was secured after Stanley publicly avowed that "the plan of apprenticeships formed part of the payment which it was intended that the proprietor should receive."[71]

The governor's diplomacy saved the island from a repetition of the episode of bloodshed and destruction that had sent shockwaves throughout Jamaica in 1831–32. Similar visits by Governor St. Leger Hill of St. Lucia were accompanied by explicit threats from him.[72] Alarmed "Inhabitants" of Trinidad begged their governor to declare martial law.[73] The council demanded that the governor apply to the commander of the Royal Navy in Barbados for a warship and two hundred men.[74] Even while facing the abuses of indignant "apprentices," the governor stayed his hand, preferring not to be driven to such an extreme, except "by the most absolute necessity."[75] Assisted by his two newly arrived special magistrates, Governor Hill (Trinidad) remonstrated with the rebels.[76] The entire day was spent in futile negotiations. At nightfall, however, the "most prominent characters" were targeted for preemptive arrests and imprisonment.[77]

After a quiet night the rebels reassembled, with reinforcements from a steady stream of new arrivals.[78] Seventeen of those arrested were sentenced to stripes and hard labor by the Crown-appointed specials.[79] As they were being escorted to prison by the cavalry, the crowd followed, encouraging them "not to mind their punishment, and avowing their own determination to submit not only to punishment, but to death itself, rather than return to work."[80] Special magistrate Captain Hay read the Riot Act to the protestors.[81] Nevertheless, it was another day of standoff, followed by another quiet night. Yet the governor insisted that "under no circumstances that presented themselves at present would he declare martial law."[82]

On the fourth day the militia was ordered to clear the streets.[83] Arrests were followed by quick summary trials by the specials. Those arrested were whipped in the public square; twenty-three apprentices received fifteen to thirty-nine stripes each.[84] Only then did the dispersals begin. If we accept the account by the *Port of Spain Gazette*, women's courage held longer than men's. An eyewitness to the retreat testified, "The mob fled and separated but then individuals, principally women, collected in little knots and still resolutely expressed their determination not to submit."[85] Unfortunately for them, the men had decided—like soldiers on the frontline—that retreat against overwhelming odds was no disgrace.

As expected, the month of August witnessed the greatest number of punishments inflicted on apprentices, with 301 persons flogged under judicial authority.[86] When compared with the close of the amelioration period, this was exceptionally high. For the six months ending 31 December 1833, 825 floggings were recorded;[87] this number represented a monthly average of slightly less than 121. Between 1 September and 31 December 1834 a total of 259 persons were flogged, representing a monthly average of almost 65;[88] this reduction reflected the rapid return of "masters" and "servants" to the battle of wits that characterized the period of amelioration.

The emancipation revolt achieved conditions of work and treatment more favorable than had been prescribed by legislation. Apprentices successfully fought against extending task work beyond 10:00 a.m., after which they were free to do as they pleased, within the limits of the law.[89] Protests were raised against the practice of imposing Saturday work as punishment for not completing an average of seven and a half hours on previous days during crop time.[90] In Cedros apprentices won contracts for a five-day work week.[91] For working Saturdays during crop time they were paid wages. Additionally, the free children of apprentices were to be maintained at the proprietors' expense.[92] Crop time 1835 was the true test of the success of those compromises. Most planters did not experience a labor shortage. Governor Hill reported that only on a few estates was there an absolute refusal by apprentices to "work beyond the Parliamentary Hours."[93]

Deceptions of Statutory Emancipation

Beyond the immediate social environment of the plantation, more sinister moves—essentially legislative and institutional—were on course to nullify the hard-won, quasi-emancipation of the enslaved. Since 1831 Trinidad legislation had made significant advances toward British juridical culture, yet its judicial administration remained highly oligarchic. During the apprenticeship crime and punishment continued to be defined according to status, free and bonded; the colonial elites persisted in framing legislation to maintain the rigid divisions between employer and laborer in postslavery "society."[94]

The legislative reconstitution of colonial society had begun with the amelioration laws. It stood to reason that the process of social engineering would be followed by a revolution in legislation to dismantle the structures of slavery and lay the foundation of a free society based on the rule of law. The Anti-Slavery Society had come to recognize what had been the crux of James Stephen's argument for the remodeling of colonial society since the turn of the century—that colonists' control of legislation was bound to make a mockery of emancipation. To preempt this situation, the society appealed to the imperial government to undertake "the final supervision of all the colonial laws affecting the condition of the coloured races."[95] Reformers had excessive faith in the power of legislation; even if "all future legislation" reflected the "just and equal principles of government,"[96] there was no guarantee of justice because the art of governing was of oligarchic design.

One of the earliest strategic developments was a postslavery immigration plan; another was the effective control of access to cultivable land. The dual policy on immigration and land grants of the early 1800s was not lost in the new aggressive immigration schemes. With the imminence of a wage labor system, immigration was a strategy to reduce the high price of labor. The preferred laborers were still Africans but with a bias toward "liberated Africans" and Creoles from the old colonies. This movement of a working-class population from the old colonies was expected to include "superior" Europeans as yeomen farmers specializing in new crops such as nutmeg.[97] In order to impact wages, however, coercive measures had to be applied to the former enslaved class.

Land control and immigration exacerbated the disenfranchisement of the emancipated. To understand the claims to justice by colonial and imperial authorities in imposing landlessness on the newly emancipated, it is necessary to return to a consideration of the overwhelming role of private property in European epistemology. To Morris Cohen "property on a large scale is power,"[98] but even on a much reduced scale, land ownership was critical to a realization of true liberty and political enfranchisement. Indeed, Cohen affirms, "to be free one must have a sphere of self-assertion in the external world. One's private property provides such an opportunity."[99] It was through the control of private property that the proprietary class intended to maintain its status quo ante emancipation.

As early as January 1834, Burnley had recommended to Stanley the linking of land control legislation with contracts for indentured immigrants. He suggested that regulations be made to prevent "the dispersion of the labouring classes over the ungranted lands of the colony."[100] His proposal included restricting the sale of private lands and preempting the subdivision of private lands into small parcels. The size of ungranted lands was estimated at 144,000 acres, as against 180,000 acres in the hands of proprietors.[101] Burnley argued that in order "to secure concentration of civilization, profitable employment of capital, and the civilization of the labouring classes," it would be necessary to employ "the now generally understood principles of colonization." These principles were articulated by Gibbon Wakefield in 1830. Wakefield appealed for a reorientation of colonial policy, which he labeled "systematic colonization," particularly to address plans for the effective colonization of Australia.[102] The Colonial Office eagerly assimilated his ideas to the postslavery Caribbean.[103] Wakefield's influence led to a halt in free land grants in all colonies from 1831.[104] When applied to Trinidad, this new policy meant the imposition of a high tax on the sale of land, to be appropriated for the financing of immigration.

Impatient for action, the colonial government initiated its own plan of control with a militia ordinance that included martial law as a permanent fixture of postslavery. Although the imperial government concurred with the imperative of controlling the emancipated, it foresaw a diminution of confidence in the "stability of Colonial Institutions" and thus sanctioned the ordinance only for the duration of the apprenticeship.[105] In order to make control more class specific, the imperial government firmly engaged the policy of restricting access to ungranted lands. In a dispatch to all colonial governors in 1836, secretary of state for the colonies Lord Glenelg declared that the more permanent interests of society must be defended by the exclusion of freedmen from land ownership.[106] Moreover, the government must convince the emancipated that this marginalization was in their best interest. Glenelg reasoned, "If therefore we are to keep up the cultivation of the staple productions, we must make it the immediate and apparent interest of the negro population to employ their labour in raising them."[107] He left details of pricing to the colonial governments so long as they were guided by the principle that the minimum price of land must be "high enough to leave a considerable portion of the population unable to buy it until they have saved some capital out of the wages of their industry, and at the same time low enough to encourage such savings by making the possession of land a reasonable object of ambition to all."[108]

In 1838 a new directive was sent to all Crown colonies to ensure that the minimum block of Crown lands they might appropriate for sale was 340 acres;

shortly after emancipation, the minimum acreage was doubled.[109] Compared to land allocation policies of the Spanish Cedula of Population or the Colonial Department under Hobart, the Glenelg plan was tantamount to a declaration of servitude in the guise of land policy. The plan placed the acquisition of land above the reach of the most industrious laborers, who might already have exhausted their savings in manumission. To assist compliance the Trinidad legislature passed an Ordinance to Establish a Rural Police Force. On the joint authority of two justices, persons arrested for "occupying waste and uncultivated lands without authority" would suffer their "plantations and cultivations cut down, rooted and torn up, burnt or otherwise utterly destroyed . . . houses pulled down . . . materials thereof burnt and destroyed."[110] This was a virtual declaration of war against the newly freed. As framed, even the older established provision grounds were targets for this scorched-earth legislation. Even the chief justice was alarmed by the draconian measures and officially condemned the package of measures as "altogether of a penal and coercive character directed against the labouring population."[111] The local ordinance was reinforced by a Suppression of Vagrancy order-in-council and another giving summary powers to special magistrates to penalize squatters who occupied Crown lands since October 1837. In addition to confiscating all property and produce, the anti-squatting order prescribed a jail term of fourteen days for contempt of notification to vacate and deliver up produce to the authorities.[112] In limiting self-employment and denying access to land, emancipated Africans were denied true compensation and restorative justice, although their enslavement was condemned by Parliament as unjust, unnatural, and criminal.

The question of compensation continues to haunt the legacy of emancipation and underscores abolitionists' self-serving pursuit of humanity and justice. From the commencement of the abolitionist movement, few abolitionists could truly be said to be free of the racist negation of African humanity; at emancipation scientific racism was engineering a new canon that denied Africans any role in world civilization, including their own. Wherever anthropologists and historians featured Africans, they were portrayed as lesser mortals. According to Rousseau, "to renounce liberty is to renounce being a man, to surrender the rights of humanity and even its duties. For him who renounces everything, no indemnity is possible."[113] This was a predicament for the newly freed: the negation of African humanity was a European invention, but it determined the distribution of compensation at the abolition of slavery.

Buxton's amelioration motion implicitly recognized the rights of property in humans, though it was carefully crafted to avoid claims for compensation. Nevertheless, compensation for deprivation of human property was justified by well-established traditions and laws. Although difficult to compute, there was no question of this debt being pecuniary. The debt owed to the enslaved population was obfuscated, however, by the long-held view of the advantages to Africans as wards of Europeans, notwithstanding abolitionists' acknowledgment that Europeans were the creators and managers of the barbarous conditions of plantation slavery. Thus, abolitionists persisted in a policy that advanced the civilizing mission as legitimate compensation to Africans. These two attitudes to compensation are exemplified in Buxton's stance on the issue. While he deferred to the notion of justice in distributing twenty million pounds to proprietors and mortgagees, the only compensation he was willing to concede to the enslaved was indoctrination: "To supply them amply with the means of instruction, to despatch missionaries, to institute schools, and to send out Bibles. It is the only compensation in our power. It is an abundant one! We may in this manner recompense all the sorrows and sufferings we have inflicted and be the means of making in the end their barbarous removal from their own land the greatest of blessings to them."[114]

Apprenticeship ensured the survival of the plantation ethos. The fear of reprisals from the emancipated class compelled legislators to focus on political stability and economic survival. To secure these objectives, Christian churches strengthened their alliances with the secular elites. The first authoritative judgment on the racial engineering of apprenticeship was that of governor Lord Harris. In a review of Trinidad society in 1848 he lamented: "One of the many errors which have been committed since the granting of emancipation is the little attention paid to legislation having for its end the formation of a society on true, sound and lasting principles"; consequently, "a race has been freed, but a society has not been formed."[115] This statement has been misunderstood by some historians. Harris's vision was obviously polarized by race, or, more precisely, a vision of two societies: the one, European and elitist; the other, African and subordinate. Indeed, this was the concept expressed by Lord Glenelg in his consideration of the "interests of society."

Although the term *plantation society* has become historical orthodoxy, the enslaved class was not a constituent integer of this construct. As de jure chattel, they were "property" and could share neither the rights nor the full moral obligations of freemen. Apprenticeship transferred the claim of property in enslaved laborers to the claim of property in their services, which they were still compelled to give. For ceding their rights to property in enslaved persons, Trinidad proprietors were granted £973,444 sterling, in addition to four to six years of largely unremunerated labor.[116] Although the recipients were condemned by natural law, moral philosophy, and Christian theology, the imperial government allowed the Trinidad council to preserve the status of the formerly enslaved as a nonperson in its apprenticeship regulations: "The interest of the master or employer in the services of the apprentice is and shall pass and be transformed and acquired and effected by Sale Donation Mortgage Inheritance and Bequest [sic] and all other lucrative & onerous titles in the same manner as other descriptions of Property."[117] Apprenticeship, therefore, perpetuated the alienation of the former chattelized class and preserved the culture of plantation slavery.

The imperative of defining colonial society is fundamental to an understanding of apprenticeship legislation and the economic and social policies of the transition. Class and race biases had deep implications for a new moral code for the whole society. Indeed, the question must be raised whether or not it was at all possible to fashion a single society. Clearly, the purpose of apprenticeship was the reordering of societal structures to preserve the plantation rationale, as the metropolitan economy progressed from mercantilism to industrial capitalism and laissez-faire. The problem of forming a postslavery society was articulated by Burnley in the run-up to Emancipation Day: "The destruction of slavery by a legislative act was easy; but the reconstruction by the same means of a free and prosperous social system on its ruins, appears enveloped in doubt and difficulty."[118] Unlike Harris, Burnley viewed the problem of social reconstruction from within; he saw himself as an integral part of the process: as a colonial. It was, however, a vision of society to which Burnley himself was not willing or able to make any real contribution. Harris's conceptualization of the reconstruction of colonial society was that of an imperialist. Yet both men agreed with the supremacist paradigm that European deployment among the general population would constitute an inherently "superior class" to "assist in [the] civilization" of "the people."[119] What few were willing to admit was that European enslavers in the sugar colonies were morally destitute; having systematically destroyed the African marriage institution, they could provide no viable model for its reconstruction.

The problem of marriage was resolved by an order-in-council dated 7 September 1838. The lateness of this ordinance was linked to the daunting problem of uniting man and wife from separate plantations. Stanley had succeeded in getting a general marriage bill to Parliament, but the government had to concede that still "insuperable objections existed to any immediate parliamentary legislation on these topics."[120] The central feature of this ordinance was the legitimizing of all forms of "slave marriage," including those conducted by sectarian missionaries.[121] Couples could legitimize their de facto marriages under this ordinance provided they solemnized them within one year of its proclamation. The law also liberated the offspring of concubinage from legal disabilities common to children born out of wedlock.[122] Yet financial obstacles remained. A fee of four shillings was demanded "for solemnizing and registering a Marriage, and transmitting the Duplicate Original to the Colonial Secretary."[123] When compared with an average wage of two shillings and seven pennies per day and the seasonality of labor in all branches of agriculture, the fee was exorbitant. When added to church fees, marriage was a luxury that few of the emancipated could afford, especially in the absence of legal compulsion or social convention. Furthermore, the hegemonic Roman Catholic Church in Trinidad did not make the same moral demands on its followers as the sectarian churches. Thus, Burke's vital cement of society was doomed to remain weak.

Admittedly, education had a potential for restorative justice—but this was not to be. From 1835 formal education meant Christian education, shaped by curricula based on religious and moral tenets of Protestantism. Before the nineteenth century education in Britain was almost exclusively a province of the church; it complemented religion, especially at lower socioeconomic strata. In the postslavery era the West Indian church maintained exclusive control over the management of schools, the appointments of teachers, and the content of curricula.

The marriage of education and religion was the ideal matrix for the indoctrination of the emancipated. Education was designed particularly to suppress freedmen's ambitions for genuine freedom, an ideology first articulated by Stanley in his introduction of the emancipation debate in 1833. His statement that it must be the duty of Parliament "to establish a religious and moral system of education for the negroes" was not remotely intended as compensation. He rightly saw that the future empire lay with the very young freedmen.[124] A more forthright articulation of this philosophy of education was that of Reverend John Sterling, who was commissioned by the British government in 1835 to inquire into the existing state of education in the colonies. Sterling was also required to make recommendations for implementing the small parliamentary grant of twenty thousand pounds sterling for the construction of schools in all colonies. Sterling emphasized the critical importance of education as a social control dynamic: "Although the negroes are now under a system of limited control, which secures to a certain extent their orderly and industrious conduct, in the short space of five years from the first of next August, their performance of the functions of a labouring class in a civilised community will depend entirely on the power over their minds of the same prudential and moral motives which govern more or less the mass of the people here."[125] For the English working class this objective represented a theory of education that was culturally acceptable and morally defensible. When transferred to the West Indies, however, this theory was clearly racist. The black factor of slavery was carried over into postslavery plantation society as the principal determinant of a laboring class; it also made the formerly enslaved the object of persistent poverty and societal marginalization. Although subliminal, the message was loud and clear: physical slavery would be followed by mental slavery. Thus, like law and justice, education and religion were designed to serve the interests of the dominant class in the postslavery era.

Wherever adopted, the onset of apprenticeship saw a frantic move by all denominations to secure as big a stake as possible in the harvest of African souls and the control of the African mind. In most colonies the principal contestants were the Church of England and sectarians. Except perhaps in Barbados, sectarian membership experienced a more rapid growth than the established church.[126] Yet there was an awareness of the need for cooperation in a common objective. As the Methodist Society expressed it, they were prepared to "engage, in common with other Missionary Societies, to aid in promoting the Government Plan of Negro Education."[127] In Trinidad this contest played out mainly between the two established churches. The threat of imminent emancipation transferred historic lethargy into revolutionary zeal. From a complement of four in 1831 the Roman Catholic clergy rose to eleven in 1833, its highest ever, and doubled by 1836.[128] Several teachers and catechists were also recruited.[129] This mobilization of missionary resources was the work of the indefatigable Bishop MacDonald. The speed and success of recruitment set back the Church of England, which had developed a similar plan for promoting Protestantism in the major centers of slavery.[130]

The alleged allegiance to Roman Catholicism of some 90 percent of the enslaved population in 1831 should have made Trinidad one of the least subject to the divisiveness of religious pluralism.[131] Aggressive Anglicization during the 1830s, however, inevitably targeted Franco-Hispanic culture, especially Roman Catholicism. Consequently, freedmen were victims of doctrinal and administrative conflict for a full decade and a half.[132] Every effort was made by the Trinidad council to limit Roman Catholic advantage and even roll it back; strategies included the distribution of "liberated" African apprentices to avoid contact with Roman Catholic planters.[133]

Vicar General Le Geoff was clearly deceived in thinking that his application for aid to educate "poor Catholic children of this Colony" would be met with sympathy simply because the council had voted a sum for education "with the view of instructing the poor generally."[134] The bishop of Barbados condoned the prejudice against Catholic children in Church of England schools.[135] Not surprisingly, although daily attendances were relatively high at the inception of mass education in 1835, Hill found a "disinclination" in the Port of Spain schools upon visiting them two years later.[136] The government maintained a rigid policy of appointing only Protestant schoolmasters even where there was clearly an overwhelming majority of Roman Catholics.[137] These schoolmasters refused to enroll Catholic children unless they consented to learn the catechism of the Church of England and read books prohibited by Catholic clergy.[138]

During the debate on the Emancipation Bill, Parliament had added to Stanley's projection a vague appeal to "liberal and comprehensive principles" as the guideline for disbursing the proposed education grant.[139] That phrase, however, was used to deny funding to the Roman Catholic Church in its education drive. In 1837 Glenelg reminded Hill of that policy. As far as Glenelg was concerned, when applied to Roman Catholics, those conditions were best met under the Mico Charity, the organization co-opted as the custodians of education of freedmen wherever a colony had a large Roman Catholic population.[140]

The emancipated class in Trinidad was thus caught in a conflict between two dominant, antagonistic colonial traditions. Because of the concerted effort to neutralize Franco-Hispanic culture, Trinidad was deprived of an early, comprehensive system of education at the dawn of emancipation. This failure further weakened the remodeling process during the apprenticeship, already marked by the lack of systems for an effective restructuring of African family life, utterly destroyed by enslavement. Consequently, in the reconstruction of civil society the imperial trustees abandoned African freedmen to their own individual whims, the whims of religious denominations, and the economic interests of the plantocracy.

12

CONCLUSION

The problem of security created by insurrectionism of the enslaved across the British colonies from the mid-eighteenth century arrested the attention of key spokesmen of empire, leading to the imperial adoption of amelioration as the flagship policy to validate and cushion the abolition of the slave trade. The dramatic failure of amelioration as a system of social control compelled metropolitans to concede general emancipation as a new security strategy. Unquestionably, the popular metropolitan movement in England was indispensable to the politics of abolitionism, goading Crown and Parliament into action. The chief parliamentary representatives of popular abolitionism were also critical, serving as links between the colonial dynamics of transformation and legislative reaction in the metropolis. But the primary social forces of abolition and emancipation must be sought among the colonies' free and enslaved populations. In exploring the pragmatic rationale for metropolitan intervention, this study has assiduously divorced the rhetoric of conscience from the economics of public security and has sought to reconcile a common ground in their deployment.

Abolitionist leaders were motivated by an awareness that a viable colonial structure needed a politically stable environment, which could best be achieved by standardizing the management of colonial slavery toward the creation of a Christianized, Creole labor force. Creolization had its own momentum, providing fodder for abolitionists' activism and a palliative to planters, but Christianization was a bitter pill for the planters to swallow. Abolition of the slave trade was a mechanism for standardizing amelioration with a fully Creole labor force while leaving emancipation to the forces of history. Yet the theory of security through amelioration and slave trade abolition proved to be a fallacy, and emancipation was won, instead, by revolution. Abolitionists had not reckoned with the possibility of an enslaved insurgency as a whole and misread the lessons of the early Creole insurgencies; they also did not anticipate the expansion of emancipationist insurgencies under Christianized Creole leadership.

Decoding the dread of revolutionary emancipationism is key to understanding the reform strategies of colonials and metropolitan abolitionists, secular and religious. The most incontrovertible evidence of this foreboding is the official policy adopted for Trinidad. Eric Williams and C. L. R. James argue that if Britain had captured St. Domingue, abolitionism would have been abandoned indefinitely. Trinidad was captured in the time it would have taken to consolidate the conquest of St. Domingue. Yet the slave trade to Trinidad was halted and every effort made to arrest the growth of the native African population in the colony, a clear case of surrender to the hysteria of black soldiery. Even though the fear of Haitian expansionism beyond the island of Hispaniola was unfounded, we cannot discredit with hindsight what was commonly thought to be true, or we discredit the forces of history. Certainly, Henry Brougham could admit of no direct connection between Haiti and the British colonies, yet he feared that "the neighbourhood of a negro state will prepare our slaves for ideas of independence."[1] It certainly did so in dramatic revolutionary style for Santo Domingo.

David Brion Davis affirms that "the sanest minds found excuses for Negro slavery."[2] The same ought not to be said of the most self-righteous, to whom slavery was anathema. The attempts by historians to make a special case for the toleration of slavery by the "saints" are unrealistic. Anstey affirms, "For the saved, slavery stood particularly condemned precisely because the concept of Redemption was central for him."[3] Yet metropolitan reformers, basking in the transcendence of personal salvation, opted for slavery over emancipation. They studiously avoided condemning the plantocracy in spite of efforts by a few to expose the futility of pursuing moral enlightenment of the enslaved under the existing immorality of the enslavers. Evangelical and Quaker reformers set back, rather than promoted, African emancipation. To sum up this aspect, the words of Canning are appropriate; in his reply to Buxton's proposals to emancipate slave children while leaving their parents in slavery, he argued: "The name of Christianity ought not to be thus used unless we are prepared to act in a much more summary manner than the honourable member now proposes. If the existence of Slavery be repugnant to the principles of the British Constitution and the Christian Religion, how can the honourable gentleman himself consent to pause even for an instant, or to allow any considerations of prudence to intervene between him and his object? How can he propose to divide the Slaves into two classes; one of which is to be made free directly while he leaves the other to the gradual extinction of their state of suffering?"[4]

Any serious discussion of this period on the fate of colonial slavery must be mindful of the established paradigms in the debate on the economic decline of the sugar plantations. Certainly, the current study strongly refutes the assertion that economic interests seem "rarely to have been a consideration" in the "humanitarian" struggle for prohibiting the slave trade and supporting African emancipation in the British colonies.[5] Metropolitan abolitionists were at the forefront in representing a new ideology of colonialism. In doing so, they were representing the spirit of change in their domestic economy in particular and in the imperial economy in general. Free trade was important to this spirit of change. But up to the 1820s the imperative to secure the Caribbean economic zone—still with great investment potential—against destructive insurrections was even more compelling. At the same time restoring economic viability by improving the efficiency of the slave system was critical. Evangelical and Quaker disciples of free trade equated the terror regime of colonial slavery with monopoly. The elimination of one meant the elimination of the other. Thus, they skillfully linked emancipation to their campaign for the equalization of East India sugar. Yet Cropper's prophecy was wrong. It was emancipation that freed the British West Indian economy of the deadweight of slave labor and provided the catalyst for liberating East India sugar from protective tariffs. Yet the extension of the West India sugar preference to India in 1835, even before full emancipation, meant that freedom occurred so much within the context of laissez-faire that the imperative of cheap labor was decisive in the construction of a new episteme of colonial society in the postslavery era.

The image of metropolitan abolitionists as defenders of property and white power remained consistent to the very end of the slavery era. Full emancipation was deferred because the image of the dangerous and vengeful African was still stamped on the minds of the saints. They later condemned apprenticeship when they saw the constructive response of the enslaved to the limited freedom it afforded them. As Brougham acknowledged early in 1838, instead of spectacles of "lurid fires of rebellion, kindled by a sense of natural though lawless revenge, and the just resistance to intolerable oppression," there were scenes of "joy, contentment, peace, and goodwill towards men."[6] Brougham confessed that he shared the general uneasiness of unconditional freedom in 1834: "I myself shared in those feelings of alarm when I contemplated the possible event of the vast but yet untried experiment."[7] He admitted that he had supported apprenticeship because immediate freedom might make the African "dangerous to the public peace."[8]

The Emancipation Act was not a charter of freedom but rather a blueprint for social control. Contrary to William Green, the betrayal of Africans did not occur in the 1840s; rather, it began with the Emancipation Act. Slavery had been jolted off its foundation but only to free the enslaved for a greater role as taxpaying, landless peasants and consumers of an aggressively expanding imperial economy. At the commencement of emancipation every Christian denomination directed its pastoral and financial resources to converting the formerly enslaved in order to ensure the survival, prosperity, and status quo of the planter class. The Colonial Office—which at that time had a full complement of "humanitarian" officials, including James Stephen Jr., one of the most renowned "Friends of the Negro"—was at the forefront of this reaction. The official conspiracy against prescriptive rights to land, even for cultivating subsistence crops, was a stratagem to preserve proprietary elitism. When combined with anti-squatting measures, it was clear that there was an all-out offensive against freedmen. By and large government allocated vastly greater funds to the militia, police, magistracy, and prisons than to education or social restitution.[9]

This assault against African liberty undermined the basis on which the formerly enslaved could reassess their identity and reestablish a true sense of community and economic prosperity. If we take Francis Hutcheson's cue that "the trust is broken" where a government fails to secure the property and lives of citizens, the imperial framework for embarking upon emancipation was an affirmation of the bond between the imperial government and colonists but a betrayal of "trust" for emancipated Africans. For them change would come only by rearming themselves with new legal and constitutional strategies and deploying the same resolve that had brought the slave system to its knees in more ways than one. Retrospectively, it was destined to be a long struggle, punctuated by militancy and occasional violence, as activists pursued cultural equality, social and economic justice, and constitutional advancements.

NOTES

Preface

1. C. L. R. James, *The Black Jacobins: Toussaint L'Ouverture and the San Domingo Revolution*, rev. ed. (1938; New York: Random House, 1963); for precursors to Williams, see William Darity Jr., "Eric Williams and Slavery: A West Indian Viewpoint?" *Callaloo* 20, no. 4 (1997), http://muse.jhu.edu/journals/callaloo/v020/20.4darity.html.

2. See, e.g., Robert Isaac Wilberforce and Samuel Wilberforce, *The Life and Times of William Wilberforce* (London, 1838); George Stephen, *Anti-Slavery Recollections: In a Series of Letters Addressed to Mrs. Beecher Stowe,* 2d ed. (1854; London: Frank Cass, 1971).

3. Frank Joseph Klingberg, *The Anti-Slavery Movement in England: A Study in English Humanitarianism* (New Haven: Yale University Press, 1926); Reginald Coupland, *The British Anti-Slavery Movement* (London: Frank Cass, 1964).

4. Eric Williams, *Capitalism and Slavery* (London: Andre Deutsch, 1964), 208.

5. Richard Hart, *Slaves Who Abolished Slavery: Blacks in Rebellion* (1985; Kingston, Jamaica: University of the West Indies Press, 2002), i–iv; an earlier published work on the subject is Richard Hart, *Black Jamaicans' Struggle against Slavery* (Kingston: Institute of Jamaica, 1977).

6. Gelien Matthews, *Caribbean Slave Revolts and the British Abolitionist Movement* (Baton Rouge: Louisiana State University Press, 2006).

7. Claudius K. Fergus, "British Imperial Trusteeship: The Reconstruction of British Colonialism with Special Reference to Trinidad, 1783–1838" (Ph.D. diss., University of the West Indies, 1996).

8. Cited in Moira Ferguson, ed., *The History of Mary Prince: A West Indian Slave (Related by Herself)* (Ann Arbor: University of Michigan Press, 1997), 17–18. For the relevance of Hegel to plantation slavery, see Orlando Patterson, *Slavery and Social Death: A Comparative Study* (Cambridge: Harvard University Press, 1982), 228–40.

9. Williams includes the African struggle for land ownership and the right to organize labor unions, among other economic struggles, in his conceptualization of Diaspora revolution (*The Negro in the Caribbean* [1942; New York: A&B Books, 1994], 83–84).

10. Roger Anstey, *The Atlantic Slave Trade and British Abolition, 1760–1810* (London: Macmillan, 1975), 387.

11. David Brion Davis, "Impact of the French and Haitian Revolutions," in *The Impact of the Haitian Revolution in the Atlantic World,* ed. David P. Geggus (Columbia: University of South Carolina Press, 2001), 6.

12. Seymour Drescher, "The Limits of Example," in *The Impact of the Haitian Revolution in the Atlantic World,* ed. David P. Geggus (Columbia: University of South Carolina Press, 2001), 10–11.

13. Seymour Drescher, "Civilizing Insurgency: Two Variants of Slave Revolts in the Age of Revolution," in *Who Abolished Slavery? Slave Revolts and Abolitionism: A Debate with João Pedro Marques,* ed. Seymour Drescher and Pieter C. Emmer (New York: Berghahn Books, 2010), 122.

14. James, *Black Jacobins,* 132–33; Williams, *Capitalism and Slavery,* 147; Eric Williams, *From Columbus to Castro: The History of the Caribbean, 1492–1969* (London: Andre Deutsch, 1983); also see Robin Blackburn, *The Overthrow of Colonial Slavery, 1776–1848* (London: Verso, 1988), 204.

1. Explicating the "Grand Evils" of Colonialism

1. Charles James Fox, qtd. in Anstey, *Atlantic Slave Trade,* 381. Rodney justifiably contends that historical correctness requires that the Atlantic slave trade be termed the "European slave trade," consistent with the contemporary Arab slave trade in the Indian Ocean (Walter Rodney, *How Europe Underdeveloped Africa* [London: Bogle L'Ouverture, 1973], 23–46).

2. Clarkson, cited in Richard Sheridan, "Slave Demography in the British West Indies and the Abolition of the Atlantic Slave Trade," in *The Abolition of the Atlantic Slave Trade: Origins and Effects in Europe, Africa and the Americas,* ed. David Eltis and James Walvin (Madison: University of Wisconsin Press, 1981), 265; Edmund Burke, in *Abolition of the Slave Trade—Motion For in the House of Commons, 12th May 1789* (London, 1789), 16–17.

3. Anstey, *Atlantic Slave Trade,* 202–7.

4. Henry Brougham, *An Inquiry into the Colonial Policy of the European Powers* (1803; New York: Kelly, 1930), 1:468.

5. Evidence of Ninian Jefferys, master in the Royal Navy, in *House of Commons Sessional Papers of the Eighteenth Century,* ed. Sheila Lambert (Wilmington, Del.: Scholarly Resources, 1975), 73:233 (hereafter cited as *Sessional Papers*).

6. Evidence of Barbados-born Rev. Robert Nicholls, *Sessional Papers,* 73:346.

7. Nicholls, *Sessional Papers,* 73:346.

8. Peter Fryer, *Staying Power: The History of Black People in Britain* (London: Pluto Press, 1984), 108.

9. Fryer lists twenty-four members in the Sons of Africa; see *Staying Power,* 108.

10. Olaudah Equiano, *The Life of Olaudah Equiano, or Gustava Vassa, the African* (1814; Mineola, N.Y.: Dover Publications, 1999), 80. I also accessed the original publication, Olaudah Equiano, *The Interesting Narrative of the Life of Olaudah Equiano, or Gustavus Vassa, The African Written by Himself* (London, 1789), www.gutenberg.org/files/17700-h.htm.

11. Ottabah Cugoano, qtd. extensively in Fryer, *Staying Power,* 99–101.

12. Ferguson, *Mary Prince,* 83; also from Mary Prince's autobiography excerpted in Karina Williamson, ed., *Contrary Voices: Representations of West Indian Slavery, 1657–1834* (Kingston, Jamaica: University of the West Indies Press, 2008), 280.

13. See James Walvin, *Slavery and the Slave Trade: A Short Illustrated History* (London: Macmillan, 1983), 8; Michael Grant, *The World of Rome* (London: Weidenfeld Press, 1974), 140.

14. Richard Ligon, *A True and Exact History of the Island of Barbados* (London, 1673), 46.

15. John Oldmixton, cited in Hilary Beckles, "A Dangerous and Unnatural Independence: The Haitian Revolution and Black Liberation in the Caribbean," in *Survivors of the Middle Passage: Affirmation and Change,* ed. Harcourt Blackett (Barbados: n.p., 1992), 36.

16. See Baron Charles Secondat de Montesquieu, *The Spirit of the Laws,* 2 vols., trans. Thomas Nugent (New York: Hafner, 1949), 1:243; also see James Ramsay, *An Essay on the Treatment and Conversion of African Slaves in the British Sugar Colonies* (London, 1784), 173.

17. Edward Long, *The History of Jamaica* (1774; London: Frank Cass, 1979), 2:431.

18. Ramsay, *Treatment and Conversion,* 173. Folarin Shyllon makes a strong case for Ramsay's humanitarianism, arguing that his ownership of slaves did not make him a hypocrite and that he measured up with the slave-owning judge Lord Mansfield, who ruled on the Somerset case condemning slavery as "odious" (*Black People in Britain, 1555–1833* [Oxford: Oxford University Press, 1977], 55).

19. Brougham, *Colonial Policy,* 2:301; the statement is repeated in *Opinion of Henry Brougham on Negro Slavery* (London, 1826), 14.

20. Laurent Dubois, *Avengers of the New World: The Story of the Haitian Revolution* (Cambridge: Harvard University Press, 2004), 210–11.

21. Augustine Shute, "Ubuntu as the African Ethical Vision," in *African Ethics: An Anthropology of Comparative and Applied Ethics,* ed. Munyaradzi Felix Murove (Scottsville, South Africa: University of KwaZulu-Natal Press, 2009), 85.

22. See Richard H. Bell, *Understanding African Philosophy: A Cross-Cultural Approach to Classical and Contemporary Issues* (New York: Routledge, 2002), 90; also see Mluleki Munyaka and Mokgethi Motlhabi, "*Ubuntu* and Its Socio-Moral Significance," in Murove, *African Ethics,* 65.

23. Stephen D. Behrendt, David Eltis, and David Richardson, "The Costs of Coercion: African Agency in the Pre-Modern Atlantic World," *Economic History Review,* n.s. 54, no. 3 (August 2001): 454–76; for several cases of ship revolts, see Maggie Montesinos, *The Slumbering Volcano: American Slave Ship Revolts and the Production of Rebellious Masculinity* (Durham, N.C.: Duke University Press, 1997); for the most famous ship revolt, see Howard Jones, *Mutiny on the Amistad: The Saga of a Slave Revolt and Its Impact on American Abolition, Law, and Diplomacy* (New York: Oxford University Press, 1988), 14–30, http://questia.com/PM.qst?a=o&d=62255635. This essay draws substantially upon the transatlantic slave trade database, first available on CD-ROM and currently at Emory State University; also see Antonio T. Bly, "Crossing the Lake of Fire: Slave Resistance during the Middle Passage, 1720–1842," *Journal of Negro History* 6, no. 3 (1998): 178–86; Lorenzo J. Greene, "Mutiny on the Slave Ships," *Phylon* 5, no. 4 (1944): 346–54; and Darold D. Wax, "Negro Resistance to the Early American Slave Trade," *Journal of Negro History* 51, no. 1 (Jan. 1966): 6–11.

24. Williams, *Negro in the Caribbean,* 84; Williams, *Columbus to Castro,* 66; Hugh Thomas, *The Slave Trade: The History of the Atlantic Slave Trade, 1440–1870* (London: Macmillan, 1998), 104; Basil Davidson, *The African Slave Trade,* rev. ed. (Boston: Little Brown, 1980), 65; Ligon, *True and Exact History,* 53.

25. See Ligon, *True and Exact History,* 46. This scenario was reiterated almost verbatim in John Oldmixton, *A History of the British Empire in America* (London, 1708), 2:135.

26. David Barry Gaspar, *Bondsmen and Rebels: A Study of Master-Slave Relations in Antigua, with Implications for Colonial British America* (Baltimore: Johns Hopkins University Press, 1985), 185; also see David Barry Gaspar, "The Antigua Slave Conspiracy of 1736: A Case Study of

the Origins of Collective Resistance," *William and Mary Quarterly*, 3d ser., 35, no. 2 (Apr. 1978): 308-33, www.jstor.org/stable/1921837.

27. Richard Dunn, *Sugar and Slaves: The Rise of the Planter Class in the English West Indies, 1624-1713* (London: Jonathan Cape, 1972), 256.

28. See Frank W. Pitman, "Slavery on the British West India Plantations in the Eighteenth Century," *Journal of Negro History* 11 (1926): 619.

29. Alvin O. Thompson, *Flight to Freedom: African Runaways and Maroons in the Americas* (Kingston, Jamaica: University of the West Indies Press, 2006), 140, 143. James Walvin interprets the reaction of whites to the Tacky war as evidence of a "permanent neurosis" (*The Trader, the Owner, the Slave: Parallel Lives in the Age of Slavery* [London: Jonathan Cape, 2007], 140). Women stood side by side with the men as supporting personnel, wives, and fighters; see Lucille Mathurin Mair, *The Rebel Woman in the British West Indies during Slavery* (Kingston, Jamaica: Dennis Ranston, 1995), chaps. 7-8.

30. R. C. Dallas, *The History of the Maroons from Their Origins to the Establishment of Their Chief Tribe at Sierra Leone* (London: Frank Cass, 1968), 46-47; Pitman, "Slavery," 619; Richard Sheridan, "The Jamaica Slave Insurrection Scare of 1776 and the American Revolution," *Journal of Negro History* 61, no. 3 (July 1986): 291-92, www.jstor.org/stable/27172255. For replication of the two Maroon treaties, see Bev Carey, *The Maroon Story: The Authentic and Original History of the Maroons in the History of Jamaica, 1490-1880* (Gordon Town, Jamaica: Agouti Press, 1997), 318-19, 353-75.

31. From an account narrated by a Maroon colonel at Accompong and recorded by the author, 8 December 2007.

32. Long, *History*, 2:444. For nuances in the concept "Creole," see Edward Brathwaite, *The Development of Creole Society in Jamaica, 1770-1820* (Oxford: Clarendon, 1971), xiv-xvi.

33. Fryer, *Staying Power*, 33-50; Williams, *Capitalism and Slavery*, chaps. 3, 5.

34. Fryer, *Staying Power*, 38-44; Williams, *Capitalism and Slavery*, 46; Davidson, *African Slave Trade*, 76-85; Thomas, *Slave Trade*, 292-300.

35. Long, *History*, 2:432. Thomas Clarkson, *An Essay on the Comparative Efficiency of Regulation or Abolition as Applied to the Slave Trade* (London, 1788), 139; J. E. Inikori, "Market Structure and the Profits of the British African Trade in the Late Eighteenth Century," *Journal of Economic History* 41 (September 1983): 723-28. For a critical overview, see Kenneth Morgan, *Slavery, Atlantic Trade and the British Economy, 1660-1800* (Cambridge: Cambridge University Press, 2000), 36-48; Williams, *Capitalism and Slavery*, 19-20, 51-53.

36. Anon., "World Is Afrika," http://home.btclick.com/jabu/ships.htm. Correspondingly, estates with paradisiacal names such as Belle Vue, Good Hope, Paradise, Plaisance, and Promised Land were common across the Caribbean.

37. John Hope Franklin and Alfred A. Moss Jr., *From Slavery to Freedom: A History of African Americans* (New York: McGraw-Hill, 1994), 35.

38. Williams, *Capitalism and Slavery*, 34-35.

39. Thomas Clarkson, *The History of the Rise, Progress and Accomplishment of the Abolition of the African Slave Trade by the British Parliament* (London: N.p., 1808), 487.

40. For an interesting poem on the subject, see Toi Derricotte, "Exits from Elmina Castle: Cape Coast, Ghana," *Callaloo* 19, no. 1 (Winter 1996): 107-10, www.jstor.org/stable/3299325.

41. Evidence of Ashley Hall, *Sessional Papers*, 72:519.

42. Equiano, *Life*, 33. An African boy taken captive at about twelve years of age told of a

similar experience to Equiano's on the overland route to the slaving port and aboard the slave ship; he had a rare opportunity to testify before a select committee of the House of Lords in 1849; see Robert Edgar Conrad, *Children of God's Fire: A Documentary History of Black Slavery in Brazil* (University Park: Pennsylvania State University Press 1994), 16–23, 37–38.

43. Evidence of Towne, *Sessional Papers,* 82:19.

44. Clarkson, *Comparative Efficiency,* 20.

45. Clarkson, *History,* 326. Muster rolls for Liverpool and Bristol confirmed Clarkson's findings; see Wilberforce in 29 *Parl. Hist.* (1791): 270. For disease-infected slavers, see Equiano, *Life,* 33.

46. Evidence of Captain Hall, *Sessional Papers,* 72:517–18; also see evidence of Ecroyde Claxton, a surgeon (*Sessional Papers,* 82:32–33).

47. Philip Curtin, *The Atlantic Slave Trade: A Census* (Madison: University of Wisconsin Press, 1969), 274–75. Paul E. Lovejoy supports Joseph C. Miller on 9–15 percent (Lovejoy, *Transformations in Slavery: A History of Slavery in Africa,* 2d ed. [Cambridge: Cambridge University Press, 2000], 64; Miller, "Mortality in the Atlantic Slave Trade: Statistical Evidence on Causality," *Journal of Interdisciplinary History* 11, no. 3 [1981]: 394–400). David Eltis applies a similar model to Miller, with similar results, in "Mortality and Voyage Length in the Middle Passage: New Evidence from the Nineteenth Century," *Journal of Economic History* 4, no. 2 (1984): 301–8.

48. "Seasoning" mortality occupies an uncertain place in slavery statistics. The figure could be as high as 46 percent; see Harry Bennett Jr., *Bondsmen and Bishops: Slavery and Apprenticeship on Codrington Plantations of Barbados, 1710–1838* (Berkeley: University of California Press, 1958), 66.

49. See bell hooks, *Ain't I a Woman? Black Women and Feminism* (London: Pluto, 1982), 27–28.

50. See Equiano, *Life,* 74.

51. Ecroyde Claxton, *Sessional Papers,* 82:36.

52. The higher numbers are from the Emory University collection: "Voyages: The Transatlantic Slave Trade Database," http://shared.web.emory.edu/emory/news/releases/2008; Hart, *Black Jamaicans' Struggle,* 4. Employing data from the Emory University database, see James A. Rawley with Stephen D. Behrendt, *The Transatlantic Slave Trade: A History,* rev. ed. (Lincoln: University of Nebraska Press, 2005), 145, table 7.3; also see 36 *Parl. Hist.* (1802): 863–64; B. W. Higman, *Slave Population and Economy in Jamaica, 1807–1834* (Baltimore: Johns Hopkins University Press, 1984), 74–77, tables 3.8 and 4.2. For import data between 1808 and 1810, see Curtin, *Atlantic Slave Trade,* 71, table 18; for re-exports from Jamaica, see 26, table 6. and 140, table 40; for end-trade populations, see 59, table 14.

53. Other orthographic renderings include *Koromantin, Koromantyn,* and *Kromanti.*

54. A sample of 201 names in Barbados yielded 62 percent Akan, 7 percent Yoruba, and 29 percent unknown; see Karl Watson, "The Trans-Atlantic Slave Trade (with Special Reference to Barbados)," in *Emancipation 1: A Series of Lectures to Commemorate the 150th Anniversary of Emancipation,* ed. Alvin O. Thompson (Cave Hill, Barbados: Learning Resource Centre, 1986), 20–22. Rawley argues for just 19.9 percent from the Gold Coast; see *Transatlantic Slave Trade,* 144, table 7.2.

55. Anon., *A Brief and Perfect Journal of the Late Proceedings and Success of the English Army in the West Indies* (London, 1655), 11; A. Caldecott, *The Church in the West Indies* (London: Frank Cass, 1970), 47.

56. William Wilberforce, *An Appeal to Religion, Justice and Humanity of the Inhabitants of the British Empire in Behalf of the Negro Slaves in the West Indies* (London, 1823), 18.

57. Carl Bridenbaugh and Roberta Bridenbaugh, *No Peace beyond the Line: The English in the Caribbean, 1624–1690* (New York: Oxford University Press, 1972), 374; Dunn, *Sugar and Slaves*, 149–50.

58. Pitman, "Slavery," 633.

59. For support of this view, see Jacky Dahomay, "Slavery and Law: Legitimations of an Insurrection," in *The Abolition of Slavery from Léger Félicité Sonthonax to Victor Schœlcher*, ed. Marcel Dorigny (New York: Berghahn Books, 2003), 7.

60. David Brion Davis, *The Problem of Slavery in Western Culture* (New York: Cornell University Press, 1966), 470.

61. Ligon, *True and Exact History*, 47.

62. Hans Sloane, "A Voyage to the Islands," in Williamson, *Contrary Voices*, 22.

63. Ligon, *True and Exact History*, 7.

64. Turnbull, "Apology for Negro Slavery" in Williamson, *Contrary Voices*, 110. For corroborating eyewitnesses, see Drewery Ottley in *Sessional Papers*, 82:163; John Greg, in *Sessional Papers*, 71:227. Despite the inevitable trauma, freed Africans often "married" enslaved females; see evidence of James Tobin, in *Sessional Papers*, 71:268.

65. Long, *History*, 2:414.

66. Warner, "Negro Slavery Described by a Negro," in Williamson, *Contrary Voices*, 267–68.

67. Warner, "Negro Slavery," 267–68.

68. Mary Prince, "The History of Mary Prince," in Williamson, *Contrary Voices*, 279.

69. Long, *History*, 2:414.

70. Long, *History*, 2:414.

71. James Walker, *Letters on the West Indies* (London, 1818), 165–66.

72. Implicit in Pitman, "Slavery," 634–35.

73. Douglas Hall, *In Miserable Slavery: Thomas Thistlewood in Jamaica, 1750–86* (Kingston, Jamaica: University of the West Indies Press, 1999).

74. Equiano, *Life*, 74, 123. John Majoribanks poetically captured these degradations in "Slavery: An Essay in Verse," in Williams, *Contrary Voices*, see esp. 162, lines 302–14.

75. Robert Wedderburn, "The Horrors of Slavery," in Williamson, *Contrary Voices*, 240; also see evidence of John Jerry, overseer and manager in Grenada, in *Sessional Papers*, 82:108, and that of Lt. Henry Dew Dalrymple, in *Sessional Papers*, 73:307.

76. Pitman, "Slavery," 635.

77. John Luffman, 28 January 1787, in *A Brief Account of the Island of Antigua* (London: J. Luffman, 1788), 45.

78. Dunn, *Sugar and Slaves*, 103.

79. Bridenbaugh and Bridenbaugh, *No Peace*, 380.

80. Bridenbaugh and Bridenbaugh, *No Peace*, 381.

81. See Bridenbaugh and Bridenbaugh, *No Peace*, 380.

82. Drawing upon Caldecott, *Church in the West Indies*, Keith Hunte reveals that in 1800 Barbados had a complement of only twenty priests, the same as Jamaica ("Protestantism and Slavery in the British Caribbean," in *Christianity in the Caribbean: Essays on Church History*, ed. Armando Lampe [Kingston, Jamaica: University of the West Indies Press, 2001], 97, 123).

83. Dunn, *Sugar and Slaves*, 252; Michael Craton, *Sinews of Empire: A Short History of British Slavery* (New York: Anchor, 1974), 216; Equiano, *Life*, 75.

84. Evidence of John Castle, *Sessional Papers*, 71:17–18.

85. Equiano, *Life*, 79.

86. Majoribanks, "Slavery," 157.

87. C. H. Haring, *The Spanish Empire in America* (San Diego, Calif.: Jovanovich, 1975), 206.

88. See John Thornton, "The Development of an African Catholic Church in the Kingdom of Kongo, 1491–1750," *Journal of African History* 25, no. 2 (1984): 150–51.

89. The quote was coined by Wilberforce, 38 *Parl. Deb.*, 1st ser. (1818): 486.

90. Cited by Vincent Brown, "Spiritual Terror and Sacred Authority in Jamaican Slave Society," *Slavery and Abolition* 24 (2003): 24.

91. See Silvio Zavala, *The Political Philosophy of the Conquest of America*, trans. Teneer Hall (Mexico City: Editorial Cultura, 1953), chaps. 1–4.

92. Cited in Davis, *Problem of Slavery*, 395.

93. James Stephen, *The Crisis of the Sugar Colonies or an Enquiry into the Objects and Probable Effects of the French Expedition to the West Indies and Their Connection with the Colonial Interests of the British Empire to Which Are Subjoined Sketches of a Plan for Settling the Vacant Lands of Trinidada* (1802; New York: Negro University Press, 1969), 72.

94. Stephen, *Crisis,* 73. Thompson defines the violence deployed by whites as "organized terror" (*Flight to Freedom,* 30).

95. Ramsay, *Treatment and Commerce,* 173.

96. Brougham, *Opinion,* 9.

97. Prince, "History," in Williamson, *Contrary Voices,* 273.

98. Prince, "History," in Williamson, *Contrary Voices,* 276–77.

99. Dunn, *Sugar and Slaves,* 258.

100. Dunn, *Sugar and Slaves,* 259. Burning was a macabre ritual of some three hours, the fire starting from the toes and progressing to the upper body.

101. Gaspar, *Bondsmen and Rebels,* 24–25, 202.

102. Cited in Thompson, *Flight to Freedom,* 165.

103. Dunn, *Sugar and Slaves,* 261.

104. Bryan Edwards, *The History Civil and Commercial of the British Colonies in the West Indies with a Continuation to the Present* (New York: AMS Press, 1966), 2:61; also discussed in Thompson, *Flight to Freedom,* 169–72.

105. Evidence of Dalrymple, *Sessional Papers,* 73:299.

106. Dalrymple, *Sessional Papers,* 73:299. For a poetic rendering of a jealous mistress's torturing of her enslaved female, see Majoribanks, "Slavery," 159.

107. Ferguson, "*Mary Prince,*" 56–57.

108. Thomas Clarkson, *An Essay on the Slavery and Commerce of the Human Species, Particularly the African* (London, 1786), 145.

109. Edwards, *History,* 2:61.

110. Equiano, *Life,* 23.

111. Brougham, *Opinion,* 9.

112. Qtd. in Patterson, *Slavery and Social Death,* 59.

113. Cited in Folarin Shyllon, *James Ramsey, the Unknown Abolitionist* (Edinburgh: Cannongate, 1977), 54–55; also see Sir S. Romilly, motion on "Treatment of Slaves in the Island of Nevis," 38 *Parl. Deb.*, 1st ser. (1818): 841.

114. Shyllon, *James Ramsay,* 54–55.

115. Evidence of Dalrymple, *Sessional Papers,* 73:299. In Barbados the term *cow-skin* was common; see William Dickson, *Letters on Slavery* (Westport, Conn.: Negro University Press, 1970), 14–15; see also 38 *Parl. Deb.*, 1st ser. (1818): 841.

116. Clarkson, *Comparative Efficiency*, 37.

117. Evidence of Lt. John Simpson and Capt. John Giles, *Sessional Papers*, 82:48 and 104, respectively.

118. Evidence of Simpson, *Sessional Papers*, 82:47.

119. Dickson, *Letters on Slavery*, 15.

120. John Wesley, *Thoughts upon Slavery* (Philadelphia, 1774), 23.

121. Clarkson, *Comparative Efficiency*, 38.

122. James Stephen, *The Slavery of the British West India Colonies Delineated as It Exists in Law and Practice and Compared with the Slavery of Other Countries, Antient and Modern* (London, 1823), 50.

123. Evidence of James Towne (carpenter, Royal Navy), *Sessional Papers*, 82:25.

124. Clarkson, *Comparative Efficiency*, 36.

125. "Slaves Sentenced by Court Marshall and Punished in George Town"; also see "Return of Negroes Admitted to the Colonial Hospital," NA, CO 111:45, 131–33.

126. Luffman, 3 October 1787, *Brief Account*, 100; Clarkson, *Comparative Efficiency*, 37.

127. Evidence Jefferys, *Sessional Papers*, 73:231.

128. Luffman, 9 November 1787, *Brief Account*, 102.

129. Clarkson, *Comparative Efficiency*, 37.

130. Buxton, 9 *Parl. Deb.*, 2d ser. (1823): 262.

131. Ramsay, *Treatment and Conversion*, 75.

132. J. R. Ward, *British West Indian Slavery, 1750–1834: The Process of Amelioration* (London: Clarendon, 1988), 157.

133. Evidence of Robert Thomas, *Sessional Papers*, 71:247.

134. See poem by M. H., "The Poor Negro Beggar's Petition and Complaint," in Williamson, *Contrary Voices*, 145–47.

135. The welfare of the elderly was dependent on friends and relatives; evidence of Simpson, *Sessional Papers*, 82:47.

136. See evidence of James Baille, *Sessional Papers*, 71:188; also see Luffman, 1 August 1787, *Brief Account*, 41.

137. Ramsay, *Treatment and Commerce*, 71–72; also see evidence of Jefferys, *Sessional Papers*, 73:233.

138. Equiano, *Life*, 75.

139. Ramsay, *Treatment and Commerce*, 82–83.

140. Luffman, 15 September 1787, *Brief Account*, 96.

141. George Pinkard, *Notes on the West Indies: Written during the Expedition under the Command of the Late General Sir Ralph Abercromby* (London, 1806), 2:114–15.

142. Dunn, *Sugar and Slaves*, 248–49; Richard B. Sheridan, *Sugar and Slavery: An Economic History of the British West Indies, 1623–1775* (Eagle Hall, Barbados: Caribbean Universities Press, 1974), 243.

143. Craton, *Sinews of Empire*, 191–92.

144. See Richard B. Sheridan, "The Crisis of Slave Subsistence in the British West Indies during and after the American Revolution," *William and Mary Quarterly*, 3d ser., 33, no. 4 (1976): 615–41.

145. For conditions up to the early eighteenth century, see Dunn, *Sugar and Slaves*, 300–324. For a wide-ranging discussion on the background of war, internal insurgency, and natural di-

sasters on the policy of greater subsistence, see Sheridan, "Crisis of Slave Subsistence," 615–41.

146. Evidence of Jefferys, *Sessional Papers*, 73:233; Equiano, *Life*, 75; Pinkard, *Notes on the West Indies*, 113; Edward Thompson, "Sailor's Letters," in Williamson, *Contrary Voices*, 62. Planters had standardized these sleeping conditions since the commencement of sugar planting; see Ligon, *True and Exact History*, 47.

147. Bridenbaugh and Bridenbaugh, *No Peace*, 118.

148. James Ramsay, *Objections to the Abolition of the Slave Trade with Answers to Which Are Prefixed, Strictures on a Late Publication, Intitled "Considerations on the Emancipation of Negroes, and the Abolition of the Slave Trade, by a West Indian Planter"* (London, 1788), 13.

149. Ramsay, *Treatment and Commerce*, 88.

150. Ramsay, *Treatment and Commerce*, 88.

151. Bridenbaugh, *No Peace*, 118.

152. This situation was rendered poetically by Edward Rushton, see "West Indian Eclogues," in Williamson, *Contrary Voices*, 366; also see Ashton Warner's account of his wife suffering, "Negro Slavery," in Williamson, *Contrary Voices*, 268, lines 19–28.

153. The long-term infant mortality in the late eighteenth century was well over 350 per 1,000; see Ward, *British West Indian Slavery*, 130.

154. Ramsay, *Treatment and Commerce*, 89; evidence of Jefferys, *Sessional Papers*, 73:233.

155. Warner, "Negro Slavery," 267–68. Mary Prince witnessed a similar flogging of her pregnant "Aunt," who was tied to a tree and flogged till she was covered with blood; see "History," in Williamson, *Contrary Voices*, 57.

156. Ramsay, *Treatment and Commerce*, 106–7. Ligon referred to thirty pounds and between twenty-five and twenty-seven pounds for males and females, respectively, since the 1640s, *True and Exact History*, 46. Prices differed depending on origins and perceived ethnicity; this was certainly the case in Jamaica in 1750, with Gold Coast captives fetching fifty pounds, while others were sold at thirty pounds; see Thomas, *Slave Trade*, 400; also see Hart, *Black Jamaicans' Struggle*, 4.

157. Craton, *Sinews of Empire*, 113–14; Sheridan, *Sugar and Slavery*, 252.

158. Long, *History*, 2:436–37.

159. See Long, *History*, 2:436–37.

2. Humanity Enchained

1. For a study of these laws, see Lawrence A. Harper, *The English Navigation Laws: A Seventeenth-Century Experiment in Social Engineering* (New York: Columbia University Press, 1939), chap. 5; also see Alan Burns, *History of the British West Indies*, 2d ed. (London: Allen & Unwin, 1965), 268–97.

2. The expression was coined by Edmund Burke; see *Speech of Edmund Burke: On Presenting to the House of Commons (on the 11th of February, 1780) a Plan for the Better Security of the Independence of Parliament*, in *Cowen Tracts* 15 (London, 1780), 58, www.jstor.org/stable/60201955.

3. Quoted in Stiv Jakobsson, *Am I Not a Man and Brother? British Missions and the Abolition of the Slave Trade and Slavery in West Africa and the West Indies, 1786–1838* (Uppsala, Sweden: Almqvist & Wilksells, 1972), 35.

4. See Jakobsson, *Am I Not a Man?*, 36.

5. F. Randolph, *A Letter to the Right Honourable William Pitt . . . on the Proposed Abolition of the African Slave Trade* (London, 1788), 9–10. This concept originated in the Puritan migration to North America during the 1620s. For the view of Puritans as the new Israelites, see K. G. Davies, *The North Atlantic World in the Seventeenth Century* (Minneapolis: University of Minnesota Press, 1974), 112, 142.

6. P. J. Marshall, *The Impeachment of Warren Hastings* (London: Oxford University Press, 1965), 13–17, 34–36, 181–86.

7. This timeline refutes Fryer's assertion that prior to the "Scramble for Africa" trusteeship was just "an ideal, not a guideline" (*Staying Power,* 184).

8. Ramsay, *Treatment and Conversion,* xiii.

9. See Davis, *Problem of Slavery,* 397.

10. Equiano, *Life,* 177.

11. *Ubuntu* is an ethical concept that presupposes that one's humanity can only be fully attained in recognizing the humanity of others; for an elaboration, see chap. 1, nn. 21–22; for the expression "humanity to humanity," see René Maunier, *The Sociology of Colonies: An Introduction to the Study of Race Contact,* trans. and ed. E. O. Lorimer (London: Routledge & Paul, 1949), 1:169.

12. Adam Smith, *The Theory of Moral Sentiment in the Essays of Adam Smith* (1759; London, 1869), 24.

13. John Wesley, *The Character of a Methodist* (Philadelphia: 1742), 9.

14. See Davis, *Problem of Slavery,* 100. Two papal bulls featured most in the historical literature on the demonization of Africans are "Romanus Pontifex" and "Sicut Dudum." For the full text of the more forthright "Sicut Dudum," see www.net/Eugene04/eugene04sicut.htm.

15. Fryer, *Staying Power,* 165.

16. Alice L. Conklin, *A Mission to Civilize: The Republican Idea of Empire in France and West Africa, 1895–1930* (Stanford, Calif.: Stanford University Press, 1997), 11. Most scholars now straddle a continuum between the Fryer-Conklin paradigm and the total rejection of self-service as espoused by Penelope Hetherington, *British Paternalism and Africa, 1920–1940* (London: Frank Cass, 1978), 45; see Knorr, *British Colonial Theories,* 246–47; Ronald Kent Richardson, *Moral Imperium: Afro-Caribbean and the Transformation of British Rule, 1776–1838* (Westport, Conn.: Greenwood, 1977), 110–18; A. P. Thornton, *Doctrines of Imperialism* (London: Wiley, 1963), 155.

17. Qtd. in Hetherington, *British Paternalism,* 53; also see Klingberg, *Anti Slavery Movement,* 26.

18. Barbados Legislature, House of Assembly, *The Report from a Select Committee of the House of Assembly, Appointed to Inquire into the Origin, Causes and Progress of the Late Insurrection* (London, 1818), 53; "Marly; or A Planter's Life in Jamaica (1828)," in Williamson, *Contrary Voices,* 256.

19. See Davis, *Problem of Slavery,* 221.

20. See "List of Subscribers," in Equiano, *Interesting Narrative.*

21. Cited in Williamson, *Contrary Voices,* 178.

22. Montesquieu, *Spirit of the Laws,* 1:ix.

23. Fryer, *Staying Power,* 100.

24. "Ottabah Cugoano," www.spartacus.schoolnet.co.uk/USAScugoano.htm.

25. Ramsay, *Treatment and Conversion,* 96.

26. For a useful exposition on the meaning of property and the connection between property and slavery in classical Europe and its continuity in medieval Europe through Saint Augustine and Thomas Aquinas, see Saint Augustine, *The City of God,* ed. R.V.G. Tasker, trans. John Healy (London: Dent, 1962), 1:xxxii–xxxiii; K. R. Popper, *The Open Society and Its Enemies,* vol. 1: *The Spell of Plato* (London: Routledge, 1966), 70–75.

27. For an elaboration of this perspective, see Robin Blackburn, "Haiti, Slavery, and the Age of the Democratic Revolution," *William and Mary Quarterly,* 3d ser., 63, no. 4 (Oct. 2006): 653–54, www.jstor.org/stable/4491574.

28. See David Brion Davis, "The Emergence of Immediatism in British and American Thought," *Mississippi Valley Historical Review* 49 (1962): 213–14.

29. H. T. Catteral, *Cases from the Courts of England, Virginia, West Virginia and Kentucky, Judicial Cases Concerning American Slavery and the Negro* (Washington, D.C.: Carnegie Institute, 1926), 9; also see James Walvin, *England, Slaves and Freedom, 1776–1838* (London: Macmillan, 1986), chaps. 2–3.

30. Catteral, *Judicial Cases,* 11.

31. Catteral, *Judicial Cases,* 11.

32. Catteral, *Judicial Cases,* 12; also see Edwards, *History,* 4:311–12.

33. Act for the More Easy Recovery of Debts, 1732, 5 Geo. 2, c. 7, in Danby Pickering, ed., *The Statutes at Large, from the Second to the Ninth Year of King George II* (Cambridge, 1765), 16:272.

34. Pearne v. Lise (1749), in Catteral, *Judicial Cases,* 12–13.

35. Pearne v. Lise, in Catteral, *Judicial Cases,* 12–13.

36. Pearne v. Lise, in Catteral, *Judicial Cases,* 12–13.

37. Pearne v. Lise, in Catteral, *Judicial Cases,* 12–13.

38. Granville Sharp, *An Appendix to the Representation of the Injustice and Dangerous Tendency of Tolerating Slavery, or of Admitting the Least Claim of Private Property in the Person of Man in England* (London, 1772), 11.

39. See excerpts in James Walvin, *The Black Presence: A Documentary History of the Negro in England, 1555–1860* (London: Opbach & Chambers, 1971), 161–63.

40. Somerset v. Stewart, in Catteral, *Judicial Cases,* 5.

41. Somerset v. Stewart, Catteral, *Judicial Cases,* 5.

42. Walvin, *England,* 42–43. Williams rightly condemned the uncritical acceptance of post-Somerset England as a province of freedom for all as "poetic sentimentality translated into modern history"; see *Capitalism and Slavery,* 45–46.

43. 9 *Parl. Deb.,* 2d ser. (1823): 269. James Stephen added another episteme, regretting that the African's skin was a "badge of infamy and vileness"; see *Slavery of the British West India Colonies,* 27.

44. Edward Long, *Candid Reflections upon the Judgement Lately Awarded by the Court of King's Bench in Westminster-Hall on What Is Commonly Called the Negro-Cause* (London, 1772), 34.

45. Long, *Candid Reflections,* 34. Interestingly, this thinking also informed the meaning of *freedom* under the apprenticeship (1834–38).

46. Long, *Candid Reflections,* 34.

47. Long, *Candid Reflections,* 56.

48. In most situations the law lost its liberalism and impartiality in issues affecting Africans and Afro-Europeans ("mulattoes" or "coloreds"); see Shyllon, *Black People in Britain,* 141.

49. Case of Grace Jones, in Catteral, *Judicial Cases,* 34.

50. Jones, in Catteral, *Judicial Cases,* 34.

51. Jones, in Catteral, *Judicial Cases,* 34.

52. Jones, in Catteral, *Judicial Cases,* 35.

53. Jones, in Catteral, *Judicial Cases,* 34.

54. Jones, in Catteral, *Judicial Cases,* 35.

55. The King v. the Inhabitants of Thames Ditton (1785), Catteral, *Judicial Cases,* 19.

56. Clarkson, *History,* 77.

57. Clarkson, *History,* 77. This opinion has been promoted by historians devoted to the myth of humanitarian idealism of English abolitionists; see, e.g., Lowell J. Ragatz, *The Fall of the Planter Class in the British Caribbean: A Study in Social and Economic History* (1928; New York: Octagon Press, 1971), 246; Anstey, *Atlantic Slave Trade,* 244–46. For a more objective assessment, see Walvin, *England,* 43–44; Jerome Nadelhaft, "The Somerset Case and Slavery: Myth, Reality, and Repercussions," *Journal of Negro History* 51 (1966): 193–208.

58. Case of Jones, in Catteral, *Judicial Cases,* 36.

59. Jones, in Catteral, *Judicial Cases,* 35.

60. Jones, in Catteral, *Judicial Cases,* 37.

61. 18 *Parl. Deb.,* 2d ser. (1826): 1037.

62. 9 *Parl. Deb.,* 2d ser. (1823): 269.

63. 9 *Parl. Deb.,* 2d ser. (1823): 255.

64. All cases cited in 119 *Parl. Deb.,* 3d ser. (1833): 1235–37.

65. Adam Smith, *Institutes,* 77.

66. Qtd. in [Long], *Candid Reflections,* 34.

3. Pragmatizing Amelioration and Abolition

1. George R. Mellor, *British Imperial Trusteeship, 1728–1850* (London: Faber & Faber, 1951), 22.

2. See W. E. B. Du Bois, *The Suppression of the African Slave-Trade to the United States of America, 1638–1870* (New York: Longmans, 1896), Gutenberg e-book, www2.hn.psu.edu/faculty/jmanis/webdubois.htm.

3. Ragatz, *Fall of the Planter Class,* 142–93; Williams, *Capitalism and Slavery,* 108–25; Selwyn H.H. Carrington, *The Sugar Industry and the Abolition of the Slave Trade 1775-1810* (Gainesville: University Press of Florida, 2002), 116–36 and 247–51; Richard Sheridan, "The Crisis of Slave Subsistence in the British West Indies during and after the American Revolution," *William and Mary Quarterly,* 3d ser., 33, no. 4 (1976): 615–41.

4. Hart, *Black Jamaicans,* 3–4.

5. Craton, *Sinews of Empire,* 113–14; Sheridan, *Sugar and Slavery,* 252; Ramsay, *Treatment and Commerce,* 106–7.

6. Ward, *British West Indian Slavery,* 155.

7. See Walvin, *Trader,* 161.

8. Ward, *West Indian Slavery,* 155.

9. Ward, *West Indian Slavery,* 156.

10. Mortality rate to birthrate was six to one; see Davis, *Problem of Slavery,* 219–21; Dunn, *Sugar and Slaves,* 324.

11. See Dunn, *Sugar and Slaves,* 324.

12. See Hilary Beckles, "An Economic Life of Their Own: Slaves as Commodity Producers and Distributors in Barbados," *Slavery and Abolition* 12, no. 1 (May 1991): 31–47.

13. From a sample of twenty-two plantations in 1781, 86 percent were owned by Creoles; by 1816 the number had increased to 91–92 percent; one of the apparent positive factors was an early sex balance (by 1687). See Watson, "Trans-Atlantic Slave Trade," 21–24; Hilary Beckles, "The Barbadian Slaves and the Struggle for Freedom," in *Emancipation 1,* 64–65; B. W. Higman, *Slave Populations of the British Caribbean, 1807–34* (Baltimore: Johns Hopkins University Press, 1984), 121–22; Elsa Goveia, *Slave Society in the British Leeward Islands* (New Haven: Yale University Press, 1965), 124. Even though Jamaica lagged behind, mortality was also down significantly from 1761 to 1805, and the number of Creoles was "actually increasing"; see Williams, *British West Indies at Westminster,* 4; also see 8 *Parl. Deb.,* 1st ser. (1807): 949–50.

14. Testimony of Equiano, *Life,* 75; also see Ramsay, *Treatment and Commerce,* 154–55.

15. Mavis C. Campbell, *The Maroons of Jamaica, 1655–1796: A History of Resistance, Collaboration, and Betrayal* (Granby, Mass.: Bergin & Garvey, 1988), 156.

16. Campbell, *Maroons of Jamaica,* 157; Long, *History,* 2:465–71; Edwards, *History,* 2: 61.

17. Long, *History,* 2:442.

18. Edwards, *History,* 2:60.

19. Equiano, *Life,* 16; also see C. Magbaily Fyle, *The History of Sierra Leone* (London: Evans Brothers, 1981), 66.

20. Long, *History,* 2:444.

21. Dunn, *Sugar and Slaves,* 257.

22. Gaspar, *Bondsmen and Rebels,* 227.

23. See Sheridan, "Jamaican Slave Insurrection," 293–304.

24. See Edwards, *History,* 3:xix.

25. Long, *History,* 2:432, 436.

26. Long, *History,* 2:405, 442; also see Long, *History,* 3:936–37.

27. Long, *History,* 2:429–30; for the likely transfer of African Christians from the Kongo to St. Domingue, see Thornton, "African Catholic Church."

28. Long, *History,* 2:441; for his faithful reproduction of the *Code Noir,* see *History,* 3:921–34.

29. Long, *History,* 2:405.

30. Long, *History,* 3:938.

31. Ramsay, *Treatment and Commerce,* 179.

32. Clarkson, *History,* 217–26.

33. Ramsay's model was the Moravian mission in the Danish colonies; see *Treatment and Commerce,* 164.

34. Ramsay, *Treatment and Commerce,* 168.

35. Ramsay, *Treatment and Commerce,* 169.

36. Ramsay, *Treatment and Commerce,* 151.

37. Ramsay, *Treatment and Commerce,* 154–55.

38. Ramsay, *Treatment and Commerce,* xiii.

39. Ramsay, *Treatment and Commerce,* 98, 171.

40. Ramsay, *Treatment and Commerce,* 168.

41. Ramsay, *Treatment and Commerce,* 114.

42. Equiano, *Life,* 178; also see Fryer, *Staying Power,* 109–10.

43. See, e.g., David Northrup, "The Compatibility of the Slave and Palm Oil Trades in the Bight of Biafra," *Journal of African History* 17, no. 3 (1976): 353–64; Robin Law, *Ouidah: The Social History of a West African Slaving "Port," 1727–1892* (Athens: Ohio University Press, 2005), 203–14.

44. Ramsay, *Objections,* 22.

45. Ramsay, *Treatment and Commerce,* 89.

46. Oliver O. Furley, "Moravian Missions and Slaves in the West Indies," *Caribbean Studies* 5, no. 1 (1965): 4.

47. Beverly Brown, "George Liele: Black Baptist and Pan Africanist, 1750–1826," *SAVACOU* 11–12 (Sept. 1975): 58–67; Melvin L. Buttler, "Dancing around Dancehalls: Popular Music and Pentecostal Jamaica and Haiti," in *Constructing Vernacular Culture in the Trans-Caribbean,* ed. Holger Henke & Karl Heinz Magister (Lanham, Md.: Lexington, 2008), 67; Silvia R. Frey and Betty Wood, *Come Shouting to Zion: African American Protestantism in the American South and British Caribbean to 1830* (Chapel Hill: University of North Carolina Press, 1998), 117–19, 131.

48. See Frey and Wood, *Come Shouting,* 131; Brian Stanley, *The History of the Baptist Missionary Society, 1792–1992* (Edinburgh: T. & T. Clark, 1992), 68–70. Another view is that London Baptists arrived in Jamaica in 1814 as a counterpoise to the Black Baptists; see Brathwaite, *Development of Creole Society,* 253–54.

49. Two outstanding examples of this pioneering cohort were "Brother Amos," of Jamaican background, who established his mission in the Bahamas, and "Black Harry," a Methodist, whose mission was in St. Eustatius; see Frey and Wood, *Come Shouting,* 115–17, 131; also see Arthur Charles Dayfort, *The Shaping of the West Indies Church, 1492–1962* (Cave Hill, Barbados: University of the West Indies Press, 1999), 129–31. For a geographical spread of these pioneer missionaries in Jamaica, see Mary Turner, *Slaves and Missionaries: The Disintegration of Jamaican Society, 1783–1834* (Urbana: Illinois University Press, 1982), 11. In Antigua two black slaveholding sisters were instrumental in spreading Christianity among the enslaved; see John Sailant, "Antiguan Methodism and Anti-Slavery Activity: Ann and Elizabeth Hart in the Eighteenth-Century Black Atlantic," *Church History* 69, no. 1 (2000), http://journals.combridge.org/action.

50. Qtd. in Barker, *African Link,* 70.

51. Wilberforce, *An Appeal to the Religion, Justice and Humanity of the Inhabitants of the British Empire in Behalf of the Negro Slaves in the West Indies* (London, 1823), 50. Der asserts that the early origin of the code (1780) was fabricated by Burke because it does not fit into his politics at the time; see Benedict Der, "Edmund Burke and Africa, 1772–1792," *Transactions of the Historical Society of Ghana* 11 (1970): 22.

52. The Grenada Guardian Act 1784, NA, CO 101:8, 305–12; the act was passed but not proclaimed. Bryan Edwards admired the Guardian Act for its "guardians of slaves"; he also realistically did not expect change because "the evidence of the slave cannot be admitted against a White person" (*History,* 172). For an overview of Jamaica's seminal ameliorative legislation, see Heather Cateau, "Management and the Sugar Industry in the British West Indies, 1750–1810" (Ph.D. diss., University of the West Indies, 1994), 218–19; also see 8 *Parl. Deb.,* 1st ser. (1807): 1042–43.

53. Clause 3, Guardian Act, NA, CO 101:8, 305–305v.

54. Clauses 7– 18, Guardian Act, NA, CO 101:8, 307–12.

55. Evidence of Lt. Henry Dalrymple, *Sessional Papers,* 73:305.

56. *Sessional Papers,* 122:151–52.

57. Evidence of Alexander Campbell (absentee planter), *Sessional Papers,* 71:149.

58. Guardian Act, NA, CO 101:8, 308v.

59. Evidence of Campbell, *Sessional Papers,* 71:149.

60. See Dalrymple, *Sessional Papers,* 73:306; *London Times,* 9 May 1788.

61. Patricia Shaubah Murphy, *The Moravian Mission to the African Slaves in the Danish West Indies, 1723–1828* (St. Croix, U.S. Virgin Islands: Prestige, 1969), 3.

62. Furley, "Moravian Missions," 4; Goveia, *Slave Society,* 220; Richard Dunn, "A Tale of Two Plantations: Slave Life at Mesopotamia in Jamaica and Mount Airy in Virginia, 1799–1828," in *The Black Diaspora: Africans and Their Descendants in the Wider World, 1800 to the Present,* ed. Black Diaspora Committee, Howard University, rev. ed. (Washington, D.C.: Ginn, 1990), 132.

63. Ramsay, *Treatment and Commerce,* 161. By 1765 the Moravians were challenging the Barbados planters; see Goveia, *Slave Society,* 273.

64. Richard Pattison to John Baxter, 1 June 1804, Wesleyan Methodist Missionary Society Reports, vol. 1: 1789–1820, box 3, School of Oriental and African Studies (hereafter cited as WMMS Reports).

65. Dr. Coke, "An Account of the Rise, Progress and Present State of the Methodist Missions," London, 1804, WMMS Reports, vol. 1, box 3. Antigua was then the leading colony in proselytizing.

66. The comment was made by one Benjamin La Trobe, a visitor to the colonies (Goveia, *Slave Society,* 273).

67. See Geoffrey Parrinder, "The African Spiritual Universe," in *Afro-Caribbean Religions,* ed. Brian Gates (London: Ward Lock, 1980), 3–25; N. S. Booth Jr., *African Religions: A Symposium* (New York: Nok, 1977).

68. Pinkard, letter 13, *Notes,* 263–64; Luffman, letter 80, 14 March 1788, *Brief Account,* 136; Fish to Benson, 26 April 1804, WMMS Archives, box 1: 2. Colonists particularly feared the "Water Mama" dance because dancers might go into a trance and receive instructions to revolt or harm their enslavers; a similar fear was associated with the "ikem" dances; see George Eaton Simpson, *Peoples and Cultures: An Anthropological Reader* (New York: Natural History Press, 1971), 491–92; Patrick Taylor, *The Narrative of Liberation: Perspectives on Afro-Caribbean Literature, Popular Culture and Politics* (Ithaca: Cornell University Press, 1989), 97–98; Michael Craton, *Empire, Enslavement, and Freedom in the Caribbean* (Kingston, Jamaica: Ian Randle Publishers, 1997), 187; Gaspar, *Bondsmen and Rebels,* 249–51.

69. Long, *History,* 2:430. Ramsay, *Treatment and Commerce,* 162–63. For evidence of adoption, see Society for the Conversion and Religious Instruction and Education of Negro Slaves in the British West India Islands, *Instructions for Missionaries to the West India Islands* (London, n.d.), 7.

70. Hesketh Bell, *Witches and Fishes* (London: Arnold, 1948), 41; also see Mulrain, "African Cosmology," 3.

71. John Savage, "'Black Magic' and White Terror: Slave Poisonings and Colonial Society in Early 19th Century Martinique," *Journal of Social History* 40, no. 3 (2007): 635, www.questia.com/PM.qst?a=o&d=5020427770; Juanita de Barros, "'Setting Things Right': Medicine and Magic in Guiana, 1803–1838," *Slavery and Abolition* 25, no. 1 (Apr. 2004): 38–41; Jerome Handler, "Slave Medicine and Obeah in Barbados, circa 1650–1834," *New West Indian Guide* 74, nos. 1–2 (2000): 57–90.

72. Bryan Edwards variously referred to it as "science," "art," and "fascinating mischief" (Edwards, *History,* 2:107–8). Also see Milton C. Sernett, ed., *African American Religious History: A Documentary Witness* (Durham, N.C.: Duke University Press, 1999), 20–24. Jerome Handler and Frederick Lange made an interesting excavation of a "revered folk doctor" at Newton Plantation in Barbados, complete with esoteric paraphernalia, including cowrie shells. They dated the burial between the late 1600s and early 1700s; cited in Charles E. Orser Jr., *A Historical Archaeology of the Modern World* (New York: Plemnum Press, 1996), 125.

73. Anne Hilton, *The Kingdom of Kongo* (Oxford: Clarendon, 1985), 94. In Kongolese *nganga* is the name of a traditional priest, *nkisi* an initiation rite.

74. Hilton, *Kingdom of Kongo,* 101.

75. Hilton, *Kingdom of Kongo,* 101.

76. Ramsay, *Treatment and Commerce,* 182.

77. Wilberforce, *Appeal,* 28.

78. Governor Woodford to Commandants of Quarters, 22 August 1823, NA, CO 295:60, 16v; Huskisson to Maj. Gen. Keane (governor of Jamaica), 22 September 1827, NA, CO 324:102, 3–7.

79. Fish to Benson, 26 April 1804, WMMS Archives, box 1: 2. "Hearers" were not counted as converts of the society.

80. "Instructions to Missionaries," instruction 7, no. 3, xii, WMMS Reports, 1828.

81. "Instructions to Missionaries," instruction 7, no. 3, xii, WMMS Reports, 1828.

82. "Instructions to Missionaries," instruction 7,, xi–xii, WMMS Reports, 1828.

83. These exhortations were contained in catechisms. See WMMS Reports, 1828, "Instructions" 7, xi–xii.

84. Instruction 7, no. 1, xi, WMMS Reports, 1828. Bible lessons were catechetical and repetitious; see Richard Nisbett, *The Capacity of Negroes for Religious and Moral Improvement Considered . . .* (1789; New York: Negro University Press, 1970), 111. For an example of an early catechism, see Nisbett, *Capacity of Negroes,* 106–7.

85. Nisbett, *Capacity of Negroes,* 123–24.

86. Nisbett, *Capacity of Negroes,* 95, 120–21.

87. Nisbett, *Capacity of Negroes,* 80.

88. Nisbett, *Capacity of Negroes,* 95, 120–21. Missionaries conned the enslaved into repudiating freedom by marronage as a quid pro quo for baptism; see Davis, *Problem of Slavery,* 215.

89. Nisbett, *Capacity of Negroes,* 98.

90. See James, *Black Jacobins,* 17–18; also see anon., *The Slave Colonies of Great Britain or a Picture of Negro Slavery Drawn by the Colonists Themselves* (London, 1825), 33; Venetia Newall, "The Hero as Trickster: The West Indian Anansi," in *The Hero in Tradition and Folklore,* ed. H. R. E. Davidson (London: Folklore Society, 1984), 66–67; Hall, *Thomas Thistlewood,* 159–60.

91. Long, *History,* 2:416–17; also Orlando Patterson, *Sociology of Slavery: An Analysis of the Origins, Development and Structure of Negro Slavery in Jamaica* (London: Cox & Wyman, 1967), 153, 173.

92. Cited by Emily Zobel Marshall, "Tracking Anansi," *Caribbean Beat* (Nov. –Dec. 2007): 53.

93. Turner, *Slaves and Missionaries,* 65; for the success of missionary strategy, see David Brailsford, *Confessions of Anansi* (Kingston, Jamaica: LMH Publishing, 2003), iv.

94. Cited in Knorr, *British Colonial Theories,* 379–80. To Maunier "the spirit is the highest point of culture" (*Sociology of Colonies,* 177).

95. Ramsay, *Treatment and Commerce,* 165.

96. Davis, *Problem of* Slavery, 215.

97. Ramsay, *Treatment and Commerce,* 162.

98. See Baxter to Pattison, 1 June 1804, WMMS Archives, box 1: 3.

99. During the 1790s, e.g., Mary Allen, a "mulatto," and Sophia Campbell, an African, held a congregation together in Antigua. Baxter to Pattison, 1 June 1804, WMMS Archives, box 1: 3.

4. Abolitionism and Empire

1. P. J. Marshall, *Problems of Empire: Britain and India* (London: Unwin, 1968), 18–24, 174, 227.

2. Marshall, *Impeachment of Warren Hastings,* xviii.

3. Marshall, *Impeachment of Warren Hastings,* 1.

4. Marshall, *Impeachment of Warren Hastings,* 13, 20.

5. Marshall, *Impeachment of Warren Hastings,* 13.

6. Marshall, *Impeachment of Warren Hastings,* 15.

7. Preamble to Burke's draft Slave Code, Windham Papers, 44:7, BL, Add. MSS 37890.

8. For an extensive discussion on this topic, see Lewis Hanke, *The First Social Experiments in America; a Study in the Development of Spanish Indian Policy in the Sixteenth Century* (Cambridge: Harvard University Press, 1935), chap. 2.

9. See Marshall, *Impeachment of Warren Hastings,* 13.

10. Burke, "West Indies," Windham Papers, 44:7, BL, Add. MSS 37890.

11. Burke, clause 22, Windham Papers, 44:9v, BL, Add. MSS 37890.

12. Burke, clause 22, Windham Papers, 44:9v, BL, Add. MSS 37890. Furthermore, clause 21 recognized cohabitation of twelve months or more—for men above eighteen years of age and for women above sixteen years of age—as de facto marriage and compelled such couples to seek out "the Minister of the District, to be married in the face of the Church."

13. Burke, clause 23, Windham Papers, 44:10, BL, Add. MSS 37890.

14. Burke, clause18, Windham Papers, 44:9, BL, Add. MSS 37890.

15. Edwards, *History,* 2:182.

16. Clarkson, *History,* 205.

17. Clarkson, *History,* 215–24.

18. Seymour Drescher,, "Paradigms Tossed: Capitalism and the Political Sources of Abolition," *British Capitalism and Caribbean Slavery: The Legacy of Eric Williams*, ed. Barbara Solow and Stanley Engerman (New York: Cambridge University Press, 1987), 200.

19. Clarkson, *History,* 113.

20. Clarkson, *History,* 118.

21. Clarkson, *History,* 476.

22. Drescher, "Paradigms Tossed," 201; also see John Ehrman, *The Younger Pitt: The Years of Acclaim* (London: Constable, 1969), 389.

23. Drescher, "Paradigms Tossed," 202.

24. See Victor C. D. Mtubani, "The Black Voice in Eighteenth-Century Britain: African Writers against Slavery and the Slave Trade," *Phylon* 45, no. 2 (1984): 93.

25. See Fryer, *Staying Power,* 108.

26. *London Times,* 29 May 1788.

27. *London Times,* 29 May 1788.

28. Clarkson, *Comparative Efficiency,* 80.

29. Clarkson, *Comparative Efficiency,* 78–82.

30. See Clarkson, *Comparative Efficiency*, 81, tables 1–5.

31. Qtd. in Davis, *Problem of Slavery*, 398.

32. The poem is reproduced in full in Williams, *Contrary Voices*, 153–71; see esp. lines 409–12 and 170 n. 45.

33. Davis, "Emergence of Immediatism," 219–20.

34. Ramsay, *Objections*, 8.

35. Ramsay, *Objections*, 11.

36. Ramsay, *Objections*, 8. For a detailed analysis of contemporary meanings of immediatism in abolition politics, see Davis, "Emergence of Immediatism," 209–29.

37. See James, *Black Jacobins*, 54.

38. *Sessional Papers*, 73:79.

39. Thomas Clarkson to John Clarkson, 3 March 1792, John Clarkson Papers, 1: 97, BL, Add. MSS 41262A.

40. Cited in George Wilson Bridges, *Dreams of Dulocracy or the Puritanical Obituary: "An Appeal," Not to the Romantic Sensibility but to the Good Sense of the British Public* (London, 1824), 8; also see Wilberforce, *Appeal*, 34–35.

41. Wilberforce, *Appeal*, 5.

42. Wilberforce, *Appeal*, 6.

43. 8 *Parl. Deb.*, 1st ser. (1807): 702–3.

44. See Davis, *Problem of Slavery*, 207.

45. See Nugent, *Spirit of the Laws*, 238–42. See explanation offered by Blackburn, "Haiti," 649.

46. Cited in Bridges, *Dream of Dulocracy*, 8.

47. Robert J.W. Horton, *The West India Question Practically Considered* (London: 1826), 2–3; also see Wilberforce *Appeal*, 48.

48. Montesquieu, *Spirit of the Laws*, 241.

49. Adam Smith, *An Enquiry into the Nature and Causes of the Wealth of Nations* (1776; New York: Random, 1937), 365, 557–83.

50. Ramsay, *Objections*, 8.

51. Ramsay, *Objections*, 8, 30–31.

52. Brougham, *Colonial Policy*, 2:120; also see Stephen, *Crisis*, 193.

53. Davis, "James Cropper and the British Anti-Slavery Movement, 1821–1823," *Journal of Negro History* 45 (Oct. 1960): 253.

54. Davis, "James Cropper," 249.

55. Davis, "James Cropper," 247–53.

56. 9 *Parl. Deb.*, 2d ser. (1823): 263, 273.

57. 9 *Parl. Deb.*, 2d ser. (1823): 263, 273.

58. Buxton to Joseph Gurney, 9 May 1825, Thomas Fowell Buxton Papers, 2:112–13, MSS. Brit. Emp. S. 444, Rhodes House Library (hereafter cited as Buxton Papers).

59. Buxton to Joseph Gurney, 9 May 1825, Buxton Papers, 2:115.

60. See Davis, "Emergence of Immediatism," 220–21.

61. See David Brion Davis, "Capitalism, Abolition and Hegemony," in *British Capitalism and Caribbean Slavery: The Legacy of Eric Williams*, ed. Barbara Solow and Stanley Engerman (New York: Cambridge University Press, 1987), 122.

62. Minutes of the Anti-Slavery Society, vol. 1, 30 April 1825, 20, MSS. Brit. Emp. S. 20, Rhodes House Library (hereafter cited as Minutes, ASS).

63. Minutes, ASS, 30 April 1825, 1:20.

64. Williams, *Capitalism and Slavery,* 151, 162, 185–88, 193–94.

65. Clarkson to Buxton, 14 May 1825, Letters from Thomas Clarkson to Thomas Fowell Buxton on Slavery, 1825–25, Add. MSS. Brit. Emp. S. 495:13, Rhodes House Library (hereafter cited as Thomas Clarkson MSS). Cropper planned every detail of Clarkson's trip; see Davis, "James Cropper," 255.

66. Clarkson to Buxton, 14 May 1825, Thomas Clarkson MSS.

67. Clarkson to Buxton, 20 September 1825, Thomas Clarkson MSS.

68. *Trinidad Guardian,* 3 February 1826, NA, CO 300:1; 23 May 1828, NA, CO 300:2. The duty had remained fixed at 27 shillings per hundredweight since 1803. *Trinidad Guardian,* 6 April 1830, NA, CO 300:3.

69. Clarkson to Buxton, 20 September 1825, 1v, Thomas Clarkson MSS.

70. The original act was followed by numerous amendments. In all of them the company's monopoly in china and tea was preserved. See Act for Expanding Private Merchants Rights, 1817, 57 Geo. 3 c. 6; also see 1821, 1 and 2 Geo. 4 c. 57.

71. An Act to Permit Entry of Sugar from Martinique, Marie Galante, Guadeloupe, St. Eustatius, St. Martin, Saba at Lower Rate of Duty than Other Non British Sugars, 1813, 53 Geo. 3 c. 62.

72. James Stephen, *England Enslaved by Her Own Colonies: An Address to the Electors and People of the United Kingdom* (London, 1826), 16.

73. 13 *Parl. Deb.,* 2d ser. (1825): 1039–40.

74. Stephen, *England Enslaved,* 14.

75. Stephen, *England Enslaved,* 15.

76. Stephen, *England Enslaved,* 15.

77. Haiti's economic recovery was dramatized in its willingness to meet France's demand for a huge indemnity equivalent to twice the value of St. Domingue's 1789 sugar crop, valued at roughly 78 million *livres.* See Horton, *West India Question,* 144–45, app. A. *Port of Spain Gazette,* 9 September 1826, reported an indemnity of 10 million dollars over a ten-year period. According to Noel Deer, the figure was 3.6 million pounds sterling, reduced from 6 million in 1817 (*History of Sugar* [London: Chapman, 1950], 2:327). Horton did not question the facts of the Haitian economy but rejected its relevance to British capitalists, who he felt ought not to be compelled to engage in undertakings less profitable than sugar (*West India Question,* 56).

78. Horton, *West India Question,* 45.

79. Horton, *West India Question,* 45.

80. Cited in Davis, "James Cropper," 244.

81. Horton, *West India Question,* 46. The press accused many leading members of the Anti-Slavery Society of profiting directly from slave labor used by the East India Company (*Trinidad Guardian,* 10 March 1826, NA, CO 300:2; also see Williams, *Capitalism and Slavery,* 184–86).

82. Horton, *West India Question,* 46.

83. 16 *Parl. Deb.,* 2d ser. (1826): 979; *Port of Spain Gazette,* 19 April 1826.

5. The Haitian Revolution and Other Emancipation Wars

1. Stephen to Wilberforce, [1803?], Wilberforce MSS, d.17, 215–17v.

2. *Sessional Papers,* 82:305–13; also see *Journals of the House of Commons,* 10 June 1806, 61:392.

3. See Blackburn, "Haiti," 644n, 1n.

4. Georges Fouron, citing Karl Marx, *The German Ideology*, in "Theories of 'Race' and the Haitian Revolution," in *Reinterpreting the Haitian Revolution and Its Cultural Aftershocks*, ed. Martin Munro and Elizabeth Walcott-Hackshaw (Kingston, Jamaica: University of the West Indies Press, 2006), 73.

5. Du Bois, *Suppression of the African Slave-Trade*.

6. The grand army was destined for North America to extend the newly acquired Louisiana Territory after completing its mission in Haiti; see Thomas Reinhardt, "200 Years of Forgetting: Hushing Up the Haitian Revolution," *Journal of Black Studies* 35, no. 4 (Mar. 2005): 247.

7. See James, *Black Jacobins*, 146.

8. George W. Brown, "The Origins of Abolition in Santo Domingo," *Journal of Negro History* 7, no. 4 (Oct. 1922): 365–76.

9. James, *Black Jacobins*, 132–33.

10. James, *Black Jacobins*, 134. James did not cite his source, but one is given in Williams, *Capitalism and Slavery*, 149.

11. James, *Black Jacobins*, 133–36.

12. Williams, *Capitalism and Slavery*, 148. The conclusion is repeated in Williams, *From Columbus to Castro*, 261–62.

13. Williams, *Capitalism and Slavery*, 148.

14. Anstey, *Atlantic Slave Trade*, 308.

15. Anstey, *Atlantic Slave Trade*, 315. For the original citation, see 32 *Parl. Hist.* (1796): 752.

16. Anstey, *Atlantic Slave Trade*, 317–18.

17. Anstey, *Atlantic Slave Trade*, 316.

18. Dale Porter, *The Abolition of the Slave Trade in England, 1784–1807* (Hamden, Conn.: Archon Books, 1970), 94–95.

19. Porter, *Abolition of the Slave Trade*, 94.

20. Cuyler to Dundas, Headquarters, Martinique, 29 March 1798, NA, WO 1:86, 62; also see "Heads of Instructions to Major Gen'l. Hunter," 26 January 1797, 59–60, NA, WO 1:86.

21. Michael Craton, *Testing the Chains: Resistance to Slavery in the British West Indies* (Ithaca: Cornell University Press, 1982), 169.

22. David Patrick Geggus, *Slavery, War, and Revolution: The British Occupation of Saint Domingue, 1793–1798* (Oxford: Clarendon Press, 1982), 150.

23. Geggus, *Slavery, War, and Revolution*, 150; also see Craton, *Testing the Chains*, 181.

24. David Geggus, "Slave Resistance and Emancipation: The Case of Saint-Domingue," in Drescher and Emmer, *Who Abolished Slavery?*, 115.

25. For Abercromby's campaign, see Roger Norman Buckley, *The British Army in the West Indies: Society and the Military in the Revolutionary Age* (Gainesville: University Press of Florida, 1998), 257; also see Buckley, *Slaves in Red Coats: The British West India Regiment, 1795–1815* (New Haven: Yale University Press, 1979), 14–15, 53, 70. In another work Buckley marginalizes the role of black fighters in the restoration of British sovereignty, especially during Ralph Abercromby's campaign in 1796–97; see Buckley, *The Haitian Journal of Lieutenant Howard, York Hussars, 1796–1798* (Knoxville: University of Tennessee Press, 1985), 257.

26. Buckley, *Slaves in Red Coats*, 57.

27. Michael Duffy, "The French Revolution and British Attitudes to the West Indian Colonies," in *A Turbulent Time: The French Revolution and the Greater Caribbean*, ed. David Barry Gaspar and David Patrick Geggus (Bloomington: Indiana University Press, 1997), 92–93.

28. Howard Temperley, "Abolition and National Interest," in *Out of Slavery*, ed. Jack Hayward (London: Frank Cass, 1985), 92.

29. Peter J. Marshall, "The Moral Swing to the East: British Humanitarianism, India and the West Indies," in *East India Company Studies: Papers Presented to Professor Cyril Philips, Centre of South Asian Studies, University of London*, ed. Kenneth Ballhatchet (Hong Kong: Asian Research Service, 1986), 73.

30. Marshall, "Moral Swing to the East," 73.

31. Burke, in anon., *Abolition of the Slave Trade—Motion For in the House of Commons, 12th May 1789* (London, 1789), 18.

32. Seymour Drescher, *Econocide: British Slavery in the Era of Abolition* (Pittsburgh: University of Pittsburgh Press, 1977), 168.

33. Cited by Jacques Adelaïde-Merlande, *La Caraïbe et la Guyane au temps de la Révolution et de l'Empire* (Paris: Karthala, 1992), 79.

34. D. M. Sutherland, *France, 1789–1815: Revolution and Counterrevolution* (London: Fontana, 1985), 354.

35. 33 *Parl. Hist.* (1797): 590.

36. 33 *Parl. Hist.* (1797): 586.

37. 31 *Parl. Hist.* (1794): 1452.

38. Williams, *From Columbus to Castro*, 261.

39. Williams, *From Columbus to Castro*, 262.

40. Drescher, *Econocide*, 168–69.

41. Craton, *Empire, Enslavement, and Freedom*, 311.

42. See Drescher, "Limits of Example," 10–11. Blackburn was reverently critical of Drescher and apologetically directs us to Drescher's affirmation of Haiti as catalyst in British emancipationism from 1823 ("Haiti," 653 n. 11).

43. Drescher, "Civilizing Insurgency," 120–44.

44. Davis, "Impact of the French and Haitian Revolutions," 6.

45. Bernard Moitt, "Slave Resistance in Guadeloupe and Martinique, 1791–1848," *Journal of Caribbean History* 25 (1991): 140.

46. 33 *Parl. Hist.* (1797): 583; also see "Correspondence with George III, 1791–1805," Melville Papers, 1:79, BL, Add. MSS 40100.

47. James, *Black Jacobins*, 135–36.

48. 33 *Parl. Hist.* (1797): 583.

49. 33 *Parl. Hist.* (1797): 584.

50. James, *Black Jacobins*, 134, 214; Williams, *Capitalism and Slavery*, 147.

51. Buckley, *British Army*, 291; A. Goodwin, *The French Revolution* (London: Hutchinson, 1970), 107–8.

52. Hart, *Slaves Who Abolished Slavery*, 157.

53. Adelaïde-Merlande, *La Caraïbe*, 73; Denis Laurent-Ropa, *Haïti, une colonie française, 1625–1802* (Paris: Éditions L'Harmattan, 1993), 192, 196; also see Blackburn, *Overthrow*, 235.

54. Laurent-Ropa, *Haïti*, 195; Blackburn, *Overthrow*, 215–16.

55. Adelaïde-Merlande, *La Caraïbe*, 63; for Guadeloupe, see Blackburn, *Overthrow*, 220.

56. Adelaïde-Merlande, *La Caraïbe*, 63. Significantly, black troops constituted a majority in the British army on the island. See Vaughan to Dundas, 24 November 1794, NA, WO 1:83, 20v.

57. James, *Black Jacobins*, 135; De Charmilly to Hobart, 16 October 1801, NA, WO 1:73, 396–97; also see Campbell, *Maroons of Jamaica*, 209.

58. De Charmilly to Hobart, 16 October 1802, NA, WO 1:73, 396–97.

59. Dundas to Maj. Gen. Forbes, 29 September 1795, NA, WO 6:6, 5; cries of woe from Capt. John Sharp laid before the Jamaican Assembly, 31 July, 1795, NA, CO 140:84, n.p.

60. Cited in *Morning Post,* 21 February 1794 (the paper was later titled the *Morning Post and Fashionable World*). By 1797 Bellay had become a deputy to the National Assembly; see Blackburn, *Overthrow,* 23.

61. James, *Black Jacobins,* 140.

62. Shanti Marie Singham, "Betwix Cattle and Men: Jews, Blacks, and Women and the Declaration of the Rights of Man," in *The French Ideal of Freedom: The Old Regime and the Declaration of Rights of 1789,* ed. Dale van Kley (Stanford: Stanford University Press, 1994), 115; Thomas, *Slave Trade,* 522.

63. Cited in *Morning Post,* 21 February 1794, 3.

64. For the port of Nantes, see Thomas, *Slave Trade,* 522.

65. *Morning Post,* 21 February 1794, 3.

66. Cited in *Morning Post,* 21 February 1794, 3; also see "Décret," 5 February 1794, DFC1A/Memoires/134/32, Centre des Archives d'Outre-mer (now Archives Nationales d'Outre-mer, hereafter cited as ANOM), Aix-en-Provence, France.

67. *Morning Post,* 26 February 1794, 2.

68. Debate on Mr. St. John's Motion for withdrawing the troops from St. Domingo, 33 *Parl. Hist.* (1797): 576–78.

69. Laurent-Ropa, *Haïti,* 193; Hart, *Slaves Who Abolished Slavery,* 158–76.

70. Long, *History,* 2:416–17; Michelle S. Laguerre, *Voodoo and Politics in Haiti* (New York: St. Martin's Press, 1989), 34, 63–65. Belief in transmigration might also have inspired extraordinary acts of military bravery; see Taylor, *Narrative of Liberation,* 109.

71. 32 *Parl. Hist.* (1796): 914; Vaughn to Dundas, 24 November 1794, NA, WO 1:83, 20v; Vaughan to Dundas, 19 November 1794, NA, WO 1:83, 17v. Vaughan also considered Guadeloupe critical to the defense of the West Indies; see Vaughan to Dundas, 19 November 1794, NA, WO 1:83, 18.

72. Gilbert Pago, "Saint-Lucie dans la Révolution Française," Spécial Bicentenaire, *France-Antilles* (Dec. 1989): 30–32, ANOM; Pago, "Saint-Lucie," 31.

73. Lucien Abenon, Jacques Cauna, and Liliane Chauleau, eds., *La Révolution aux Caraïbe* (Paris: Société des Études Robespierristes, 1989), 171.

74. Abenon, Cauna, and Chaleau, *La Révolution aux Caraïbe,* 175.

75. Pago, "Saint Lucie," 31.

76. Elizabeth Landi, "Les Evénements—Chronologie," Spécial Bicentenaire, *France-Antilles* (Dec. 1989): 29; Adelaïde-Merlande, *La Caraïbe,* 60–61.

77. Vaughan to Dundas, 24 November 1794, NA, WO 1:83, 20v; Geggus, *Slavery, War, and Revolution,* 191. General Irving to Dundas, 8 July 1795, NA, WO 1:84, 13–14; and Irving to Lt. Col. Dickson, August 1795: 190; Landi, "Les Evénements—Chronologie," 28–29. Symbolically, its main port, Point-à-Pitre, was renamed "Port de la Liberté"; Memoires, Dossier 450, DFC/VI : 4, ANOM.

78. Vaughan to Dundas, 22 December 1794, NA, WO 1:83, 52v.

79. 33 *Parl. Hist.* (1797): 586–87. This report was confirmed in Vaughan to Dundas, 16 April 1795, NA, WO 1:83, 170. James and Blackburn agree on a slightly higher figure of fifteen hundred men; see *Black Jacobins,* 143; Blackburn, "Haiti," par. 5. The vast majority of Hughes's colonial armies consisted of emancipated recruits; see Laurent Dubois, *A Colony of Citizens: Revolution*

and Slave Emancipation in the French Caribbean, 1787–1804 (Chapel Hill: University of North Carolina Press, 2004), 227–33; also see Ragatz, *Fall of the Planter Class,* 219.

80. Proclamation, Guadeloupe, *18 prairial l'annèe 3* (6 June 1795), F3/234, dossier 5, ANOM.

81. Vaughan to Dundas, 16 April 1795, NA, WO 1:84, 170–72; also see I. E. Kirby and C. I. Martin, *The Rise and Fall of the Black Caribs* (Kingstown, St. Vincent: St. Vincent and the Grenadines National Trust, 1995), 35–40; Charles Shepherd, *An Historical Account of the Island of Saint Vincent* (London: Frank Cass, 1975), 80–94.

82. Vaughn to Dundas, 16 April 1795, NA, WO 1:83, 170; "De la Revolution Opérée en L'isle de la Grenade," 2 March 1795, C10A/4: 247, ANOM; Edward L. Cox, "Fedon's Rebellion, 1795–96: Causes and Consequences," *Journal of Negro History* 67, no. 1 (Spring 1972): 7–19.

83. Craton, *Testing the Chains,* 189.

84. Vaughan to Dundas, 24 January 1794, NA, WO 1:83, 20–21; President John Stanley to Home Secretary Portland, 22 March 1795, 90; Minutes of Council, 25 March 1795, NA, CO 152:77, 209–10.

85. See Adelaïde-Merlande, *La Caraïbe,* 62; also see James Millette, *The Genesis of Crown Colony Government: Trinidad, 1783–1810* (Curepe, Trinidad: Moko Enterprises, 1970), 28–31, republished under the title *Society and Politics in Colonial Trinidad* (San Fernando, Trinidad: Omega, 1985).

86. *Morning Post,* 29 June 1795, 3.

87. Williams, *Capitalism and Slavery,* 149.

88. See Claudius Fergus, "War, Revolution, and Abolitionism," in *Capitalism and Slavery Fifty Years Later: Eric Eustace Williams—A Reassessment of the Man and His Work,* ed. Heather Cateau and S.H.H. Carrington (New York: Peter Lang, 2000), 173–95.

89. Vaughan to Dundas, 24 November 1794, NA, WO 1:83, 20v.

90. "Returns of Killed and Wounded . . . 14 October to 10 December 1794," in Vaughan to Dundas, 18 December 1794, NA, WO 1:83, 43–44.

91. Dundas to Vaughan, 19 February 1795, NA, WO 1:83, 97.

92. Vaughn to Dundas, 12 December 1794, NA, WO 1:83, 57–59v.

93. Dundas to Vaughan, 19 February 1795, NA, WO 1:83, 97.

94. See, e.g., Vaughan to President Edward Byam, 15 March 1795, NA, CO 152:77, 94.

95. Stanley to Portland, 22 March 1795, NA, CO 152:77, 90.

96. Vaughan to Dundas, 16 April 1795, NA, WO 1:83, 172.

97. Vaughan to Dundas, 16 April 1795, NA, WO 1:83, 172.

98. Maj. Gen. White to Vaughan, letter no. 14, 17 April 1795, NA, WO 1:83, 121v–23.

99. Council Meetings, 23 March 1795 and 26 March 1795, NA, CO 152:77, 110–16.

100. "Resolution of Committee," 4 October 1795, NA, WO 1:84, 525.

101. See Minutes of House of Assembly of Dominica, 13 October 1794, NA, CO 71:27, 41v.

102. Council Minutes, Jamaica House of Assembly, Portland to Forbes, 25 August 1795, NA, CO 140:84 (hereafter cited as JCM; this volume was not paginated).

103. Copy of contract signed by S. Chollet and C. Cuyler enclosed in Dundas to Cuyler, 18 January 1798, NA, WO 1:86, 619; also see Cuyler to Dundas, 4 April 1798, NA, WO 1:86, 671. Age was flexible, up to thirty years, depending on ability to bear arms; "Heads of Instructions to Major Gen'l Hunter," 26 January 1797, NA, WO 1:86, 59; also see "Heads of Instructions to Brig. General Moore," 18 January 1797, NA, WO 1:86, 67.

104. See Craton, *Testing the Chains,* 169.

105. Dundas to Abercromby, "Heads of Instructions," 18 January 1797, NA, WO 1:86, 63; also see "Heads of Instructions to Major Gen'l. Hunter," 26 January 1797, NA, WO 1:86, 60.

106. Cuyler to Dundas, 3 April 1798, NA, WO 1:86, 656; the conversion rate was one hundred pounds local currency to fifty-eight pounds sterling.

107. "Heads of Instructions," 26 January 1797, NA, WO 1:86, 59–60; also see Chollet to Cuyler, 21 March 1798, NA, WO 1:86, 627; Cuyler to Dundas, 29 March 1798, NA, WO 1:86, 631–33; Dundas to Cuyler, 18 January 1798, NA, WO 1:86, 523; Irving to Lt. Gen. Dickson, NA, WO 1:84, 192. For plans to purchase from the African coast, see Abercromby to Dundas, 28 March 1796, NA, WO 1/85, 299–300.

108. The regiment in question comprised 172 officers plus 760 privates; actual sum, £416,468 10d. The estimate was signed by John Wigglesworth, commissary general; Portland to Maj. Gen. Simcoe, 7 July 1797, NA, WO 1:66, 315.

109. Trigge to Hobart, 22 November 1801, NA, WO 1:90, 613. The West India Regiment constituted one third of the total British military strength in the Caribbean and was acquired at a cost of almost one million pounds sterling; see Duffy, "French Revolution and British Attitudes," 88, 95.

110. Craton, *Testing the Chains,* 169.

111. "State of the Nation Debate," 32 *Parl. Hist.* (1796): 914.

112. Debate on Fox's Motion, 31 *Parl. Hist.* (1794): 1379.

113. 33 *Parl. Hist.* (1797): 576–80; also see JCM, 17 January 1795, NA, CO 140:84, n.p.

114. 33 *Parl. Hist.* (1797): 580.

115. 33 *Parl. Hist.* (1797): 580.

116. Mr. Martin at the St. Domingue office to John Sullivan, 12 January 1804, NA, WO 1:73, 29–45; Dundas to Maj. Gen. John Knox, 22 August 1798, NA, WO 6:6, 234.

117. Dundas to Knox, 22 August 1798, NA, WO 1:90, 231–34.

118. Stephen, *England Enslaved,* 50, 139–40.

119. Debate on Mr. St. John's Motion for withdrawing the troops from St. Domingo, 576–77.

120. See 33 *Parl. Hist.* (1797): 581. James Fox estimated the total loss of lives and deserters at nine thousand; see 33 *Parl. Hist.* (1797): 589.

121. Geggus, *Slavery, War, and Revolution,* 362, 403, app. F.

122. Blackburn, *Overthrow,* 239; also see Stephen, *England Enslaved,* 50; and 15 *Parl. Deb.,* 2d ser. (1826): 249.

123. Duffy, "French Revolution and British Attitudes," 85; for an estimate of twice the fatalities in the Leeward Islands compared to St. Domingue, see Blackburn, *Overthrow,* 239.

124. Williams, *Capitalism and Slavery,* 147; Michael Duffy, *Soldiers, Sugar, and Seapower: The British Expeditions to the West Indies and the War against Revolutionary France* (Oxford: Clarendon Press, 1987), 327; David Patrick Geggus, "Slavery, War, and Revolution in the Greater Caribbean, 1789–1815," in *A Turbulent Time: The French Revolution and the Greater Caribbean,* ed. David Barry Gaspar and David Patrick Geggus (Bloomington: Indiana University Press, 1997), 24–25.

125. Geggus, "Slavery, War, and Revolution," 25. James cited 100,000 British fatalities in the West Indies by 1799 but without stating his source; see C. L. R. James, *A History of Negro Revolt* (1938; London: Race Today, 1985), 12.

126. David Geggus, "Yellow Fever in the 1790s: The British Army in Occupied St. Domingue," *Medical History* 23 (1979): 52; also see Buckley, *Slaves in Red Coats,* 99–105.

127. "Debate on Fox's Motion for a Committee on the State of the Nation," 31 *Parl. Hist.* (1794): 1352–53.

128. Stephen to Wilberforce, 24 June 1796, Wilberforce MSS, d.15: 55v.

129. Dundas to Cuyler, 18 January 1798, NA, WO 1:86, 523.

130. *Morning Post,* 21 August 1794, 3.

131. *Morning Post,* "From St. Domingo," 9 January 1795, 3.

132. *Morning Post,* 9 January 1795, 4.

133. Drescher, "Limits of Example," 12.

134. High Command to Abercromby, letter no. 1, September 1796, NA, WO 1:65, 278–79; Maitland to Dundas, 8 May 1797, NA, WO 1:67, 130v–31.

135. Buckley, *British Army,* 157.

136. "Return of the Army under the Command of Major General Sir Ralph Abercromby," 7 November 1795, NA, WO 1:84, 287; JCM, Portland to Forbes, 25 August 1795, NA, CO 140:84, n.p.; also see JCM, Dundas to Horse Guards, 26 August 1795, NA, CO 140:84, 37–38. Buckley cites twenty thousand troops (*British Army,* 257). Duffy estimates thirty-two thousand troops ("French Revolution," 85).

137. "Secret Instructions to Ralph Abercromby," 9 October 1795, NA, WO 1:84, 245–47 (hereafter cited as "Secret Instructions").

138. Dundas to Duke of York, "Secret & Confidential," 28 July 1795, Melville Papers, 3:9, BL, Add. MS 40102.

139. See "Secret," Dundas to Abercromby, 10 January 1796, NA, WO 1:85, 9–13; 175v. The King, 27 January 1796, Melville Papers, 1:175v, BL, Add. MSS 40102.

140. The King, 27 January 1796, Melville Papers, 1:175, BL, Add. MSS 40,100.

141. "Secret Instructions," 272; also see Buckley, *Haitian Journal,* 141, app. A.

142. "Secret Instructions," 275–76.

143. "Secret Instructions," 275–76.

144. Horse Guards, "Secret," 10 January 1796, NA, WO 1:85, 12–13.

145. Pago, "Saint-Lucie," 32.

146. Duffy, "French Revolution," 85.

147. Adelaïde-Merlande, *La Caraïbe,* 66–67.

148. Pago, "Saint-Lucie," 32.

149. Council Chamber, 9 December 1794, NA, CO 71:27; Meeting of Privy Council, 10 December 1794, CO 71:27; Pago, "Saint-Lucie," 32.

150. Although most imperial reinforcements were destined for the eastern Caribbean, the Second Maroon War in Jamaica also tied up "desperately needed reinforcements for St. Domingue"; see Buckley, *Haitian Journal,* 257; also see Blackburn, *Overthrow,* 239.

151. See 33 *Parl. Hist.* (1797): 587.

152. For an analysis of Tacky's War, see Hart, *Slaves Who Abolished Slavery,* 130–56.

153. Landi, "Les Evénements—Chronologie," 29; Adelaïde-Merlande, *La Caraïbe,* 60–61.

154. Lord Grenville, in 8 *Parl. Deb.,* 1st ser. (1807): 658.

155. Williams, *Westminster,* 8–11.

156. W. Major to Wilberforce, 20 February 1792, "Correspondence with George III, 1791–1805," Melville Papers, 1:23v, BL, Add. MSS 40,100.

157. Williams, *Westminster,* 23.

158. Williams, *Westminster,* 23.

159. Williams, *Westminster,* 23.

160. Drescher, *Econocide,* 168; Anthony P. Maingot cited in Franklin W. Knight, "The Haitian Revolution," *American Historical Review* 105, no. 1 (2000), par. 27, www.historycooperative.org/journals.

161. High Command to Abercromby, 13 November 1796, NA, WO 1:85, 643–47; also see John Ehrman, *The Younger Pitt: The Reluctant Transition* (London: Constable, 1986), 634; Abercromby to Dundas, 16 January 1797, NA, WO 1:86; 41; Picton to Rear Admiral Harvey, 20 February 1799, Letter Book of Colonel Thomas Picton, 1799, letter 9; and Picton to Dundas, 30 July 1799, letter 35, BL, Add. MSS 36870 (hereafter cited as "Picton's Letter Book").

162. High Command to Abercromby, 13 November 1796, NA, WO 1:85, 643–47.

163. George Rose to General Cuyler, 8 July 1797, NA, WO 1:86, 295.

164. Anstey, *Atlantic Slave Trade,* 322.

165. See "Memorials of Planters and Merchants of St. Vincent to William Pitt," 9 May 1795, NA, WO 1:84, 327–33. The document claimed that they were the "Negroe invaders & destroyers of the original Charaibs."

166. Lipscomb, "Party Politics," 448.

167. 33 *Parl. Hist.* (1797): 251–69.

168. 33 *Parl. Hist.* (1797): 276.

169. Anstey, *Atlantic Slave Trade,* 328; for the debate on the motion, see 36 *Parl. Hist.* (1802): 860–61.

170. 33 *Parl. Hist.* (1797): 276.

171. 33 *Parl. Hist.* (1797): 276.

172. See Stephen Alexis, *Black Liberator: The Life of Toussaint Louverture,* trans. William Stirling (London: Ernest Benn, 1949), 159.

173. Stephen, *Crisis,* 64.

174. Stephen, *Crisis,* 165.

175. John K. Thornton, "African Soldiers in the Haitian Revolution," *Journal of Caribbean History* 25, nos. 1–2 (1991): 60–61; Patterson, *Sociology of Slavery,* 119–22.

176. For one of the earliest postcolonial scholars' address of the problem, see Basil Davidson, *Black Mother: The Years of the African Slave Trade* (Boston: Little, Brown, 1961), 81, 112, 153–55, 226–2, www.questia.com/PM.qst?a=o&d=10559140. For a more comprehensive study, see J. E. Inikori, "The Import of Firearms into West Africa: A Quantitative Analysis," *Journal of African History* 18, no. 3 (1977): 339–49, www.jstor.org/stable/180637. Another good essay on the subject, building on Inikori's work, is W. A. Richards, "The Import of Firearms into West Africa in the Eighteenth Century," *Journal of African History* 21, no. 1 (1980): 43–59.

177. Stephen, *Crisis,* 69.

178. Stephen, *Crisis,* 52.

179. Laurent-Ropa, *Haiti,* 195.

180. Brougham, *Colonial Policy,* 2:301

181. Brougham, *Colonial Policy,* 1:119.

182. Brougham, *Colonial Policy,* 1:310.

183. Brougham, *Colonial Policy,* 1:310.

184. Brougham, *Colonial Policy,* 1:310.

185. 36 *Parl. Hist.* (1802): 691.

186. 36 *Parl. Hist.* (1802): 694.

187. 36 *Parl. Hist.* (1802): 694.

6. From Revolution to Abolition

1. For a discussion on the motion, see 36 *Parl. Hist.* (1802): 860–61; also see Anstey, *Atlantic Slave Trade*, 327–29.

2. 33 *Parl. Hist.* (1797): 272.

3. See "Extract of a Royal Proclamation, 1792," in *A Collection of the Private Acts* (London, 1827), 10:542–55.

4. Abercromby to Dundas, 16 January 1797, NA, WO 1:86, 41; Picton to Rear Admiral Harvey, 20 February 1799, letter 9, and Picton to Dundas, 30 July 1799, letter 35, Picton's Letter Book.

5. Millette, *Genesis*, 30.

6. Brig. Gen. Nicholls to Maj. Gen. Leigh, 21 February 1796, NA, WO 1:85, 253.

7. See Millette, *Genesis*, 70.

8. Picton to Dundas, 30 July 1799, letter 35, Picton's Letter Book.

9. Pierre M'Callum, *Travels in Trinidad during the Months of February, March, and April 1803 in a Series of Letters to a Member of the Imperial Parliament of Great Britain* (Liverpool, 1805) 17; Lionel M. Fraser, *History of Trinidad* (London: Frank Cass, 1971), 1:192.

10. See Bridget Brereton, *The History of Modern Trinidad, 1783–1962* (London: Heinemann, 1981), 47.

11. 36 *Parl. Hist.* (1802): 865.

12. Stephen, *Crisis,* 158. This claim was rejected by Brougham, arguing for no more than 25 percent (*Colonial Policy,* 1:533); also see Anstey, *Atlantic Slave Trade,* 333.

13. Cecil Ashton Goodridge, "Land, Labour and Immigration into Trinidad, 1783–1833" (Ph.D. diss., University of Cambridge, 1969), 113.

14. Goodridge, "Land, Labour and Immigration," 113. For lower imports, see Curtin, *Atlantic Slave Trade,* 71.

15. For a different reading of the strategies implied in the terms *main question* and *subordinate question,* see Anstey, *Atlantic Slave Trade,* 376–78.

16. See Millette, *Genesis,* 79–82; also see Addington in 36 *Parl. Hist.* (1802): 880.

17. Peter Dixon, *Canning: Politician and Statesman* (London: Weidenfeld and Nicolson, 1976), 30.

18. Canning to Windham, 23 May 1802, "Letters from George Canning, 1797–1807," Windham Papers, 3:295v–297, BL, Add. MSS 37844.

19. Buckley, *Slaves in Red Coats,* 59.

20. 36 *Parl. Hist.* (1802): 875.

21. 36 *Parl. Hist.* (1802): 875.

22. 36 *Parl. Hist.* (1802): 876.

23. Anstey, *Atlantic Slave Trade,* 333.

24. 36 *Parl. Hist.* (1802): 855, 865; also see entry 4350, "Resolutions," *Sessional Papers,* 82:305–9.

25. 36 *Parl. Hist.* (1802): 855.

26. Anstey, *Atlantic Slave Trade,* 333.

27. William F. Lewis, "Simon Bolivar and Xavier Mina: A Rendezvous in Haiti," *Journal of Inter-American Studies* 11, no. 3 (July 1969): 48–65; also see Blackburn, "Haiti," 645, 648; Brown, "Abolition in Santo Domingo," 376.

28. See Buckley, *Slaves in Red Coats,* 88.

29. 36 *Parl. Hist.* (1802): 869.

30. 36 *Parl. Hist.* (1802): 869–70.

31. 36 *Parl. Hist.* (1802): 859–61.

32. 36 *Parl. Hist.* (1802): 871–72.

33. 36 *Parl. Hist.* (1802): 871–72.

34. 36 *Parl. Hist.* (1802): 873.

35. 36 *Parl. Hist.* (1802): 877.

36. 36 *Parl. Hist.* (1802): 380.

37. Stephen, *Crisis,* 157.

38. Stephen, *Crisis,* 186.

39. Stephen, *Crisis,* 194.

40. Stephen, *Crisis,* 186.

41. Stephen, *Crisis,* 186–87.

42. Stephen, *Crisis,* 186.

43. Stephen, *Crisis,* 186.

44. Stephen, *Crisis,* 189.

45. Stephen, *Crisis,* 189.

46. Brougham, *Colonial Policy,* 2:402.

47. Perceval to Wilberforce, 24 June 1803, Wilberforce MSS, d.17, 125–25v. Symbolically, Perceval sent a hot-off-the-press copy of *Colonial Policy* to Wilberforce.

48. Brougham, *Colonial Policy,* 2:420–21.

49. Brougham, *Colonial Policy,* 2:413; repeated in Brougham, *Opinions,* 5.

50. Brougham, *Colonial Policy,* 2:419.

51. Brougham, *Colonial Policy,* 2:455–56.

52. Brougham, *Colonial Policy,* 2:429.

53. Brougham, *Colonial Policy,* 2:403. Brougham's assessment was also informed by his conviction that Africans were "fit only for a state of slavery"; see Davis, *Slavery and Human Progress,* 133.

54. Brougham, *Colonial Policy,* 2:450.

55. Brougham, *Colonial Policy,* 2:451.

56. Ellis to Wilberforce, 27 August 1801, Wilberforce MSS, d.13, 175.

57. Brougham, *Colonial Policy,* 1:468.

58. Wendy Hinde, *George Canning* (London: Collins, 1973), 102; Lord Grenville on the Definition Treaty, 36 *Parl. Hist.* (1802): 691–94.

59. "Memorandum," 1803, NA, BT 6:70; "Outline of a Plan for the Better Cultivation, Security and Defense of Our West Indian Colonies," 6 June 1806, BT 6:70. Most folios in this volume were not enumerated.

60. See Stewart, "Religion and Society," esp. chaps. 3 and 4; also see Turner, *Slaves and Missionaries,* esp. chaps. 1–3.

61. Castlereagh to Governors of "Conquered Colonies," 21 August 1805, NA, CO 324:103, 51v–52. For the order-in-council, see Castlereagh to Governors, 21 August 1805, NA, CO 324:103, 60v–64. The edict became effective on proclamation of governors; see Proclamation of the Governor of Berbice, 30 November 2005, reproduced in *Sunday Starbroek* (Guyana), 6 August 2006, 19.

62. Speech of Attorney General, 7 *Parl. Deb.,* 1st ser. (1806): 598. Castlereagh to Governors, 21 August 1805, NA, CO 324:103, 52, 60v.

63. Castlereagh to Governors, 21 August 1805, NA, CO 324:103, 52v.

64. Charles Grey to Dundas, 28 July 1794, NA, CO 71:27, 287.

65. Grey to Dundas, 28 July 1794, HO 30:1, 287.

66. For the evidence of Henry A. Wise, American minister to Brazil and high-ranking naval officers, see Warren S. Howard, *American Slavers and the Federal Law, 1837–1862* (Berkeley: University of California Press, 1963), 10–12; also see 8 *Parl. Deb.,* 1st ser. (1807): 805.

67. Trigge to Hobart, 11 November 1801, NA, WO 1:90, 593.

68. Drescher, "Limits of Example," 10–11.

69. Winston F. McGowan, "The French Revolutionary Period in Demerara-Essequibo, 1793–1802," *History Gazette,* no. 55 (Apr. 1993): 11–13.

70. Pitt to Liverpool, 9 July 1799, Liverpool Papers vol. 3, BL, Add. MSS 38192: 101–101v, British Library.

71. Castlereagh to Governors, 21 August 1805, NA, CO 324:103, 53–54. For Grenada and Jamaica, see Ward, *West Indian Slavery,* 123 and 133, respectively. The African Institution found a depletion rate of 14 percent (*Reasons for Establishing a Registry of Slaves in the British Colonies, Being a Report of a Committee of the African Institution* [London, 1815], 28). On the other hand, Curtin claims that the rate of decline for native Africans up to 1808 was about 3 percent, while the overall decrease was only 1.5 percent (*Atlantic Slave Trade,* 71).

72. Castlereagh to Governors, 21 August 1805, NA, CO 324:103, 53.

73. Castlereagh to Governors, 21 August 1805, NA, CO 324:103, 54.

74. Castlereagh to Governors, 21 August 1805, NA, CO 324:103, 55.

75. Castlereagh to Governors, 21 August 1805, NA, CO 324:103, 56.

76. Castlereagh to Governors, 21 August 1805, NA, CO 324:103, 56v–57.

77. Castlereagh to Governors, 21 August 1805, NA, CO 324:103, 59v–60.

78. Castlereagh to Governors, 21 August 1805, NA, CO 324:103, 57.

79. See Millette, *Genesis,* 215–16.

80. Drescher, "Limits of Example," 10–11.

81. 3 *Parl. Deb.,* 1st ser. (1805): 661.

82. *The Speech of the Rt. Hon. Chas. James Fox, in the House of Commons, June 10, 1806 on a Bill for the Abolition of the Slave Trade* (Newcastle, 1824).

83. 8 *Parl. Deb.,* 1st ser. (1807): 660.

84. 8 *Parl. Deb.,* 1st ser. (1807): 701–2.

85. 8 *Parl. Deb.,* 1st ser. (1807): 954.

86. 2 *Parl. Deb.,* 1st ser. (1804): 455.

87. 2 *Parl. Deb.,* 1st ser. (1804): 455.

88. 8 *Parl. Deb.,* 1st ser. (1807): 702.

89. 8 *Parl. Deb.,* 1st ser. (1807): 702.

7. Imperatives of Creole Colonization

1. Hobart to Picton, 18 July 1802, NA, CO 296:1, 27v–28.

2. Hobart to Picton, 18 July 1802, NA, CO 296:4, 28–28v.

3. Hobart to Commission, 16 October 1802, encl. no. 20, NA, CO 296:4, 64–72.

4. Hobart to Commission, 16 October 1802, encl. no. 20, 72, NA, CO 296:4, 70.

5. Hobart to Commission, NA, CO 296:4, 70.

6. See Millette, *Genesis,* 134–35.

7. Hobart to Picton, 18 July 1802, NA, CO 296:4, 28v.

8. See Minutes of Council, Dominica, 15 October 1794, NA, CO 71:27, 53–54; also see 5 December 1794, NA, CO 71:27, 66.

9. Hobart to Picton, 18 July 1802, NA, CO 296:4, 28v.

10. John Sanderson, *Emancipation in Disguise; or, The True Crisis of the Colonies* (London, 1807), 137, 177.

11. Colonial Department to Kenneth Mc Queen (Most Secret), 21 April 1803, BT 6:70. The spelling Mc Queen is variously rendered Macqueen, Mcqueen, McQueen, and MacQueen. For relevant excerpts concerning the plan, see Walton Look Lai, *The Chinese in the West Indies, 1806–1995: A Documentary History* (Kingston, Jamaica: University Press of the West Indies, 1998), 22–46.

12. "Remarks on Mr. Farquhar's Observations of Settling Chinese," NA, BT 6:70.

13. Memorandum Relating to the Introduction of Chinese Settlers into the West India Islands, 1803, NA, BT 6:70.

14. "Secret Memorandum from Mr. I Sullivan to the Chair," 18 February 1803, letter 1; "Secret Orders to Bengal," 21 April 1803, letter 2; Hobart's "Instructions to K. Mac Queen," April 1803, letter 3, encl. in "List of Papers Respecting the Introduction of a Colony of Chinese in the Island of Trinidad," BT 6:70.

15. "Speculative Observations of Mr. Farquhar, Lieutenant Governor of Prince of Wales Island and Agent to the Governor General of the Malay States, on the Proposed Plan of 'Introducing Chinese Settlers at Trinidad and Other West Indian Islands . . . .'" N.d., NA, BT 6:70.

16. Some secondary sources carry different information on the numbers of Chinese arriving in Trinidad: Williams, e.g., cites 145 and 192 immigrants in *History of the People of Trinidad and Tobago* (Trinidad: PNM, 1962), 77; E. L. Joseph cites 193 (see *History of Trinidad* [1838; London: Frank Cass, 1970], 231–33); Trevor M. Millett cites "194 of 192" (see *The Chinese in Trinidad* [Trinidad: Inprint, 1993], 17).

17. Hobart to Commissioners, 16 October 1802, encl. no. 20, NA, CO 296:4, 72v.

18. Barry Higman, "The Chinese in Trinidad, 1806–1838," *Caribbean Studies* 12, no. 3 (1972): 29.

19. Sanderson, *Emancipation in Disguise,* 134.

20. Headmen were paid fifteen dollars per month, while others received six dollars. All were guaranteed return passage to China; they were also provided with facilities for remitting money and letters to China. See "Article of Agreement between the Honourable the Governor and Council of Prince of Wales Island . . . and Chinamen," NA, BT 6:70.

21. Higman, "Chinese," 33.

22. *Trinidad Guardian,* 4 July 1826, NA, CO 300:1; Higman, "Chinese," 31; also see John Sanderson, *An Appeal to the Imperial Parliament upon the Claims of the Ceded Colony of Trinidad &sc* (London, 1812), 50.

23. Colonial Department to Macqueen, 21 April 1803, NA, BT 6:70.

24. Millette, *Genesis,* 215.

25. Woodford to Bathurst, 3 October 1814, NA, CO 295:33, 240–40v.

26. "Report of the Honourable William Burnley with Regard to the Best Method of Improving the Colony by the Establishing of a Free Population of Agriculturists" (1814), NA, CO 295:37, 100–101v.

27. "Report of the Honourable William Burnley," NA, CO 295:37, 101v.

28. Act for Punishing Mutiny and Desertion; and for Better Payment of the Army and Other Quarters, 1807, 47 Geo. 3 c. 32. See also Buckley, *Slaves in Red Coats,* 110–11; Brian Dyde, *The Empty Sleeve: The Story of the West India Regiments of the British Army* (St. John's, Antigua: Hansib Caribbean, 1977), 28–29.

29. Buckley, *Slaves in Red Coats,* 135.

30. Buckley, *Slaves in Red Coats,* 113, 137; encl., Minutes of the Law Commissioners of the Treasury, 24 February 1819, NA, CO 296:8, 82.

31. The actual number landed is therefore uncertain; see Woodford to Bathurst, 5 August 1815, NA, CO 295:37, 139–39v. This account was first sourced from Duplicate Dispatches at the Trinidad and Tobago National Archives (hereafter cited as TTNA, DD), a useful assortment of duplicate correspondence, but many of the documents were rescued from near destruction, which sometimes obscured or obliterated the filing and/or folio numbers. Also see Woodford to Bathurst, 5 August 1815, TTNA, DD 113; K. O. Laurence, "The Settlement of Free Negroes in Trinidad before Emancipation," *Caribbean Quarterly* 9.1 (1963): 27; Noel Titus, *The Amelioration and Abolition of Slavery in Trinidad, 1812–1834: Experiments and Protests in a Slave Colony* (Bloomington, Ind.: AuthorHouse, 2009), 43.

32. Laurence, "Free Negroes," 27.

33. Laurence, "Free Negroes," 27; Jean-Baptiste Philippe, *Free Mulatto,* with a new introduction by Selwyn R. Cudjoe (Wellesley, Mass.: Calaloux Publications, 1996), 178.

34. Laurence, "Free Negroes," 31; Woodford to Bathurst, 10 November 1816, TTNA, DD 205.

35. Laurence, "Free Negroes," 33–34; Edward Bean Underhill, *The West Indies: Their Social and Religious Condition* (London: Frank Cass, 1970), 45–46.

36. See Philippe, *Free Mulatto,* 178–84.

37. Woodford to Bathurst, 8 November 1815, TTNA, DD 131.

38. Woodford to Bathurst, 8 November 1815, TTNA, DD 131.

39. Laurence refers to the carriage of loads on their backs, but such porterage is not typically African and not logical for very long distances; see "Free Negroes," 32. The retention of the authentic African tradition is confirmed by Long (*History,* 2:413).

40. Woodford to Bathurst, 10 November 1816, TTNA, DD 205.

41. Carl Campbell, "Mohammedu Sisei of Gambia and Trinidad, c. 1778–1838," *African Studies Association of the West Indian Bulletin* 7 (1974): 32.

42. For case examples, see "Trinidad, 23 May 1802," Cumberland Papers, 9: 97v, BL, Add. MSS 36499.

43. *Trinidad Guardian,* 29 August 1828, NA, CO 300:2.

44. Catteral, *Judicial Cases,* 1:29–46.

45. Stephen, *Anti-Slavery Recollections,* 8.

46. Stephen, *Anti-Slavery Recollections,* 9.

47. Act for Rendering More Effectual . . . the Abolition of the Slave Trade, 1811, 51 Geo. 3, c. 23.

48. Stephen to Perceval (Pte. & Conf.), 10 April 1810, Perceval Papers, 2:149, BL, Add. MSS. 49183.

49. Stephen to Perceval, 10 April 1810, Perceval Papers, 2:150v–51, BL, Add. MSS. 49183.

50. Stephen to Perceval, 10 April 1810, Perceval Papers, 2:149v, BL, Add. MSS. 49183.

51. See Stephen, *Recollections,* 24.

52. All direct references to the registration order are from A. Meredith John, *The Plantation*

Slaves of Trinidad, 1783–1816: A Mathematical and Demographic Enquiry (Cambridge: Cambridge University Press, 1988), 217–42; for this reference, see 218.

53. Stephen, *Recollections*, 18.

54. Eric Williams, "The British West Indian Slave Trade after the Abolition in 1807," *Journal of Negro History* 27 (1947): 175–91.

55. Howard, *American Slavers*, 11–12. English schooners also continued to be sighted off the coast of Africa.

56. Stephen to Perceval, 10 April 1810, Perceval Papers, 2:149v, BL, Add. MSS. 49183.

57. Stephen to Perceval, 10 April 1810, Perceval Papers, 2:149v–50, BL, Add. MSS. 49183.

58. John, *Plantation Slaves*, 40; Woodford to Bathurst, 18 March 1814, TTNA, DD 23.

59. Woodford to Bathurst, 18 March 1814, TTNA, DD 23, 143.

60. David Eltis, "The Traffic in Slaves between the West Indian Colonies," *English Historical Review* 25, no. 1 (1992): 21.

61. See, e.g., Williams, "Slave Trade," 175–91.

62. John, *Plantation Slaves*, 217–18, 241.

63. John, *Plantation Slaves*, 240.

64. Memorandum of Henry Gloster to Edward Stanley, NA, CO 295:105, 162. The office of registrar was united with that of the protector of slaves.

65. Gloster to Stanley, NA, CO 295:105, 162.

66. Gloster to Stanley, NA, CO 295:105, 238.

67. Gloster to Stanley, NA, CO 295:105, 233.

68. Gloster to Stanley, NA, CO 295:105, 241.

69. James Stephen, "Registry of Slaves in Trinidad: Facts and Observations as to the Execution of the Order in Council of March 26, 1812," NA, CO 295:34, 14–29.

70. Woodford to Bathurst, 4 January 1814, TTNA, DD 1, 88.

71. Stephen, "Facts and Observations," NA, CO 295:34, 14–29.

72. Woodford to Bathurst, 18 March 1814, TTNA, DD 23, 144.

73. Murray to Woodford, 20 April 1814, encl. in Woodford to Bathurst, 20 April 1814, TTNA, DD 5, 159–61. A mathematical study confirms that the additional numbers were new imports; see John, *Plantation Slaves*, 165–66.

74. Murray to Woodford, 20 April 1814, TTNA, DD 5, 75–76.

75. Murray to Woodford, 20 April 1814, Encl. 77, TTNA, DD 5.

76. Woodford to Bathurst, 4 January 1814, TTNA, DD 5, 75, 78.

77. Woodford to Bathurst, 4 January 1814, TTNA, DD 5, 77.

78. Solicitor General Henry Fuller to Woodford, 27 July 1814, TTNA, DD, 340–44; encl. in Chief Judge John Bigge to Woodford, 28 April 1814, TTNA, DD 14, 495–526.

79. Fuller to Woodford, 27 July 1814, TTNA, DD, 75, 78.

80. Brereton, *Modern Trinidad*, 64; Anthony de Verteuil, *Seven Slaves and Slavery, 1777–1838* (Port of Spain, Trinidad: Inprint, 1992), 38.

81. Cited in Brereton, *Modern Trinidad*, 53.

82. Fuller to Woodford, 29 July 1814, TTNA, DD; Fuller to Woodford, 1 July 1814, TTNA, DD.

83. See Williams, "Slave Trade," 178; Higman, "Population Geography," 156; Eltis, "Traffic in Slaves," 57.

84. Bathurst to Woodford, 8 September 1821, NA, CO 296:6.

85. Williams, "Slave Trade," 181.

86. Williams, "Slave Trade," 181.

87. See Higman, "Population Geography," 157, table 3.6; also see Williams, "Slave Trade," 178. Re-exports were minimal; see Eltis, "Traffic in Slaves," 58, table 1.

88. See "Landholders of Trinidad," 7 November 1816, Liverpool Papers, 314, BL, Add. MS 38263.

89. Protector's Report, July–December 1826, NA, CO 300:21, 17–20.

90. Consolidated Slave Trade Act, 1824, 5 Geo. 4, c. 113; also see Act to Continue an Act for Amending and Consolidating the Laws Relating to the Abolition of the Slave Trade, 1827, 9 Geo. 4, c. 84.

91. Williams, "Slave Trade," 178.

92. See Higman, *Slave Population,* 154. Many people were also active in their own behalf, staking claims to freedom on allegations of breaches of various aspects of the slave trade laws; for examples, see Protector of Slaves Report, NA, CO 300:21, 17–20.

8. New-Modeling in Action

1. John Norris Brierley, *Trinidad: Then and Now* (Trinidad: Franklin, 1912), 65–67.

2. Brierley, *Trinidad: Then and Now,* 66–68.

3. For the Cedula, see John, *Plantation Slaves,* 206–11. For a printed French version, see *Gazette de la Martinique,* 3 September 1784, F/3/62: 328, ANOM.

4. Keith Kevin Radhay, "Conspiracy and Contraband: Trinidad and the Spanish Main, 1797–1802" (M.Phil. diss., University of Calgary, Alberta, 1983), 11. For French strategic interest in Trinidad, see Mémoire sur l'Isle de la Trinité par M. de Lery," January 1786, F/3/62: 330, ANOM.

5. Brierley, *Trinidad: Then and Now,* 96–97.

6. Millette, *Genesis,* 67–69.

7. See M'Callum, *Travels,* 131.

8. "At the Court of St. James," Memorandum on Picton, 21 November 1805, NA, CO 295:13, 241; M'Callum, *Travels,* 133.

9. Memorandum, NA, CO 295:13, 249; M'Callum, *Travels,* 133.

10. Millette, *Genesis,* 128.

11. Trinidad Board of Council, 13 July 1803, NA, CO 298:1, 19v, 28–33 (hereafter cited as TBC).

12. See Millette, *Genesis,* 167–82.

13. TBC, 29 November 1804, NA, CO 298:1, 202.

14. TBC, 29 November 1804, NA, CO 298:1, 202v.

15. See Brown, "Origins of Abolition in Santo Domingo," 368, 373.

16. TBC, 29 November 1804, NA, CO 298:1, 202v; Philippe, *Free Mulatto,* 226–27; for a description of severe punishments for minor infractions of anti-freedmen laws, see Philippe, *Free Mulatto,* 76–77; Titus, *Experiments and Protests,* chap. 5.

17. Stephen to Perceval, 24 September 1810, Perceval Papers, 2:164, BL, Add. MSS 49183.

18. Stephen to Perceval, 24 September 1810, Perceval Papers, 2:164, BL, Add. MSS 49183.

19. Stephen to Perceval, 24 September 1810, Perceval Papers, 2:164, BL, Add. MSS 49183.

20. Stephen to Perceval, 24 September 1810, Perceval Papers, 2:164, BL, Add. MSS 49183.

21. Stephen to Perceval, 24 September 1810, Perceval Papers, 2:164, BL, Add. MSS 49183.

22. Millette, *Genesis,* 76–77. In Borde's view the problem was more religious than political; see *History,* 156.

23. Millette, *Genesis,* 72–74.

24. Stephen, *Crisis,* 121–23.

25. Stephen, *Crisis,* 189.

26. Stephen to Perceval, 9 September 1809, Perceval Papers, 2:136, BL, Add. MSS 49183.

27. Smith to Liverpool, 14 February 1810, UWI/CO 295:23, 16. This document and some of the CO 295 series were sourced from a collection in the History Department of the University of the West Indies (St. Augustine Campus); the documents were reproduced in typescript, thus folio numbers might not correspond with the original documents (hereafter cited as UWI/CO 295).

28. Smith to Liverpool, 14 February 1810, UWI/CO295:23, 17.

29. Smith to Liverpool, 14 February 1810, UWI/CO 295:23, 17.

30. TBC, 18 July 1810, NA, CO 298:4, 211–14, and 199–200, respectively.

31. TBC, 7 July 1810, NA, CO 298:4, 202–3v.

32. TBC, 7 July 1810, NA, CO 298:4, 202–03v.

33. See Millette, *Genesis,* n.p., table 6 (inserted between 191–92).

34. TBC, 28 July 1810, NA, CO 298:4, 216v–17.

35. TBC, 4 January 1811, NA, CO 298:5, 6v; also, Liverpool to Hislop, 27 November 1810, NA, CO 295:61, 200–202. The actual date of the order-in-council was 17 November 1810. For a complete reproduction of the order, see Philippe, *Free Mulatto,* 230–33.

36. TBC, 4 January 1811, NA, CO 298:5, 6v.

37. "Trinidad," 23 May 1802, Cumberland Papers, 97.

38. "Trinidad," 23 May 1802, Cumberland Papers, 97. One Frenchman had to go to Grenada to marry his colored fiancé; see Philippe, *Free Mulatto,* 110–11.

39. Liverpool to Hislop, 4 January 1811, NA, CO 298:5, 4.

40. Liverpool to Hislop, 4 January 1811, NA, CO 298:5, 5–5v. For the Articles of Capitulation, see NA, CO 295:61, 198–99v, app. B.

41. Liverpool to Hislop, 4 January 1811, NA, CO 298:5, 6.

42. Liverpool to Hislop, 4 January 1811, NA, CO 298:5, 5v.

43. See Stephen, *Crisis,* 205, app. l.

44. William Burnley, *Observations on the Present Condition of the Island of Trinidad and the Actual State of Experiment of Negro Emancipation* (London, 1842), 5–6.

45. Stephen, *England Enslaved,* 10–11.

46. See Stephen to Perceval (Pte. & Conf.), 10 April 1810, Perceval Papers, 2:148, BL, Add. MSS 49183; Wilmot Horton to Wilberforce, 7 October 1823, NA, CO 296:6, 92–92v.

47. Stephen Jr. to Horton, 18 April 1823, NA, CO 298:6, 90v.

48. See, e.g., clause 13 of the Royal Order, 10 March 1824, NA, CO 318:69, 229, app. D.

49. See Patrick Nerhot, "Interpretation in Legal Science: The Notion of Narrative Coherence," in *Law, Interpretation, and Reality: Essays in Epistemology, Hermeneutics, and Jurisprudence,* ed. Patrick Nerhot (Dordrecht, Neth.: Kluwer Academic Publishers, 1990), 201–4.

50. Pierre-Gustave Louis Borde, *The History of the Island of Trinidad under Spanish Rule* (Trinidad: Paria, 1982), 461.

51. Sanderson, *Appeal,* 94.

52. For a list of disabilities and punishments, see Commission of Legal Enquiry in the West Indies, 1827, vol. 13, Trinidad Report, NA, CO 318:69, 70.

53. Smith to Stephen, encl. in Stephen to Perceval (Pte. & Conf.), 10 April 1810, 2:58, BL, Add. MSS 49183. For Picton's Code, see NA, CO 295:13, 49–55.

54. Sanderson, *Appeal*, 197.

55. Report from the Commissioners of Enquiry on the Administration of Civil and Criminal Justice in the West Indies and South American Colonies, 1825–29, *British Parliamentary Papers*, vol. 3: Colonies, West Indies, 290.

56. Franklin W. Knight, *Slave Society in Cuba during the Nineteenth Century* (Madison: University of Wisconsin Press, 1970), 123.

57. Smith to Stephen, 10 April 1810, 2:160, BL, Add. MSS. 49183.

58. Encl. no. 527, Drafts of Proposal for Amelioration Order in Council, 5 December 1823, NA, CO 295:60, 218–19.

59. Encl. no. 227, NA, CO 295:60, 220.

60. Mellafe, *Negro Slavery*, 106.

61. See Davis, *Problem of Slavery*, 102.

62. Seventh *Partida*, third law, qtd. in "Laws Referred to by the Cabildo as the Punishment Now Provided for Cruelty," appended to "Copy of Remonstrance of Three of the Members of His Majesty's Council," encl. no. 4, in Woodford to Bathurst, 26 May 1824, TTNA, DD 550.

63. Davis, *Problem of Slavery*, 103.

64. Millette, *Genesis*, 49.

65. Sanderson, *Appeal*, 17. In reality Picton and Chacon were equally absolute in their exercise of civil and military powers, except that under Spanish rule every subject of the king, including a slave, had the right of appeal to the *Audencia* against the judgment of the intendant, whereas under early British rule this right did not exist.

66. Brierley, *Trinidad*, 87.

67. Calculated from Millette's data, *Genesis*, n.p., table 5.

68. Excluded from official, religious censuses were the Chinese, African Muslims, and African American Baptist settlers.

69. Haring, *Spanish Empire*, 167.

70. Hobart to Picton, 29 June 1801, encl. in "Commission and Instructions," 1 June 1801, NA, CO 296:4, 11.

71. Vincent Leahy, *History of the Catholic Church in Trinidad, 1797–1820* (Arima, Trinidad: St. Dominic, 1980), 54.

72. John Harricharan, *The History of the Catholic Church in Trinidad, 1498–1852* (Port of Spain, Trinidad: Imprint, 1975), 1:40.

73. Act for Exempting Their Majesties Protestant Subjects . . . from Penalties of Certain Laws, 1688, 1 W & M, c. 18.

74. Woodford to Bathurst, 28 August 1816, TTNA, DD 189.

75. See, e.g., Liverpool to Governors, 7 November 1811, NA, CO 324:103, 126–27; also see Huskisson to Governor Keane, Jamaica (Pte.), 22 September 1827, NA, CO 324:102, 6.

76. Woodford to Bathurst, 8 February 1815, TTNA, DD 157.

77. Woodford to Bathurst, 16 September 1823, TTNA, DD 504; also see Woodford to Bishop of London, 16 May 1825, Fulham Papers, Howley Collection, 3:8780, Lambeth Palace (hereafter cited as Fulham Papers).

78. Woodford to Bathurst, 25 April 1825, TTNA, DD 615, 151–53.

79. Woodford to Bishop of London, 5 November 1823, Fulham Papers, 866.

80. Woodford to Bishop, 8 October 1824, Fulham Papers, 871.

81. Woodford to Bishop, 8 October 1824, Fulham Papers, 871.

82. Woodford to Bathurst, 7 May 1825, TTNA, DD 616:155–59.

83. See Leahy, *Catholic Church,* 51.

84. Woodford to Bathurst, 17 June 1815, TTNA, DD 105; Woodford to Bathurst, 10 July 1816, TTNA, DD 183; also see Woodford to St. Yago Marino, 3 August 1816, TTNA, DD. For reports of large-scale marronage to the Main, see Woodford to Bathurst, 28 August 1816, TTNA, DD 193.

85. Woodford to Bathurst, 29 August 1815, TTNA, DD 117.

86. Woodford to Bathurst, 23 April 1816, TTNA, DD 167.

87. Woodford to Bathurst, 8 February 1815, TTNA, DD 157.

88. Talboys to Dr. Fin, 30 June 1812, box 1: 19, WMMS Archives.

89. Talboys to Fin, 30 June 1812, box 1: 19, WMMS Archives.

90. WMMS Reports, 1811, 10.

91. 5 December 1817, box 1: 50, WMMS Archives.

92. Petition of missionary from Spanish Town, 9 November 1816, box 1: 42, WMMS Archives.

93. 5 December 1817, box 1: 50, WMMS Archives.

94. "The Proceedings in the Island of Trinidad against Thomas Talboys Methodist Preacher in the Year 1811," box 2: 77, WMMS Archives.

95. TBC, 20 April 1811, NA, CO 298:5, 76; also see box 1: 78, WMMS Archives.

96. TBC, 20 April 1811, NA, CO 298:5, 76v.

97. TBC, 20 April 1811, NA, CO 298:5,76v.

98. TBC, 20 April 1811, NA, CO 298:5, 76–77.

99. TBC, 20 April 1811, NA, CO 298:5, 77.

100. TBC, 20 April 1811, NA, CO 298:5, 77.

101. Trinidad belonged to the District of St. Vincent, which was also a district headquarters; see "The Directions to the West-India Missionaries," in *The Report of the Wesleyan-Methodist Missionary Society* (London, 1828), xvii.

102. District Meeting, 3 April 1815, box 1: 38, WMMS Archives.

103. Most were children of free parents; see 5 December 1817, box 1: 50, WMMS Archives.

104. 5 December 1817, box 1: 50, WMMS Archives.

105. 5 December 1817, box 1: 50, WMMS Archives.

106. 5 December 1817, box 1: 50, WMMS Archives.

107. Woolley to Missionary Committee, 18 April 1820, box 3: 112, WMMS Archives.

108. Woolley to Missionary Committee, 18 April 1820, box 3: 112, WMMS Archives.

109. Bathurst to Woodford, 5 February 1818, NA, CO 296:5.

110. Bathurst to Woodford, 8 November 1817, NA, CO 296:5; Woolley to Missionary Committee, 18 April 1820, box 3: 112, WMMS Archives.

111. Woolley to Missionary Committee, 18 April 1820, box 3: 112, WMMS Archives.

112. Millette, *Genesis,* 68.

113. Millette, *Genesis,* 68.

114. Millette, *Genesis,* 68.

115. Millette, *Genesis,* 68.

116. See 28 March 1825, box 6: 261; 24 August 1826, box 6: 286, WMMS Archives.

117. Woolley to Butterworth, 12 December 1822, box 4: 155, WMMS Archives.

118. Woolley to Butterworth, 8 May 1822, box 4: 160, WMMS Archives. Woolley wrongly estimated forty miles.

119. Woolley to Butterworth, 8 May 1822, box 4: 160, WMMS Archives. The ceremony for the cornerstone of the Port of Spain chapel was conducted by the protector of slaves, Henry Gloster; see *Port of Spain Gazette,* 4 March 1826.

120. Woolley to Butterworth, 8 May 1822, box 4: 160, WMMS Archives.

121. Woolley to Butterworth, 8 May 1822, box 4: 160, WMMS Archives.

122. 2 June 1823, box 4: 189, WMMS Archives.

123. 21 December 1826, box 6: 294, WMMS Archives,

124. Woodford to Bishop of London, 5 November 1823, Fulham Papers, 3:866.

125. 20 August 1825, box 5: 234, WMMS Archives.

126. See WMMS Reports, 1825, 49.

127. See Roger Anstey, "Slavery and the Protestant Ethic," *Historical Reflections: Roots and Branches, Current Directions in Slave Studies* 6, no. 1 (1979): 167.

128. 20 August 1825, box 5: 234, WMMS Archives.

129. 20 August 1825, box 5: 234, WMMS Archives.

130. WMMS Reports, 1829, 61.

131. WMMS Reports, 1830, 65.

132. De Verteuil, *Seven Slaves,* 77.

133. WMMS Reports, 1833, xix.

134. The first Emancipation Act applied to the West India Regiments, previously addressed. Full emancipation was achieved earlier in the Crown colonies and grudgingly slower in the legislative colonies; see Charles H. Wesley, "The Emancipation of the Free Colored Population in the British Empire," *Journal of Negro History* 1, no. 2 (Apr. 1934): 157–61. Enfranchisement came with hurdles; see Murray to Grant, 1 March 1830, NA, CO 296:8, 144.

9. The Launch of Imperial Amelioration

1. M'Callum, *Travels,* 17; Borde, *Trinidad,* 316.

2. Millette, *Genesis,* 122; Brereton, *Modern Trinidad,* 69

3. See, e.g., *Blue Books Trinidad 1823,* NA, CO 300:37, 78v–79; *Blue Books Trinidad, 1830,* CO 300:44, 76v–77; also see Anthony de Verteuil, *The Years Before* (Port of Spain, Trinidad: Inprint, 1975), 22, 27–30.

4. Ragatz, *Fall of the Planter Class,* 335; *Trinidad Guardian,* 6 April 1830, NA, CO 300:3.

5. Luffman, letter 11, 28 January 1787, *Brief Account,* 49; also see Stephen, *England Enslaved,* 33–34.

6. TBC, 7 October 1824, NA, CO 298:6, 140.

7. 9 *Parl. Deb.,* 2d ser. (1823): 334–35.

8. Williams, *History,* 76.

9. Campbell, "Free Coloureds," 53, table 3, 109.

10. "Personal slaves" included those owned by family members on plantations and also by persons with no other form of property. Of the 25,717 recorded enslaved persons in the first registration (1813), 8,630, or 36.6 percent, were classed as "Personal"; see Woodford to Bathurst, 18 March 1814, TTNA, DD 23, 156.

11. De Verteuil, *Seven Slaves,* 42.

12. For examples in St. Domingue, see Edwards, *History,* xix. For a moving story on Trinidad planter Nolly Beaubrun's experience, see Anthony de Verteuil, *Begorat Brunton: A History of Diego Martin, 1784–1884* (Trinidad: Inprint, 1897), 21.

13. Commandant (Com't) Brunton to Woodford, 30 August 1823, NA, CO 295:60, 30.

14. Com't Danglade to Woodford, 3 October 1823, NA, CO 295:60, 106.

15. Com't Peschier to Woodford, 14 July 1823, NA, CO 295:60, 42v–43.

16. Peschier to Woodford, 14 July 1823, NA, CO 295:60, 42v–43.

17. Peschier to Woodford, 14 July 1823, NA, CO 295:60, 42v–43.

18. Picton to Melville, 21 June 1804, Melville Papers, 2:109.2.

19. See Portland to Governors, 6 May 1797; 12 July 1799, NA, CO 324:103, 2–2v and 10–10v, respectively.

20. See esp. articles 10 and 14. For a copy of the ordinance, see Gertrude Carmichael, *The History of the West Indian Islands of Trinidad and Tobago, 1498–1900* (London: Redman, 1961), 379–83, app. 18.

21. Leahy, *History,* 49.

22. John, *Plantation Slaves,* 119.

23. This compared with a fee of eighteen pounds for whites. See NA, CO 295:61, 216, app.; Philippe, *Free Mulatto,* 248.

24. Woodford to Bathurst, 6 November 1823, TTNA, DD 518.

25. Curtin, *Atlantic Slave Trade,* 71.

26. Woodford to Bathurst, 23 November 1816, TTNA, DD 214.

27. Woodford to Bathurst, 7 February 1824, UWI/CO 295:62, 30.

28. "Memorial of Cocoa Planters of Trinidad," 9 January 1819, CO 295:49, 162–63.

29. Woodford to Bathurst, 7 February 1824, UWI/CO 295:62, 30.

30. Woodford to Goulbourn, 3 August 1817, UWI/CO 295/44, 40.

31. Burke, Draft Code, Windham Papers, 3–11.

32. Ramsay, *Objections,* 66.

33. Ramsay, *Objections,* 8–9.

34. 27 *Parl. Hist.* (1791): 274.

35. Ramsay, *Objections,* 147.

36. Slave trade debate, 1791, qtd. in Robert J. W. Horton, *The West India Question Practically Considered* (London, 1826), 28.

37. Horton, *West India Question,* 28–29.

38. Horton, *West India Question,* 28–29.

39. Anstey, *Atlantic Slave Trade,* 327.

40. Horton, *West India Question,* 29.

41. See Portland to Governors, 6 May 1797, NA, CO 324:103, 2–2v.

42. "Resolutions of the Whole House," *Sessional Papers,* 82:309.

43. Brougham, *Colonial Policy* 2:433.

44. Brougham, *Colonial Policy* 2:432.

45. Lt. Dalrymple, *Sessional Papers,* 73:306.

46. *London Times,* 24 February 1788.

47. 11 *Parl. Deb.,* 2d ser. (1824): 1211.

48. 11 *Parl. Deb.,* 2d ser. (1824): 1211.

49. 15 *Parl. Deb.,* 2d ser. (1826): 1312.

50. Grant, *World of Rome,* 141, 143–44.

51. *The Oxford Companion to Law* (Oxford: Clarendon, 1980), 896.

52. Long, *History,* 2:422.

53. Gaspar, *Bondsmen and Rebels,* 239; Craton, *Empire, Enslavement, and Freedom,* 187.

54. Law 13, title 16, part 3, of the *Recopilación* was reproduced from the Justinian Code of the sixth century. See Marquis and Regis v. the State, NA, CO 295:62, 201–8.

55. 15 *Parl. Deb.*, 2d ser. (1826): 1312.

56. "Report of a Committee of the Anti-Slavery Society, August 1823," in *Substance of the Debates in the House of Commons on the 15th May, 1823, on a Motion for the Mitigation and Gradual Abolition of Slavery throughout the British Dominions* (1823; New York: Negro University Press, 1969), xxxiv.

57. Brougham, *Colonial Policy*, 2:432.

58. 15 *Parl. Deb.*, 2d ser. (1826): 1286.

59. Stewart, "Religion and Society," 365.

60. 9 *Parl. Deb.*, 2d ser. (1823): 265-66.

61. 9 *Parl. Deb.*, 2d ser. (1823): 263, 273.

62. 9 *Parl. Deb.*, 2d ser. (1823): 265.

63. 9 *Parl. Deb.*, 2d ser. (1823): 269-70.

64. 9 *Parl. Deb.*, 2d ser. (1823): 263, 273.

65. Regarding the enslaved, see Bathurst to Woodford, 28 May 1823, NA, CO 296:6, 82v-83; regarding the proprietors, see Bathurst to Woodford, 9 July 1823, NA, CO 296:6, 83v-84.

66. Woodford to Commandants, 23 August 1823, NA, CO 295:60, 16-18.

67. See, e.g., Woodford to Brunton, 15 August 1823; Woodford to Com't Gray, 15 August 1823; Com't St. Bresson to Woodford, 10 July 1823, NA, CO 295:60, 25, 48v, 60v.

68. See, e.g., Woodford to Com't Goin, 15 August 1823; Woodford to Brunton, 15 August 1823, NA, CO 295:60, 31v-32, 25.

69. Woodford to Commandants, 22 August 1823, NA, CO 295:60, 166.

70. Linda A. Newson, *Spanish Colonial Trinidad: a Study in Culture Contact* (London: Academy, 1976), 181, 190, table 14; de Verteuil, *Begorat Brunton*, 26; A. C. Carmichael, *Domestic Manners and Social Conditions of the White, Coloured and Negro Population of the West Indies* (London, 1833), 2:80.

71. *Code Noir*, in John, *Plantation Slaves*, 206-11.

72. Horton strongly disapproved of this liberalism; Horton to Woodford, 24 January, Private Letters, NA, CO 324:98, 3v-4.

73. Woodford to Bathurst, 5 December 1823, NA, CO 295:60, 3v-4.

74. Brunton to Woodford, 22 July 1823, NA, CO 295:60, 23.

75. Examples include St. Bresson to Woodford, 10 July 1823; Peschier to Woodford, 14 July 1823; Montgommerie, Charles, and Collins to Peschier, NA, CO 295:60, 60v, 42v, 44.

76. Opinions of Members of Council, 5 December 1823, NA, CO 295:60, 151.

77. Opinions of Members of Council, 5 December 1823, NA, CO 295:60, 153v.

78. Bathurst to Woodford, 20 November 1823, CO 296:6.

79. "Opinions," 5 December 1823, NA, CO 295:60, 137.

80. "Opinions," 5 December 1823, NA, CO 295:60, 142v.

81. "Opinions," 5 December 1823, NA, CO 295:60, 163v.

82. "Opinions," 5 December 1823, NA, CO 295:60, 163v.

83. "Opinions," 5 December 1823, NA, CO 295:60, 163v.

84. Horton to Woodford, 7 October 1823, NA, CO 296:6, 92.

85. Horton to Woodford, 7 October 1823, NA, CO 296:6, 92.

86. Horton to Woodford, 7 October 1823, NA, CO 296:6, 92. Woodford regretted his failure to get approval for this key measure. He consoled himself, however, with an alternative proclamation "to show the *ladies,* that they would be kept in order"; Woodford to Bishop of London, 8 October 1824, Fulham Papers, 870-71.

87. Bathurst to Woodford, 9 October 1823, NA, CO 296:6, 93.

88. Bathurst to Woodford, 9 October 1823, NA, CO 296:6, 93.

89. Stephen to Robert Wilmot, 18 April 1823, NA, CO 295:61, 90v.

90. See Carmichael, *History,* 398, app. 16; also see TBC, 7 July 1825, NA, CO 298:6, 25–26.

91. See clauses 29 and 30 of the Trinidad Order in Council, 1824, NA, CO 318:69. 232–33; also see Woodford to Bishop of London, 27 November 1826, Fulham Papers, 3:883.

92. Fuller to Bathurst, 19 August 1824, NA, CO 295:63, 199v.

93. Fuller to Bathurst, 19 August 1824, NA, CO 295:63, 200.

94. "Memorial of Inhabitants," appended to Fuller to Bathurst, 19 August 1824, NA, CO 295:63, 203; the influence of Burnley was evident in this document; see TBC, 29 July 1824, NA, CO 298:6, 54.

95. Philippe, *Free Mulatto,* 75.

96. "Memorial of Inhabitants," NA, CO 295:63, 203.

97. "Memorial of Inhabitants," NA, CO 295:63, 203. The memorialists argued that neither Spanish nor English law conferred such powers on a magistrate as the royal order.

98. Clause 3, Order-in-Council, 10 March 1824, NA, CO 318:69, 226.

99. Fuller to Bathurst, 19 August 1824, NA, CO 295:63, 201v.

100. See Gloster to Stanley, 12 January 1834, NA, CO 295:105, 162; also see *Blue Book,* 1823, NA, CO 300:37, 20v.

101. Gloster to Stanley, 12 January 1834, NA, CO 295:105, 164v.

102. Gloster to Stanley, 12 January 1834, NA, CO 295:105, 164v.

103. Order-in-Council, 10 March 1824, NA, CO 318:69, 231; *Trinidad Guardian,* 27 February 1828, NA, CO 300:2. Woodford was acting on instructions from an imperial dispatch; see TBC, 2 August 1827, NA, CO 298:7, 32–33.

104. See Copies of Reports from Protector of Slaves, 1828, NA, CO 300:24, 12–13, app. D.

105. Clauses 1–3, "A Proclamation," 23 June 1824, NA, CO 318:69, 236–37 (hereafter cited as "Proclamation").

106. Horton to Woodford, 9 October 1823, 93–93v; Bathurst to Woodford, 20 November 1823, NA, CO 296:6, 94–94v.

107. Woodford to Bathurst, 3 June 1824, query to Clause 13, TTNA, DD 551, app.

108. Illustrious Cabildo to Woodford, 1824, TTNA, DD.

109. The protest by Burnley, Alexander Duncanson, and Francis Peschier, 20 May 1824, TTNA, DD; also see Woodford to Bathurst, 2 July 1824, query to clauses 14–16, TTNA, DD, app.

110. See *The Present State of the Law: the Speech of Henry Brougham . . . on Thursday, February 7, 1828* (London, 1828).

111. "Clarifications" enclosed in "Proclamation," NA, CO 318:69, 239.

112. "Clarifications," 239.

113. "Clarifications," 238.

114. Woodford to Commandants, 21 August 1824, TTNA, DD.

115. Summary of the revised order in Carmichael, *History,* 399, app. 17.

116. Carmichael, *History,* 399, app. 17.

10. Constitutional Militancy

1. In this sense protectors were also magistrates; see clauses 6 and 7 of the Trinidad Order, NA, CO 318:69, 226–27.

2. Commission of Legal Enquiry, 3–26.

3. "Proclamation," 237.

4. "Proclamation," 237.

5. "Proclamation," 237.

6. See Brougham, *Present State of the Law,* 1.

7. Funso Aiyejina, "Esu Elegbara: A Source of an Alter/Native Theory of African Literature and Criticism," 4, http://sta.uwi.edu/newspics.2009.Esu20%Elegbara3.pdf.

8. Examples include Collin v. enslaver, and Anne v. enslaver, 20 March 1832, NA, CO 300:29, 59–61, 61v; Josephine v. enslaver Julie de Verteuil, and Marianne v. enslaver Jean Charles Raymond, NA, CO 300:32, 82–84v.

9. See Carmichael *Domestic Manners,* 192–93. Widespread strikes followed news of the 1831 order-in-council. The concept "positive action" is taken from the political vocabulary of Kwame Nkrumah; see June Milne, *Kwame Nkrumah: A Biography* (London: Panaf, 1999), 52–54.

10. Protector's Report, January 1828 to June 1830; computed from NA, CO 300:24, 28–30, app. D, E.

11. Carmichael, *Domestic Manners,* 10–11; also see Goin to Woodford, 9 October 1823, NA, CO 295:60, 32v.

12. See Protector's Report, July–December 1826, NA, CO 300:21, 62v–64.

13. See, e.g., Protector's Report, July–December 1826, NA, CO 300:21, 62v–64; also see Nancy v. enslaver Mrs. Nugent, *Trinidad Guardian,* 15 May 1827, NA, CO 300:1; Maria Rose v. enslaver, Protector's Report, July–December 1831, NA, CO 300:30, 307–10v. Some men also subscribed to those reports; see Carmichael, *Domestic Manners,* 180.

14. See evidence of Maj. Gen. Tottenham, *Sessional Papers,* 82:125.

15. Carmichael, *Domestic Manners,* 10–11.

16. Protector's Report, August 1834, NA, CO 300:33, 301. For a more comprehensive study of female resistance through litigation, see Claudius Fergus, "A Civilianization Experiment: Women as Litigants and Defendants during the Imperial Amelioration in Trinidad, 1823–1834," special issue, *Jamaican Historical Review* 25 (2011): 4–33.

17. Clause 35, the Trinidad Order, 10 March 1824, NA, CO 318:69, 234.

18. Protector's Report, January–June 1827, NA, CO 300:22.

19. *Trinidad Guardian,* 10 March 1826, NA, CO 300:1.

20. Evidence of Chief Judge, Commission of Legal Enquiry, 8.

21. TBC, Burnley's complaint, 7 October 1824, NA, CO 298:6, 103–4.

22. Burnley's complaint, NA, CO 298:6, 103–4. Often when the enslaved felt public justice had not been done, they resorted to private justice by poisoning their enslavers' livestock and other acts of discreet retaliation; see de Verteuil, *Begorat,* 21.

23. All cases, Protector's Report, January–June 1827, CO 300:22.

24. *Port of Spain Gazette,* 7 April 1827.

25. *Port of Spain Gazette,* 2 August 1826.

26. Protector's Report, January–June 1828, NA, CO 300:24, 43, app. A, no. 1.

27. TBC, 7 July 1825, NA, CO 298:6, 51–67.

28. TBC, 7 July 1825, NA, CO 298:6, 67.

29. *Port of Spain Gazette,* 8, 12, and 19 October 1825.

30. *Trinidad Guardian,* 6 January 1826, NA, CO 300:1.

31. Bathurst to D'Urban (Pte.), 6 October 182, NA, CO 324:73, 163v–64.

32. Bathurst to Woodford (Pte. and Conf.), 1 November 1826, NA, CO 318:74, 59–59v.

33. For both examples, see Protector's Report, January–June 1827, NA, CO 300:22.

34. See Carmichael , *Domestic Manners,* 25.

35. Protector's Report, July–December 1826, NA, CO 300:21, 22v–23. Throughout the nationalist war in Venezuela (launched in 1810) there was a well-organized underground operation facilitating runaways to Guiria (northeastern Venezuela); see Woodford to Bathurst, 28 August 1816, TTNA, DD 193.

36. TBC, 7 October 1824, NA, CO 298:6, 105.

37. TBC, 7 October 1824, NA, CO 298:6, 103–4.

38. TBC, 7 October 1824, NA, CO 298:6, 105.

39. Eugene D. Genovese, *From Rebellion to Revolution: Afro-American Slave Revolts in the Making of the Modern World* (New York: Vintage Books, 1981), 37.

40. Philippe, *Free Mulatto,* 118–19.

41. TBC, 9 September 1826, NA, CO 298:6, 101–2.

42. Protector of Slaves Report, 1831, NA, CO 300:26, 3v.

43. See *Port of Spain Gazette,* 14, 17, and 21 April 1830.

44. All direct references to this code are to the publication in the *Port of Spain Gazette,* 19 January 1832.

45. Grant to Goderich, 25 January 1832, NA, CO 295:92, 121. Although they were declassified as "domestic offences," they were reclassified as "misdemeanours" punishable by criminal law.

46. Woodford to Bathurst, 5 November 1823, TTNA, DD 518.

47. TBC, 7 June 1804, NA, CO 298:1, 129v; for the Hislop trials, see Brereton, *Modern Trinidad,* 48–49.

48. Grant to Goderich, 3 July 1832, UWI/CO 295:93, 53.

49. Grant to Goderich, 26 March 1832, UWI/CO 295:92, 52.

50. For 1809, see Brereton, *Modern Trinidad,* 47; for 1829, see evidence of Joseph Marryat, "Select Committee Reports and Correspondence on the Trade and Commerce of the West Indies Together with Minutes of Evidence," *British Parliamentary Papers,* vol. 2: Slave Trade, 1806–49, 284.

51. See TBC, 4 June 1830, 6 June 1830, NA, CO 298:8, 165–66, 170–80. For Berbice, see Alvin O. Thompson, A *Documentary History of Slavery in Berbice* (Georgetown, Guyana: Free Press, 2002), 238–39.

52. Grant to Howick, 26 May 1832, NA, CO 295:92, 296–304. For the Concord fire, see excerpt of *Gazette Extraordinaire,* 25 March 1832, NA, CO 295:92, 241.

53. See, e.g., Marie and Jeanne Louise v. enslaver Vincent Monier, Protector of Slaves Report, 22 February 1832; Cecile v. enslaver Guadin de Heurré, Protector of Slaves Report, 10 February, 1832, NA, CO 300:28, 170, 151–54.

54. Grant to Goderich, 18 and 20 January and 26 March 1832, NA, CO 295:92.

55. Trinidad Council of Government, 29 October 1832, NA, CO 298:9, 199–200.

56. TCG, 29 October 1832, NA, CO 298:9, 199–200.

57. TCG, 29 October 1832, NA, CO 298:9, 189–90, 195.

58. Evidence of Robert Bushe, proprietor and attorney, "Report from the Select Committee on West India Colonies Together with Minutes of Evidence," *British Parliamentary Papers,* vol. 1: Colonies, West Indies, 1842, 288.

59. Bushe, *Parliamentary Papers,* 1842, 288, 289.

60. *Port of Spain Gazette,* 7 December 1825.

61. Ordinance no. 1, *Trinidad Ordinances, 1832 to 1834,* NA, CO 297:1, 4–20v.

62. Ordinance no. 1, *Trinidad Ordinances,* 7–12v.

63. Ordinance no. 1, *Trinidad Ordinances,* 9.

64. Ordinance no. 1, *Trinidad Ordinances,* 10v–11.

65. Ordinance no. 1, *Trinidad Ordinances,* 10v–18v.

66. Preamble, May 1832 Ordinance, NA, CO 297:1, 4–4v.

67. May 1832 Ordinance, NA, CO 297:1, 16–16v; for offenses, see 19–36. The maximum penalty was set at thirty-nine lashes, indicating the serious economic threat they represented.

68. Gloster to Grant, 2 December 1833, NA, CO 295:101, 11.

69. De Verteuil, *Years Before,* 286, 290–91.

11. Breaking the Chains

1. See Long, *History,* 2:444.

2. Bridenbaugh and Bridenbaugh, *No Peace,* 352.

3. 9 *Parl. Deb.,* 2d ser. (1823): 246.

4. 9 *Parl. Deb.,* 2d ser. (1823): 246.

5. Michael Craton, "Emancipation from Below? The Role of the British West Indian Slaves in the Emancipation Movement, 1818–34," in *Out of Slavery: Abolition and Its Aftermath, 1833–1983,* ed. Jack Hayward (London: Frank Cass, 1985), 113; Turner, *Slaves and Missionaries,* 152–53.

6. *Trinidad Guardian,* 19 August 1828, NA, CO 300:2.

7. For the original version, see Brereton, *Trinidad,* 48.

8. See Craton, "Emancipation," 117; Blackburn, *Overthrow,* 249.

9. Evidence of William Anand and John M'Intyre, "Copy of the Report of a Committee of the House of Assembly of Jamaica, Appointed to Inquire into the Causes, and Injury Sustained by, the Recent Rebellion in That Colony; Together with the Examinations on Oath, Confessions and Other Documents Annexed to the Report," *British Parliamentary Papers,* vol. 47: Slave Trade, no. 80: 1831–34, 211, 235 (hereafter cited as Committee of the HAJ).

10. Robert Morris, "The 1816 Uprising—A Hell-Broth," *Journal of the Barbados Museum and Historical Society* 46 (2000): 9–10. Morris disputes claims made by Beckles and others for Bussa as generalissimo of the rebellion.

11. Craton, "Emancipation," 112; also see Morris, "1816 Uprising," 1–39; Hilary McD. Beckles, "Bussa: The 1816 Revolution in Barbados" (Cave Hill, Barbados: University of the West Indies and the Barbados Museum and Historical Society, 1998), 15–16, 83–88. During the month of April 2000 Jerome S. Handler and Hilary Beckles engaged in a heated debate over the identity of Bussa in the two main Barbadian newspapers, the *Advocate* and the *Nation,* with a spillover in the *Sunday Sun.*

12. Craton, "Emancipation," 116–17. For a much more conservative estimate, see Blackburn, *Overthrow,* 428.

13. See Durban to Bathurst, 12 July 1825, NA, CO 111:50, 8v–9.

14. Craton, *Testing the Chains,* 291; Mathieson's tally was approximately fifty thousand, *British Slavery,* 214. Again, Blackburn gave a much more conservative estimate of twenty to thirty thousand (*Overthrow,* 430).

15. Committee of the HAJ, 184, 215.

16. Horton to Woodford, 8 October 1825, NA CO 324:78, 104v–6v.

17. See Anstey, "Protestant Ethic," 168–69.

18. Craton, "Emancipation," 121.

19. Letter to Wilberforce, encl. in Clark to Wilberforce, 30 July 1830, Wilberforce MSS, d.17, 288v; Turner, *Slaves and Missionaries,* 171.

20. Blackburn, *Overthrow,* 439; Mathieson, *British Slavery,* 206.

21. Minutes, 23 April 1831, 3:87, ASS.

22. Stephen, *England Enslaved,* 58.

23. Minutes, 9 December 1828, 3:146, 10 February 1829, 3:4, ASS.

24. Testimony of Linton, M'Kinlay, and Donald Malcolm, Committee of the HAJ, 206–9.

25. Hart, *Blacks in Rebellion,* 227.

26. Minutes, 11 April 1832, 3:132, ASS.

27. Minutes, 11 April 1832, 4 July 1832, 3:132, 152, ASS.

28. Buxton to Buxton, 23 June 1832, Buxton Papers, 3:29.

29. Minutes, 19 September 1832, 3:104, ASS.

30. Buxton to Buxton, 15 October 1832, Buxton Papers, 3:31.

31. 13 *Parl. Deb.,* 3rd ser. (1832): 48.

32. 9 *Parl. Deb.,* 2d ser. (1823): 264.

33. Buxton to Buxton, 15 October 1832, Buxton Papers, 3:31.

34. Minutes, ASS, 2 April 1833, 4:17.

35. Minutes, ASS, 2 April 1833, 4:17.

36. Minutes, ASS, 13 May 1833, 5:37.

37. William Green, "Was British Emancipation a Success? The Abolitionist Perspective," in *Abolition and Its Aftermath: The Historical Context,* ed. David Richardson (London: Frank Cass, 1985), 189.

38. Minutes, ASS, 1 January 1837, 5:143.

39. See preamble to the act in Kenneth N. Bell and W. P. Morrell, eds., *Select Documents on British Colonial Policy, 1830–1860* (Oxford: Clarendon Press, 1968), 389.

40. William A. Green, *British Slave Emancipation: The Sugar Colonies and the Great Experiment, 1830–1865* (Oxford: Clarendon, 1976), 119; David Brion Davis, "Slavery and Progress," in *Anti-Slavery, Religion, and Reform: Essays in Memory of Roger Anstey,* ed. Christine Bolt and Seymour Drescher (Folkestone, Eng.: Dawson, 1980), 352.

41. 9 *Parl. Deb.,* 2d ser. (1823): 286.

42. Edward Stanley first proposed that Parliament consent to a loan of fifteen million pounds sterling as compensation; see Roy Augier, ed., *Debates in Parliament on the Motion to Abolish Slavery* (N.p.: University of the West Indies, n.d.), 62.

43. In Buckingham's estimation the total compensation package was worth roughly seventy-five million pounds in the original proposal, including twenty million pounds cash, twelve years of apprenticeship, and protecting duties worth twenty-four million pounds; see 19 *Parl. Deb.,* 3d ser. (1833): 1067–68.

44. Clause 15, Bell and Morrell, *Select Documents,* 394. Eventually, 132 magistrates were dispatched; see W. L. Burn, *Emancipation and Apprenticeship in the British West Indies* (New York: Johnson, 1970), 199.

45. Although mainly concerned with Jamaica, the standard work on the subject is still Burn; see *Emancipation,* chap. 3.

46. "Proposed Code for Regulating the Apprenticeship," NA, CO 295:101, 195v. The number proposed for the rural settlements alone was ninety-two.

47. Marginal comment in George Hill to Lefevre, 24 May 1834, NA, CO 295:102.

48. See *Port of Spain Gazette,* 5 August 1834; Claude Levy, "Barbados: The Last Years of Slavery, 1832–1833," *Journal of Negro History* 44 (Oct. 1959): 340. Only in Jamaica did the governor desist from making appointments from among possessors of "apprentice property"; see Burn, *Emancipation,* 198; Mathieson, *British Slavery,* 255–56.

49. TCG, 21 July 1834, NA, CO 298:9, 26–29.

50. *Port of Spain Gazette,* 25 July 1834.

51. Council Minutes, 27 May 1834, NA, CO 298:9, 51–53.

52. There were two different classes of "apprentice" in Trinidad: those freed by the Emancipation Act of 1833 and those liberated from the slave trade. Each class was under different apprenticeship laws. See Apprenticeship Ordinance, NA, CO 297:1, 317.

53. *Port of Spain Gazette,* 25 July 1834. An earlier plan had envisaged only five police districts, including Port of Spain; see "Proposed Code for Regulating Apprenticeship," CO 295/101,191–91v, app.; also see Minutes of Council, 17 July 1834, NA, CO298:9, 20; Minutes of Council, 15 May 1835, NA, CO 298:10, 350–55.

54. "Proposed Code," NA, CO 295, 101, 200.

55. "Proposed Code," NA, CO 295, 195–96.

56. TCG, 20 August 1838, NA, CO 298:13, 113.

57. TCG, 23 June 1834, NA, CO 298:9, 72–74; "Extract of Proceedings in Council," 23 June 1834, NA, CO 295:103, 90–91. The cost of a station varied from a thousand pounds sterling for Port of Spain to three hundred pounds sterling for the Southern District. TCG, 15 May 1835, NA, CO 298:10.

58. "Extract of Proceedings," 91–92.

59. TCG, 23 June 1834, NA, Co 298:9, 73–74.

60. TCG, 23 June 1834, NA, Co 298:9, 73–74.

61. TCG, 23 June 1834, NA, Co 298:9, 73–74.

62. George Hill to Spring Rice, 30 July 1834, NA, CO 295:102.

63. *Port of Spain Gazette,* 5 August 1834.

64. See Augier, *Debates,* 55–60, 63–66.

65. George Hill to Spring Rice, 7 August 1834, NA, CO 295:103, 3.

66. Ferguson, *Mary Prince,* 17–18. For the relevance of Hegel to plantation slavery, see Patterson, *Slavery and Social Death,* 228–40.

67. See WMMS Reports, 1835, 50–51. For St. Lucia, see "Proclamation," 25 July 1834, NA, CO 253:46, 248v. For British Guiana, see "Proclamation," 15 July 1834, NA, CO 111:132, 442–42v.

68. George Hill to Spring Rice, 7 August 1834, NA, CO 295:103, 8.

69. *Port of Spain Gazette,* 5 August 1834.

70. George Hill to Spring Rice, 7 August 1834, NA, CO 295:103, 3.

71. Augier, *Debates,* 186.

72. Governor St. Leger Hill, in *Saint Lucia Gazette,* 30 July 1834, NA, CO 253:46, 248–49.

73. Hill visited several estates from 6 to 9 August 1834, NA, CO 253:46, 248v–49.

74. TCG, 3 August 1834, NA, CO 298:9, 59. Barbadian authorities also increased the number of imperial troops; see Levy, "Barbados," 334.

75. TCG, 4 August 1834, NA, CO 298:9.

76. George Hill to Spring Rice, 7 August 1834, NA, CO 295:103, 4v.

77. George Hill to Spring Rice, 7 August 1834, NA, CO 295:103, 5.

78. George Hill to Spring Rice, 7 August 1834, NA, CO 295:103, 4v.

79. *Port of Spain Gazette,* 5 August 1834.

80. *Port of Spain Gazette,* 5 August 1834.

81. *Port of Spain Gazette,* 5 August 1834. The law defined a "riot" as an assembly of three or more apprentices.

82. TCG, 4 June 1834, NA, CO 298:9, 73.

83. George Hill to Spring Rice, 7 August 1834, NA, CO 295:103, 5v.

84. George Hill to Spring Rice, 7 August 1834, NA, CO 295:103, 6v–7.

85. *Port of Spain Gazette,* 5 August 1834; also qtd. in George Hill to Spring Rice, 7 August 1834, NA, CO 295:103, 27–28.

86. Papers Relative to the Abolition of Slavery in the British Colonies, in *Slavery in the British Colonies* (official publication), NA, CO 295:106, 146–46v (hereafter cited as Abolition Papers).

87. Abolition Papers, 146–46v.

88. Abolition Papers, 146–46v.

89. Report of Robert Schick, "an intelligent gentleman," 30 August 1834, enclosed in Hill to Spring Rice, 3 September 1834, NA, CO 295:103, 120–22v.

90. Schick, 120–22v.

91. Schick, 120–22v.

92. Schick, 120–22v.

93. George Hill to Aberdeen, 3 March 1835, NA, CO 295:106, 144–45.

94. See *Permanent Laws of the Emancipated Colonies* (London, 1838), 10–12. Also see Minutes, ASS, 5:96–97, 6 July 1838; "Report from the Select Committees to Enquire into the Working of the Apprenticeship System in the Colonies," *British Parliamentary Papers,* 1836–37, Slave Trade, no. 3, app. no. 2 (6–10).

95. Minutes, ASS, 5:71, 10 February 1838.

96. Minutes, ASS, 5:99, 6 July 1838.

97. Burnley to Stanley, 24 January 1834, NA, CO 295:105, 34–43v.

98. Morris R. Cohen, *Law and the Social Order: Essays in Legal Philosophy* (1933; Hamden, Conn.: Archon Books, 1967), 62.

99. Cohen, *Law and the Social Order,* 53.

100. Burnley to Stanley, 24 January 1834, NA, CO 295:105, 34–43v.

101. Burnley to Stanley, 24 January 1834, NA, CO 295:105, 34–43v.

102. Knaplund, *James Stephen,* chap. 4.

103. Knaplund, *James Stephen,* 31.

104. Knaplund, *James Stephen,* 73.

105. "Military Ordinance № 9," NA, CO 295:106, 27–35v; for the imperial dispatch, see Colonial Office to Hill, 10 October 1835, NA, CO 295:106, 20v–22.

106. *British Parliamentary Papers,* 1836–37, Slave Trade, no. 3, app. 19, [224–25].

107. Report on Apprenticeship, 224.

108. Report on Apprenticeship, 225.

109. Mellor, *Imperial Trusteeship,* 132.

110. TCG, 20 August 1838, NA, CO 298:13, 113–26.

111. TCG, 20 August 1838, NA, CO 298:13, 113–14.

112. *Laws of Trinidad, 1831 to 1848: The Orders in Council, and Ordinances of the Council of Government from 1831 to 1848* (1852), 82–84, 89–90.

113. Rousseau, *Social Contract,* 8.

114. Cited in Williams, *Capitalism and Slavery,* 192.

115. Bell and Morrell, *Select Documents,* 432.

116. Williams, *From Columbus to Castro,* 332.

117. "Proposed Code for Regulating Apprenticeship," NA, CO 295:101, 228v, chap. 7. The precedent was in the imperial act itself, which equated the "services" of an apprentice with those of a slave (cl. 2).

118. Burnley to Stanley, 27 January 1834, NA, CO 295:105, 44–45.

119. Bell and Morrell, *Select Documents,* 433. For Burnley's view, see Burnley to Stanley, 24 January 1834, NA, CO 295:101, 34–43v.

120. WMMS Reports, 1837, 51.

121. Marriage Order-in-Council 1838, *Laws of Trinidad,* 69.

122. Marriage Order, *Laws of Trinidad,* 71.

123. Marriage Order, *Laws of Trinidad,* 68.

124. See Augier, *Debates,* 65–66.

125. Shirley C. Gordon, *A Century of West Indian Education: A Sourcebook* (London: Longmans, 1963), 21; and Gordon, *Reports and Repercussions in West Indian Education, 1835–1933* (London: Ginn, 1968), 59.

126. See WMMS Reports, 1836, 54; WMMS Reports, 1838, 81.

127. See WMMS Reports, 1836, 55.

128. Harricharan, *Catholic Church,* 74.

129. Harricharan, *Catholic Church,* 74.

130. Harricharan, *Catholic Church* 107–8.

131. De Verteuil, *Seven Slaves,* 77.

132. The prejudice against funding of Catholic education was temporarily resolved by Lord Harris's policy of secular education through state-controlled ward schools in 1851; see Gordon, *Reports and Repercussions,* 48–49.

133. For the policy of council, see TCG, 18 April 1835, NA, CO 298:10, 279–84; for "Names of Estates with 100 or More Apprentices," see TCG, 18 April 1835, 297.

134. Le Geoff to George Hill, 28 March 1837, NA, CO 295:106, 165– 65v.

135. Bishop to George Hill, 3 November 1836, NA, CO 295:114, 182v–83.

136. George Hill to Bishop, 21 February 1837, NA, CO 295:114.

137. Hill to Bishop of Barbados, 21 February 1837, NA, CO 295:114.

138. Le Geoff to Hill, 28 March 1837, NA, CO 295:106, 165–65v.

139. Cited in Carl Campbell, "Towards an Imperial Policy for the Education of Negroes in the West Indies after Emancipation" (Kingston, Jamaica: University of the West Indies, n.d.), 1.

140. Glenelg to Hill, 13 July 1837, NA, CO 295:114, 172–74.

12. Conclusion

1. Brougham, *Opinion,* 13.

2. Davis, *Problem of Slavery,* 321.

3. Anstey, "Protestant Ethic," 159.

4. Anon., *Substance of the Debates,* 29.

5. James Walvin, "Freeing the Slaves: How Important Was Wilberforce?" in *Out of Slavery,* ed. Jack Hayward (London: Frank Cass, 1985), 38.

6. *Lord Brougham's Speech in the House of Lords on Tuesday, the 20th of February, 1838, for the Immediate Emancipation of the Negro Apprentices* (London, 1838), 13–14.

7. *Lord Brougham's Speech,* 11.

8. *Lord Brougham's Speech,* 12–13.

9. On police settlements for the start of the apprenticeship, see NA, CO 298:10, 218, 351–55. The chief justice admitted that the new measures would require "a large outlay of public money," the details of which would have exceeded the imperial education grant for all colonies. See Ordinance to Establish a Rural Police, NA, CO 298:13, 115–16; and Militia Ordinance, NA, CO 295:106, 27–35v.

GLOSSARY

akomfo: Traditional priest or priestess of the Ashanti; a sacred oath.

alcalde: Magistrate.

alcalde de barrio: Justice of the peace of a ward or district in the town.

alcalde ordinario: Leading magistrate of a Cabildo.

Anansi: Spider god of the Ashanti; their most renowned trickster-hero.

asiento: Spanish royal contract for the supply of slaves.

audencia: The highest Spanish colonial court.

babalawo: Priest of Ifa, the Yoruba sacred tradition known as Orisha and Santería in the Caribbean.

cédula real: Spanish royal decree; that of 1789 was equivalent to the French *Code Noir.*

corregidor: Official in charge of a native or Amerindian mission.

corps de chasseur: Light infantry; rangers.

Esu/Eshu: A Yoruba deity; guardian of the crossroads; a trickster.

fanega: Land about 6.5 acres (ca. 2.6 hectares).

hungan: Priest of the Ewe-Fon traditional religion.

Legba: An Ewe-Fon deity, tester of human will; also assimilated to Esu.

manbo: Priestess of the Ewe-Fon traditional religion.

nganga: Traditional priest in the Kingdom of Kongo.

nkisi: Kongolese talisman or sacred charm.

obeah: A wide range of West Africa esoteric practices.

okomfo: See *akomfo.*

onus probandi: Burden of proof.

peon: A destitute laborer in Spanish America.

procurador síndico: A city attorney; guardian of the rights of the people.

quantum valeat: Literally, "according to one's worth."

Recopilación: The Spanish legal compilations of 1680 for colonial governance.

regidor: A council member of a Cabildo.

Siete Partidas: Spanish code of laws compiled in the thirteenth century.

ubuntu: A southern African Bantu concept of the primacy of humanity.

villein en gros: English peasant of servile status legally tied to the land.

villein regardant: English serf legally tied to a feudal landowner but not the land.

SELECTED BIBLIOGRAPHY

Primary Sources

This study relied heavily on manuscripts and other archival sources in the United Kingdom and Trinidad and Tobago. Archival sources in France provided valuable insights into the revolutionary 1790s in the Caribbean. In the United Kingdom the Public Record Office, British Library, Colindale Newspaper Library, Lambeth Palace, School of Oriental and African Studies (SOAS) at the University of London, Bodleian Library, and Rhodes House Library were all invaluable in allowing me to develop the revisionist approach taken in the study. The Main Library of the St. Augustine Campus of the University of the West Indies has built up an impressive collection of duplicate archival sources and was also useful in providing extensive material about the nineteenth century. The National Archives of Trinidad and Tobago also has a wealth of sources on the early nineteenth century, although many volumes are plagued with mere fragments of documents. Only the most valuable sources are listed here.

MANUSCRIPTS

Anti-Slavery Society. Papers. Minute Books, 1823–39. Rhodes House Library, Oxford, England.

Buxton, Thomas Fowell. Papers. Rhodes House Library, Oxford, England.

Clarkson, John. Papers. British Library.

Clarkson, Thomas. Papers. Letters to T. F. Buxton, 1825–28. Rhodes House Library.

———. Papers. British Library.

Colonial Office. Papers. Public Record Office, National Archives, Kew Gardens, London. A wide range of call numbers for different territories were consulted, in addition to special correspondents and reports.

Colonies. Papers. Archives Nationales d'Outre-Mer, Aix-en-Provence, France.

Colony. Original copies of Official Correspondences to the Colonial Office. National Archives. Trinidad and Tobago.

Cumberland Papers. Correspondence on Trinidad, 1802. British Library.

Fulham Papers. Howley Collection. Lambeth Palace, London.

Liverpool. Papers. British Library.

Melville. Papers. Correspondence with George III, 1791–1805. British Library.

———. Papers. Trinidad, 1802–4. Rhodes House Library, Oxford, England.

Perceval, Spencer. Papers. Letters from James Stephen, 1807–10. British Library.

Picton, Thomas. Letter Book. British Library.

Wesleyan Methodist Missionary Society. Papers. Stations in the West Indies, 1803–28. School of African and Asian Studies, London University.

Wilberforce, William. Papers. Bodleian Library, Oxford, England.

Windham Papers. Edmund Burke's Draft Slave Code, [1780]. British Library.

PRINTED DOCUMENTS

British Parliamentary Papers. Vol. 47. Copy of the Report of a Committee of the House of Assembly of Jamaica, Appointed to Inquire into the Causes, and Injury Sustained by, the Recent Rebellion in That Colony; Together with the Examinations on Oath, Confessions and Other Documents Annexed to the Report. Slave Trade, no. 80: 1831–34. Shannon: Irish University Press, 1969.

Brougham, Henry. *An Inquiry into the Colonial Policy of the European Powers.* 2 vols. 1803. New York: Kelly, 1930.

Clarkson, Thomas. *An Essay on the Comparative Efficiency of Regulation or Abolition as Applied to the Slave Trade (Showing That the Latter Only Can Remove the Evils to Be Found in That Commerce).* London, 1789.

———. *An Essay on the Slavery and Commerce of the Human Species, Particularly the African, Translated from a Latin Dissertation Which Was Honoured in the University of Cambridge, for the Year 1785, with Additions.* London, 1786.

Cobbett's Parliamentary History. London, 1820. Vols. 28–36.

Equiano, Olaudah. *The Life of Olaudah Equiano, or Gustava Vassa, the African.* 1814. Mineola, N.Y.: Dover Publications, 1999.

Hansard's Parliamentary Debates. London, T. C. Hansard. Vols. 1–40.

Lambert, Sheila, ed. *House of Commons. Sessional Papers of the Eighteenth Century.* Select Committee of Parliament on the Slave Trade, 1791–92. Scholarly Resources, 1975. Several volumes on the inquiry into the slave trade.

Long, Edward. *History of Jamaica.* 3 vols. 1774. London: Frank Cass, 1979.

Nisbett, Richard. *The Capacity of Negroes for Religious and Moral Improvement Considered: with Cursory Hints, to Proprietors and Governments, for the Immediate Amelioration of the Condition of Slaves in the Sugar Colonies: to Which Are Subjoined Short and Practical Discourses to Negroes, on the Plain and Obvious Principles of Religion and Morality.* 1789. New York: Negro University Press, 1970.

Permanent Laws of the Emancipated Colonies. London, 1838.

Prince, Mary. *The History of Mary Prince: a West Indian Slave (Related by Herself)*. Edited by Moira Ferguson. Ann Arbor: University of Michigan Press, 1997.

Ramsay, James. *An Essay on the Treatment and Conversion of African Slaves in the British Sugar Colonies*. London, 1784.

Sanderson, John. *An Appeal to the Imperial Parliament upon Claims of the Ceded Colony of Trinidad to Be Governed by a Legislature and Judicature Founded upon Principles Sanctioned by Colonial Precedents and Long Usage . . . .* London, 1812.

Society for the Conversion and Religious Instruction and Education of Negro Slaves in the British West India Islands. *Instructions for Missionaries to the West India Islands*. London, [1824?].

Stephen, James. *The Slavery of the British West India Colonies Delineated as It Exists in Law and Practice and Compared with the Slavery of Other Countries, Ancient and Modern*. London, 1823.

―――. *The Crisis of the Sugar Colonies or an Enquiry into the Objects and Probable Effects of the French Expedition to the West Indies and Their Connection with the Colonial Interests of the British Empire to Which Are Subjoined Sketches of a Plan for Settling the Vacant Lands of Trinidada*. 1802. New York: Negro University Press, 1969.

NEWSPAPERS

London Times, select issues from 1788 and 1789. British Library.

Morning Post and Fashionable World, 1793–1798. Colindale Newspaper Library, London.

Port of Spain Gazette, 1825–37. Trinidad and Tobago National Archives.

Trinidad Guardian. Public Record Office. National Archives. London.

Selected Secondary Sources

Anstey, Roger. *The Atlantic Slave Trade and British Abolition, 1760–1810*. London: Macmillan, 1975.

Barker, Anthony J. *The African Link: British Attitudes to the Negro in the Era of the Atlantic Slave Trade, 1550–1807*. London: Frank Cass, 1978.

Beckles, Hilary McD. *Bussa: The 1816 Revolution in Barbados*. Cave Hill, Barbados: Department of History, University of the West Indies, 1998.

Bly, Antonio T. "Crossing the Lake of Fire: Slave Resistance during the Middle Passage, 1720–1842." *Journal of Negro History* 6, no. 3 (1998): 178–86.

Brereton, Bridget. *The History of Modern Trinidad, 1783–1962*. London: Heinemann, 1981.

Brown, Beverley. "George Liele: Black Baptist and Pan-Africanist, 1750–1826." *Savacou* 11–12 (Sept. 1975): 58–67.

Buckley, Roger Norman. *The British Army in the West Indies: Society and the Military in the Revolutionary Age.* Gainesville: University Press of Florida, 1998.

———. *Slaves in Red Coats: The British West India Regiments, 1795–1815.* New Haven: Yale University Press, 1979.

Carrington, Selwyn H. H. "'Econocide'—Myth or Reality: The Question of West Indian Decline, 1783–1806" and "Postscriptum." *Boletin de estudios latinoamericanos y del Caribe* 36 (June 1984): 13–38 and 66–67.

Craton, Michael. *Testing the Chains: Resistance to Slavery in the British West Indies.* Ithaca: Cornell University Press, 1982.

Dallas, R. C. *The History of the Maroons from Their Origins to the Establishment of Their Chief Tribe at Sierra Leone.* 1803. London: Frank Cass, 1968.

Davis, David Brion. "James Cropper and the British Anti-Slavery Movement, 1821–1823." *Journal of Negro History* 45 (Oct. 1960): 241–58.

———. *The Problem of Slavery in Western Culture.* New York: Cornell University Press, 1966.

Dixon, Peter. *Canning, Politician and Statesman.* London: Weidenfeld and Nicolson, 1976.

Drescher, Seymour. *Econocide: British Slavery in the Era of Abolition.* Pittsburgh: University of Pittsburgh Press, 1977.

———. "Econocide, Capitalism, and Slavery: A Commentary." (Response to Carrington.) *Boletin de estudios latinoamericanos y del Caribe* 36 (June 1984): 49–65.

Dubois, Laurent. *A Colony of Citizens: Revolution and Slave Emancipation in the French Caribbean, 1787–1804.* Chapel Hill: University of North Carolina Press, 2004.

Duffy, Michael. *Soldiers, Sugar, and Seapower: The British Expedition to the West Indies and the War against Revolutionary France.* Oxford: Clarendon Press, 1987.

Furley, Oliver W. "Moravian Missions and Slaves in the West Indies." *Caribbean Studies* 5, no. 1 (1965): 3–16.

Geggus, David P. *Slavery, War, and Revolution: The British Occupation of Saint Domingue, 1793–1798.* Oxford: Clarendon Press, 1982.

Hart, Richard. *Slaves Who Abolished Slavery: Blacks in Rebellion.* 1985. Jamaica: University of the West Indies Press, 2002.

James, C. L. R. *The Black Jacobins: Toussaint L'Ouverture and the San Domingo Revolution.* 2d ed. New York: Random, 1963.

Knorr, Klaus E. *British Colonial Theories, 1570–1850.* London: Frank Cass, 1968.

Lipscomb, Patrick. "Party Politics, 1801–1802: George Canning and the Trinidad Question." *Historical Journal* 12 (1969): 442–66.

Maunier, René. *The Sociology of Colonies: An Introduction to the Study of Race Contact.* Trans. and ed. E. O. Lorimer. 2 vols. London: Routledge and Kegan Paul, 1949.

M'Biti, John. *African Religion and Philosophy.* London: Heineman, 1969.

Millette, James. *The Genesis of Crown Colony Government: Trinidad, 1783–1810.* Trinidad: Moko, 1970.

Morris, Robert. "The 1816 Uprising—A Hell-Broth." *Journal of the Barbados Museum and Historical Society* 46 (2000): 1–39.

Parrinder, Geoffrey. "The African Spiritual Universe." In *Afro-Caribbean Religions*, ed. Brian Gates. London: Ward Lock, 1980.

Richardson, Ronald Kent. *Moral Imperium: Afro-Caribbeans and the Transformation of British Rule, 1776–1838*. Westport, Conn.: Greenwood, 1987.

Schuler, Monica. "Akan Slave Rebellions in the British Caribbean." In *Caribbean Slave Society and Economy: A Student Reader*, ed. Hilary McD. Beckles and Verene Shepherd, 373–86. Kingston, Jamaica: Ian Randle Publications, 1991.

Stewart, Robert. "Religion and Society in Jamaica, 1831–1880: Conflict, Compromise and the Christian Churches in a Post-Slave Colony." Ph.D. diss., University of the West Indies, 1983.

Thornton, John K. "African Soldiers in the Haitian Revolution." *Journal of Caribbean History* 25, nos. 1–2 (1991): 51–80.

———. "The Development of an African Catholic Church in the Kingdom of Kongo, 1491–1750." *Journal of African History* 25, no. 2 (1984): 147–67.

Williams, Eric. *Capitalism and Slavery*. 1944. London: Andre Deutsch, 1964.

Williamson, Karina, ed. *Contrary Voices: Representations of West Indian Slavery, 1657–1834*. Jamaica: University of the West Indies Press, 2008.

INDEX

labor: free labor, 60–61, 63, 65–66, 101, 110–16; labor unions, 203n9; and land policies, 190–92; natural increase of, 37, 42, 43, 45, 59, 60, 89, 104, 128, 145, 146, 171. *See also* British colonial slavery; creolization of labor

laissez-faire doctrine, 60–66, 181, 194, 201

land ownership: exclusion of freedmen from, 190–92, 202; and land grants, 98, 100, 115, 124, 190–91; Williams on, 203n9

Law of Nations, 129–30

Layman, William, 111–12

Leeward Islands, 12, 81–83, 91, 108, 226n123

Lesser Antilles, xii, 71, 75–77, 79, 85, 88

Liele, George, 43–44

Ligon, Richard, 3, 10, 211n156

Liverpool Anti-Slavery Society for the Amelioration and Gradual Abolition of Slavery, 61

London Anti-Slave Trade Society, 27

Long, Edward: on Anansism, 50; on Atlantic slave trade, 56; on conditions of slavery, 43; on creolization of labor, 8, 36, 38–41, 89, 91, 106; on economics of British colonial slavery, 89; on enslaved Africans' marriages, 10, 11; on enslaved Africans' secret meetings, 177; on enslaved Africans' spiritual beliefs, 149–50; on mortality of enslaved Africans, 21–22; and pseudoscientific racism, 3; on slave insurrections, 108; on Somerset case, 31; and status of Africans under common law, 32; and statutory amelioration, 44, 45; on Tacky's War, 5, 39

Lushington, Stephen, 34, 149

Mansfield, Lord (William Murray), 30, 31, 32, 33, 34, 38, 205n18

manumission, 62, 119, 151, 155, 157, 167, 192

Maroons: and Anansism, 50; and guerrilla warfare, 93; and imperial amelioration, 168–69; and missionism, 51, 218n88; punishment for, 125, 166; and revolutionary emancipationism, 5, 77, 78, 206n29; and Venezuela, 136

Maroon Treaty (1739), 38

marriage: and Burke's plan, 53–54, 195; and Church of England, 53, 219n12; conceptions of, 9–11, 48, 194; and emancipation, 194–95; enforcement of, 62, 151, 153; and imperial amelioration, 157; and slavery conditions, 11, 13, 194

Marshall, Peter, 52–53, 72–73

Martinique, 63, 75, 77, 80–84, 94, 105, 127, 223n56

Mauritius, 63, 65, 114

mercantilism, 6, 65, 194

Methodism: and missionism, 23, 25, 46, 48–49, 216n49; in Trinidad, 131, 134, 136–41, 171

Methodist Society, 48, 63, 196

metropolis and metropolitans: and abolitionism, xii, 3, 22, 24, 26, 28, 39, 52–60, 61, 95, 169–70, 179, 199–202; and amelioration, 43, 118, 176; and emancipation, 184, 199; on enslaved Africans, 16; and free trade, 61; and imperial amelioration, 152, 173; and missionism, 44, 46, 140; and remodeling of colonial system, xiii; and Trinidad, 113

Middle Passage, 4, 6, 12, 17, 50, 56

missionism: and apprenticeship system, 196–97; and baptism, 47–48, 143, 218n88; and catechisms, 49, 218n83, 218n84; and Church of England, 41, 45, 48, 134–35, 196; and emancipation, 193, 202; and enslaved Africans' use of Christianity, 179; focus on West Indies, 104; government support of, 42; and imperial amelioration, 171; and marriages, 195; and Methodism, 23, 25, 46, 48–49, 216n49; persecution of, 131; and prohibition of dancing, 46, 217n68; and Protestants, 23, 43–44, 179; and quietism, 140, 177; and remodeling of colonial system, xiii; and sectarians, 47, 48–50, 51, 196; as social control, 40, 45–51; and subservience, 163, 176; in Trinidad, 134–39

monopoly, 60–62, 64–66, 179, 201, 221n70

Montesquieu, Charles Secondat de, Baron, 3, 27, 59, 60

moral imperium, ix–x, 23–24, 30, 52, 141

Moravian missionaries, 43, 46, 215n33

mortality: in Atlantic slave trade, 6–7, 21,